# CHRISTIAN THEOLOC

## SERIES EDITORS

TIMOTHY GORRINGE   SERENE JONES   GRAHAM WARD

# CHRISTIAN THEOLOGY IN CONTEXT

Any inspection of recent theological monographs makes plain that it is still thought possible to understand a text independently of its context. Work in the sociology of knowledge and in cultural studies has, however, increasingly made obvious that such divorce is impossible. On the one hand, as Marx put it, 'life determines consciousness'. All texts have to be understood in their life situation, related to questions of power, class, and modes of production. No texts exist in intellectual innocence. On the other hand, texts are also forms of cultural power, expressing and modifying the dominant ideologies through which we understand the world. This dialectical understanding of texts demands an interdisciplinary approach if they are to be properly understood: theology needs to be read alongside economics, politics, and social studies, as well as philosophy, with which it has traditionally been linked. The cultural situatedness of any text demands, both in its own time and in the time of its rereading, a radically interdisciplinary analysis.

The aim of this series is to provide such an analysis, culturally situating texts by Christian theologians and theological movements. Only by doing this, we believe, will people of the fourth, sixteenth, or nineteenth centuries be able to speak to those of the twenty-first. Only by doing this will we be able to understand how theologies are themselves cultural products—projects deeply resonant with their particular cultural contexts and yet nevertheless exceeding those contexts by being received into our own today. In doing this, the series should advance both our understanding of those theologies and our understanding of theology as a discipline. We also hope that it will contribute to the fast developing interdisciplinary debates of the present.

# *Maximus the Confessor*

Jesus Christ and the Transfiguration
of the World

Paul M. Blowers

OXFORD
UNIVERSITY PRESS

# OXFORD
### UNIVERSITY PRESS

Great Clarendon Street, Oxford, OX2 6DP,
United Kingdom

Oxford University Press is a department of the University of Oxford.
It furthers the University's objective of excellence in research, scholarship,
and education by publishing worldwide. Oxford is a registered trade mark of
Oxford University Press in the UK and in certain other countries

© Paul M. Blowers 2016

The moral rights of the author have been asserted

First published 2016
First published in paperback 2018

Published in the United States of America by Oxford University Press
198 Madison Avenue, New York, NY 10016, United States of America

British Library Cataloguing in Publication Data
Data available

Library of Congress Cataloging in Publication Data
Data available

ISBN 978-0-19-967394-0 (Hbk.)
ISBN 978-0-19-967395-7 (Pbk.)

To the memory of
*Sergius Epifanovich (1886–1918)*
*Polycarp Sherwood, OSB (1912–1969)*
*Hans Urs von Balthasar (1905–1988)*
*Lars Thunberg (1928–2007)*
pioneers in the modern study of Maximus the Confessor

# Acknowledgments

Another monograph on Maximus the Confessor was already in the works for me when Tom Perridge of Oxford University Press put me in contact with Graham Ward, now Regius Professor of Divinity at Oxford, about the possibility of submitting this book to the "Christian Theology in Context" series. I am very grateful to both, since this fine series has given me a marvelous opportunity not only to revisit and reassess Maximus' achievement in its own context but also to investigate the various retrievals and recontextualizations of the Confessor in later Christian thought.

Here and in my other publications on Maximus I have benefited immensely from the scholarship that has accrued since the likes of Sergius Epifanovich of the Kiev Theological Academy, Polycarp Sherwood of the Benedictine Abbey of St. Meinrad in southern Indiana, and the prolific Swiss theologian Hans Urs von Balthasar blazed the trail of the modern study of Maximus in the first half of the twentieth century. At the 1995 Oxford Patristics Conference I had the good fortune of visiting at length with another pioneer in modern Maximus studies, Lars Thunberg, a brilliant Swedish interpreter of Maximus who was also a great encourager of younger scholars working on the Confessor.[1] My notes and bibliography will certainly indicate all my debts. But much more intensely in this study than before, especially in my first chapter, I have made myself the student of an eminent cadre of cultural historians of Byzantium who have, especially over the last half-century, greatly expanded our knowledge of major developments in the sixth and seventh centuries and thereby enriched our understanding of the world in which Maximus made his mark: among others Averil Cameron, Walter Kaegi, John Haldon, Paul Magdalino, James Howard-Johnston, Mary Whitby, Michael Maas, and Derek Krueger.

I am especially grateful to two indispensable conversation partners in producing this book. Fr. Maximos (Nicholas) Constas, of the

---

[1]  See Vladimir Cvetković's fine tribute to Thunberg's work in "Saint Maximus the Confessor in Scandinavia: Homage to Lars Thunberg (1928–2007)," *Candela Nordului* 5 (2012): 29–35.

Simonos Petras Monastery (Mount Athos) and of the faculty of Holy Cross Greek Orthodox Seminary in Boston, has helped me in ongoing exchanges about the *Ambigua ad Johannem* and about literary and rhetorical features in Maximus' works. He read Chapter 2, and his invaluable criticisms and suggestions definitely improved it. Phil Booth at Oxford, who kindly sent me a pre-publication draft of his excellent monograph *Crisis of Empire*, carefully read my first chapter and offered extensive comments and criticisms, saving me from some historical errors and challenging me to strengthen my account.

Others to thank include Marek Jankowiak, who provided me a copy of his 2009 University of Warsaw dissertation in advance of its publication; Prof. Ed Siecienski, who sent me his unpublished Fordham University dissertation on the use of Maximus' writings at the Council of Florence; Fr. Andrew Louth and Fr. Joshua Lollar, both of whom furnished me with pre-publication drafts of their essays for *The Oxford Handbook of Maximus the Confessor*; and Profs. Pauline Allen and Bronwen Neil, who allowed me access to the page proofs of *The Oxford Handbook of Maximus the Confessor* just before its publication.

I am also profoundly indebted to Bishop Maxim Vasiljević for the invitation to present a lecture in the international conference on Maximus in Belgrade, Serbia, in October 2012. This conference's presentations, rich discussion, and celebratory events were a sheer gift to me and many others. Fr. Nikolaos Loudovikos and Fr. Demetrios Harper were gracious hosts and marvelous conversation partners while I attended a conference in Thessaloniki in May 2014, and I have bene-fited much from their recent work on Maximus. Prof. Doru Costache and other friends at St. Andrews Theological College in Sydney, along with Prof. Adam Cooper of the John Paul II Institute in Melbourne, and Profs. Pauline Allen and Bronwen Neil at Australian Catholic University in Brisbane, have also on two long visits Down Under been wonderful hosts and colleagues in Maximus studies, and I thank them for their hospitality (and contagious Aussie humor).

At the Oxford University Press, I am grateful for the encourage-ment and superlative work of Tom Perridge, Karen Raith, Gayathri Manoharan, my copy editor Joanna North and my proofreader Hayley Buckley. Far from Oxford, here in the Emmanuel Christian Seminary at Milligan College in northeast Tennessee, I have been greatly aided by assistant librarian Sarah Arndt and by graduate assistants Stefanie Coleman and Tom Tatterfield.

Finally, I also wish to acknowledge Peeters Publishing in Leuven for granting me permission to use material from my essay "The Passion of Jesus Christ in Maximus the Confessor: A Reconsideration," *Studia Patristica* 37 (2001) for Chapter 7 of this monograph. I am also grateful to E. J. Brill Publishing in Leiden for permission to use material from my essay "The Dialectics and Therapeutics of Desire in Maximus the Confessor," *Vigiliae Christianae* 65 (2011), 425–5. Lastly, I thank Sage Publishing for permission to use material from my essay "Aligning and Reorienting the Passible Self: Maximus the Confessor's Virtue Ethics," *Studies in Christian Ethics* 26 (2013), 333–50, especially in Chapter 8 of the present study.

TRANSLATION NOTE: I have made some use of preexisting translations of ancient texts and of Maximus, including my own, but in certain cases slightly emended previous translations (as will be indicated in my footnotes). All other translations are my own.

Paul M. Blowers

*Emmanuel Christian Seminary at Milligan College*
*October 2015*

# Contents

## Part III: Maximus' Vision for the Transfigured Creation

# List of Abbreviations

## ABBREVIATIONS OF MAXIMUS THE CONFESSOR'S WORKS

| | |
|---|---|
| *Amb. Jo.*[*] | *Ambigua ad Johannem* |
| *Amb. Th.* | *Ambigua ad Thomam* |
| *Car.* | *Capita de caritate* |
| *Disp. Pyrr.* | *Disputatio cum Pyrrho* |
| *Ep./Epp.* | *Epistula/Epistulae* |
| *Exp. Ps. 59* | *Expositio in psalmum LIX* |
| *LA* | *Liber asceticus* |
| *Myst.* | *Mystagogia* |
| *Opusc.* | *Opuscula theologica et polemica* |
| *Or. dom.* | *Expositio orationis dominicae* |
| *QD* | *Quaestiones et dubia* |
| *Q. Thal.* | *Quaestiones ad Thalassium* |
| *Th. Oec.* | *Capita theologica et oeconomica* |

## ABBREVIATIONS OF SERIES, PRIMARY WORKS, AND SECONDARY STUDIES

| | |
|---|---|
| ACO II, 1 | *Acta conciliorum oecumenicorum*, series secunda, vol. 1 (ed. R. Reidinger) |
| ACO II, 2 | *Acta conciliorum oecumenicorum*, series secunda, vol. 2 (ed. R. Reidinger) |
| Allen and Neil | Pauline Allen and Bronwen Neil, eds. and trans., *Maximus the Confessor and His Companions: Documents from Exile* |
| Berthold | George Berthold, trans., *Maximus Confessor: Selected Writings*, Classics of Western Spirituality |
| Blowers and Wilken | Paul Blowers and Robert Wilken, trans., *On the Cosmic Mystery of Jesus Christ: Selected Writings from St. Maximus the Confessor* |
| BSGRT | Bibliotheca scriptorum graecorum et romanorum teubneriana |

[*] For the text of the *Ambigua ad Johannem*, I am using Maximos Constas's corrected version of the PG edition, though retaining (as does Constas) its column/section designations.

| | |
|---|---|
| CCCM | Corpus Christianorum, continuatio mediaevalis |
| *CCEB* | Averil Cameron, *Changing Cultures in Early Byzantium* (collected studies) |
| CCSG | Corpus Christianorum, series graeca |
| CCT | Corpus Christianorum in Translation |
| Constas I, II | Maximos (Nicholas) Constas, ed. and trans., *On Difficulties in the Church Fathers: The* Ambigua *of Maximos the Confessor* |
| GCS | Griechischen christlichen Schriftsteller der ersten drei Jahrhunderte |
| GCS NF | GCS Neue Folge |
| GNO | Gregorii Nysseni Opera |
| LCL | Loeb Classical Library |
| *MC* | Felix Heinzer and Christoph Schönborn, eds., *Maximus Confessor Actes du Symposium sur Maxime le Confesseur, Fribourg, 2–5 septembre 1980* |
| Neil and Allen | Bronwen Neil and Pauline Allen, eds. and trans., *The [Greek] Life of Maximus the Confessor: Recension 3* |
| NETS | Albert Pietersma and Benjamin Wright, eds., *New English Translation of the Septuagint* |
| *OHMC* | Pauline Allen and Bronwen Neil, eds., *The Oxford Handbook of Maximus the Confessor* |
| PG | Patrologia Graeca |
| PL | Patrologia Latina |
| PO | Patrologia Orientalis |
| PTS | Patristische Texte und Studien |
| SC | Sources Chrétiennes |
| TTH | Translated Texts for Historians |
| Vasiljević | Maxim Vasijević, ed., *Knowing the Purpose of Creation through the Resurrection: Proceedings of the Symposium on St. Maximus the Confessor, Belgrade, October 18–21, 2012* |

# Introduction

As one of the most prolific theologians of the late ancient and early medieval periods in Christian history, and as a towering figure in Orthodox tradition, competing with John Damascene for the title of "Thomas Aquinas of the East," Maximus the Confessor's thought has been analyzed through and through in its properly theological, philosophical, and ascetical dimensions. There is an enormous bibliography of secondary studies of Maximus in numerous languages, and a new international burst of energy in Maximian studies has unfolded within the past two decades alone.[1] Other than the famous positions that he articulated in the last great phase of the ancient controversies concerning the natures, person, operations, and wills of Jesus Christ, however, Maximus' larger theological achievement has not always been so closely scrutinized with respect to the immediate background and foreground of his writings or the concrete contexts in which he was formed and spent his career. Historical and dogmatic theologians, meanwhile, perpetually run the risk of extrapolating systems of ideas from historic Christian thinkers like Maximus and disembodying them from the messy world of vital theology where those thinkers staked their claims and where their speculations and insights first began to take on trajectories of their own.

One striking example of this interpretive risk can be found in the longstanding profile of Maximus as an essentially or systematically anti-Origenist theologian. The profile is not completely unwarranted, to be sure, given his sustained criticism of radical Origenists, explored many years ago by Polycarp Sherwood and investigated by many

---

[1] See the excellent bibliographic compilation by Mikonja Knežević, *Maximus the Confessor (580–662): Bibliography*, Bibliographia serbica theologica 6 (Belgrade: Institute for Theological Research, 2012).

others since. Maximus clearly considered systematized Origenism to be flawed as a reimagining of the economy of creation and redemption. But in fact there were multiple "Origenisms" afloat in the wake of both Origen himself and his influential fourth-century devotee Evagrius Ponticus, some more controversial than others. One was the radicalized version of Origenist cosmology and eschatology circulating in certain Palestinian monasteries in the sixth century. This is the version presumably most problematic for Maximus and other critics, and it provided a foil for important features of his own mature thinking on the origins and destiny of creation. Another stream, however, was the legacy of Origen's own ascetical gospel, his compelling vision of the spiritual life, wherein Christ the Logos is the romancer and educator of souls who entices the deep-seated *erôs* of human nature toward the transcending beauty and goodness of God. In his devotion to this particular legacy, Maximus was himself a certain kind of Origenist, and so were many others before and after him, including the likes of Gregory of Nyssa and Dionysius the Areopagite, two of the Confessor's most crucial sources. And yet some of the scholarship on Maximus, in its zeal to profile him as a philosophical anti-Origenist in the wake of the anathematization of Origenism at the Council of Constantinople of 553, has downplayed the recontextualization of Origen that still lay at the core of his spiritual teaching. In doing so it risks belittling a crucial thread linking Maximus to the earliest traditions of Greek Christian asceticism, as well as Maximus' own unique improvisations on Origenist–Evagrian ascetical theology.

What is demanded, especially in assessing the work of a thinker whose theology is as intricate and nuanced as Maximus', is the kind of thick description that elicits not only the internal intelligibility or consistency in his literary corpus but also the often subtle signals that his work has once been addressed to live audiences, that it has stood on the cusp of inherited traditions and new interpretive contexts, and that it is the product of personal commitments to networks of mentors, friends, and sympathizers as well as of carefully refined intellectual judgments developed over long periods of time. In most of his spiritual and theological works, unlike some of his letters and christological *Opuscula*, Maximus normally does not furnish an accompanying commentary on the live circumstances in which he was writing. Like other theologians of his age, and unlike many postmodern Christian thinkers sensitized to remain aware of their own cultural and historical location, he was not a *self-consciously* contextualizing theologian. This complicates the task of penetrating more than simply the general background and foreground of his works.

In the case of the *Ambigua to John*, for instance, we know that Maximus is rebutting Origenism, but we long to know more from him about the exact provenance and character of the Origenism that he is refuting. In the *Questions and Responses for Thalassius*, we see him developing elaborate exegetical and theological responses to scriptural queries posed to him by a friend who was the abbot of a Libyan monastery, but we wish he would reveal more about what has prompted this particular set of questions on this particular set of ambiguous or perplexing biblical texts. At one level, the *Questions and Responses for Thalassius* is rather predictable and transparent. Thalassius's monks want to know how certain obscure biblical texts are still relevant to their ascetical disciplines, and Maximus uses classic Alexandrian forms of "spiritual" interpretation, well-tested within monastic tradition, imaginatively to answer the queries in ways that are edifying, in the manner of what later became known as *lectio divina*. And yet we are left wanting for a word from Maximus on the antecedent debates in patristic exegesis over the possible abuses of non-literal exegesis, or on why he is so secure, now that Origen's legacy has become controversial, in carrying forward the tradition of Alexandrian–Origenian allegory and anagogy, especially when these kinds of interpretation had been employed in support of speculative and controversial features of Origenist doctrine. More to the point, we would love for Maximus to articulate more explicitly the kind of "Origenist" he still allows himself to be in an age of multiple Origenisms. A "corrected" form of Origenist–Evagrian spiritual doctrine and asceticism is, after all, still an appropriation, still indebted to a chemistry uniquely and organically related to these controversial thinkers of an earlier period. The issue is all the more acute when we consider just how much Maximus gleans from Evagrius, the most touted Origenist thinker after Origen himself. I will take up the issue again in Chapter 2.

Still another example from the earlier part of Maximus' literary corpus is his *Dialogue on the Ascetical Life* (*Liber asceticus*), a work clearly resembling the "conferences" recorded in the *Sayings of the Desert Fathers* (*Apophthegmata patrum*) from an earlier generation. There is much in the work consistent with the "classic" Maximus, such as the emphasis on divine kenosis and incarnation as the ultimate rationale of the ascetical life (and of all created existence), and on the double love commandment as formative for all Christian virtue and praxis. But why does Maximus see fit to deploy this literary throwback to the older desert monastic tradition, and boldly to retrieve the stringent model of penitential discipline and self-mortification typical of that tradition? Has he experienced this model for himself in Palestine or Egypt, or is this perhaps just one among other alternative literary artifices for expounding on the exigencies of the ascetical life?

These kinds of questions especially arise in conjunction with works from Maximus' early monastic career, prior to his deep public involvement in the christological crisis of the mid-seventh century. They are all the more imposing because, as we shall see in Chapter 1, there is extensive new biographical debate on his precise background and monastic provenance. At least with his more christologically-focused works from the latter decades of his career, we have abundant evidence of the immediate foreground of imperial and ecclesiastical politics in North Africa, Rome, and Constantinople.

Meanwhile, there are great challenges for bringing together the pieces of Maximus' life to form a complete portrait, one in which his early work as a monastic theologian and spiritual pedagogue is fully integrated with his more controversial public persona in the monothelete controversy that preoccupied him from the 640s to the end of his life. Juan Miguel Garrigues has attempted one such portrait, claiming to find an evolution in Maximus' thought commensurate with distinctive phases of his career. Garrigues maps five stages in Maximus' development. First is "the monk" deeply engaged with Origenist spiritual doctrine and its strongly existentialist doctrine of human freedom enhanced by Gregory of Nyssa, the troubling elements of which Maximus supposedly corrected by appeal to the stabilizing ontology of Dionysius the Areopagite. Second is "the nomad" cast into monastic exile (*xeniteia*) in Africa by the Arab invasions, taking on a more eschatological outlook and preparing, under the guidance of his spiritual father Sophronius, for the emerging battle with imperially-supported monothelete Christology. Third is "the theologian" matured through the refiner's fire of the monothelete controversy. Fourth is "the confessor" whose commitment to dyothelete Christology leads him ultimately to Rome and a dangerous alliance with the Roman Church against Constantinople. Fifth and finally is "the martyr," Maximus' destiny after having been taken into custody, tried, tortured, and exiled by the imperial authorities in Constantinople, giving his life for his Orthodox confession.[2] Commensurate with all this, Garrigues argues, was Maximus' doctrine of deification, the very skeleton of his theology. Maximus had to overcome the "intellectualism" and Platonic dualism of Evagrius, and to transcend the "dramatic existentialism" of Gregory of Nyssa, whose eschatological spirituality focused on the fulfillment of "nature" through free will. At last he discerned the superiority of "person" to "nature," and re-envisioned deification as *personal* adoption in the Son" through the kenosis of divine love.[3]

Garrigues's reconstruction is imaginative but far too tidy, and presupposes an artificial gap between the allegedly immature monk and the mature theologian; it also oversimplifies or misrepresents authentic elements of development in Maximus' thinking.[4] Garrigues is one among other scholars, moreover, who have tended to view Maximus as a precursor of Aquinas, anticipating the definition of deification more as a fruition of infused grace than of nature's own aspiration in keeping with its true *telos*.

Meanwhile, I do not disparage Garrigues's attempt to construct a coherent portrait of Maximus in his context, but my own goal in this book is to take fuller account of the complexities in his formation as a theologian. Like Garrigues, I write as a historical theologian, not as a social or cultural historian of Byzantium, and yet I am obliged to begin this study in Chapter 1 with an extended examination of the difficulties faced in reconstructing Maximus' life. Here I rely heavily on the best recent scholarship on seventh-century Byzantium, and on the newer studies analyzing the rival Greek and Syriac *Vitae* of Maximus, though recognizing that Byzantinists and historical theologians have their differences of interest and perspective.[5] I also try in the first two chapters to set the historical stage for my exploration, in subsequent chapters, of some of the principal themes and guiding leitmotifs of his theology. We will investigate, in Chapters 3 through 5, the "cosmic landscapes" of his thought, including his conceptualization of the

[2] Juan Miguel Garrigues, *Maxime le Confesseur: La charité, avenir divin de l'homme* (Paris: Beauchesne, 1976), 35–75.

[3] Ibid., 79–199.

[4] See Marcel Doucet's convincing criticism of Garrigues in "Vues récentes sur les 'métamorphoses' de la pensée de saint Maxime le Confesseur," *Science et Esprit* 31 (1979): 267–302.

[5] On this difference, see Averil Cameron, "The Cost of Orthodoxy," *Church History and Religious Culture* 93 (2013): 339–61, esp. 340–3.

basic architecture of the created cosmos, the christocentric focus of his cosmology, and the eschatological interfaces between his vision of the world and his vision for the Church. In these chapters I intend to enhance what Hans Urs von Balthasar first began to develop as a "theo-dramatic" reading of Maximus, with Christ the New Adam as the principal actor in the drama of the salvation and transfiguration of the world. I shall describe as well what I call Maximus' "cosmo-politeian" perspective, which sees all (especially rational) creatures, in their *particularity* both in the structure of the cosmos and in concrete history, undertaking their subsidiary performances in the new *politeia* of creaturely existence inaugurated by Jesus Christ.

In the next section, Chapters 6 through 8, I examine elements of Maximus' theological anthropology, his teaching on the precise character of Christ's redemptive work, and the yield of these things for his instruction in the moral and spiritual life of the Christian. My aim in these chapters is not to revisit all the subordinate doctrinal themes already treated in detail in other studies, but to demonstrate how Maximus' overarching teleological and eschatological (and preeminently christocentric) perspective is determinative of his understanding of creation, human nature, and the fall. Humanity, I will argue, is for Maximus a theo-dramatic work-in-progress. His protology, or doctrine of "beginnings," is thoroughly conditioned by anticipation of the revelation of the new eschatological humanity of Jesus Christ. The human creature's own *politeia*, the parameters and protocols of performing her or his role in the denouement of the drama of Christ, is marked by forms of love and virtue—new life in the Spirit—that divulge the indwelling Christ, the Christ who (in a famous image that Maximus expands from Origen) "incarnates" himself in the virtues.

In the final section, having considered Maximus at length in his own context, I turn to some of the historic attempts to recontextualize his work in new theological settings both East and West. These diverse receptions go far in disclosing the breadth of his thought and the ongoing prospects of critical but constructive retrieval of his legacy. In my closing Epilogue, I attempt to integrate the different aspects and phases of his career into a refreshed portrait of his achievement as a contextual theologian—a portrait that commends itself to continuing engagement of Maximus as a "Confessor" for East, West, and Global South.

# Part I

# Backgrounds

# 1

## Maximus in His Historical Setting: Betwixt and Between

They were neither the best of times nor the worst of times for the Byzantine Empire. They were, however, unsettled and unsettling. Maximus the Confessor's life as a monk, churchman, and theologian fell betwixt and between certain definitive historical developments in Byzantium in the late sixth and seventh centuries. Born in 580, he lived just past the grand age of Justinian (r. 527–65), the peak period of Byzantine power and imperial expansion. The Byzantium that Maximus knew was an empire aspiring to reclaim an already elusive greatness after the severe instabilities that dogged it during the troubled regimes of Justinian's successors. And yet Maximus died in 662, well before the alternating expansions and shrinkages of the Byzantine Empire devolved into a final, fateful trajectory of decline.

### FROM JUSTINIAN TO HERACLIUS: BYZANTINE ASPIRATIONS TO A CHRISTIAN WORLD ORDER

Justinian's own imprint on Maximus' world was enormous, since he had much to do with the overall configuration of Christianity in the Mediterranean basin in the sixth and seventh centuries.[1] During his reign, a subtle transformation of the Roman Empire emerged, a

[1] For an excellent overview, see John Meyendorff, *Imperial Unity and Christian Divisions: The Church 480–680 A.D.* (Crestwood, NY: St. Vladimir's Seminary Press, 1989), 207–50.

"Byzantine alloy, a world in which Christian, Roman, Greek, and many local elements fused to create a new medieval civilization within imperial borders."[2]

Justinian, to be sure, inherited his fair share of monumental challenges to advancing such a civilization. But he also created new ones of his own. Endorsing a mode of interpreting Chalcedonian Christology in terms that invoked the revered (if controversial) legacy of Cyril of Alexandria, Justinian, with the counsel of his influential wife Theodora, set a precedent for later emperors maneuvering to draw the miaphysite churches of the East back into the fold of Chalcedonian orthodoxy even as that same "orthodoxy" was still being defined. But his mixed signals in dealing with the miaphysites, strong-arming them but also trying to appease them in the imperially orchestrated Council of Constantinople of 553, backfired badly, alienating those churches all the more while also deepening frictions with the Roman Church. The destabilizing fall-out of all of this lasted well into Maximus' own time.

The westward military campaigns undertaken by Justinian's illustrious commander Belisarius took back Roman Africa from Arian Vandal occupation,[3] so that the region was securely under Byzantine control during the years Maximus later spent with the Eukratas monastic circle near Carthage. But this military reconquest and cultural disruption only commenced a long process of "Roman" reclamation,[4] a yet-to-be negotiated Byzantino-African identity that significantly muddied the African churches' relation to Constantinople. Not all Catholics in North Africa were enthused about the arrival of a "Byzantine" orthodoxy, and even pushed back against some of Justinian's theological initiatives and endorsements. Justinian was equipped with an extensive dossier of imperial legislation, the *Corpus juris civilis*, and even with a semi-official handbook of scriptural interpretation composed by his senior legal minister or Quaestor, Junillus Africanus, who sought to demonstrate the Bible's support for the divine right of the emperor and the official

[2] Michael Maas, "Roman Questions, Byzantine Answers: Contours of the Age of Justinian," in Michael Maas, ed., *The Cambridge Companion to the Age of Justinian* (Cambridge: Cambridge University Press, 2005), 4.

[3] Recounted in Procopius, *De bellis, lib.* 3–4 (LCL 81).

[4] On the political, administrative, and social challenges of this reclamation, see Jonathan Conant, *Staying Roman: Conquest and Identity in Africa and the Mediterranean, 439–700* (Cambridge: Cambridge University Press, 2012), 196–251.

imperial orthodoxy.[5] With these sources at his disposal, Justinian projected a reconsecrated symbiosis of Church and state. Expressed in virtually mythic terms in his sixth *Novella*,[6] this symbiosis would have Constantinople, capital and home to the rebuilt patriarchal basilica of Hagia Sophia, as the sacral center of gravity for Byzantium's Christian world order. But at the level of the provinces, where the emperor remained dependent on governors, exarchs, other political or military officials, and even bishops to carry out his universally binding will, this elusive ideal was constantly tested. One reason was the sheer weight of its own hubris. The historian Procopius famously lampooned this in his *Secret History*, vilifying Justinian as a capricious rogue and "prince of demons,"[7] a hard label to make completely stick given, among other things, Justinian's personal studiousness with regard to matters theological and ecclesiastical.[8] In the long run, however, local resistance in all its forms (religious, political, cultural, etc.) was an enduring and destabilizing reality on the ground.

This situation prompted Justinian's nephew and successor, Justin II (r. 565–78), to implement a policy whereby provincial governors would no longer be sent out from Constantinople but elected by local aristocrats and bishops.[9] These kinds of appeasements, however,

---

[5] See Junillus's *Handbook of the Basic Principles of Divine Law*, ed. and trans. with introduction and notes by Michael Maas, *Exegesis and Empire in the Early Byzantine Mediterranean: Junillus Africanus and the* Instituta Regularia Divinae Legis (Tübingen: Mohr Siebeck, 2003). On the Bible and imperial power in Junillus's hermeneutics, see Maas's discussion ibid., 65–71.

[6] For the text from the sixth *Novella* propounding the perfect concert of the "divine gifts" (*dona Dei*) of *imperium* and *sacerdotium*, see Ernest Barker, *Social and Political Thought in Byzantium* (Oxford: Oxford University Press, 1957), 75–6; for further Byzantine imperial texts building on such a precedent and moving beyond it, see ibid., 84–5, 89–104.

[7] See Procopius's *Historia arcana* 12.14–32; 18.1–44, trans. Anthony Kaldellis, *The Secret History with Related Texts* (Indianapolis: Hackett, 2010), 58–61, 80–6; and specifically on the "demonic" accusation, see Averil Cameron, *Procopius and the Sixth Century* (Berkeley: University of California Press, 1985), 56–8.

[8] See Procopius, *De aedificiis* 1.1.9 (LCL 343:4). Meyendorff (*Imperial Unity and Christian Division*s, 245–8) notes how modern secular historians have also been hard on Justinian for his "zig-zagging" policies and maneuvers. Many have doubtless struggled to imagine how Christology in its own right (which Justinian himself addressed in writing), rather than sheer political self-interest, could have played such a central role in the controversies of the time. For Justinian's own christological treatises, see Kenneth Wesche, trans., *On the Person of Christ: The Christology of Emperor Justinian* (Crestwood, NY: St. Vladimir's Seminary Press, 1991).

[9] See here Peter Sarris, *Empires of Faith: The Fall of Rome to the Rise of Islam, 500–700* (Oxford: Oxford University Press, 2011), 226–8.

did little to quell the resurgence of local unrest. Meanwhile, Byzantium was headed toward unrelenting pressures on its imperial borders by Lombards, Slavs, Avars, Persians, and Arabs, and the specter of new upsets to an already fragile imperial equilibrium. These external challenges would have much to do, then, with the strongly defensive posture that the empire assumed, but not before Justinian's immediate successors attempted some awkwardly aggressive measures. Warren Treadgold appropriately titles the period between Justinian and Heraclius, 565–610, the era of "the danger of overextension." Justin II not only further strained relations with the provinces, he also learned little from Justinian's stormy relation with the miaphysite churches, repeating the calamitous mixture of negotiation and force in dealing with them. Justin prematurely attacked the Persians on the eastern front and thrust the empire into a very precarious position. His successor Tiberius II (r. 578–82) dipped lavishly into the imperial treasury to try to resolve problems of government and military security. Maurice (r. 582–602), an able military commander, nonetheless had "one major army and three major wars to fight," and despite a glorious victory against the Persians, he presided over a dramatic depletion of resources and manpower. In the melee of trying to stage an army to ward off the impending threat on Constantinople from Slavs and Avars amassed in the Balkans, Maurice and five of his sons were captured and cruelly executed by co-conspirators of his successor Phocas (r. 602–10), whose subsequent reign saw a sustained famine and an even more disastrous weakening of the empire's borders.[10]

The seventh century, Maximus the Confessor's century, truly set the stage for the "reduced medieval state" that Byzantium was destined to become.[11] In this respect, Heraclius (b. 575, r. 610–41), the emperor of Maximus' early and middle career, was a crucial transitional figure who desired to reestablish the grandiosity of the reigns of his predecessors Constantine and Justinian while negotiating the fault line between imperial idealism and the stark realities of political, economic, military, and religious upheaval. Shortly after

[10] Warren Treadgold, *A History of the Byzantine State and Society* (Stanford: Stanford University Press, 1997), 218–41; see also Sarris, *Empires of Faith*, 169–204, 226–45; John Haldon, *Byzantium in the Seventh Century: The Transformation of a Culture*, revised edn. (Cambridge: Cambridge University Press, 1990), 31–40.
[11] James Howard-Johnston, "Byzantium and Its Neighbors," in Elizabeth Jeffreys, ed., *The Oxford Handbook of Byzantine Studies* (Oxford: Oxford University Press, 2008), 939.

Heraclius's ascendancy, the Persians handed the Byzantine army a devastating defeat near Antioch, and eventually marched on Jerusalem in 614.[12] There they allegedly attacked (but, it seems, did not destroy) the Church of the Holy Sepulchre, Eastern Christianity's holiest shrine. They captured the Patriarch Zacharias, massacred hundreds of Christians, and stole the cherished relic of the True Cross.[13] The event was symbolically enormous, signaling the heightened stakes of controlling the empire's borders. It is rightly compared to the sack of Rome by the Visigoths in 410, which sent shockwaves across the Christian population in the West and signaled the end of an era of security.[14]

In the meantime, another Persian army advanced through Asia Minor as far as Chalcedon, just across the Sea of Marmara from Constantinople. By 615 dispatches were sent to the Persian ruler Chosroes II to try to negotiate a settlement. The anonymous *Paschal Chronicle* quotes one of the dispatches as an appeal to Chosroes to recognize the divinely bestowed "providence" protecting the earthly "kingdom" (generically speaking) and deeming it worthy of freedom from disturbance. In highly deferential terms it blames Heraclius's predecessor Phocas for having failed to pay due diplomatic respect to the Persian monarch, and begs "forgiveness" in order to appease Chosroes and obviate further Persian aggression.[15] This appeal fell on deaf ears, and was probably laughable to the Persians who were doing well in battle and confident of further decisive victories against the Byzantines.[16] Compounding difficulties, the Slavs and Avars were strengthening in the Balkans and poised to strike

[12] See Theophanes, *Chronographia, Anno Mundi 6103–6106*, ed. and trans. Cyril Mango and Roger Scott, *The Chronicle of Theophanes Confessor: Byzantine and Near Eastern History AD 284–813* (Oxford: Oxford University Press, 1997), 429–31.

[13] See the report of the Judean monk Antiochus Strategius, trans. from a Georgian MS by F. C. Conybeare, "Antiochus Strategos' Account of the Sack of Jerusalem (614)," *English Historical Review* 25 (1910): 502–17. Details of Strategos's report have nonetheless been contested by James Howard-Johnston, *Witnesses to a World Crisis: Historians and Histories of the Middle East in the Seventh Century* (Oxford: Oxford University Press, 2011), 164–7, 422. Cf. also Nicephorus, *Breviarium historicum* 12, Greek text ed. and trans. Cyril Mango, *Nikephoros, Patriarch of Constantinople: Short History* (Washington, DC: Dumbarton Oaks, 1990), 54, 55.

[14] Jan Drijvers, "Heraclius and the *Restitutio Crucis*: Notes on Symbolism and Ideology," in Gerrit Reinink and Bernard Stolte, eds., *The Reign of Heraclius (610–641): Crisis and Confrontation* (Leuven: Peeters, 2002), 175.

[15] *Chronicon Paschale*, ed. Ludwig Dindorf (Bonn: E. Weber, 1832), 1:707–9.

[16] See Nicephoros, *Brev. hist.* 6–8 (Mango, 44–8). For fuller analysis see Walter Kaegi, *Heraclius: Emperor of Byzantium* (Cambridge: Cambridge University Press, 2003), 58–99.

Constantinople. In June of 623, feigning a diplomatic mission to Heraclius at Selymbria just west of the capital, the Avars ambushed the imperial party, forcing Heraclius to don plain clothes, grab his crown, and escape back to Constantinople.[17] Only a hastily negotiated peace treaty, with the enemy receiving a massive sum of tribute money, temporarily staved off the Avar threat.

Heraclius's rocky first decade was not to have the last word on his reign. He had not been able for long to capitalize on the opprobrium cast on his predecessor Phocas, and had been thrust from the outset into a military and diplomatic nightmare. Technically, moreover, he was a usurper and had to prove his legitimacy.[18] His political and military prowess, however, was to be vindicated in a new and decisive campaign against the Persian Sassanid dynasty beginning in 624. Intermittently, the Persian support of, and involvement in, a coalition of Slavs and Avars that laid siege to Constantinople in 626 sent a clear signal that the very viability of Byzantium was in question.[19]

Though the capture of Jerusalem was disastrous for Heraclius, Byzantine historians and the esteemed panegyrist George of Pisidia predictably amplified the drama of Heraclius's Persian campaign, hailing the conquering hero and quoting alleged speeches of the emperor in which he exhorted his troops to a spiritual as well as material showdown. They played it up as a crusade against infidels who had committed sacrilege by desecrating the Holy City and stealing the priceless relic of the True Cross,[20] though the harsh reality, as Walter Kaegi notes, was a testing of military wits in "expeditionary warfare of maneuver over vast distances" across Asia Minor, the Caucasus, western Iran, and ultimately Mesopotamia.[21] All the while Heraclius employed biblical

---

[17] Nicephoros, *Brev. hist.* 10 (Mango, 50–2).

[18] As emphasized by Ralph-Johannes Lilie, *Byzanz: Das zweite Rom* (Berlin: Siedler, 2003), 84.

[19] On the 626 siege of Constantinople, see *Chron. Pasch.* (Dindorf 1:715–26); Nicephoros, *Brev. hist.* 13 (Mango, 58–60). According to the *Chronicon*, the ultimate aversion of the Avar threat was credited to the intercession of the Theotokos. For further analysis of this dramatic event in the survival of Byzantium, see James Howard-Johnston, "The Siege of Constantinople in 626," in Cyril Mango and Gilbert Dagron, eds., *Constantinople and Its Hinterland* (Aldershot: Variorum, 1995), 131–42.

[20] Fiercely defending the application of "crusade" and "holy war" to Heraclius's exploits against the Persians is Geoffrey Regan, *First Crusader: Byzantium's Holy Wars* (New York: Palgrave Macmillan, 2001), 53–134.

[21] *Heraclius: Emperor of Byzantium*, 122–55, quoted at 125. Kaegi abundantly cites the historians' and panegyrists' claims concerning Heraclius's military and spiritual heroics.

prophecy, especially Daniel, to prove how his campaign was divinely sanctioned, which helped justify, in turn, his intolerance and cruelty toward enemies who showed contempt for his aura as Christian emperor.[22] Help came as well from the Syriac Christian *Alexander Legend* (c.629), a work that retold the story of Alexander the Great as a prophet of the Messiah who vowed to place his throne in Jerusalem, and whose own conquest of the Persians adumbrated Heraclius's exploits and redemption of the Holy City.[23] In 627–8, having forged an alliance with Kök Turks, Heraclius at last invaded the Persian heartland in Mesopotamia, defeated Chosroes II, and negotiated the Persians' withdrawal from the Levant and Egypt. As important as the military victory was the recovery of the True Cross and its associated relics, which thoroughly sealed the religious interpretation of the Persian campaign.

## HERACLIUS, THE RISE OF ISLAM, AND THE COSMOS OF BYZANTINE CHRISTIAN CULTURE IN THE SEVENTH CENTURY

Heraclius's ceremonial restoration of the True Cross to Jerusalem in 630 was no simple ceremonial accent mark on his defeat of the Persians. It was part of a concerted ideological campaign to retrieve the legacy of Constantine, for whose regime the cross also famously had unique meaning as a sign of sanctified dominion. With this powerful public gesture, Heraclius "aspired to the renewal of his reign, a new beginning, and the start of a new age after a successfully concluded war."[24] The poet laureate George of Pisidia,[25] a deacon of

---

[22] Ibid., 144–5, 147. On the prophetic apocalypticism surrounding Heraclius's exploits against the Persians, see Gerrit Reinink, "Heraclius, the New Alexander: Apocalyptic Prophecies," in Reinink and Stolte, *The Reign of Heraclius (610–641)*, 81–94.

[23] Trans. in E. A. Wallis Budge, *The History of Alexander the Great: Being the Syriac Version of the Pseudo-Callisthenes* (Cambridge: Cambridge University Press, 1889; reprinted Piscataway, NJ: Gorgias Pres, 2003), 144–58.

[24] Drijvers, "Heraclius and the *Restitutio Crucis*," 186.

[25] For excellent overviews of George's poetic corpus in context, see Howard-Johnston, *Witnesses to a World Crisis*, 16–35; also Joseph Frendo, "The Poetic Achievement of George of Pisidia," in Ann Moffatt, ed., *Maistor: Classical, Byzantine, and Renaissance Studies for Robert Browning* (Canberra: Australian Association for

Hagia Sophia, in turn contributed to crafting an imperial myth according to which Heraclius's reign was not only a new beginning but indeed, a "new creation." In his poem *On the Restoration of the True Cross*, George set out the event's eschatological significance as a signal of the emperor's cosmic sovereignty on Christ's behalf.[26] Indeed, among his various panegyrics on Heraclius was an elegant epic entitled the *Hexaemeron*, which used the six-day creation story in Genesis 1 as the thematic backdrop for eulogizing the cosmic dimensions of the emperor's military and political achievement. In the Creator's struggle to bring new order and "rhythm" ($\acute{\rho}\upsilon\theta\mu\acute{o}s$) out of the material chaos of nascent creation, George envisions a compelling analogy with the new cosmic order inaugurated by Heraclius's victory over the Persians.[27] In one segment of the *Hexaemeron*, George styles an address on the lips of Sergius, Patriarch of Constantinople, extolling the Creator as Architect of the wonders of the world, and bidding the Creator to open wide the "lower gates" of the earthly city, the imperial capital, for Heraclius now to pass through as the "deliverer of the cosmos" ($\kappa o\sigma\mu o\rho\acute{\upsilon}\sigma\tau\eta s$).[28] In another panegyric, the *Heraclias*, George praises the emperor in virtually apocalyptic terms as "commander of cosmic rebirth" ($\sigma\tau\rho\alpha\tau\eta\gamma\acute{o}s$ $\kappa o\sigma\mu\iota\kappa o\hat{\upsilon}$ $\gamma\epsilon\nu\epsilon\theta\lambda\acute{\iota}o\upsilon$).[29]

As Averil Cameron has demonstrated in her learned and prolific studies of early Byzantine literary culture, there was already a transformation underway in Christian discourse and rhetoric well before Heraclius's time. The developing Christian "rhetoric of empire" registered itself in manifold ways, from the writing of history to the writing of hagiography, seeking to surmount classical rhetorical forms both by exploiting them and creatively integrating figural language and religious symbols drawn from Scripture.[30] "Imperial

---

Byzantine Studies, 1984), 159–87; Mary Whitby, "George of Pisidia's Presentation of the Emperor Heraclius and His Campaigns," in Reinink and Stolte, *The Reign of Heraclius (610–641)*, 157–73.

[26] *In restitutionem Sanctae Crucis*, ed. Agostino Pertusi, *Giorgio di Pisidia Poemi, I. Panegirici Epici* (Murnau, Germany: Buch-Kunstverlag Ettal, 1959), 225–30. On the significance of George's two poems on the restoration, see also Phil Booth, "Sophronius of Jerusalem and the End of Roman History," in Philip Wood, ed., *History and Identity in the Late Antique Near East* (Oxford: Oxford University Press, 2013), 10–11.

[27] *Hexaemeron*, ll. 248–69 (PG 92:1453A–1455A).

[28] *Hex.*, ll. 1838–1910 (PG 92:1574B–1578B).

[29] *Heraclias* I, ll. 201–6 (ed. Pertusi, 249).

[30] *Christianity and the Rhetoric of Empire: The Development of Christian Discourse* (Berkeley: University of California Press, 1991), passim.

historians and poets who had previously striven to keep up 'classical' styles of writing now presented their subjects unblushingly within the terms of Old Testament typology."[31]

George of Pisidia both capitalized on this pattern and took it to all new heights in eulogizing Heraclius's bid to inaugurate a world order even greater than that of his predecessors. Already in the opening lines of his early poem *On Heraclius's Return from Africa*, which praises Heraclius's extermination of Phocas, George had admitted a poetic inadequacy to use human words (*logoi*) to describe one who was so clearly ordained by the very Logos of God himself. The thrust here and elsewhere in George's works was rhetorically to galvanize the interconnections between the divine Word, the word of Scripture, the word of the emperor, the word of the patriarch, and his own words of poetic eulogy in order to spin a sophisticated web of meaning that sealed the legitimacy, sanctity, and prophetic aura of the Heraclian regime.[32]

Historical critics may well want to drive a wedge here between the rhetoric and the reality. This was a ruler, after all, with much unfinished business. But the cultural power of this religious and political myth of Heraclius's reign should not be underestimated. Divine sanction and public confidence were things the Byzantine emperor both wanted and desperately needed. As Kaegi argues, Heraclius, before and after restoring the True Cross to Jerusalem in 630, traveled about in the Middle East and Mesopotamia, and thereby gained "a richer perspective on his contemporary world than any emperor since Theodosius I," which likely enhanced his own deeply religious as well as political and military vision.[33] With these travels abroad, including a survey of the ecclesiastical as well as strategic landscapes of his domains, Heraclius imagined moving the empire at last toward the elusive resolution on Christology and the reconsolidation of Chalcedonian and non-Chalcedonian churches that his predecessors had so grievously failed to attain. The

---

[31] Averil Cameron, "Images of Authority: Elites and Icons in Late Sixth-Century Byzantium," *Past and Present* 84 (1989): 4.

[32] See here Frendo, "The Poetic Achievement of George of Pisidia," 171–2; Mary Whitby, "George of Pisidia and the Persuasive Word: Words, Words, Words," in Elizabeth Jeffreys, ed., *Rhetoric in Byzantium: Papers from the Thirty-Fifth Spring Symposium of Byzantine Studies, Exeter College, University of Oxford, March 2001* (Aldershot: Ashgate, 2003), 181–7; ead., "George of Pisidia's Presentation of the Emperor Heraclius and His Campaigns," in Reinink and Stolte, *The Reign of Heraclius (610–641)*, 159–60, 163.

[33] *Heraclius: Emperor of Byzantium*, 201–10, quoted at 210.

historian Theophanes indicates that, while in Hierapolis (of Syria), Heraclius was met by Athanasius, the Patriarch of the Jacobite (Syrian miaphysite) churches. The Emperor allegedly promised him that if the Jacobites would embrace the Council of Chalcedon, he would make him (Chalcedonian/Melkite) Patriarch of Antioch. Athanasius at first feigned agreement with the dyophysite definition of Christ, but further inquired of the emperor whether there might yet be a single "energy" and "will" in Christ. Finding that this "monenergist" position was the emerging view of Patriarch Sergius of Constantinople, himself of Syrian origin, Heraclius authorized Athanasius's orthodoxy. With this, the Jacobites and their miaphysite counterparts in Alexandria claimed to have won a victory, boasting that the Chalcedonian establishment had effectively conceded "one nature" of Christ by virtue of affirming a single energy ($\dot{\epsilon}\nu\dot{\epsilon}\rho\gamma\epsilon\iota\alpha$) in Christ.[34] The situation was an embarrassment to Heraclius, who hoped to create a viable doctrinal consensus, and though there were other intervening developments not mentioned in Theophanes's account, the result was the *Ekthesis* (638), the emperor's declaration, endorsed by Patriarch Sergius shortly before he died, that all language of one or two energies in Christ should be entirely avoided, and that the two natures of Christ were rather joined in a single *will*.[35] Other evidence from Michael the Syrian's *Chronicle* (in Syriac) suggests instead that Athanasius remained dead-set against conciliation with Chalcedon and that Heraclius tried to force conformity by persecuting miaphysite communities in Syria.[36]

We will return later to the monothelete controversy that subsequently erupted, in which Maximus the Confessor would also be thoroughly embroiled. For now I want simply to emphasize Heraclius's recognition of Christology as an indispensable factor in the direction of establishing a viable doctrinal—and cultural—consensus throughout the empire. As Heraclius and Maximus realized from their very different perspectival locations, Christology, even in its most precise definitions, was crucial to the web or "cosmos" of Byzantine culture and religion. For Heraclius it nurtured the Eusebian myth of divinely sanctioned imperial rule and of the emperor's prerogatives as Christ's cosmic viceroy. For Maximus, as we will see in more detail later in this study, Christology grounded and

---

[34] See Theophanes, *Chron.*, A.M. 6121 (Mango and Scott, 460–1).
[35] Ibid. (Mango and Scott, 461). See p. 48 in this volume.
[36] On Michael's testimony, see Phil Booth, *Crisis of Empire: Doctrine and Dissent at the End of Late Antiquity* (Berkeley: University of California Press, 2014), 202–3.

shaped the specific moral and ascetical disciplines that he commended to his fellow monks, and more broadly those "modes of existence" (τρόποι ὑπάρξεως), or christocentric ways-of-being-in-the-world, that he envisioned for all Christians, indeed *for all created beings in heaven and on earth.* The reconcilability, if any, between the "cosmic Christologies" of Heraclius and Maximus, emperor and monk, also remains for investigation further on.

Heraclius's window of opportunity after the Persian wars to work toward christological consensus in the empire closed rather quickly, for beginning in the 630s he faced a whole new external threat to the security of the Byzantine cultural cosmos: the Arab invasions of imperial territories and the rise of Islam. The presence of Islam would put the Byzantine Empire into a defensive posture that persisted, with greater or lesser intensity, until the collapse of Constantinople to the Ottoman Turks in 1453. Early Arab incursions into the Negev and the victories in the region where Palestine, Syria, and Jordan converge, climaxing in the Arabs' devastating defeat of the Byzantines at Yarmuk in August of 636, presaged the loss of most Byzantine territories in the Middle East and North Africa. Damascus had already fallen in 634–5, and Tiberias (Galilee) in 635. Muslim control of most of Syria, Transjordan, and Palestine (including Jerusalem) was secured by 638; Mesopotamia by 640; Egypt by 641; Armenia by 645. Beginning in 647, the Muslim conquest of North Africa took much longer, but by the end of the seventh century a large portion of the region had been secured.

John Haldon appropriately emphasizes that, in comparison with the Persian wars, the Arab conquests and rise of Islam "dislocated Byzantine society much more fundamentally and dramatically, and at all levels—political, economic, and in terms of beliefs and ideas about the world."[37] Well-worn arguments about God's providential punishment of his people's infidelity were easily recalled, such as when Sophronius, Patriarch of Jerusalem, urged Patriarch Sergius to pray fervently for Heraclius to prevail "over all barbarians but especially the Saracens [Arabs], destroying their pride [since] through our sins they have now unexpectedly risen up against us, and are carrying everything off as booty with cruel and savage intent and impious and godless daring."[38]

---

[37] *Byzantium in the Seventh Century,* 364.
[38] *Epistola synodica* (ACO II, 1:490–2); trans. Pauline Allen, *Sophronius of Jerusalem and Seventh-Century Heresy: The Synodical Letter and Other Documents* (Oxford: Oxford University Press, 2009), 152–5. Sophronius displays the same penitent spirit in

For not a few Byzantine Christians, including the monks, the Arab invasions represented a veritable apocalypse.[39] Maximus, who met up in Africa with numerous monks fleeing the Arab onslaught, reflected with severe foreboding on the specter of the Arab advances in a letter to Peter the Illustrious, possibly the same person as Peter the Byzantine *strategos* (general) in Numidia,[40] dating to around 634, after Maximus' relocation near Carthage:

> What is more upsetting than the evil now taking hold of the world? What is more dreadful than what has happened? What is more tearful or fearful to those suffering it than to see a desert-inhabiting and barbarian people overrun another land as though it were its own? And see these rough and wild beasts who have only the thinnest surface with a human form outside overrun this sophisticated and luxuriant state?
>
> ... it announces the coming of the Anti-Christ, because they truly do not know the Saviour. It signifies the bad and the lawless, hating men and hating God, because they are haters of mankind and haters of God, and because they inveigh against the saints...
>
> What is more monstrous to the eyes and ears of Christians? Because you see this rough and uncouth people born to license raising up its hand against God's inheritance. But this mass of things has happened to us because of our sins.[41]

Maximus' opprobrium for the Arabs was reminiscent of the Spanish Christian poet Prudentius's earlier depiction of Europe's barbarian peoples as "wild beasts" and "four-footed creatures" in comparison

---

his *Christmas Sermon* of 634, ed. Hermann Usener, "Weihnachtspredigt des Sophronios," *Rheinisches Museum für Philologie* 41 (1886): 506–7, 514–15. See also Kaegi's analysis of this sermon in "Initial Byzantine Reactions to the Arab Conquests," *Church History* 38 (1969): 139–41.

[39] For the literary evidence of this apocalypticism, see Kaegi, "Initial Byzantine Reactions to the Arab Conquests," 141–9.

[40] For the prosopography of Peter the Illustrious, see Marek Jankowiak and Phil Booth, "A New Date-List of the Works of Maximus the Confessor," *OHMC*, 24–5, 44.

[41] *Ep.* 14 (PG 91:540A–B, 541B), trans. with analysis by Walter Kaegi, *Muslim Expansion and Byzantine Collapse in North Africa* (Cambridge: Cambridge University Press, 2010), 113–15. Polycarp Sherwood assumes, I think rightly, that Maximus was reacting in this letter to the Arab invasion of Syria. See his *Date-List of the Works of Maximus the Confessor* (Rome: Herder, 1952), 40–1. Grigory Benevich notes that Maximus' anti-Islamic rhetoric is actually "more moderate, even laconic" compared with Sophronius's, attacking the Muslims' barbarity rather than their religion. See his "Christological Polemics of Maximus the Confessor and the Emergence of Islam onto the World Stage," *Theological Studies* 72 (2011): 338–9.

with Romans.[42] Such labels may well offend modern sensitivities, but they were a function less of hardcore ethnocentrism than of the pervasive conviction that the Romano-Byzantine cultural cosmos was the protective bosom of true civilization and, of course, of Christianity as well. The same holds true of Maximus' fierce denunciations, also in his epistle to Peter the Illustrious, of the Jews' glee over Arabs spilling Christian blood.[43] The targeting of alleged Jewish collaboration in, or sympathy with, the persecution of Christians by Byzantium's enemies was rather typical from earlier chroniclers,[44] and served to amplify the apocalyptic aura of these grave periods in which Byzantine cultural security was sorely tested. When, in 632, Heraclius instigated the forced baptism of Jews in territories that were militarily or politically vulnerable, Maximus balked. Compromising a sacrament of the Church on unbelieving Jews could very well initiate the horrible apostasy predicted by Paul (2 Thess. 2:3):

> I am fearful lest [the apostasy] begin through contact between these [Jews] and the believing peoples, which will enable them to spread the evil seed of the stumbling-blocks among the most innocent folk, and there appear that manifest and undisputed sign of the end, discussed by all; according to this, they expect great temptations and struggles for the sake of the truth, for which they prepare themselves by prayers, by entreaties, by many tears, and by the changes necessary for righteousness.[45]

Compelling Jews to be baptized would thus augment rather than alleviate the sins for which God was punishing the empire.

Maximus' responses to crisis in these instances display a tension between his nervous loyalty to Byzantium's Christian imperial ideal, which assumed the emperor to be the unrivaled protector of the empire's religious and cultural security, and his readiness to appeal to a higher divine providence and judgment comprehending world

---

[42] *Contra Symmachum* 2.807–19 (LCL 398:70).     [43] *Ep.* 14 (PG 91:540A).

[44] See the accusation of Jewish participation in the Persian conquest of Jerusalem (614) in Antiochus Strategos, trans. Conybeare, "Antiochus Strategos' Account of the Sack of Jerusalem (614)," 508–9.

[45] *Ep.* 8 [end], ed. Robert Devreesse, "La fin inédite d'une lettre de saint Maxime: Un baptême forcé de juifs et de samaritains à Carthage en 632," *Revue des sciences religieuses* 17 (1937): 35, trans. Joshua Starr, "St. Maximos and the Forced Baptism at Carthage in 632," *Byzantinisch-neugriechische Jahrbücher* 16 (1940): 195. See also Starr, "Note on the Crisis of the Early Seventh Century C.E.," *Jewish Quarterly Review* NS 38 (1947): 97–9.

history and thoroughly relativizing that security. The same tension is more graphic in the later seventh-century *Apocalypse* of Pseudo-Methodius (originally in Syriac), which, on the one hand, interprets the Arab invasions as God's weapon against Byzantium's licentiousness while, on the other hand, predicting the ultimate ruination of the Arabs at the hands of the last Byzantine emperor, when

> all the fury of the wrath of the king of the Greeks shall be completed upon those who have denied Christ . . . [and] the king of the Greeks shall go up and stand on Golgotha and the holy Cross shall be placed on that spot where it had been fixed when it bore Christ. The king of the Greeks shall place his crown on the top of the holy Cross, stretch out his hands toward heaven, and hand over the kingdom to God the Father. And the holy Cross upon which Christ was crucified will be raised up to heaven, together with the royal crown.[46]

Not surprisingly, this same kind of apocalyptic reading of Byzantium's woes was destined to be applied to the empire's *doctrinal* sins as well, specifically christological heresy. Maximus himself, in his later trial in Constantinople, was to be accused (though denying the charge) of having a vision of an angelic host proclaiming that Gregory, the Byzantine exarch in Africa, could prevail as Augustus—presumably a reference to Gregory's insurrection in the 640s against the monothelete emperor.[47] Maximus' younger contemporary, the monastic theologian Anastasius of Sinai, declares in a sermon that God had granted the Arabs devastating victories against the Byzantines precisely because "Heraclius's grandson"—the monothelete emperor Constans II—exiled and brutalized Pope Martin I, the very pope with whom Maximus was allied in the Lateran Council in Rome (649) to defy the imperially-sponsored monotheletism. The imperial authorities, says Anastasius, "sent for and arrested the men in the Roman synod [i.e. Lateran Council], and excised their tongues and cut off their hands."[48] While other evidence indicates that Martin died shortly after he was taken to Constantinople, tried, and exiled, descriptions of his punishment in

---

[46] Ps-Methodius, *Apocalypse* 13:15; 14:2–4, trans. Sebastian Brock in Andrew Palmer et al., eds. and trans., *The Seventh Century in the West-Syrian Chronicles*, TTH 15 (Liverpool: Liverpool University Press, 1993), 238, 240. See also Kaegi, "Initial Byzantine Reactions to the Arab Conquests," 143–6; and Paul Alexander, *The Byzantine Apocalyptic Tradition* (Berkeley: University of California Press, 1985), 13–60 (on Ps-Methodius), 151–84 (on the motif of the "Last Roman Emperor").
[47] *Relatio motionis* §2 (Allen and Neil, 50–2).        [48] *Sermo* 3 (PG 89:1156C–D).

other sources do not mention this specific fate. Sources positively confirm this fate, however, for Maximus and his close disciples.[49] For Anastasius, meanwhile, God's final punishment for this grievous injustice was Constans II having been "slain by the sword in Sicily," which was followed by the restoration of tranquillity and order under Constantine IV.[50]

In the end we must resist inferring utterly polarized trajectories of imperial ideology and apocalypticism, since in early Byzantine Christian culture they more or less grew up together. Apocalyptic traditions and texts could prophetically vilify the emperor and his associates, cast doubt on their competence and fidelity, and hold them up for special divine judgment; but they could also serve the "imperial eschatology,"[51] portraying the (virtuous, orthodox) emperor, or the "last" emperor in Pseudo-Methodius's case, as an agent of God committed to the much-coveted security and vitality of the Byzantine cultural cosmos. And yet, as Haldon rightly cautions, we dare not underestimate the social and rhetorical power of *any* new narrative seriously challenging imperial authority in this volatile period of the breathtaking spread of Islam. Direct appeal to the prerogatives of the all-provident Creator fit with broader religious trends in the age of Heraclius, as popular trust and devotion were being invested in ostensibly more "effective" sources of supernatural power and access to God.[52] Already before the time of Heraclius and Maximus, the

---

[49]  See p. 62 in this volume.     [50]  *Sermo* 3 (PG 89:1156D).

[51]  An apt phrase used by Reinink ("Heraclius, the New Alexander," 83ff. and n. 15) and other Byzantinists, referring to the ancient and abiding Christian view that the Roman Empire was the "fourth empire" from Daniel's prophecy. See also Gerhard Podskalsky, *Byzantinische Reichseschatologie: Die Periodisierung der Weltgeschichte in der vier Grossreichen (Daniel 2 und 7) und dem tausendjährigen Friedensreiche (Apok. 20): Eine motivgeschichtliche Untersuchung* (Munich: W. Fink, 1972), esp. 51–61, 70–6; and Paul Magdalino, "The History of the Future and Its Uses: Prophecy, Policy and Propaganda," in Roderick Beaton and Charlotte Roueché, eds., *The Making of Byzantine History: Studies Dedicated to Donald M. Nichol* (Aldershot: Variorum, 1993), 3–34. On Byzantine imperial eschatology's probable influence on early Islam, see Stephen Shoemaker, "'The Reign of God Has Come': Eschatology and Empire in Late Antiquity and Early Islam," *Arabica* 61 (2014): 530, 535–50; more apprehensive about this influence, in view of problems precisely defining apocalypticism and eschatology in late antiquity, is Avril Cameron, "Late Antique Apocalyptic: A Context for the Qur'an," posted to Academia.edu but forthcoming in Hagit Amirav, Emmanouela Grypeou, and Guy Stroumsa, eds., *Visions of the End: Apocalypticism and Eschatology in the Abrahamic Religions, 6th–8th Centuries* (Leuven, 2015).

[52]  Haldon, *Byzantium in the Seventh Century*, 355–71.

charismatic ascetical sage or holy man had surfaced in Byzantine society as a unique mediator before God, a religious rallying-point.[53] The cult of the intercessory Virgin Mother, the Theotokos, though closely aligned with the imperial prestige, had grown rapidly and exercised profound influence in and beyond Constantinople.[54] By the late sixth and seventh centuries, moreover, the holy icons were also intervening as yet another crucial form of mediation between God and humanity, and with immense social and cultural consequences leading into the age of imperial iconoclasm.[55]

The question that will occupy us further on in this study is whether Maximus' developed "cosmic theology"—his "theory of everything" as Doru Costache calls it,[56] which aspires to articulate, in highly nuanced form, the interrelations between "universal" and "particular" realities under the guidance of Christ the Logos—worked to undergird the Byzantine imperial and cultural order, to challenge or even upset the security of that order, or to project a healthy dialectic of trust and distrust. Averil Cameron, for one, contends that Maximus' theological oeuvre fits into the campaign to conserve and standardize theological knowledge so as to fortify Byzantine Christian culture against the twin threats of Islam from without and heresy from within.[57] But does this do justice to the ascetical and eschatological dimensions of his work? There is the rub; and the difficulties of interpretation are considerable, since, apart from his letters, rarely in his ascetical and theological writings does Maximus explicitly refer to, or reflect on, the political and cultural foreground of his literary enterprise.

---

[53] As explicated in Peter Brown's influential study, "The Rise and Function of the Holy Man in Late Antiquity," *Journal of Roman Studies* 61 (1971), 80–101.

[54] On its roots at the imperial capital, see Vasiliki Limberis, *Divine Heiress: The Virgin Mary and the Creation of Christian Constantinople* (New York: Routledge, 1994); also Averil Cameron, "The Cult of the Theotokos in Sixth-Century Constantinople," *Journal of Theological Studies* NS 29 (1978): 79–108; ead., "Images of Authority," 18–23.

[55] See Averil Cameron, "The Language of Images: The Rise of Icons and Christian Representation," *CCEB* XII, 1–42.

[56] "Seeking Out the Antecedents of the Maximian Theory of Everything: St. Gregory the Theologian's *Oration 38*," *Phronema* 26 (2011): 27–45. Columba Stewart has used the same phrase, a "unified theory of everything," to describe Evagrius Ponticus's contemplative theology: "Imageless Prayer and the Theological Vision of Evagrius Ponticus," *Journal of Early Christian Studies* 9 (2001): 174–82.

[57] See pp. 64–5 in this volume.

BETWEEN EAST AND WEST:
MAXIMUS' PROVENANCE AND MIGRATIONS

Having viewed Maximus broadly within the cosmos of Byzantine Christian culture in the seventh century, my purpose now is to go back and pinpoint the crucial contexts and turning points in his unfolding career. Not only did he live in the "betwixt and between" of some major transitions in the history of the Byzantine Empire, geographically too he moved betwixt and between, destined to become one of the few truly ecumenical figures of his age—a fact all the more significant because he was not a bishop. Maximus was an Eastern monk who nonetheless migrated to Byzantine-occupied North Africa, from which location he was drawn into the fray of christological controversy and eventually aligned himself with the Roman Church, contributing (perhaps in person) to the Lateran Council hosted by the papacy in 649, before being taken into imperial custody and transported to Constantinople for the final legal proceedings against him. All this, however, comes with substantial historical questions about Maximus' precise provenance, about the setting and character of his monastic formation, about the personal networks in which he operated, and about fundamental issues of chronology.

As for Maximus' origins and early biography, we are presently limited to two quite disparate traditions. One is the highly tendentious and polemical Syriac *Life* of Maximus composed by George (or Gregory) of Reshʿaina, a monothelete cleric from Jerusalem in the company of Patriarch Sophronius, which has the advantage of a seventh-century dating and claims close proximity to the action.[58] Despite its caustic aspects, it contains genuinely credible elements, as noted very early by the esteemed Maximus specialist Sergius Epifanovich.[59] We shall consider these elements later. The other tradition consists in three recensions of the Greek *Life* of Maximus which provide a very different and unabashedly hagiographical account, but which also date from a later

---

[58] Syriac text ed. and trans. with notes and commentary by Sebastian Brock, "An Early Syriac Life of Maximus the Confessor," *Analecta Bollandiana* 91 (1973): 299–346. George is insistent on his own veracity: "I have set down these records for (the benefit of) the faithful: they represent what I have seen, heard, and taken over from persons who are worthy of credence" (§5, p. 315). A number of Byzantinists favor the Syriac *Vita*, including Haldon, *Byzantium in the Seventh Century*, 306.

[59] Grigory Benevich, "Maximus' Heritage in Russia and Ukraine," *OHMC*, 464, 465.

time, the earliest not sooner than the tenth century.[60] The Greek *Life* too has come under increasing scrutiny and criticism for a variety of reasons, and these too I will take up in due course.

The Syriac *Life* describes Maximus as of inglorious Palestinian birth, the illegitimate child of a Samaritan father, a linen-maker, and a Persian Jewish slave-girl. The parents were baptized by a priest, Martyrios, who befriended the couple and granted them space on church property to live and raise their children. Martyrios renamed Maximus "Moschion" at his baptism,[61] and later enrolled him and his younger brother for the novitiate of the Old Lavra (St. Chariton) monastery. There the abbot Panteleon, a "wicked Origenist," "poured out and filled this disciple of his, Maximos, with the entire bitterness of evil teaching, finding in him a vessel capable of receiving all the foul dregs of his blasphemy."[62] George's pro-monothelete account next jumps to his association with Sophronius, blaming Maximus (Moschion), an impudent sophist, for implicating Sophronius in the "error" of dyothelete Christology, a striking claim given our knowledge that Sophronius was Maximus' spiritual father, not vice versa. Overall, the tendentiousness of the Syriac *Life* has brought severe criticism of its credibility, well-summarized by Jean-Claude Larchet.[63]

The account of Maximus' early years in the recensions of his Greek *Life* could not be more different from the Syriac narrative. Here he is described as born in Constantinople to parents of celebrated nobility and Christian piety, who raised him with ascetical austerity and set him on a path to virtue. Maximus accordingly received an excellent private education in grammar, rhetoric, and

---

[60] For discussion of the background and differences of the three recensions, see Neil and Allen, 5–8, 22–31; and Bronwen Neil, "The Greek *Life* of Maximus the Confessor (*BHG* 1234)," *Studia Patristica* 36 (2001): 46–53. Neil and Allen provide a helpful synopsis of all the extant documentation for Maximus' early life. They build on the pioneering work of Robert Devreese, "La *Vie* de S. Maxime le Confesseur et ses recensions," *Analecta Bollandiana* 46 (1928): 5–49; and Wolfgang Lackner, "Zu Quellen und Datierung der Maximosvita," *Analecta Bollandiana* 85 (1967): 285–316; also Sherwood's still useful *Date-List of the Works of Maximus the Confessor* (1952).

[61] The name Moschion appears tantalizingly close to "Moschus," and in fact the Syriac *mwsky* can be translated Moschus. But there is no proof that George of Resh'aina was trying retroactively to identify Maximus with the pro-Chalcedonian monk John Moschus. See Booth, *Crisis of Empire*, 144, n. 14.

[62] Syriac *Vita* §§1–7 (Brock, 302–5, 314–15).

[63] *La divinisation de l'homme selon saint Maxime le Confesseur* (Paris: Cerf, 1996), 8–12.

especially philosophy,[64] in which he thrived and (unlike the Syriac account) proved himself an enemy of sophistry. On his good repute he was drafted into imperial service under Heraclius as the "chief secretary of imperial records," a post at which he excelled until overcome with desire for the true "philosophical" and "hesychastic" life of the monk.[65] To render credibility to this claim, scholars have sometimes cited Maximus' statement in *Epistle* 12, where, extolling the superiority of the ascetical life, he states (self-referentially?) that "it is better and more honorable to occupy the lowest rank before God than to hold the highest ranks in the service of the emperor (βασιλεῖ) here below among the things of earth"; and he then identifies that lowest but worthiest rank precisely with the life of ascetical serenity or hesychasm (καθ᾽ ἡσυχίαν).[66] I would note as well that in *Amb. Jo.* 32, Maximus reveals a seemingly internal familiarity with the insignias (σήμαντρα) proper to various ranks within Byzantine imperial government:

> Every government—for it is good to draw on examples from our own life to point to the truth of the realities that are above us—has distinctive insignia, which make their bearers known to all as persons who have received authority from the emperor. Here one thinks of the so-called *codicilli*, which are borne by the provincial governor, or the sword that is the sign of the duke, or the distinctive signs and standards belonging to others in different offices.[67]

Maximos Constas observes that the term *codicillus* is extremely rare in patristic literature, but is attested fifteen times in Justinian's legal *Novellae*.[68] And yet it is plausible that Maximus knew the insignias through his interactions with government officials, not necessarily from intimacy with the imperial court.

The Greek *Life* next reports that Maximus entered a monastery at Chrysopolis (*c.*613/14), across the Bosphorus Strait from Constantinople, where he was quickly urged to become abbot, which he humbly accepted, assiduously attending to the spiritual care of his disciples.[69]

---

[64] Maximus alludes to his private education in *Mystagogia* Prol. (CCSG 69:5), suggesting that it did not include rhetoric, though this may simply be a show of humility.

[65] Greek *Vita* §§1–5, Recension 3 (Neil and Allen, 38–48). Recension 2 speaks of his embrace of "hesychastic living" (τοῦ καθ᾽ ἡσυχίαν βιῶναι) (PG 90:72D).

[66] *Ep.* 12 (PG 91:505B). The "autobiographical" character of this statement is disputed by, among others, Booth, *Crisis of Empire*, 146.

[67] *Amb. Jo.* 32 (PG 91:1284A–B), trans. Constas II, 57.     [68] Constas II, 356, n. 6.

[69] Greek *Vita* §§1–6, Recension 3 (Neil and Allen, 38–50).

The model of faithful service in the imperial court seamlessly transitions into a model of ascetical piety, betraying the strong hagiographical tone of the Greek *Life*.

The contradictory accounts of the Syriac and Greek *Lives* continue in their treatment of Maximus' mid-career and transition to North Africa, though again we have helpful information from his personal correspondence. The Greek *Life* moves expeditiously from Maximus' ministry as an abbot at Chrysopolis to his involvement in the monothelete crisis. Its obvious goal is to exalt him as the predestined champion of christological orthodoxy,[70] especially when, as it suggests, the powerful figures of the Emperor Heraclius and the Patriarch Sergius of Constantinople, in league with the Jacobite Patriarch Athanasius of Antioch and the overly conciliatory Melkite (Chalcedonian) Patriarch Cyrus of Alexandria, had succumbed to heresy. According to the Greek *Life*, Maximus resolved to go to Rome because the papacy had already come out publicly against monotheletism, and en route he stopped to aid orthodox-minded (dyothelete) bishops in North Africa.[71]

Traditionally it has been inferred from certain of Maximus' letters, however, that before going to Africa, he intermittently spent a brief but meaningful time (*c*.624/5) in another monastery, St. George's in Cyzicus (modern Erdek, Turkey), located south across the Sea of Marmara from Constantinople, along the northwest coast of Asia Minor. In *Epistle* 3 Maximus thanks John the Chamberlain for his benefaction to "the illustrious monastery of the glorious saint and martyr George," which Polycarp Sherwood connected via *Epistles* 28–31 (addressed to one assumed to be the bishop of Cyzicus) as evidence of Maximus' forced exile (with others) from St. George's in Cyzicus.[72] Sherwood presumed this to be the bishop John of Cyzicus, to whom Maximus addressed the earlier set of *Ambigua* (= *Ambigua* 6–71), begun while Maximus and John were still in conversation in Cyzicus.[73] Another conclusion has been that Maximus was forced with other monks to abandon St. George's in view of the Slav–Avar

---

[70] In the Greek *Vita* §5, Recension 3, the biographer even suggests that Maximus' original zeal for the monastic vocation was motivated by alarm about monotheletism, a clear anachronism since this christological proposal was not even on the scene yet when Maximus became a monk in the 610s. See Neil and Allen, 12, and 185, n. 8.

[71] Ibid. §§7–14 (Neil and Allen, 50–62).

[72] See *Ep.* 3 (PG 91:408C); also Sherwood, *Date-List*, 25, 27.

[73] I will take up the issue of the disputed identity of John of Cyzicus later in this chapter.

siege of Constantinople in 626, and that he longed to return to its warm community. Momentarily we shall turn to the justified skepticism lately expressed toward this reconstruction, but I hold it up now as that which, until recently, was the prevailing view in deference to the Greek *Life*.

Maximus' relocation to North Africa also poses problems for precise reconstruction and interpretation. The Syriac *Life* knows nothing of Maximus spending time in monasteries in Asia Minor, and instead portrays him as grounded squarely in Palestine and fully assimilated into the inner circle of Sophronius, whom he advised, as a prestigious monk, to rally episcopal support against monotheletism. With Sophronius's impetus, in turn, a synod was convened in Cyprus (mid-630s) by its bishop Arcadius. George, author of the Syriac *Life*, claims to have been present at the synod, and asserts that, though Maximus himself was not there in person, he was represented by his disciple Anastasius the Monk, and still had a significant—if failed—voice along with Sophronius for the dyenergist/dyothelete position in the negotiations.[74] The Syriac *Life* further suggests that Maximus spread his heresy into Syria, but that, because of the Arab invasions, and since there was already rebellion against the monothelete emperor afloat in North Africa, he departed for Africa with Anastasius and some other monks. There, it is claimed, Maximus and his company took up residence in a Nestorian monastery whose monks fully embraced them as kindred spirits in their christological beliefs.[75]

Primarily under the influence of Polycarp Sherwood's seminal *Date-List* (1952) of the works of Maximus, scholars have understood the Greek *Life*, together with certain allusions in Maximus' own writings, to present a different picture of his transition to Africa as well as his friendship with Sophronius. Accordingly, after leaving St. George's in Cyzicus, Maximus was ostensibly in Crete, where he clashed with bishops associated with the great miaphysite bishop Severus of Antioch over whether, according to the *Tome of Leo*, the text at the core of the Chalcedonian definition of 451, there were one or two energies and wills in Christ.[76] Relocated in Africa presumably in the years 628–30, Maximus says that he came into contact with "the divine Sophronius,

---

[74] Syriac *Vita* §§7–14 (Brock, 308–9, 315–17).

[75] Ibid. §§17–19 (Brock, 309–11, 317–18). The identification of the dyothelite Maximus with Nestorianism, the perceived extreme of dyophysite Christology, clearly betrays again the polemical thrust of the Syriac *Life*. These monks may well have simply been Chalcedonian dyophysites in natural sympathy with Maximus.

[76] *Opusc.* 3 (PG 91:49C).

who, with me and all the other exiled monks (*peregrinis monachis*), spent time in the land of the Africans."[77] In *Epistle* 12 (*c*.641) he reminisces on "the many exceedingly pious monks who are in exile (ἐπιξενουμένων) there, and especially the blessed servants of God, our fathers called the Eukratades."[78] This refers to the intimate circle of monastic disciples of John Moschus (d. 634), the revered Cilician-born monk in Palestine who had become the spiritual father of Sophronius, and who shared with him the surname "Eukratas."[79] Maximus (perhaps already connected with Sophronius) attached himself to Sophronius's circle near Carthage and developed a deep bond with Sophronius during the latter's short stay in Africa. This relationship, which has now become the subject of a rich body of newer scholarship that aspires rather dramatically to revise the picture of Maximus' provenance, would decisively shape Maximus' subsequent career, especially his public role in the monothelete controversy. I shall return to this relationship in more detail later in this chapter.

The Greek *Life* of Maximus for its part dwells at length on Maximus coaching the African bishops in christological orthodoxy rather than on his monastic connections. It goes out of its way to extol his theological and rhetorical prowess above that of the local episcopal authorities:

> For the very wise man knew that we had need of great skill and powers of debate if we were to throw down our adversaries *and destroy their every height, which they had raised against true knowledge* (2 Cor. 10:5). This is why he encouraged them in every way, applauded them, stimulated them verbally to fortitude, filled them with a nobler spirit (cf. 2 Macc. 7:21). For although the bishops were superior because of their throne, they were inferior and lacking in wisdom and intellect—not to speak of his other virtue, and the renown of the man in every respect. Hence they both submitted to his words and were persuaded without dispute by the other exhortations and counsels which contained such great value . . . Because of all these factors, not only all those who were priests and bishops, but also all the laity and all the first ranks of the multitude completely relied on him in everything.[80]

---

[77] Ibid. 12 (= an extract in Latin trans. from a letter to Peter the Illustrious) (PG 91:142A).

[78] *Ep.* 12 (PG 91:461A).

[79] This surname appears in the addressee line of some MSS *Ep.* 8, "to the monk Sophronius, surnamed Eukratas," but in other sources too. See Booth, *Crisis of Empire*, 149 and n. 41.

[80] Greek *Vita* §14, Recension 3 (Neil and Allen, 62–5).

While this might sound like hagiographical hyperbole, it is not altogether implausible if we consider the background of the African churches' disposition toward Constantinople in the period of the Byzantine occupation in the sixth and seventh centuries. These churches, which in their history had already known a sustained resistance to Roman political and ecclesiastical intervention,[81] and which had experienced the Donatist movement's fierce expression of African independence, did not instantly embrace the theological initiatives of their Byzantine overlords. When, for example, Justinian, in another bid to appease miaphysite churches in the East, campaigned to condemn the so-called "Three Chapters" (a trio of allegedly quasi-Nestorian authors) before and after the Council of Constantinople of 553, the initiative alienated numerous Western and African bishops who saw it as a threat to the legacy of Chalcedon.[82] By the time Sophronius and Maximus were in Africa, Latin culture there was declining while the emerging, Greek-speaking Byzantino-African Christian culture was in its infancy.[83] For this reason, as Cameron remarks of the immigration of these highly literate Byzantine refugee monks, "their arrival was a tonic," with the Africans welcoming them rather than resenting their presence.[84] Quickly they provided a rallying point for many African church leaders zealous to find a voice in resisting imperial overextension and articulating christological orthodoxy. Once Sophronius left Africa, Maximus became the center of gravity, enjoying increasing prestige through his network of friendships not only with the monks, for whom he became a kind of liaison with the civil administration,[85] but also with numerous bishops and clerics, and with leading government officials like Peter the Illustrious, George the eparch (prefect) of Carthage, and later on the imperial exarch Gregory.[86]

---

[81] On the mixed bag of resistance and appeal in the African bishops' relations with Pope Gregory the Great (590–604), see Conant, *Staying Roman*, 324–30.

[82] On the African resistance to Justinian's condemnation of the Three Chapters, see Averil Cameron, "Byzantine Africa: The Literary Evidence," *CCEB* VII, 25–32; and Conant, *Staying Roman*, 316–24.

[83] Cameron, "Byzantine Africa," 32–8.     [84] Ibid., 38–43.

[85] Ibid., 42–3.

[86] On Maximus' relatively extensive correspondence with government office-holders, see Daniel Sahas, "The Demonizing Force of the Arab Conquests: The Case of Maximus (ca. 580–662) as a Political 'Confessor,'" *Jahrbuch der österreichischen Byzantinistik* 53 (2003): 98–110.

## SOPHRONIUS, MAXIMUS, AND
## MONASTIC DISSENT

In examining Maximus' friendship with Sophronius, we should pay close attention to the language of a shared experience of monastic "exile" or peregrination (ξενιτεία; *peregrinatio*) that appears in Maximus' own writing. This is a rich theme in late ancient and early medieval Christian monastic tradition both East and West, variously manifesting itself in ideals of religious migrancy,[87] spiritual pilgrimage,[88] and ascetical mission in remote places.[89] Evagrius Ponticus calls *xeniteia* the "first of the illustrious contests" of the ascetical life.[90] Intrinsic to the mythos of exile was the idea that it was simultaneously "imposed" and voluntary. The exiled ascetic was passive to God's discipline of upheaval, alienation, and marginal identity in the world, but also challenged actively to embrace this vocation and the exigencies it entailed. Spiritual formation and active duty were therefore of a piece, and under the shadow of eschatological judgment. For Sophronius and Maximus, however, this exile was not just a matter of geographic removal to a foreign land (Africa) to carry on there the protocols of the ascetical life in which they were already rooted; it now gestured a common, crucial mission to work with bishops and to defend the Chalcedonian faith and to evangelize the ignorant or the complacent in the deeper ramifications of that faith for Christian piety as well as for the very integrity of the Church itself.

Sophronius, a peregrinator par excellence, was born in Damascus (*c*.550) and was a trained instructor in rhetoric (thus his early epithet "the Sophist"), destined to become a model of the scholar-monk. Most likely while on pilgrimage to the Holy Land, he encountered, at the monastery of St. Theodosius in the Judean desert east of

---

[87] See Daniel Caner, *Wandering, Begging Monks: Spiritual Authority and the Promotion of Monasticism in Late Antiquity* (Berkeley: University of California Press, 2003), 24–30; also Antoine Guillaumont, "Le dépaysement (*xeniteia*) comme forme d'ascèse dans le monachisme ancien," in his *Aux origines du monachisme chrétien: pour une phénoménologie du monachisme* (Bégrolles en Mauges: Abbaye de Bellefontaine, 1979), 89–116.

[88] See Brouria Bitton-Ashkelony, *Encountering the Sacred: The Debate on Christian Pilgrimage in Late Antiquity* (Berkeley: University of California Press, 2005), 110–15.

[89] See Hans von Campenhausen, "The Ascetic Idea of Exile in Ancient and Early Medieval Monasticism," in his *Tradition and Life in the Church: Essays and Lectures in Church History*, trans. A. V. Littledale (Philadelphia: Fortress Press, 1968), 231–51.

[90] *Ad Eulogium* 1, Greek text ed. and trans. Robert Sinkewicz, *Evagrius of Pontus: The Greek Ascetic Corpus* (Oxford: Oxford University Press), 29–30, 310–11.

Bethlehem, the remarkable figure of John Eukratas, better known as John Moschus, who, though probably only slightly older than Sophronius, assumed the role of his spiritual father and mentor. The two were inseparable traveling companions for decades.[91] Around 578, John and Sophronius went to Egypt for an extended period and spent time in Alexandria under the tutelage of reputed Christian intellectuals, all paupers, like Abba Theodore the Philosopher, a gifted teacher but with few books, Zoïlus the Lector, renowned for his *xeniteia* and ascetical solitude, and Cosmas Scholasticus, who, though poor, maintained and shared an enormous library, and had a passion to confute and convert Jews.[92] They also sought instruction from Stephen ("the Sophist") of Alexandria, a renowned commentator on Aristotle, Galen, and other Greco-Roman thinkers.[93] John also led Sophronius to visits with desert sages in some remote lavras in Egypt.

As Christoph Schönborn notes, Sophronius had aspired not only to the *paideia* of the rich Hellenistic-Christian culture of Alexandria but also the *paideia* of the desert,[94] and after he and John returned to Palestine, Sophronius ostensibly took monastic vows at St. Theodosius. Thereafter, Sophronius was probably with John in Sinai for at least part of the decade he spent there. The two returned to Palestine for a time at the New Lavra in Judea, but with the mounting dangers of the Persian wars, traveled north to Antioch and to Cilicia (southeastern Turkey) before sailing again to Alexandria, where they developed a deep friendship with the (Melkite) Patriarch John the Almsgiver. Sometime after the fall of Jerusalem to the Persians in 614, Moschus and Sophronius made a protracted journey, via "various islands" (νήσοις διαφόροις), toward Rome, a friendly haven for Chalcedonian monks from the East.[95] Sophronius's own bond with the Roman Church would later

---

[91] On the character of their friendship, see Henry Chadwick, "John Moschus and His Friend Sophronius the Sophist," *Journal of Theological Studies* NS 25 (1974): 41–74. On the pattern of their sustained companionship as a celibate intimacy marked by the *erôs* of agapeistic affection and mutual edification in the ascetic life, see Derek Krueger, "Between Monks: Tales of Monastic Companionship in Early Byzantium," *Journal of the History of Sexuality* 20 (2011), esp. 28–31, 33–8, 56, 58–61.

[92] John Moschus, *Pratum spirituale* 171–2 (PG 87:3037B–3041B); ibid. 77 (PG 87:2929D). On the early travels of John and Sophronius, see also the fine study of Christoph von Schönborn, *Sophrone de Jérusalem: vie monastique et confession dogmatique* (Paris: Beauchesne, 1972), 53–71.

[93] *Pratum spirituale* 77 (PG 87:2929D).       [94] *Sophrone de Jérusalem*, 60–4.

[95] Anonymous Prologue to John Moschus's *Pratum spirituale*, Greek text ed. Hermann Usener, *Der heilige Tychon* (Leipzig and Berlin: Teubner, 1907), 91–2

prove important when he was the politically, geographically, and christo-logically isolated anti-monothelete patriarch of Jerusalem. John perhaps died in Rome as late as 634, and Sophronius went there to convey his remains to Palestine.[96]

So where does the time of exile in Africa fit into this scheme? By one reconstruction, Maximus, having a history with Sophronius and Moschus going back to Palestine, was already in monastic retreat in Africa with these two in the late 620s before either went on to Rome. Theoretically, then, Maximus could have been with Sophronius and Moschus when they left via "various islands" for Rome, but the three retreated for a time in Africa; Maximus stayed in Africa, then, when Moschus and later Sophronius went on to Rome.[97] By another account, however, these monks were not together in Africa until Sophronius had fled there from the East much later, in the wake of the Arab advance in the 630s.[98] The historical circumstances and chronology will continue to be debated. For our purposes, meanwhile, the focus will be on the crucial role of this exile with the "Eukratas" circle not only for Maximus' spiritual and doctrinal development but also for his percep-tion of Rome as a headquarters of Chalcedonian orthodoxy.

We now turn to Maximus' intimacy with this circle, the subject of considerable recent scholarship and the focus now of a compelling alternative reinterpretation of his early and middle career, one in which the Syriac *Life* and Maximus' Palestinian provenance have been rehabilitated. This account assumes that, even though the Syriac *Life* is recognizably polemical and misleading in places (e.g. Maximus' dishonorable birth; his touting of Origenism; his relocation to a Nestorian monastery in Africa), it still credibly reports Maximus' emergence in a Palestinian monastery and his early prominence as a

---

(ll. 3–29). Arguments have been advanced that when the author refers to Moschus going to "the great city of the Romans" (τὴν τῶν Ῥωμαίων μεγάλην πόλιν), he might actually be referring to the "Second Rome," Constantinople. In *Crisis of Empire*, 106–10, Booth has convincingly argued that it was indeed Rome itself.

[96] See the Prologue to the *Pratum spirituale* (Usener, 92–3, ll. 38–74). On the journey to Rome and the dating of Moschus's death, see Booth, *Crisis of Empire*, 110 (and n. 96)–115. Booth believes, moreover, that Moschus went to Rome alone long before Sophronius arrived to collect his remains c.634 (ibid., 231–2).

[97] See Booth, *Crisis of Empire*, 109–11, 149–51. Booth suggests that Maximus' own friendship with the priest Marinus of Cyprus could have been connected with Sophronius's and Moschus's journey via "various islands" toward Rome (*Pratum spirituale* Prol.).

[98] Schönborn, *Sophrone de Jérusalem*, 72–8.

monastic theologian, while also plausibly establishing a relationship between Maximus and Sophronius much earlier than their time together in Africa.

This reconstruction has naturally entailed contesting much of the Greek *Life* and the longstanding assumptions about Maximus' connections both with Constantinople and with monasteries in Asia Minor.[99] One especially powerful argument is that the Greek *Life*, late as it is, also shows evidence, in its narration of Maximus' earliest years, of hagiographical conformation with one of the traditions of the *Life* of Theodore the Studite, the revered Constantinopolitan monk of the ninth century.[100] Another argument, less compelling, is that Maximus' philosophical literacy, particularly in Neoplatonism, links him much more to Alexandria than Constantinople,[101] as does the fact that the addressees of certain of his letters were in Alexandria and among the city's Christian "scholastics."[102] But it is plausible that Maximus, if in fact he was early on a member of Sophronius's learned Palestinian circle, had spent time in Alexandria with him, indicating at one point his knowledge of Sophronius's abundance of books.[103] Sophronius, moreover, was quite possibly the true addressee of *Epistle* 8, in which Maximus expresses his desire to be (either in Alexandria or in Palestine) with the one who had been

[99] For a good overview of accumulated arguments against the veracity of the Greek *Life* and the reasons for an alternative account on the basis of the Syriac *Life*, see Booth, *Crisis of Empire*, 143–9.

[100] See Lackner, "Zu Quellen und Datierung der Maximosvita," 315–16; Bram Roosen, "Maximi Confessoris Vitae et Passiones Graecae: The Development of a Hagiographic Dossier," *Byzantion* 80 (2010): 446–51; Booth, *Crisis of Empire*, 145–6. Roosen has also postulated ("Maximi Confessoris Vitae," 427–33) that there was an *Urpassio* produced in Palestine, coordinated with the Greek *Vita* of Pope Martin I, which propagated that Maximus had once served in Constantinople as a "first secretary" (πρωτοασηκρῆτις).

[101] See here Christian Boudignon, "Maxime était-il constantinopolitain?" in Bart Janssens, Bram Roosen, and Peter van Deun, eds., *Philomathestatos: Studies in Greek and Byzantine Texts Presented to Jacques Noret for his Sixty-Fifth Birthday* (Leuven: Peeters, 2004), 13–22.

[102] e.g. *Ep.* 17 (PG 91:580C–584D), to Julian the Scholastic (mentioning also Christopemptus the Scholastic); and Maximus addressed his *Quaestiones ad Theopemptum* to Theopemptus the Scholastic, who must have been connected with Alexandria (cf. *Ep.* 18, PG 91:589A) (Boudignon, "Maxime était-il constantinopolitain?" 15).

[103] *Ep.* 13 (PG 91:532D–533A). Here Maximus refers his addressee, Peter the Illustrious, who must have been in Alexandria at the time, to his own "father and teacher, lord abba Sophronius, prudent and wise advocate of truth, and invincible defender of divine dogmas... who is rich with a plethora of books."

to him a true pastor and instructor in the ascetical life, and who similarly faced the dangerous bites of the "wolves of Arabia."[104] An additional argument for Maximus' Palestinian provenance is that, even though the Syriac *Life* distorts his allegiance to Origenism, his positive and negative responses to the legacy of Origen make much more sense in the afterglow of controversy over Origenist theology that had fomented in certain Palestinian monasteries in the sixth century.

Obviously the closer Maximus appears connected, via Sophronius and the Eukratades, to Palestine and Alexandria, the more remote appear his links to monastic communities in Asia Minor. Especially problematic is the link (noted earlier) with St. George's monastery thought to be in Cyzicus, and with the assumed bishop of Cyzicus, John. In only one letter, to John the Chamberlain, does Maximus explicitly refer to this monastic community and there is no indication here that this community is in Cyzicus.[105] In two of his letters, one to a mysterious bishop Cyrisicius, another to bishop John (of Cyzicus?), considered by Sherwood to be one and the same person,[106] Maximus encourages his addressee to provide compassionate care for those monks who have been displaced, and to do so once the threat of danger from unidentified "enemies" has subsided.[107] In a related letter he praises this John for having followed through in drawing these involuntarily expatriated monks under his care.[108] While the traditional reading has been that Maximus was speaking on behalf of his fellow monks longing to be back under John's pastoral care in Cyzicus,[109] Christian Boudignon has instead argued that Maximus,

---

[104] *Ep.* 8 (PG 91:441B–444C). In one of the MSS but not all, Sophronius is the addressee of *Ep.* 8. On the probability of this, see Boudignon, "Maxime était-il constantinopolitain?" 17–20. Boudignon argues that the "wolves of Arabia" signal *both* the physical threat of the Arab hordes and the spiritual threat of sin assailing the ascetical life. He also postulates that Maximus had temporarily rejoined Sophronius in Alexandria during the years 614–617 for a time of further intellectual formation (ibid., 21). Booth discounts the reference to Arabs since the full phrase is "wolves of Arabia, that is, of the West," probably referring to some *pastoral* threat (*Crisis of Empire*, 231, n. 20).

[105] *Ep.* 3 (PG 91:408C). See also Jankowiak and Booth ("A New Date-List," 38), controverting Sherwood's account (*Date-List*, 25, 27).

[106] *Date-List*, 27, concurring with the view of Maximus' seventeenth-century editor François Combefis that "Cyrisicius" was a copyist's corruption of "Cyzicenus" (i.e. bishop "of Cyzicus").

[107] *Ep.* 28 (to Cyrisicius) (PG 91:621A): "Make haste, then, to gather together into oneness those children of God who have been scattered abroad." Also *Ep.* 30 (to Bishop John) (PG 91:624C).

[108] *Ep.* 29 (PG 91:621C–624A).    [109] Sherwood, *Date-List*, 27–8.

writing in third- rather than first-person-plural of his fellow monks, was simply referring to a monastic community of St. George that he had known in Africa, without having shared their flight into exile. Strictly speaking, moreover, he does not refer to their "return" to their home but of their being gathered under John's care—quite possibly still in Africa.[110] As for John himself, Maximus dedicated to him his earlier set of *Ambigua*, in which he claims to have originally studied Gregory Nazianzen's orations in person with John.[111] Boudignon asserts, however, that the two, having been peers as students, later saw John elevated to an archiepiscopate in Cyzicus,[112] even though the city may have not been his original home. Maximus' connections with John, then, would not necessarily have been based on mutual time together in that city.[113]

With these and other arguments,[114] defenders of the Syriac *Life* of Maximus and of his Palestinian provenance have cast tremendous doubt on the Greek *Life*, but have not been free of guesswork and hypothetical claims of their own. A clear problem, if the Constantinopolitan and Anatolian trajectory of Maximus' formative monastic career is in dispute, is explaining how he would have known and corresponded with significant court officials at the imperial capital like John the Chamberlain and Constantine Sacellarius.[115] Maximus wrote his famous encomium on Christian love as *Epistle* 2 to John the Chamberlain, and one could easily infer from this a sustained period in which the two were together as friends in Constantinople. Maximus' plea to this John on behalf of George, eparch of Africa, when the latter was in serious trouble with the Empress Martina and imperial authorities in the early 640s, would likewise hint of a history and depth of friendship. Boudignon instead surmises that Maximus could have taken

---

[110] Boudignon, "Maxime était-il constantinopolitain?" 23–4; cf. Booth, *Crisis of Empire*, 165–9.

[111] *Amb. Jo.* (PG 91:1064B).

[112] This because Maximus acknowledges John's ordination to the "high priesthood" (ἀρχιερωσύνη), *Ep.* 29 (PG 91:621C–624A).

[113] Boudignon, "Maxime était-il constantinopolitain?" 25–6.

[114] See Boudignon, "Maxime était-il constantinopolitain?" 26–43; Booth, *Crisis of Empire*, 143–55.

[115] e.g. Booth (*Crisis of Empire*, 150–1) hypothesizes within a hypothesis when suggesting that Maximus may have accompanied Moschus and Sophronius via "various islands" en route to Rome (see Moschus, *Pratum spirituale*, Prol.), and possibly on this trip went to Constantinople for a time where he made connections with imperial officials like John the Chamberlain.

brief refuge at Constantinople after being in Alexandria and Cyprus, and that he was hosted there by John.[116] In that event, could he have already been a companion of John Moschus and Sophronius? Phil Booth suggests as much:

> It is possible, therefore, that the monastic triumvirate of Moschus, Sophronius and Maximus had been together for a far longer period than the Constantinopolitan tradition of Maximus's origins permits: acquaintance in Palestine; withdrawal to Antioch and then to Alexandria; flight (perhaps) to the capital, and then the Aegean; retreat to North Africa. That the three monks shared this experience is of course speculative; but it is nevertheless not impossible, and there is evidence enough in the sources to support it. But however we wish to reconstruct the movements of the group in the 620s, it is clear that towards the end of that obscure decade Sophronius and Maximus (and perhaps also Moschus) were united as exiles in North Africa.[117]

Over and beyond the tensions between the approaches to Maximus' biography respectively privileging his Constantinopolitan and Palestinian origins, the strength of the more recent readings of his *vita* is to have thrown into sharper relief his critically important relation to Sophronius and to the circle of the Eukratades, since this friendship was unquestionably formative for Maximus' public career as a monastic dissenter in the developing monothelete controversy.

Indeed, the character of the monastic dissent taking shape from among Moschus, Sophronius, and Maximus has been the subject of a compelling reconstruction by Phil Booth, a strong advocate for the Confessor's Palestinian origins. Booth frames their dissent, first, within the context of emerging models of a more ecclesially-engaged and sacramentally-focused asceticism in the sixth and seventh centuries. The sixth-century controversy over Origenism in Palestinian monasteries brought to light, in Booth's judgment, a tension between the older pioneering asceticism, with its emphasis on individual striving and rigorous contemplation, and more institutionally accountable models— that is, models answerable not only to the larger monastic system itself but to the hierarchy of the Church and even to the empire.[118] Such models found favor with hagiographers like Cyril of Scythopolis and, even more significant for our purposes, with the prolific Pseudo-Dionysius the Areopagite, one of Maximus' principal sources of mystical

---

[116]  Boudignon, "Maxime était-il constantinopolitain?" 35–6.
[117]  Booth, *Crisis of Empire*, 151.          [118]  Ibid., 10–22.

theology and spiritual doctrine. Dionysius ranked the monks within a strictly defined ecclesiastical hierarchy, where, to be sure, they were honored for their role in spiritual contemplation and communion, but also viewed as thoroughly dependent on and accountable to the bishops as the trustees of the holy sacraments.[119] For Booth, in turn, Maximus' own reorientation to this more ecclesial, sacramental, and hierarchical asceticism shows up in his commentary on the liturgy, the *Mystagogia*[120]—a thesis that I will assess later in Chapter 5.

Booth furthermore frames the monastic dissent of Moschus, Sophronius, and Maximus in terms of proactive support for an ecclesiastically and sacramentally grounded christological orthodoxy that could stand up to emperors who, in their anxiety over stabilizing the empire amid political and military calamities, maneuvered to force doctrinal consensus on a Church wracked by post-Chalcedonian divisions. Moschus and Sophronius had endeared themselves to Patriarch John ("the Almsgiver") of Alexandria, served him as advisors, and eventually even penned a *Life* of John.[121] They viewed him as a staunch Chalcedonian ally and patron, and their friendship demonstrated the power of a coalition of monastics and ecclesiastics. Moschus's *Spiritual Meadow*, with its vignettes of the Christian virtues and fidelity of monastics, clerics, and seculars alike, expanded the boundaries of true holiness beyond the desert so as to include those of various vocation who upheld Chalcedonian orthodoxy and Chalcedonian sacraments.[122]

No matter when and where his association with them precisely began—and I am greatly swayed by arguments for a Palestinian provenance—Maximus was definitely nurtured in this circle of the Eukratades in North Africa, most likely in the late 620s, and Sophronius played a decisive role in mentoring and encouraging his high-profile debut as a monastic protagonist in the monothelete crisis. In the company of Moschus and Sophronius, Maximus learned all the more the importance of monks cultivating patrons in high ecclesiastical or even political positions in order to exercise a strong public voice in this rapidly intensifying conflict over Christology. Maximus' relationship with George, the African eparch, is the most striking example of this kind of networking, not only because the two men developed an abiding

---

[119] Ibid., 27–33.     [120] Ibid., 170–85.
[121] Ibid., 49–59, 100–5.     [122] Ibid., 121–39.

friendship, with Maximus serving as George's spiritual director, but because George ultimately became a sponsor of the anti-monothelete monks, and put his own reputation on the line for Chalcedonian orthodoxy.

George had apparently already experienced tensions with Constantinople when, in late 641, soon after Heraclius's death, he was formally caught up in a serious dispute with the controversial Empress Martina over the treatment of some refugee miaphysite nuns who had agitated in strong support of the Syrian bishop Severus of Antioch from the convents in which they had been relocated in Alexandria.[123] At a loss over what to do about them, George, who had at first shown hospitality to the nuns, looked for advice from the Emperor Heraclius, and even contacted the local archbishop, the pope , and the Patriarch of Constantinople. The eventual response was an encouragement to purge heresy, and George proceeded to relocate the recalcitrant nuns in orthodox monasteries, though some were successfully reconciled to Chalcedonian orthodoxy.[124] When, however, the Empress Martina (the "Patricia"), had demanded the nuns' release from custody, George dismissed her letter as a forgery.

At some point in this melee, George was actually summoned to appear in Constantinople. Maximus in turn sought to advocate on the eparch's behalf to authorities in the capital, most notably his friend John the Chamberlain, to whom he addressed three urgent letters about the affair.[125] Maximus had wanted to support George's claim that the Empress's letter was a forgery. How could a woman so firmly grounded in the orthodox faith possibly exculpate heresy? And yet he acknowledged the seeming integrity of the individual who had delivered the letter with an oath about its authenticity. Maximus confessed his nervous uncertainty (ἀμφιβολία) to John, and his fear that perhaps, like King Rehoboam of Judah (2 Chron. 10:1–12:16), the Empress had forsaken the counsel of her wise elders and been duped by the advice of younger persons, in this case some doctrinally

---

[123] As Sherwood points out (*Date-List*, 47), Maximus seems to be alluding in *Ep.* 12 to Heraclius's death when he refers to the one who has now become "the companion among saints" (ὁ ἐν ἁγίοις γεγόμενος σύμβιος, PG 91:461A). The actual dispute over the miaphysite nuns had likely begun, however, well before Heraclius died.

[124] For the details on this episode, see *Ep.* 12 (PG 91:460A–465B). There are differences of timing of this crisis between Sherwood (*Date-List*, 45–51) and Booth, *Crisis of Empire*, 254–9; cf. also Jankowiak and Booth, "A New Date-List," *OHMC*, 51–6.

[125] *Epp.* 12, 44, 45.

deluded nuns. Rehoboam's punishment, as Maximus reminded John, was the forfeiture of most of his kingdom![126]

Leading in George's defense, Maximus even went so far as to assume the eparch's persona in a letter to the miaphysite nuns. He argued to them the hypostatic rather than natural unity of Jesus Christ, and shamed the nuns for betraying the true faith in order to return to their own vomit (Prov. 26:11).[127] The letter, which indicates how George had corresponded with patriarchs, bishops, ruling officials, and emperors over this situation, clearly demonstrates Maximus' intimate knowledge of George's affairs and the deep bond of friendship which enabled this insinuation of identities. Maximus went much further, however, than justifying George's dissent and dropping hints of a growing African resistance to Constantinople. He lauded the eparch as a fellow ascetic in an all-out spiritual battle for the Chalcedonian faith. In *Epistle* 1, addressed to George after he had been called to Constantinople, Maximus shows himself as the eparch's spiritual director, discoursing at length on the challenges of cultivating virtue and knowledge in the refiner's fire of earthly existence and in the face of divine judgment.[128] The gist of it is that George is already advanced in virtue but will need to hold strong amid his current trials, with the promise that his loyal monks in Africa will be praying unceasingly for his well-being.[129] In an additional letter to John the Chamberlain from the time of George's summons to the capital, Maximus asks God to forgive the emperors the injustice of detaining a man of such virtuous reputation, so genuine a servant of the empire, whose people crowded around him at his departure as if trying to block his boat from leaving Africa.[130] Why?

---

[126] *Ep.* 12 (PG 91:461B–464A). Upon Heraclius's death in 641, Martina, his niece and also, quite controversially, his second wife (as of *c.*622), had maneuvered to position herself in the transition of power, supporting Heraklonas, her own son by Heraclius, against Heraclius Constantine (= Constantine III), Heraclius's son (and co-regent) by his first wife, Eudokia. Later Byzantine chroniclers like Theophanes (*Chron.* 6121, Mango and Scott, *Chronicle*, 461) even accused her of having poisoned Constantine III, who ruled only 103 days. For her political machinations, the empress incurred much wrath from the populace of Constantinople, while her fervent monotheletism likewise tainted her reputation in subsequent decades in Byzantium. On the context of Martina's actions, including those against the eparch George, see Lynda Garland, *Byzantine Empresses: Women and Power in Byzantium AD 527–1204* (London and New York: Routledge, 1999), 61–72.

[127] *Ep.* 18 (PG 91:584D–589B).     [128] *Ep.* 1 (PG 91:364A–392A).
[129] Ibid. (PG 91:392A–B).     [130] *Ep.* 44 (PG 91:645B–648C).

for those in need, he is a provider, for others a steward of their
abundance; for the widows he is a guardian; for orphans, their father;
for the poor, a lover of the poor; for strangers, a giver of hospitality; for
brothers, the lover of brothers; for the diseased, their healer; for those in
sore straights, their consolation . . .[131]

In yet another letter to John the Chamberlain, Maximus extols these
and other virtues of George, including now his utter zeal for the
Church and its genuine orthodox faith.[132]

The upshot of all these letters is the sense that, together with the
monks and other faithful, and with Maximus' crucial assistance and
support, George galvanized African opposition to the imperial establishment's inability to protect and defend the Chalcedonian faith. As
Phil Booth observes, we cannot know the precise grounds of George's
summons to Constantinople, whether it was political—the fruit of
imperial perceptions of growing unrest in Africa—or properly doctrinal.[133] So far as the African Church's strained relationship with the
capital is concerned, it really does not matter. This whole episode,
against the background of the chaotic state of the imperial court immediately after Heraclius's death, manifested an alienation that would only
deepen as the monothelete crisis broke wide open later in the 640s.

## MAXIMUS' PUBLIC ROLE IN THE MONENERGIST–MONOTHELETE CONTROVERSY

The intensifying drama of the monenergist–monothelete controversy, the last phase of the ancient christological debates, repositioned
Maximus the Confessor on a whole new public—*and ecumenical*—
stage. It thoroughly dominated his later years, leaving an exclamation
mark on a career spent "betwixt and between" in the political and
ecclesiastical geography of the seventh century.

The Chalcedonian definition (451)—Christ as "one person in two
natures"—had not only given rise to sustained conflicts between and
within pro- and anti-Chalcedonian parties in the East, it had also strained
relations between Eastern Chalcedonians, who largely considered the

[131] Ibid. (PG 91:648B).    [132] *Ep.* 45 (PG 91:649A).
[133] See Booth, *Crisis of Empire*, 256.

definition a workable interpretation of the Nicene faith,[134] and Western Chalcedonians (beginning with Pope Leo I himself), who judged it an immutable dogmatic formula.[135] In the East, monenergism and monotheletism held forth the real possibility—or futility, to its critics—of retaining the Chalcedonian language of Christ's two unconfused natures while refocusing the core unity of his personal agency and volition such as might prove acceptable to miaphysites. The resulting public controversy, lasting roughly from 610 to 681, was an extraordinary display of the profound interplay of imperial and ecclesiastical interests in Byzantium.[136] It should not be reduced, however, solely to the desperate *political* maneuvers of Byzantine emperors and patriarchs to reconcile the alienated miaphysite churches for the sake of solidarity in an empire wracked with military and political crises. This extension of christological debate could never have persisted had it not found fuel in serious and longstanding doctrinal issues, including the precise "physiology" of Christ and the concomitant soteriological ramifications of his natural and hypostatic constitution.

Monenergist terminology already had roots as far back as the fourth century, and we must keep in mind that it was not from the outset perceived as necessarily intrinsically inconsistent with Chalcedon. But it acquired all new sophistication in the anti-Chalcedonian context,

---

[134] During his brief imperial tenure, the Emperor Basilicus (r. 475–6), reaching out to miaphysites, told the exiled miaphysite Patriarch Timothy Aelurus of Alexandria that the creed of Nicea (325) and the additional decrees of Ephesus (431) were alone normative for orthodoxy, whereas "the so-called tome of Leo, and all things declared and transacted at Chalcedon" constituted "innovation" (καινοτομία) (*Encyclical*, recorded in Evagrius Scholasticus, *Historia ecclesiastica* 3.4, PG 86.2:2600D–2601A). Basilicus's usurper Zeno, in his more famous *Henotikon* (482) sent to the churches in Egypt and Libya, affirmed the sufficiency of the Nicene faith while avoiding, however, the debunking of Leo's *Tome* and the Chalcedonian definition.

[135] Pauline Allen has rightly emphasized this point in her *Sophronius of Jerusalem and Seventh-Century Heresy*, 3; ead. and C. T. R. Hayward, *Severus of Antioch* (London: Routledge, 2004), 3.

[136] For the substance of this extended controversy, Friedhelm Winkelmann, *Der monenergetisch-monotheletisch Streit* (Frankfurt: Peter Lang, 2001), 45–184 (register of documentation), 185–279 (prosopography of major figures in the crisis); Allen, *Sophronius of Jerusalem*; Cyril Hovorun, *Will, Action and Freedom: Christological Controversies of the Seventh Century* (Leiden: Brill, 2008), esp. 53–167; Marek Jankowiak, "Essai d'histoire politique du monothélisme" (Ph.D. dissertation, University of Warsaw, 2009). Good historical overviews are found in Meyendorff, *Imperial Unity and Christian Divisions*, esp. 165–292, 333–80; Andrew Ekonomou, *Byzantine Rome and the Greek Popes* (Lanham, MD: Lexington Books, 2007), 79–112; and Andrew Louth, *Maximus the Confessor* (London: Routledge, 1996), 12–16, 54–62.

especially in the richly-developed miaphysite Christology of the Patriarch Severus of Antioch in the early sixth century.[137] For miaphysites, the idea of "one activity" (μία ἐνέργεια) was not an option or an afterthought, it was intrinsic to the doctrine of a single nature of Jesus Christ. But could not a single *energeia* operate from out of two hypostatically conjoined natures? Cyrus, formerly a bishop in Lazica (in the Caucasus) who, upon Heraclius's nomination, became Patriarch of Alexandria as well as the city's imperial prefect, had been convinced both by the emperor and by Patriarch Sergius of Constantinople of the legitimacy of the monenergist option.[138] As a Chalcedonian moderate who was able to earn trust from moderate Egyptian miaphysites, Cyrus celebrated a Eucharist attended by some important miaphysite clergy and bishops, from which issued a formal *Pact of Union* (633). The *Pact* strategically recalled the venerated figure of Cyril of Alexandria, whose doctrine of divine incarnation and the unity of Christ (the "one incarnate nature of God the Logos") it deemed a rallying-point; but more famously, it stated "that one and the same Christ and Son performed things befitting God and things human *by one theandric activity* (μιᾷ θεανδρικῇ ἐνεργείᾳ) according to Dionysius [now] among the saints."[139] As the later anti-monothelete Lateran Council (649) would point out,[140] the key phrase here deviated slightly from Dionysius's actual wording, "a *new* theandric activity" (καινὴ θεανδρικὴ ἐνέργεια),[141] a formulation that even Maximus himself, as a committed Chalcedonian, was able to give a strikingly positive interpretation.[142]

At this point we pick up again with the crucial role of Sophronius and his disciple Maximus in challenging the monenergist and monothelete options. Encouraged by the *Pact of Union* of 633 in Alexandria, but concerned about enduring tensions over monenergism, Patriarch Sergius sent a letter to Pope Honorius containing the substance of a new *Psephos*, or "Judgment" (633 or early 634), subsequently endorsed by the

---

[137] On the roots of monenergist language, see Hovorun, *Will, Action and Freedom*, 5–51.

[138] For the documentation, see Allen, *Sophronius of Jerusalem*, 26–8, 161–7.

[139] *Announcement* (Πληροφορία), Art. VII, Greek text ed. with trans. in Allen, *Sophronius of Jerusalem*, 170–2 (emphasis added).

[140] ACO II, 1:152, lines 30–9.          [141] *Ep.* 4 (PTS 36:161).

[142] *Amb. Th.* 5 (CCSG 48:29–32); cf. *Disputatio cum Pyrrho* (PG 91:345C–348B). Maximus' interpretation of the "new theandric energy" is further discussed on pp. 132, 151, 164, 293 in this volume.

emperor.[143] In it, he noted that Sophronius had been in Alexandria at the time of the *Pact* and vehemently protested its article on "one activity" of Christ, at which point Cyrus urged that the article should not cause contention since the Fathers who spoke of a single *energeia* had done no harm to the integrity of the traditional faith. Sergius further indicates that Sophronius journeyed to Constantinople and appealed to him in person to remove the controversial article, but that he thought this reactionary since the phrase was so vital to the unity achieved in the *Pact*, and since the affirmation of "two activities" in Christ was itself offensive to many. Sophronius was asked to produce documentation from the Fathers for dyenergism, and allegedly failing to do so, was instructed not to press for it, in respect for the Fathers who had in fact used monenergist language. Henceforth, however, *neither one activity nor two activities* were to be espoused,

> but rather, just as the holy, ecumenical synods have handed down, a person should profess that one and the same only-begotten Son, our Lord Jesus Christ, true God, performs both the divine and the human activities, and that every activity, both fitting for God and fitting for a human being, proceeds without division from one and the same incarnate God.[144]

Having become Patriarch of Jerusalem in 634, Sophronius outlined a formal response to monenergism in his *Synodical Epistle*, specifying that there could be neither a single *energeia* emerging after the union of the divine Son with his humanity, nor a single *energeia* deriving from a single nature, but only an *energeia* proper to each of Christ's natures, with "every utterance and activity" proceeding from his composite person.[145] We see here a brief window for conciliation. Sergius's *Psephos* had advised a cessation of debate over the number of *energeiai* in Christ, and Sophronius initially agreed to this, and probably sought to be discreet when he worded his view in the *Synodical Epistle*, even if it was a strong salvo against monenergism.[146] We must remember that, at the inception of this controversy, there was no strong inherited consensus in the East

---

[143] Greek text and trans. of the letter in Allen, *Sophronius of Jerusalem*, 182–95.

[144] Ibid., 188–9.

[145] *Epistula synodica* 2.10–11, Greek text with trans. by Allen, *Sophronius of Jerusalem*, 102, 103.

[146] Noted by Meyendorff, *Imperial Unity and Christian Divisions*, 348–9, 351; cf. Louth (*Maximus the Confessor*, 15), who emphasizes Sophronius's avoidance of "counting" *energeiai* in his *Synodical Epistle*.

over the concrete outworking of the Chalcedonian definition with respect to Christ's activity and volition.[147] Little wonder that the emerging "Neo-Chalcedonian" options struggled to be reconciled.

Maximus became fully aware of Sophronius's protest of the Alexandrian *Pact of Union*, of Sergius's response in the *Psephos*, and of Sophronius's initial diplomacy toward the *Psephos*. He too was at first positive about the document's urgency to suspend debate over energies in Christ. In a letter to the monastic abbot Pyrrhus (future Patriarch of Constantinople), Maximus called the *Psephos* a safeguard on the teaching handed to the churches by the "God-bearing Fathers," and even praised its author Sergius as a new "Moses"[148]—all of which approval Maximus tried years later to retract.[149] But at the time Maximus saw Sergius as protecting the reciprocity of divine and human operations in Christ whereby, in his incarnational kenosis, "he performed divine things humanly (σαρκικῶς)...and human things divinely (θεϊκῶς)."[150] Further in this letter to Pyrrhus, Maximus asked him, out of his expertise in christological matters, to clarify the precise semantics of ἐνέργεια, the distinction between this term and ἐνέργημα, or between "performance" (πρᾶξις) and "achievement" (ἔργον), since the "God-inspired Fathers" may have differed on wording but never on meaning.[151] This question actually cut to the heart of the controversy. The term *energeia* long carried an ambiguity about whether it applied solely to instrumental activity itself (ἐνέργεια) or also included its accomplished effect (ἐνέργημα). If the latter, monenergists seemed to have the obvious advantage in establishing the pure congruence between Christ's activity and ultimate achievement. Sergius's *Psephos* held out hope that, however many *energeiai* were operative in Christ, there might still be consensus on the "effect" of his work in the economy of salvation.

Despite the initial irenics, however, Maximus went on the offensive against monenergism. Either before the *Psephos* was issued or more

---

[147] On this lack of an antecedent consensus, see Karl-Heinz Uthemann, "Der Neuchalkedonismus als Vorbereiten des Monotheletismus: Ein Beitrag zum eigentlichen Anliegen des Neuchalkedonismus," in Elizabeth Livingstone, ed., *Studia Patristica* 29 (Leuven: Peeters, 1997), 373–413; also Booth, "Sophronius of Jerusalem and the End of Roman History," 15–17.

[148] *Ep.* 19 (PG 91:592B–C).

[149] *Opusc.* 9 (PG 91:129C–132C). For analysis see Booth, *Crisis of Empire*, 213–18.

[150] *Ep.* 19 (PG 91:592D–593A). This phrase is paralleled in the text of *Amb. Th.* 5 (CCSG 48:28–29) from the same time period.

[151] *Ep.* 19 (PG 91:596B–C).

likely after its promulgation,[152] having decided to ignore its mandate about avoiding "energies" language altogether, he composed a brief response to three perceived rationales of monenergism. To those who argued that the divine *energeia* effectively overruled the human one in Christ, Maximus countered, on the basis of the Aristotelian category of relation (Πρός τι), that such would merely lead to the diminution of *both*, since whatever rules is invariably subject to the thing ruled in order to rule it.[153] Second, to monenergists proposing that there was one activity by which the divinity used the humanity like an instrument (ὄργανον), he replied that such would require, by "natural" instrumentality, that the Logos and his flesh (instrument) were contemporaneous, or that his flesh was coeternal with him—both of which options defied the distinction between the uncreated and the created.[154] Finally, to those monenergists claiming that in Christ there was a "composite activity" (σύνθετος ἐνέργεια), Maximus answered that such could only arise from a "composite nature" (συνθέτου φύσεως), a nature whose constituent parts, by necessity, were "locally" circumscribed and synchronous, so that by this ontological definition there could presumably be a multitude of "Christs."[155]

Maximus' early and public role in the mounting controversy is enhanced by the Syriac *Life*, which, as noted briefly earlier, refers to a synod convened on Cyprus by its bishop Arcadius, sometime between late 634 and mid-636,[156] in which Sophronius (now Patriarch of Jerusalem) was in attendance seeking to controvert the monenergism being endorsed by Cyrus and even by Pope Honorius through a papal deacon. The account alleges that Maximus, represented by his disciple Anastasius, was himself the inspiration of the dyenergist/ dyothelete teaching that Sophronius defended, and that after the synod had condemned their views, a letter was sent to Heraclius reporting their dangerous teaching.[157]

Whatever hopes remained for monenergism as a basis for reconciliation among disparate parties evaporated by 640. Pope Honorius, responding to the letter in which Sergius had outlined the substance of the *Psephos*, fatefully suggested that "we confess *one will* (ἕν θέλημα) of

---

[152] A point on which I fully concur with Booth, *Crisis of Empire*, 213 and n. 103.
[153] *Opusc.* 5 (PG 91:64A–B).     [154] Ibid. (PG 91:64B–C).
[155] Ibid. (PG 91:64D–65A).
[156] Booth's dating is 636 (*Crisis of Empire*, 239). It must have been after Sophronius had become Patriarch of Jerusalem in late 634.
[157] Syriac *Vita* §§10–15 (Brock, 306–9, 316–17).

the Lord Jesus Christ, since manifestly our nature was assumed by the Godhead."[158] Perhaps as early as 636, the monothelete phase of the controversy was formally inaugurated when Heraclius issued the *Ekthesis*, a text actually authored by Sergius, and reflecting imperial frustration with efforts at rapprochement.[159] The decree rather unsurprisingly condemned miaphysitism and Nestorianism again in the name of protecting the Nicene and Chalcedonian faith; but it also reinforced the *Psephos*'s declaration about the inappropriateness of numbering *energeiai* in Christ. In so doing, it shifted attention to Christ's volition, and formally ratified Pope Honorius's monotheletism as true to patristic teaching.[160]

> How is it possible that those who confess the correct faith and glorify one Son, our Lord Jesus Christ, true God, also accept . . . *two contrary wills* (δύο ἐναντία θελήματα) in him? Hence, following the holy Fathers closely in all things and in this too, we confess *one will* (ἕν θέλημα) of our Lord Jesus Christ, true God, such that at no time did his rationally ensouled flesh separately and on its own initiative perform its natural movement in a manner contrary (ἐναντίως) to the command of God the Word, hypostatically united to it, but God the Word himself decided at the time and according to the nature and the extent [of the movement].[161]

Sophronius, however, died as Patriarch of Jerusalem in March of 638, months before the *Ekthesis* was promulgated as law in November of that year. Maximus would now assume Sophronius's mantle as the premier Eastern challenger to imperially-sponsored monotheletism, further galvanizing the monastic dissent in Africa and strengthening its alliance with the Roman Church against Constantinople. At the death of Sergius in December 638, Maximus' former correspondent Pyrrhus, with the aging Heraclius's strong endorsement, became Patriarch in the imperial capital, wasting no time in assembling a dossier of documents to validate monotheletism as true to patristic

---

[158] Honorius, *First Letter to Sergius*, Greek text with trans. by Allen, *Sophronius of Jerusalem*, 196–9 (emphasis added). The letter was fateful in the sense that it would be read publicly as evidence when the Council of Constantinople of 681 anathematized monotheletism and condemned Honorius.

[159] Traditional dating of the *Ekthesis* has been 638, but Jankowiak ("Essai d'histoire," 155–60), has made a strong case for an earlier dating in 636.

[160] Greek text of the *Ekthesis* (= ACO II, 1:156–62), trans. Allen, *Sophronius of Jerusalem*, 208–17.

[161] Ibid. (Allen, *Sophronius of Jerusalem*, 214–15; emphasis added).

and episcopal tradition.[162] Around the same time, Maximus posted one among other short treatises to Marinus, a priest he knew in Cyprus, seeking to show him how some superficially monenergist–monothelete passages in three significant authorities (Anastasius of Antioch, Gregory Nazianzen, and Pope Honorius) should be given a dyenergist–dyothelete reading.[163] Maximus was fully sympathetic with the urgency (already expressed in the *Ekthesis*) to avoid any hint of "opposition" in the operations or wills in Christ, but as he would insist more than once in writings from this period, a duality of wills in Christ's composite hypostasis need only indicate *difference, not opposition*—a truth he claimed was already present in Gregory Nazianzen, a patristic authority second to none.[164] In another of his short treatises to Marinus, Maximus refers to the emerging imperial monotheletism as "betrayal" ($\pi\rho o\delta o\sigma i\alpha$) of the teaching of the Fathers and of the very reality of divine incarnation.[165]

Especially striking at this juncture, however, was Maximus' zeal to exonerate the deceased Pope Honorius, whose *First Letter to Sergius* had explicitly affirmed a singular will of Christ. He explained that Honorius was referring simply to the divine will in its freedom from a sinful or carnal human will, not its displacement of Jesus's natural human will.[166] Maximus' defense of Honorius paralleled that of Pope John IV, who also set out to vindicate Honorius's dyothelete orthodoxy, and in fact Maximus indicates how his disciple Anastasius the Monk had gone to Rome and reported back to him both the embarrassment of the Roman clergy and the claim of a certain Abba John, Latin transcriber of Honorius's letter, that the Greek translators of Honorius's letter to Sergius had interposed the mention of one will of Christ.[167] Be that as it may, this episode provides further evidence, as Marek Jankowiak and Phil Booth have emphasized, of the increasing presence of dissident Eastern monks in Rome and its strategic and diplomatic importance for the consolidation of the anti-monothelete cause.[168]

In the tempestuous events of the imperial succession after Heraclius's death in February 641, Pyrrhus's alignment with the ill-fated Empress

---

[162] See Hovorun, *Will, Action and Freedom*, 75–6.

[163] *Opusc.* 20 (PG 91:228B–245D).

[164] Ibid. (PG 91:232D–233B); cf. *Opusc.* 6 (PG 91:65A–68D); *Opusc.* 7 (PG 91:80C–84A); *Opusc.* 3 (PG 91:48B–49A).

[165] *Opusc.* 7 (PG 91:72C–73A).          [166] *Opusc.* 20 (PG 91:237C–245A).

[167] Ibid. (PG 91:244B–D).

[168] See Jankowiak, "Essai d'histoire," 183–91; Booth, *Crisis of Empire*, 266–9.

Martina and her son Heraclius Constantine spelled the end of his patriarchate. Claiming he would no longer serve a "disobedient people," Pyrrhus left Constantinople for Africa,[169] most likely hoping that Gregory, the Byzantine exarch in Carthage, who was primed for a coup d'état amid the political chaos in the imperial capital, would help restore him to his episcopate. Among the Africans, however, Pyrrhus was a shamed figure. Peter the Illustrious consulted Maximus about retaining honorific titles for the expatriated bishop. Maximus' response is an astounding sign of the loyalty of the African monks to Rome. No bishop who had forsaken the Catholic faith, and been condemned by the Roman Church, deserved the title "most holy" (*sanctissimus*); and so

> [Pyrrhus] should above all hasten to give satisfaction to Rome . . . [f]or he simply thinks in vain if he thinks that men like me need to be persuaded, and he does not satisfy and implore the most blessed pope of the most sacred Church of the Romans, that is, the apostolic see, which from the incarnate Word itself, but also in all the sacred synods, according to the sacred canons and definitions, has received and holds the rule, the authority and the power of binding and loosing (*imperium, auctoritatem et potestatem ligandi et solvendi*) of the universal, holy Churches of God throughout the entire world, through and in all things.[170]

In an event of monumental importance for Maximus' ecumenical visibility in the monothelete controversy, he engaged in a public debate with Pyrrhus in Carthage (July 645), with the exarch Gregory presiding. The author of the *Disputation with Pyrrhus* dramatizes a clash of titans,[171] beginning with Pyrrhus thoroughly on the defensive, entreating Maximus to explain why he had everywhere accused him of heresy, especially when they had never even met face to face.

---

[169] Nicephorus, *Brev. hist.* 31 (ed. Mango, 82); cf. Theophanes, *Chron.* 6133 (Mango and Scott, *Chronicle*, 475). For the circumstances surrounding Pyrrhus's loss of the patriarchate, see Jankowiak, "Essai d'histoire," 191–200.

[170] *Opusc.* 12 (PG 91:144B–C), trans. Booth with analysis in *Crisis of Empire*, 271. This opuscule consists in excerpts of Maximus' letter to Peter the Illustrious culled in the West in the ninth century by the scholar-abbot Anastasius Bibliothecarius, sometime archivist of the papal library and the key figure in the Latin MS tradition of those works relating to Maximus' career and trials that proved his loyalties to the Roman see.

[171] *Disp. Pyrr.* (PG 91:288A–353B). Booth (*Crisis of Empire*, 196, 285–6) believes the text of the *Disputation* to be no exact account of the debate but a "meditation on the Christological wills and operations" written long afterward.

Maximus for his part explicitly denounced Heraclius's *Ekthesis*, insisting that the monothelete doctrine was a dangerous innovation on the traditional (apostolic and patristic) faith.[172] The debate turned primarily on the issue of the seat of Christ's volition, Pyrrhus arguing that his one will was a function of his single *hypostasis*, and Maximus that his two wills were grounded squarely in his two *natures*. Maximus propounded what became a major theme of his mature Christology, distinguishing the wills themselves from the "mode of willing" ($\tau\grave{o}$ $\pi\hat{\omega}\varsigma$ $\theta\acute{\epsilon}\lambda\epsilon\iota\nu$) or "mode of use" ($\tau\rho\acute{o}\pi o\varsigma$ $\tau\hat{\eta}\varsigma$ $\chi\rho\acute{\eta}\sigma\epsilon\omega\varsigma$) of the wills as intrinsic respectively to Christ's divine and human natures.[173] His hypostasis had to do only with the modality of the wills, not the volitional faculties themselves.

At the end of the debate Pyrrhus conceded to Maximus the folly of a single operation or will in Christ, and reversed himself, pledging to go to Rome to worship at the tombs of the preeminent apostles, even personally delivering to the pope a *libellus* (certification) of his recantation.[174] Over and beyond the high drama of this reversal, the whole scene carried enormous symbolic significance politically and ecclesiastically. As Phil Booth astutely observes:

> The author of the *Disputation with Pyrrhus* thus enacts an implicit conception of the proper relationship between representatives of monasticism, Church, and state. Despite holding no clerical position, Maximus debates the faith in open, reasoned dialogue with a (deposed) patriarch; his eventual triumph, however, is not definitive but requires the ratification of Rome, and the exarch, for his part, facilitates and presides over the debate but does not attempt to interfere in the discussions. The *Disputation* constitutes, therefore, both a cogent defense of the "two operations" and "two wills," and an implicit condemnation of the comparative doctrinal authoritarianism and secularism of Constantinople.[175]

As it so happens, when the penitent Pyrrhus did go to Rome, perhaps with aspirations that the papacy would now help him recover his patriarchate, he and his *libellus* were received by Pope Theodore I, one of the so-called "Greek" popes, of Palestinian origin, whose father had been a bishop under Sophronius during the latter's campaign

---

[172] See the opening salvos, ibid (PG 91:288B C).    [173] Ibid. (PG 91:292D ff.).
[174] Ibid. (PG 91:352D–353A); cf. Greek *Vita* of Maximus §16, Recension 3 (Neil and Allen, 66).
[175] *Crisis of Empire*, 286.

against monenergism.[176] Andrew Ekonomou speculates that through his father, Theodore, like Maximus, was a former disciple of Sophronius, and had been exiled with his father from Palestine because of monenergist–monothelete strong-arming.[177] This early connection of Theodore with Sophronius cannot be confirmed since it is not mentioned in the *Liber Pontificalis*. As pope (642–9), nevertheless, he was an ardent protagonist for dyotheletism, and in letters to the Constantinopolitan Patriarch Paul II vociferously rebuked Pyrrhus, demanding that, since he had not been canonically deposed during the political chaos of 641, this should still be done, if not by the bishops in Constantinople (with the participation of emissaries from the pope), then in Rome itself.[178] Paul II courteously resisted Theodore's strong overtures. But now presented with a contrite Pyrrhus in his own see, the pope took strategic advantage of the situation, initially acknowledging him as rightful Patriarch of Constantinople. Nevertheless, when Pyrrhus went on to Ravenna, the Byzantine exarchate in Italy, he once again reversed himself and resumed his loyalty to the imperially-supported monotheletism,[179] at which point Theodore excommunicated him and further declared his official deposition from the see of Constantinople.[180] What is more, when Paul II continued to balk at papal pressure to renounce the *Ekthesis* and the whole monothelete crusade, Theodore gathered a synod in Rome in 648 and excommunicated the patriarch, prompting an open ecclesiastical schism.[181] Meanwhile in Constantinople, Paul II drafted a new statement in 647 or 648, the *Typos*, sanctioned by the Emperor Constans II, which aimed to silence all talk of one or two wills in Christ, though clearly intending to undermine the anti-monothelete dissent.[182]

---

[176] See the *Liber Pontificalis* 75.3, trans. Raymond Davis, *The Book of the Pontiffs*, 2nd edn., TTH 6 (Liverpool: Liverpool University Press, 2000), 69.

[177] On Pope Theodore and his connections with Sophronius, see Ekonomou, *Byzantine Rome and the Greek Popes*, 96–8. Ekonomou stresses the likelihood that Theodore would have had access to Sophronius's *Synodical Epistle* and other of his works that Maximus also knew.

[178] Theodore, *Ep. ad Paulum* (PL 87:75C–80B; = PL 129:577–82). See also Jankowiak, "Essai d'histoire," 209–10.

[179] Greek *Vita* of Maximus §16, Recension 3 (Neil and Allen, 66–8).

[180] Theophanes, A.M. 6121 (Mango and Scott, *Chronicle*, 462). See also Jankowiak, "Essai d'histoire," 231–3.

[181] *Liber pontificalis* 75.3 (Davis, *Book of the Pontiffs*, 69–70). On these events, see Ekonomou, *Byzantine Rome and the Greek Popes*, 98–9; Jankowiak, "Essai d'histoire," 215–20.

[182] Text of the *Typos* in ACO II, 1:208–10.

With a Greek with Palestinian connections being pope, the geographic arc of the Chalcedonian-dyothelete opposition, crossing East and West, and enfolding activist monks and clerics from Palestine, Africa, and Rome, appeared complete. Maximus ostensibly traveled to Rome immediately after Pyrrhus (*c*.646) and worked with Pope Theodore I to assemble a dossier of patristic authorities for bolstering the dyothelete cause.[183] Around this time, Maximus dispatched to the dyothelete bishop Stephen of Dor in Palestine an extensive florilegium of patristic citations to this same effect, and such was easily integrated into the sources collected at the later Lateran Council of 649.[184] Meanwhile, Maximus' victory over Pyrrhus in debate and his increasingly public alignment with the Roman see helped bring to a head the growing unrest in Africa. We know from letters placed in evidence at the Lateran Council that African bishops as well as monks, in full knowledge that Constantinople suspected their rebellious ways, had vigorously demanded the deposition of Paul II in a virtual ecclesiastical coup.[185] In the same period, the emboldened exarch Gregory instigated a failed political coup against the empire—a revolt in which Maximus was later accused of seditious participation.[186] Jankowiak does not exaggerate when he posits that Maximus' audacious plan was precisely "to recreate in the West an orthodox Empire whose fidelity to the Fathers would be a gauge of the divine protection so obviously withdrawn from the court in

---

[183] The Greek *Vita* of Maximus §§16, 18, Recension 3 (Neil and Allen, 68, 70), has Maximus in Rome after Pyrrhus's repentance and eventual relapse into monotheletism, since it claims that he and Pope Theodore I met to condemn Pyrrhus's infidelity, and that Maximus lived in Rome from that point because he had long desired to make it his home. For a listing of the principal anti-monenergist/monothelete florilegia, including Maximus' own, see Alois Grillmeier, *Christ in Christian Tradition*, 2/1, trans. Pauline Allen and John Cawte (Atlanta: John Knox Press, 1987), 73–5.

[184] *Opusc.* 15 (PG 91:153C–184C). Bram Roosen has produced a new critical edition of *Opusc.* 15 (publication forthcoming in a volume in the "Studies in Byzantine History and Civilization" series from Brepols). I am grateful to Roosen for furnishing me a pre-publication draft of this edition.

[185] See especially the letter from African bishops, *Ep. ecclesiarum Africanorum ad sanctum Theodorem* (PL 87:81D–86D). On these letters and their background, see Jankowiak, "Essai d'histoire," 221–7; Booth, *Crisis of Empire*, 287–8.

[186] Theophanes, *Chron.* A.M. 6138 (Mango and Scott, *Chronicle*, 477), cf. also the Syriac *Vita* of Maximus §18 (Brock, 310, 317). For discussion, see Conant, *Staying Roman*, 355–6. For the accusation of Maximus' involvement, see *Relatio motionis* §2 (Allen and Neil, 50–2).

Constantinople, reduced as it was to desperation over the Arab invasions."[187] And yet, ironically, that same Arab onslaught would also rapidly undermine the resistance of the African churches.

## FINAL YEARS BETWIXT AND BETWEEN: ROME, CONSTANTINOPLE, LAZICA

Pope Theodore I did much to set the stage for a long-awaited pontifical synod specifically to condemn the *Ekthesis* and the *Typos* and to register a formal protest against the pro-monothelete policies of the emperor. Such was the Lateran Council of 649, presided over by Theodore's successor, Pope Martin I, an Italian who had served as a papal *apocrisiarius* (emissary) to Constantinople in the midst of the mounting tensions that led to his own expulsion from the capital.[188] Martin came to the papacy without imperial approval, but with the strong support and trust of the assembled council. Rudolf Riedinger has suggested that the Lateran Council was certainly not a council as we normally know them by their dogmatic transactions. It was more like a rubber stamp on the cumulative antecedent work of Sophronius, Maximus, and Theodore I, which needed no debate since the members of the council—including not only the clerics but at least thirty-eight Greek monks—were already thoroughly agreed on its substance.[189]

Indeed, this Western council's Greek aura is, in retrospect, its most arresting feature, since the documentation it endorsed was already in Greek, with Latin translation expeditiously completed for the bishops,[190] and since the contingent of Greek monks was so large,

[187] "Essai d'histoire," 220–1.
[188] See *Liber pontificalis* 76.1–2, 4 (Davis, *Book of the Pontiffs*, 70–1).
[189] For the official documentation of the Council, see ACO II, 1. For analysis see Rudolf Riedinger, "Die Lateransynode von 649 und Maximos der Bekenner," in Felix Heinzer and Christoph Schönborn, eds., *Maximus Confessor: Actes du Symposium sur Maxime le Confesseur, Fribourg, 2–5 septembre 1980* (Fribourg: Éditions Universitaires, 1982) (hereafter *MC*), 111–21; Ekonomou, *Byzantine Rome and the Greek Popes*, 113–57, esp. 128–41; Jankowiak, "Essai d'histoire," 258–64; Hovorun, *Will, Action and Freedom*, 83–6 (who insists *pace* Riedinger that it was a "real" council and not contrived); also the still useful survey by Charles Hefele, *A History of the Councils of the Church*, trans. William Clark (Edinburgh: T. & T. Clark, 1896), 5:97–116.
[190] See Riedinger, "Die Lateransynode von 649 und Maximos der Bekenner," 119–20.

bespeaking the tremendous number of refugee Eastern and African monks settled into monastic communities in Rome in the wake of the Arab invasions.[191] By episcopal delegation it was definitely not an "ecumenical" council. Only one of its 105 bishops was an Easterner, Stephen of Dor, from a diocese north of Caesarea Maritima. Stephen was a Palestinian disciple of Sophronius and his former envoy to Rome, and gave witness to the assembly of his vow to Sophronius on the holy mount of Golgotha to return to the Apostolic See and help rid the empire once and for all of the monothelete heresy.[192] With Stephen and all the Eastern monks, therefore, the council could still claim to be ecumenical at least in geographical, if not episcopal, representation.

Questions linger over whether Maximus himself was actually present in the sessions of the Lateran Council. He is registered among its members, and he implied his presence at the council when he was later tried in Constantinople.[193] The Syriac *Life*, furthermore, scorns Maximus for having rallied dyothelete support in Africa and the Mediterranean islands before ending up at the council, where "he anathematized the patriarchs of Constantinople because they did not agree with him."[194] And yet Maximus' physical presence at the council is not confirmed, and besides, he may well have desired to retain a low profile in the council's proceedings since the imperial court considered him a menace.[195]

Given its background, the canons of the Lateran Council are predictable. They frame dyothelete Christology as the organic extension of the Nicene and Chalcedonian faith, dismiss the *Ekthesis* and *Typos*, anathematize the monothelete protagonists (Theodore of Pharan, Cyrus of Alexandria, Sergius, Pyrrhus, and Paul II), redeem Dionysius's language of the "new theandric energy" of Christ, and

---

[191] The Lateran Council included an anathematization of the Patriarchs Sergius, Pyrrhus, and Paul II by abbots of four Eastern monastic communities: John, of the Mar Saba monastery in the Judean Desert; Theodore, of a Sabaite lavra in "Christ-loving" Africa; Thalassius, of the community of Armenian monks in the Renatus monastery in Rome; and George, abbot of the Cilician monks resident in the Aqua Silva monastery in Rome (ACO II, 1:50). See also Jean-Marie Sansterre, *Les moines grecs et orientaux à Rome aux époques byzantine et carolingienne* (Brussels: Palais des Académies, 1983), 1:9–31; and Jankowiak, "Essai d'histoire," 231–4.

[192] ACO II, 1:41; see also Winkelmann, *Der monenergetisch-monotheletische Streit*, 125–7 (No. 110).

[193] *Relatio motionis* §12 (Allen and Neil, 68–70).

[194] Syriac *Vita* §21 (Brock, 312, 318).     [195] Allen and Neil, 19.

treat all the assembly's declarations as those of a legitimate ecumenical council in line with the earlier ones.[196] The mark of Maximus' Christology is especially conspicuous in canon 10:

> If anyone does not properly and truthfully confess according to the holy Fathers that one and the same Christ our God had two wills, divine and human, cohering in union, and that, on this basis, through each of his natures, the same Christ of his own free will effected our salvation, let him be condemned.[197]

The canons as a whole are a mirror on Maximus' Christology, and a thorough testament of the effectiveness with which this unordained Byzantine monk had amalgamated monastic and ecclesiastical forces to counteract the power of an empire.

Pope Martin I moved quickly to broadcast the Lateran Council's actions to the emperor and to all churches East and West,[198] and immediately encouraged the Frankish bishops to follow suit with their own synodical condemnation of monotheletism.[199] In an additional series of epistles, he congratulated the African churches for holding firm,[200] and appointed the Eastern bishop John of Philadelphia to represent the papacy in deposing monothelete clergy and ordaining dyothelete clergy in the Middle East.[201] He posted another encyclical specifically to the churches under the patriarchates of Antioch and Jerusalem to foster their reception of the council's decisions.[202] Perhaps most striking, however, is Martin's letter directly to the teenage Emperor Constans II, in which he not only forces the issue of the emperor's responsibility to genuine orthodoxy but also ties victory over the invading barbarians (Arabs) to the upholding of the orthodox faith.[203]

---

[196] ACO II, 1:368–88. Maximus himself seems to have considered the Lateran Council genuinely ecumenical in his remarks about it in *Opusc.* 11 (PG 91:137–40).

[197] ACO II, 1:374.

[198] See the text of Martin I's encyclical in ACO II, 1:404–20.

[199] *Ep. ad Amandum* (ACO II, 1:422–4).

[200] *Ep. ad ecclesiam Carthaginensem* (PL 87:145C–154A).

[201] *Ep. ad Joannem episcopum Philadelphiae* (PL 87:153B–164A). Earlier, Pope Theodore I had charged Stephen of Dor with this same mission, which encountered substantial resistance. See Jankowiak, "Essai d'histoire," 235–7; Booth, *Crisis of Empire*, 295–7.

[202] *Ep. ad ecclesiam Jerosolymitanam et Antiochenam* (PL 87:175A–180D).

[203] *Ep. ad Constantem Imperatorem* (PL 87:137D–146C, and esp. 146A–B). For analysis of Martin's letters, see Jankowiak, "Essai d'histoire," 265–77; Hefele, *History of the Councils of the Church*, 5:116–18.

Needless to say, the imperial court interpreted the actions of Maximus and Pope Martin I as a brazen interference in matters of state. While papal interventions in affairs of the Eastern churches were certainly not unprecedented, the empire had never seen the likes of a monastic–ecclesiastical alliance of this geographic extent and ideological robustness. Indeed, ecclesiologically this coalition was absolutely unprecedented, even if short-lived.[204] Maximus the monk had encouraged and sanctioned the idea of a pope, not an emperor, convening an ecumenical council—a total break with tradition.[205] The lingering instability of the imperial throne and the unrelenting stresses of Arab expansion drastically intensified the volatility of the situation. The emperor predictably responded through the Byzantine exarchate in Ravenna. Even before the Lateran Council was ended, Constans II sent his newly appointed exarch Olympius to Rome to demand that the pope and assembled bishops embrace the *Typos*, although the *Liber Pontificalis* states that Olympius was commissioned specifically to assassinate the pope while he was administering the Eucharist, and that, when a soldier was miraculously blinded trying to kill Martin I, the remorseful Olympius and his troops were reconciled with the pope and revealed their original plan to him.[206] According to a record of Martin's later trial, however, he was accused by one witness of conspiring with Olympius to murder the emperor, and by another of preparing Olympius's soldiers to take an oath of allegiance to the exarch, a patent gesture of insurrection.[207] The emperor appointed a new exarch, Theodore Calliopa, who led an army into Rome in July 653 and arrested Martin in the Church of St. John Lateran, deporting him to Constantinople to be tried for treason.[208]

---

[204] Ekonomou, *Byzantine Rome and the Greek Popes*, 118–19. Ekonomou further remarks, "the germ of an ecclesiological conscience that would come to conceive of papal authority in juridical terms had been planted. Although wholly foreign to the East, these novel importations had ironically been the product of Eastern minds bent on combating a heresy of Eastern origin."

[205] Ibid., 136–7. Ekonomou notes that precisely here Maximus broke from Dionysius the Areopagite's own notion of ecclesiastical-political hierarchy.

[206] *Liber pontificalis* 76.5–7 (Davis, *Book of the Pontiffs*, 72). On the principal sources for Martin's demise, see Bronwen Neil, *Seventh-Century Popes and Martyrs: The Political Hagiography of Anastasius Bibliothecarius* (Leuven: Brepols, 2006), 93–133.

[207] *Narrationes de exilio sancti papae Martini* 16 17, Latin text with trans. by Neil, *Seventh-Century Popes and Martyrs*, 194–6.

[208] Ibid. 5–13 (Neil, *Seventh-Century Popes and Martyrs*, 172–88); *Liber pontificalis* 76.8 (Davis, *Book of the Pontiffs*, 72).

As for Maximus himself, the sources do not thoroughly concur on the time or precise circumstance of his arrest and deportation to the imperial capital.[209] But thanks to Anastasius Bibliothecarius in the ninth century, who assembled crucial sources for Maximus' later career, and more recently to Pauline Allen and Bronwen Neil, who have produced the critical edition of that cluster of documents,[210] the sequence of events of Maximus' and Martin's demise is clearer, as is the compelling drama that earned Maximus his epithet "Confessor." Most likely he was arrested in Rome very soon after Martin, and Martin's trial occurred in Constantinople in late 653 before Maximus' in 655. Following Martin's being sentenced to death for treason, he was publicly humiliated and paraded through the streets by an executioner, until the dying Patriarch Paul II intervened with the emperor to commute his sentence, so that he was sent into exile.[211]

The trials of both Martin and Maximus were "show trials," carefully orchestrated by the Byzantine senate to undercut the dyothelete opposition by framing it as sedition pure and simple.[212] Especially telling, given the earlier claims of Sophronius and other dyotheletes that the Arab onslaught was providential punishment on the (theological) sins of the empire, was the very first charge leveled at Maximus by the imperial *sacellarius*, accusing him of betraying Byzantine territories to the Arabs:

"From what you have done it has become clear to everyone that you hate the emperor and his empire. I say this because single-handedly you betrayed Egypt, Alexandria, Pentapolis, Tripolis and Africa to the Saracens."

"And what's the proof of those charges?" [Maximus] said.

[209] By one recension of Maximus' Greek *Vita*, he and his companions, Anastasius the Monk and Anastasius the Apocrisiarius, were arrested in Rome together with Martin, which would mean in 653 (Greek *Vita*, Recension 2, PG 90:85D–88A). By another recension, they were all arrested when Constans II was completing the ninth year of his reign, which suggests 650 (Greek *Vita* §22, Recension 3, in Neil and Allen, 78).
[210] Critical edition in CCSG 39; Greek text reproduced with translation in Allen and Neil, 48–175.
[211] *Narrationes de exilio* 20–6 (Neil, *Seventh-Century Popes and Martyrs*, 202–16); cf. Theodore Spoudaeus, *Hypomnesticon* §8 (Allen and Neil, 158).
[212] Allen and Neil, 22; also citing Wolfram Brandes, "'Juristische' Krisenbewälti-gung im 7. Jahrhundert? Die Prozesse gegen Martin I. und Maximos Homologetes," in Ludwig Burgmann, ed., *Fontes Minores* 10 (Frankfurt: Löwenklau-Gesellschaft, 1998), 141–212, at 212.

And they produced John, the former finance minister of Peter, the former general of Numidia in Africa, who said: "Twenty-two years ago the emperor's grandfather [Heraclius] ordered blessed Peter to take an army and go off to Egypt against the Saracens, and he wrote to you, as if he were speaking to a servant of God, having confidence in you as a holy person, [to inquire] if you counselled him to set off. And you wrote back to him saying that he should do nothing of the sort, because God did not approve lending aid to the Roman empire during the reign of Heraclius and his kin."[213]

When Maximus, confessing having exchanged letters with Peter, asked for documentary evidence of the correspondence mentioned in the charge, the *sacellarius* admitted not having it, and the trial moved on. On the face of it, the charge appears far-fetched; and yet it makes perfect sense in the atmosphere of the time, amid the urgency to explain why the empire was being divinely chastised with the Arab onslaught.[214] Even the Syriac *Life* claimed that "following the wicked Maximus, the wrath of God punished every place which had accepted his error."[215]

A second charge of treason—also denied by Maximus—alleged that he had claimed to have a dream of the African exarch Gregory prevailing against Constans II, effectively making him an accessory of Gregory's coup in 646.[216] A third charge purported that Maximus had made contemptuous comments about the emperor.[217] A fourth accused his companion, Anastasius the Monk, of denying, in Maximus' presence, that the emperor was himself a priest ($\iota\epsilon\rho\epsilon\upsilon\varsigma$) when an imperial secretary had proposed to them the reunion of Rome and Constantinople on the basis of the *Typos*. Answering, Maximus recalled the conversation with the envoy, repudiating not only the *Typos*, and its inconsistency with the Nicene faith, but the envoy's appeal to Melchizedek as a biblical *typos* (prefiguration) of the emperor as priest-king, since that *typos* applied exclusively to Christ.[218]

The further proceedings of the trial pressed the issue of Maximus' ecclesiastical divisiveness, inducing him to admit being out of communion with Constantinople, and blaming him for standing in the way of an allegedly imminent reconciliation between Rome and the

---

[213] *Relatio motionis* §1 (Allen and Neil, 48 51).
[214] Jankowiak, "Essai d'histoire," 280.     [215] Syriac *Vita* (Brock, 312–13, 318).
[216] *Relatio motionis* §2 (Allen and Neil, 50–2).
[217] Ibid. §3 (Allen and Neil, 52–4).     [218] Ibid. §4 (Allen and Neil, 54–8).

imperial capital.[219] The thorough insinuation of ecclesiastical and political interests was epitomized in the words of one of his accusers, the patrician Troilus: "You've anathematized the *Typos*—you've anathematized the Emperor."[220] But the climactic question posed to him was, "Why do you love the Romans and hate the Greeks?"—to which Maximus famously replied, "I love the Romans because we share the same faith, whereas I love the Greeks because we share the same language."[221] This was no gesture toward conciliation but a capstone of the historic coalition of Greek monks and the Roman see, and a last-ditch plea to Constantinople to rectify its Christology.

Sensing the judicial impasse, the imperial authorities exiled Maximus to a fortress at Bizya in Thrace, separating him from his disciple and confidant, Anastasius the Monk.[222] Here, in August 656, the elderly Maximus engaged in a debate with the bishop Theodosius of Caesarea Bithyniae, engineered by the emperor and patriarch to pursue yet again a reconciliation. Interestingly, the dispute began with Theodosius querying Maximus about divine foreknowledge and predestination. When Theodosius insinuated that his exile might be divine retribution against doctrinal error, Maximus retorted that his sufferings might rather be the refiner's fire for courage.[223] But the exchange quickly cut to Christology, with Maximus emphasizing that monotheletism confused the registers of *theologia* and *oikonomia* by forcing the singularity of the divine will into the incarnational economy, evoking a divine "Quaternity" since the fleshly Christ would have to be connatural with the Logos. Theodosius nonetheless betrayed a genuine urgency for conciliation, especially when he said that the *Typos* was not "ratified teaching" (κύριον δόγμα) but only an "accommodation" (οἰκονομία),[224] and promised that if Maximus

---

[219]  Ibid. §§6–8 (Allen and Neill, 60–4).
[220]  Ibid. §11 (Allen and Neil, 68, 69).        [221]  Ibid. (Allen and Neil, 70, 71).
[222]  For the details of Maximus' exiles, see Booth, *Crisis of Empire*, 313–28.
[223]  *Disputatio Bizyae* §3 (Allen and Neil, 76–81).
[224]  Ibid. §3; also §12 (Allen and Neil, 84, 110). An "accommodation," a term already used in Sergius's *First Letter to Honorius* containing the *Psephos* (see Allen, *Sophronius of Jerusalem*, 186), means the attempt to achieve consensus on the substance of doctrine without bogging down in the wording: namely, the attempts of the *Ekthesis* and *Typos* to uphold the Chalcedonian of distinction of natures, while discreetly avoiding language of energies/wills so as to protect the integrity of Christ's action and the absence of any internal opposition in him. On this theme, see Heinz Ohme, "*Oikonomia* im monenergetisch-monotheletischen Streit," *Zeitschrift für Antikes Christentum* 12 (2008): 308–43, esp. 332–43. Ohme for his part accuses Maximus

would resume communion with Constantinople, the emperor would revoke the *Typos* altogether.[225] Maximus balked at this and reasserted that emperors do not define orthodoxy; the truth stands on its own and is recognized by councils (including regional synods) whose fidelity is confirmed ex post facto within ecclesiastical tradition.[226] At last, like Pyrrhus eleven years earlier, Theodosius admitted being convinced by Maximus' arguments, and pledged to commit his dyotheletism to writing, at which point Maximus directed him, along with the emperor and Patriarch Peter of Constantinople, to appeal directly to the pope if they were serious about reunion.[227]

Despite Theodosius's efforts toward a breakthrough, Maximus' woes were merely protracted. Subsequently detained at a monastery near Constantinople, two imperial representatives met him— ironically—in the section of the monastery church reserved for cat- echumens, where they promised him extraordinary public repute if he was compliant:

> Since all the West and those in the East who are causing subversion look to you, and they all stir up strife because of you, refusing to be recon- ciled with us in the cause of faith, may God compel you to enter into communion with us on the terms of the *Typos* which was published by us, and we will go out of our own accord to the Chalke [at the entrance of the imperial palace], and we will embrace you, and we will lay our hands on you, and with every mark of honor and glory we will lead you into the Great Church [Hagia Sophia].[228]

Maximus recoiled yet again, and soon, together with the two Anastasii, found himself once more exiled in two locations in Thrace. From Thrace he issued a letter (658) to his fellow-exile Anastasius the Monk indicating that he had received a message from the patriarch asking him whether he belonged to the united Church of all the patriarchates, *including Rome*. That Rome was included here may be sheer rhetoric,

---

of having distorted the arguments of his opponents who were also arguing from tradition, of ignoring their points of agreement, and of implacably holding up his own doctrinal insights as the self-evident orthodoxy.

[225] *Disputatio Bizyae* §4 (Allen and Neil, 88).

[226] Ibid. §4 (Allen and Neil, 88–90). Booth rightly discerns a shift of emphasis from the *Record* of his first trial, where Maximus attacked the "priestly" identity of the emperor in assuming the clerical privilege of debating doctrine, and his argument in Bizya that orthodoxy is orthodoxy even apart from clerical debate (*Crisis of Empire*, 314).

[227] *Disputatio Bizyae* §§4, 8 (Allen and Neil, 98, 104).

[228] Ibid. §10 (Allen and Neil, 108, 109).

but probably betrays the fact that Pope Vitalian (elected 657) had intermittently reneged on the dyothelete alliance and restored communion with Constantinople. Maximus may have known this, for he replies to the patriarch by interpreting the "rock" on which the Church is built not as Peter (the papacy) but as Peter's orthodox confession of the Christ (cf. Matt. 16:16).[229]

Maximus was returned to Constantinople for a second trial in 662. There he had his tongue excised and his right hand cut off, and he was paraded in his mutilated state around Constantinople, then banished to a mountain fortress in Lazica (western Georgia),[230] wherefore later Orthodox tradition remembered him "like a Greek *pharmakos* [scapegoat] taking all the sins of the Monothelite church to the Diothelite world at the eastern end of the Black Sea."[231] In Lazica Maximus allegedly prophesied his own death, and miracles were associated with his death and burial, which did much to immortalize him in Georgian hagiographical tradition.[232] Thus too began his aggrandizement as a "Confessor."

Not, however, until the Council of Constantinople in 680–1 was Maximus the Confessor's imprint on the seventh century and on ecumenical theological tradition finally sealed. Constans II's son, Constantine IV, who had secured the throne in 668 aided by the papacy, reopened communication between the rival patriarchates, and invited a delegation to come to Constantinople from Rome to resume discussion of Christology. The delegation, eventually sent by Pope Agatho, included some Roman and Italian clergy, but also four Greek monks, signaling that the dyothelete alliance remained alive despite Pope Vitalian's earlier defection. Once convened by Constantine IV, the Council of Constantinople quickly became a contest of dyothelete and monothelete florilegia. The monothelete position was eroded, however, when Patriarch Macarius of Antioch, its principal spokesman, was accused of producing falsified texts from

[229] Maximus, *Ep. ad Anastasium monachum disciplum* (Allen and Neil, 120). See also Allen and Neil, 25, 185, n. 4; Booth, *Crisis of Empire*, 320–1, 332, 341.
[230] *Disputatio Bizyae* §17 (Allen and Neil, 118); Theodore Spudaeos, *Hypomnesticon* §4 (ibid., 150–2).
[231] Geoffrey Carr-Harris, "The Folklorization of Maximus the Confessor," in Tamila Mgaloblishvili and Lela Khoperia, eds., *Maximus the Confessor and Georgia* (London: Centre of the Exploration of Georgian Antiquities, 2009), 202.
[232] Theodore Spudaeos, *Hypomnesticon* §§5, 9 (Allen and Neil, 154, 162).

the Fathers.[233] In the end, the council confirmed Christ's two *energeiai* and wills, and yet Maximus' name was never mentioned in its documentation, sparing the imperial throne public embarrassment over Constans II's ill-treatment of the very architect of the council's christological verdict.

Maximus ended his life a shamed figure, a political prisoner of Byzantium, put away in a remote fortress in the Caucasus on imperial hopes that the memory of him would fade. But his legacy in the Church was already secure. He had moved to the very forefront of the Greek monastic dissent. Together with Sophronius, he had consolidated an unprecedented monastic–ecclesiastical coalition that spread itself across East and West in defiance of the empire. And he had personally articulated the final contours and nuances of Neo-Chalcedonian christological orthodoxy. In the chapters to follow, I will explore more directly how his larger theology and asceticism fit into the landscapes of a life lived "betwixt and between" in the turbulent seventh century.

---

[233] Documentation of the council is in ACO II, 2. On its background and internal workings, see Jankowiak, "Essai d'histoire," 427–88.

# 2

# Writing Theology in Early Byzantium

Byzantium in the seventh century was locked in nothing short of a political, cultural, and religious identity crisis. So argues Averil Cameron in her depiction of a Christian Empire striving both to carry on the legacy of Hellenic civilization and to consolidate itself in the face of the external challenge of Arab invasion (and emerging Islam) and the internal challenge of religious dissent and heresy. Heraclius and his successors, as we observed in the last chapter, struggled to fortify the Byzantine cultural cosmos, pursuing an elusive equilibrium of its political, geographical, ecclesiastical, and not least theological extremities. In Cameron's judgment, writers like Dionysius the Areopagite, Maximus, and later John Damascene answered the need for a new paradigm of knowledge itself. She observes that in early Byzantium, "What mattered was the achievement of a discourse that provided for a secure sense of total order, the perception that all knowledge could be contained in one system embracing all things divine and human."[1]

The early Byzantine "systematization of knowledge,"[2] as Cameron calls it, evolved as a hardening consensus based on biblical, patristic, and conciliar authorities and manifested across an array of literary genres: poetic and homiletic works with staged dialogues to amplify the Christian narrative and to demonstrate its internal coherence;[3] prose disputations (not only those pitting learned Christians against Jews or Manichaeans or Muslims, but also intramural Christian debates,

---

[1] "Byzantium and the Past in the Seventh Century: The Search for Redefinition," *CCEB* V, 271.
[2] "Disputations, Polemical Literature, and the Formation of Opinion in the early Byzantine Period," *CCEB* III, 100; cf. "Byzantium and the Past," *CCEB* V, 255 ("a complete synthesis of knowledge"), 261 ("codification and synthesis"), 270 ("a redefinition of knowledge").
[3] e.g. the *Kontakia* of Romanos the Melodist in the sixth century.

climaxing in Maximus' historic disputation with Pyrrhus at Carthage); the broad variety of question-and-response literature of this era (well represented again by Maximus); and finally, the plethora of catenae, florilegia, and conciliar documents.[4] Cameron proposes that Maximus, in his public role in the christological crisis, and John Damascene in the battle against imperial iconoclasm a century later,

> both produce complete systems of knowledge—based of course on precisely this repertoire. Christian history and Christian authority is [sic] defined, as it is [sic] in the works of ps-Dionysius the Areopagite, as consisting in the Scriptures, the Councils, and the works of approved, or select, Fathers. All necessary human knowledge is to be found and confined in that chain of authority.[5]

> In each case the end product was to be a total discourse in which all Christian knowledge should be contained.[6]

This profile of Maximus as a proto-scholastic works well as a retrospect on his role and his writing in the last phase of his career, the monothelete controversy, and it befits a cultural-historical perspective like Cameron's, which focuses on intellectual elites as instrumental to Byzantium's cultural stability. I will discuss it further later in this chapter. It is nonetheless inadequate as a historical-theological portrait of the making of a Confessor out of a monk, and falls short of comprehending the creativity of Maximus' synthesis in addressing new theological and ecclesiastical crises. Maximus was not just a sophisticated compiler or standardizer. Only a thick description, I suggest, can do justice to his conception of the proper disciplines of the theologian as an interpreter of sacred history and tradition. Only a thick description can bring together the different strands of Maximus' formation as a monk and a theologian in a profile that integrates the early, middle, and later phases of his life, and that avoids viewing his public involvement in ecclesiastical controversy as a transcending of his monastic vocation.[7]

---

[4] "Disputations, Polemical Literature," 92–108; more recently, Cameron's *Dialoguing in Late Antiquity* (Washington, DC: Center for Hellenic Studies, 2014).

[5] "Disputations, Polemical Literature," 106.

[6] "Byzantium and the Past," 269. Cf. ibid., 255 ("a complete synthesis of knowledge"), 261 ("codification and synthesis"), 270 ("a redefinition of knowledge").

[7] Even as circumspect a historian as Cameron does not elude the temptation to alienate Maximus' monastic and ecclesiastical involvements when she writes, "whereas perhaps at first he moved mainly in monastic circles and had contact with the Greek administration, during the time that the Monothelite question developed he quickly assumed leadership of the African church and after Gregory's defeat and

We begin, then, by examining Maximus' formation as a monastic theologian and writer, as this was his core formation and laid the foundation for his entire career. In his earlier writings pre-640s he developed discursive and interpretive habits that endured throughout his career, even though there was a marked change in the genre, tenor, and thrust of his writing after he entered fully into the fray of christological controversy. I wish to propose that the ultimate force of his argumentation in the heat of the monothelete crisis depended at bottom not merely on acquired support from clerics and government officials, or on the momentum of urgency for doctrinal consensus, but on the *charismatic authority* that accrued to Maximus through his monastic background and connections. Without this authority, the monumental monastic dissent challenging monothelete emperors and patriarchs would have been unimaginable.

## WRITING WISDOM: MONASTIC *ASCÊSIS* AND THE QUEST OF *PHILOSOPHIA*

Questions considered in the last chapter about Maximus' early life and monastic provenance loom large when trying to reconstruct his formation as an ascetical and theological author. A key preliminary issue is Maximus' precise relation to the heritage of Origen, for especially through the teaching of Evagrius Ponticus, which Maximus clearly admired and used, Origen's teaching had been elemental for monastic *philosophia*. Even if Origenist sources are scarce at best after the conciliar condemnation of Origen in 553, it is certainly easy to imagine how Origenism's myth of the beginning and end of the world could have remained compelling for monks.[8] Some scholars, perhaps prematurely, have dismissed the claim of the Syriac *Life* that Maximus began in an Origenist monastery in Palestine, and Polycarp Sherwood long ago opposed Hans Urs von Balthasar's (retracted) claim that Maximus the monk had once undergone a "crisis" of infatuation with Origenist

death went with the bishops as their leader to the Lateran Council in Rome" ("Byzantine Africa," *CCEB* VII, 44).

[8] Irénée-Henri Dalmais, "Saint Maxime le Confesseur et la crise de l'origénisme monastique," in *Théologie de la vie monastique* (Paris: Aubier, 1961), 411–21.

thought.[9] If the Syriac *Life* is at least correct about his Palestinian provenance, it would help explain Maximus' familiarity with the forms of monastic Origenism against which he writes in the *Ambigua to John* and other texts. If the Greek *Life* is given precedence, the logical conclusion must be that Maximus learned of these later forms of Origenism secondhand either in monastic residence in Asia Minor or in travels in the East.

Either way, Maximus engages Origenist thought critically but also constructively. The hagiographic *Record of the Trial* has him at last publicly repudiating Origen and his sympathizers. When one of his cross-examiners tells him that he is being punished by God for deluding others with the teachings of Origen, Maximus responds, "Anathema on Origen and his teachings, and on everyone of the same mind as himself."[10] Reductionistic accusations of "Origenism" were nevertheless thrown around consistently in Eastern monasticism, in which case Maximus' response here might be more his reaction to a familiar innuendo than a wholesale repudiation of all things Origenian.[11] Numerous scholars acknowledge Maximus' use of Origen and Evagrius, but are quick to point out that he meticulously screened his Origenist influences and drew out only the redeemable elements.[12] Larchet emphasizes the overriding influence of the Cappadocians, while Garrigues argues that Maximus looks mainly to Dionysius the Areopagite as a corrective to Origenist cosmology. Both Larchet and Garrigues also

---

[9] Von Balthasar, in his first edition of *Kosmische Liturgie* (Freiburg: Herder, 1941), 42, suggested the possibility that Maximus temporarily underwent his own personal Origenist "crisis," supposedly while in Alexandria with Sophronius; Sherwood's criticism (*Date-List*, 4–5) and demonstration of Maximus' anti-Origenism led von Balthasar to retract this claim in the second edition of *Kosmische Liturgie* (Einsiedeln: Johannes-Verlag, 1961), 12–13.

[10] See *Relatio motionis* §5 (Allen and Neil, 58, 59), where one of his cross-examiners tells him that he is being punished by God for deluding others with the teachings of Origen, to which Maximus responds: "Anathema on Origen and his teachings, and on everyone of the same mind as himself."

[11] On the context of this common Origenist innuendo, see Peter Hatlie, *The Monks and Monasteries of Constantinople, ca. 350-850* (Cambridge: Cambridge University Press, 2007), 136–40.

[12] Sherwood, *Date-List*, 4–5; id., Introduction to Maximus, *The Ascetic Life: Four Centuries on Charity*, Ancient Christian Writers 21 (Westminster, MD: Newman Press, 1955), 8–9, 85–91; Larchet, *La divinisation de l'homme*, 30–1, 451–2, 518–20; Walther Völker, *Maximus Confessor als Meister des geistlichen Lebens* (Wiesbaden: Franz Steiner, 1965), passim; Lars Thunberg, *Microcosm and Mediator: The Theological Anthropology of Maximus the Confessor*, 2nd edn. (Chicago: Open Court, 1995), passim.

highlight Maximus' deference to other distinctive streams of monastic theology, especially the Pseudo-Macarian tradition.[13] The risk, however, is to underplay his debt to Origen's legacy, and to treat his engagement of Origenist thought and *philosophia* mainly as an early phase through which Maximus passed, or which he had to overcome.

After all, even more than Clement of Alexandria, it was Origen who had built an entire cosmology and eschatology around the Christ-centered ascetical gospel, the *imitatio Christi*, and who projected a compelling vision of Christ the Logos as the divine Paramour romancing souls at the level of their deep-seated *erôs*, and as the ubiquitous divine Pedagogue educating embodied spirits (νόες) toward transcendent glory.[14] Under the sway of the Cappadocians, especially Gregory of Nyssa and Gregory Nazianzen,[15] who filtered out problematic elements in Origen's cosmology, Maximus still envisioned Christian—and all the more so *monastic*—existence as a training and reorientation of desire and will to the image of Christ, and as a perennial quest for divine wisdom, the true *philosophia*. Around this model of assimilative communion with Christ, he shaped his own kaleidoscopic vision of the deification of the whole of human nature through the ascetical inculcation of the virtues and the contemplative journey of the mind (νοῦς) into the fullness of the mystery of Christ and the Trinity. In so doing, as several detailed studies have shown, he availed himself of the legacies of Irenaeus, Athanasius, the Cappadocians, Cyril of Alexandria, and a wide range of Eastern ascetical authors.[16]

[13] Garrigues, *Maxime le Confesseur*, 37–8; Larchet, *La divinisation de l'homme*, 11–12. Cf. also Marcus Plested, *The Macarian Legacy: The Place of Macarius-Symeon in the Eastern Christian Tradition* (Oxford: Oxford University Press, 2004), 213–54.

[14] Maximus on at least one occasion, in the *Disputatio cum Pyrrho*, cited Clement of Alexandria's *Stromateis* (PG 91:317C), but he never cites Origen (for obvious reasons). Maximus' knowledge of Origen's own writings has long been debated. Von Balthasar, in his annotations on Maximus' *Th. Oec.*, believed that he had read some of them directly (*Kosmische Liturgie*, 2nd edn., 509–26), and Polycarp Sherwood agreed in his *The Earlier Ambigua of Saint Maximus the Confessor and His Refutation of Origenism* (Rome: Herder, 1955), 88–9. I suggest that this direct knowledge is not only possible but likely.

[15] Maximus' reverence for Gregory Nazianzen is obvious especially in the *Amb. Jo.* See Andrew Louth, "St. Gregory the Theologian and St. Maximus the Confessor: The Shaping of Tradition," in Sarah Coakley and David Pailin, eds., *The Making and Remaking of Christian Doctrine: Essays in Honour of Maurice Wiles* (Oxford: Oxford University Press, 1993), 117–30; also George Berthold, "The Cappadocian Roots of Maximus the Confessor," *MC*, 51–9.

[16] e.g. Larchet, *La divinisation de l'homme*, passim; Thunberg, *Microcosm and Mediator*, passim.

## Deference to an Elder Sage and the Tradition
## of Charismatic Wisdom

From his more immediate monastic background, meanwhile, certain ascetical protocols proved formative for Maximus as a theological thinker and writer. One of these was deference to an elder, be it a spiritual father or an esteemed authority within antecedent patristic tradition. For Maximus, the integrity of religious and doctrinal tradition was entrusted not only to bishops and preeminent theologians but also to charismatic sages, the kindred spirits of the Bible's own authors and characters, assumed to be far advanced in contemplation (θεωρία) and in the mystery of deification. Already by Maximus' time, hagiographical literature narrated how sanctity and spiritual power could be transferred mimetically from the biblical exemplars themselves to venerable recent saints and to living Christian ascetics. But the primary vehicle of this re-inscription of holiness and spiritual insight was the abba–disciple relation that Maximus would have experienced in his own background, and most intensely in the intimate Moschus–Sophronius circle, the Eukratades. A scholion in the *Questions and Responses for Thalassius* defines the role of a spiritual father thus:

> Spiritual fathers, [Maximus] is saying, are established through their teaching, being voluntary fathers of voluntary sons, forming them in a godly way by their word and life. Spiritual sons, consenting, become as their disciples voluntary sons of voluntary fathers, deliberately (γνωμικῶς) submitting to being formed in a godly manner by their fathers' word and life. For the grace of the Spirit makes the birth of begetters and begotten a matter of free will, which is something that fathers according to the flesh do not have, since they are involuntary fathers of involuntary sons, inasmuch as the formation of those who give birth and those who are born physically is a result of nature and not of free choice.[17]

Maximus' *Liber asceticus*, or *Dialogue on the Ascetical Life*, crafted in the genre of monastic "conferences" between the desert abbas/ammas and their disciples in the *Sayings of the Desert Fathers [and Mothers]*, presents an idealized portrait of this relationship, an extended exchange between an elder (γέρων) and a disciple on the ultimate

---

[17] Q. Thal. 54, scholion 7 (CCSG 7:469, ll. 38–48). My thanks to Maximos Constas for pointing this text out to me.

rationale of the ascetical life. Were it autobiographical, and there is no textual evidence that it is, one could imagine Maximus being the abba instructing his disciple (namely his long-time companion Anastasius the Monk), or else Maximus as himself the humble novice schooled by a spiritual father (Sophronius). As in the *Sayings*, the core question of Maximus' *Dialogue* is a variation on the rich young man's query to Jesus (Matt. 19:16–22). The disciple asks his abba, "I beseech you, father, what was the purpose of the Lord's incarnation?"—followed by "What commandments ought I to perform, that I may be saved?"[18] The abba outlines at length how Christ's own kenosis is the template of the ascetical journey toward deification.[19] Salvation hangs on the abba's own word to the extent that it births the divine Word in his disciple's heart and advances him in the mystery of Christ. Maximus thereby honors a tradition of charismatic wisdom that lies alongside dogmatic (and episcopal) tradition and provides privileged commentary on it. If the sage speaking in the *Dialogue* is his own voice, his composing the conference in third person would be an act both of humility and of respect for a charismatic tradition that is much larger than him or any lone voice.

In the *Ambigua to John*, a work still relatively early in his career, Maximus refers seven times to a "wise elder" (γέρων σοφός) whose identity he never discloses.[20] The very fact that Maximus is commenting on difficult passages from the orations of a recognized master, Gregory Nazianzen, "the Theologian," demands accountability to a senior wisdom. Most likely this elder was not a literary artifice, but an enduring profile to Maximus of the perfectly balanced life of praxis and contemplation leading to the knowledge of God (θεολογία).[21] There are compelling reasons to see this figure as Sophronius, who also bore the aura of John Moschus, the Eukratades' revered link to the ascetical wisdom of Palestinian and Sinaitic anchorites. Similarly in the *Mystagogia*, his

---

[18] *LA* (CCSG 40:5, 7). For this same pattern of questioning in fourth-century monastic conferences, cf. *Apophthegmata patrum*, Anthony 19 (81B); Ares 1 (PG 65:132C); Hierax 1 (232C–D); Poemen 153 (360B); Poemen 162 (361A); Poemen 163 (361B).

[19] Ibid. (CCSG 40:23–37).

[20] *Amb. Jo.* 27 (PG 91:1269D); ibid. 28 (1272B); ibid. 29 (1272D); ibid. 35 (1288D); 39 (1301B); 43 (1349B); ibid. 66 (1393B).

[21] Maximos Constas suggests that this elder was Maximus' actual guide to Nazianzen's work, as well as his living model of the spiritual life depicted in *Amb. Jo.* 10 and *Amb. Jo.* 30 (Constas II, xix–xx). An identification with Sophronius seems most natural but cannot be confirmed.

commentary on the Divine Liturgy, Maximus references "a grand elder (τινὶ μεγάλῳ γέροντι), truly wise in divine truths concerning both the holy Church and the holy synaxis performed therein," a man ostensibly known to the person to whom he addresses this work.[22] While it is plausible that this "elder" too is Sophronius, other candidates cannot be discounted,[23] and it is also possible that he is a fictitious character, whom Maximus honors as his "live" mediator of the teachings of the preeminent visionary of ecclesiastical and sacramental mysteries, Dionysius the Areopagite. Christian Boudignon calls this a ruse on Maximus' part to maintain the "'mythic' ambiance of admonitions and teachings from the Fathers of the desert" and to sustain—*in writing*—an authority that is properly *oral*.[24] But if Sophronius is in fact Maximus' "grand elder," there is no ruse here. Finally, a "wise man"—Sophronius, or perhaps Cyril of Alexandria—shows up as well in Maximus' *Opusculum 7* (*c.*642), credited with eloquently upholding the duality of natures and energies in Christ.[25]

### Mediating Holiness and Wisdom through Text

Maximus' reverence for a larger, older charismatic tradition from the desert is also in evidence in what I shall call his pattern of authorial κένωσις, or self-abasement, paralleling the kenosis of the Logos in his incarnation, and the kenosis of the Spirit in the lives of revered saints. In an incisive study of the nature of authorship in early Byzantine Christianity, Derek Krueger observes that especially with hagiographers, most of them monks, an author was already discouraged from being visibly self-assertive, hiding himself within his writing but

---

[22] *Myst.* prooemium (CCSG 69:4, ll. 9–11).

[23] See Theodore Nikolaou, "Zur Identität des μακάριος γέρων in der *Mystagogia* von Maximos dem Bekenner," *Orientalia Christiana Periodica* 49 (1983): 407–18. Nikolaou analyzes different candidates for the "wise elder," especially Dionysius the Areopagite (whom many have suggested), and argues that he was instead probably an unidentified monk and spiritual teacher in one of Maximus' early monastic residences, Chrysopolis or Cyzicus. Clearly this hypothesis rests on Nicolaou's trust in the dubious Greek *Life.*

[24] "Maxime le Confesseur et ses maîtres: À propos du 'bienheureux ancien' de la *Mystagogie*," in Giovanni Filoramo, ed., *Maestro e Discepolo: Temi e problemi della direzione spirituale tra VI secolo a.C. e VII secolo d.C* (Brescia: Morcelliana, 2002), 317–23.

[25] *Opusc.* 7 (PG 91:88A–B). Louth (*Maximus the Confessor*, 217, n. 27) sees this figure as Cyril.

also working to conform himself to its subject matter: holy lives.[26] Mortification and transformation went hand in hand in the ascetical project of composing a text, since it too was an *embodiment* of holiness and wisdom just like the person of the illustrious saint. With many hagiographers, in turn, the goal was a robust humility, an authorial kenosis imaging the incarnation. The author had to decrease in order for his subject matter to increase, doing literary and rhetorical justice to his subject without showcasing his self-investment in the work. Authorial self-deprecation was one element in this process, and while it may have been a rhetorical convention, it still had a quite precise theological and ascetical purpose here.[27] A comparable dynamic is operative, I would propose, in Maximus' writing. His only supposed foray into hagiography was a *Life of the Virgin* ascribed to him, dubiously it seems,[28] through a Georgian translation tradition.[29] But in other genres too, Maximus demonstrates this kenotic mimesis. I have already discussed his self-concealment in the *Dialogue on the Ascetical Life*, and in numerous other works and letters he abases himself as author, confessing his own poverty of linguistic or intellectual ability and moral virtue while esteeming that of his addressee,[30] or else contrasting his own incapacity with the magnitude of the subject at hand.[31] Introducing his *Mystagogia*, he casts his authorial cares *"upon the Lord* [Ps. 54:23, LXX; 1 Peter 5:7, who is the only miracle-worker [Ps. 135:4, LXX], the one who *teaches man knowledge* [Ps. 93:10, LXX], who clears up the speech of stammerers [Isa. 35:6; Wis. 10:21], who contrives a way for those who are without resources [Wis. 14:2], *who lifts up the poor from the earth and raises the needy from the dunghill* [Ps. 112:7, LXX; 1 Kgdms. 2:8, LXX]."[32] In the opening of his *Commentary on the Lord's*

---

[26] *Writing and Holiness: The Practice of Authorship in the Early Christian East* (Philadelphia: University of Pennsylvania Press, 2004), esp. 2–3, 27–32, 35–48, 63–93.

[27] On the dynamics of this humility in "textual performance," see Krueger, ibid., 94–106.

[28] See Phil Booth, "On the *Life of the Virgin* Attributed to Maximus the Confessor," *Journal of Theological Studies* NS 66 (2015): 149–203. I thank Phil Booth for allowing me to read pre-publication proofs of this essay.

[29] See Stephen Shoemaker, trans., *The Life of the Virgin* (New Haven: Yale University Press, 2012).

[30] e.g. *Q. Thal.* Intro. (CCSG 7:17–21); ibid. 10 (p. 87); ibid. 65 (CCSG 22:253); *Amb. Jo.* Prol. (PG 91:1061A–1065B); *Amb. Th.* Prol. (CCSG 48:3–5); *Opusc.* 21 (PG 91:245D–248A); ibid. 7 (69B–C); ibid. 10 (133B–D); ibid. 1 (12B).

[31] e.g. *Q. Thal.* 20 (CCSG 7:125); ibid. 48 (p. 331); ibid. 50 (p. 391).

[32] *Mystagogia* Prol. (CCSG 69:5, ll. 44–7); trans. Berthold, 184.

*Prayer*, he aligns at once his reticence to write, his obligation to write, and the gracious condescension of the Logos to aid the venture:

> I write then because I must, writing not what I think, *since the thoughts of men are vile* [Wis. 9:14] . . . but what God wants and grants through grace to begin this undertaking. Indeed, *the counsel of God*, says David, *remains forever, the thoughts of his heart from generation to generation* [Ps. 32:11, LXX]. Undoubtedly he calls *counsel* of God the Father the mysterious self-abasement (κένωσιν) of the only-begotten Son with a view to the deification of our nature, a self-abasement in which he holds enclosed the limits of all history; while by *thoughts of the heart* he means the principles (λόγους) of providence and judgment according to which he directs with wisdom as different generations our present life and the life to come, imparting differently to each the mode (τρόπον) of activity which is proper to it.[33]

For Maximus, ascetical or theological writing may not be revelation, but it is a derivative participation in the grand *oikonomia* of divine revelation. Authorship is participating—with appropriate fear and trembling—in the self-disclosure of the Logos-Christ, the Word who authors all truth, goodness, and beauty, and who "always and in all things desires to realize the mystery of his embodiment."[34] In the broader framework of Maximus' "Logology," as we might call it, the Word alone enjoys the pure freedom to inscribe or incarnate himself in any and all "holy texts," whether the text be creation, Scripture, flesh, the scripts of virtuous conduct, or even human writings striving to emulate and transmit the sanctity and wisdom of the Logos.[35] Committing a "pious word" (εὐσεβὴς λόγος) to writing is paired with practical asceticism.[36] Given Maximus' strong emphasis on how the Logos constantly "thickens himself" (παχύνεται) in penetrating and transfiguring materiality and corporeality,[37] it only follows that he would be utterly self-conscious about his own writing serving as a conduit, however broken and partial, of the pedagogy of the Word.

---

[33] *Or. dom.* Prol. (CCSG 23:28–9, ll. 35–49), trans. Berthold, 101–2 (slightly altered).

[34] *Amb. Jo.* 7 (PG 91:1084D).

[35] These multiple "incarnations" will be discussed later in this study. Specifically on the Logos's "incarnation" in scriptural *text*, see. *Amb. Jo.* 33 (PG 91:1285D–1288A); *Th. Oec.* 2.61 (PG 90:1152A–B).

[36] *Amb. Jo.* 13 (PG 91:1209A).

[37] See esp. *Amb. Jo.* 33 (PG 91:1285B–1288A), based on Gregory Nazianzen, *Or.* 38.2 (SC 348:106); also Adam Cooper, *The Body in Maximus the Confessor: Holy Flesh, Wholly Deified* (Oxford: Oxford University Press, 2005), 39–42.

## Ethical, Natural, and Theological *Philosophia*

Maximus' self-consciousness about submitting with humility and docility to the pedagogy of the Logos is especially evident in his writings prior to the monothelete crisis. He is diligent to place himself under inherited disciplines conducive to wisdom and moral perfection. From its respective variations in Origen, Evagrius, and other sources, Maximus appropriated a traditional scheme of three integrated conventions governing the moral, intellectual, and spiritual life of the Christian. Origen's early model of *ethics, physics, and epoptics* (metaphysics)[38] had inspired similar triads of *practice, contemplation, and (mystical) theology*,[39] or else *ethical (or practical), natural, and theological philosophy*.[40] Such constituted the core curriculum, as it were, of monastic paideia, and indicated early Christian ascetical theologians' revamping of the Greco-Roman ideal of the "philosophical life" (βίος φιλοσοφικός).[41] Cultivation of moral virtues, insight into the "nature" of things as registered in creation and in sacred history, and mystagogical initiation in the mysteries of Christ and the Trinity together constituted, in their deep interconnection, the circulatory system of a well-ordered life. Even the apostle Peter was charged to observe these disciplines when he saw the great sheet teeming with animals descend from heaven, and was told to "rise" (ascetically from worldly attachments), "kill" (by penetrating the superficial to contemplate the deep *logoi* of "natural" creatures), and "eat" (so as to be "filled with theological power") (cf. Acts 10:9–16).[42]

---

[38] *Comm. in Canticum Canticorum*, Prol. 3.1, 6 (SC 375:128, 132).

[39] These are fairly pervasive in Evagrius, who is Maximus' most immediate ascetical source for them. See the shared vocabulary already analyzed by Völker, *Maximus Confessor als Meister des geistlichen Lebens*, 236–48; Thunberg, *Microcosm and Mediator*, 332–73.

[40] Maximus uses this triad fairly frequently, indicating that praxis, contemplation of nature, and mystical theology are all determinative for true Christian *philosophia*. See e.g. *Amb. Jo.* 10 (PG 91:1129A–B, 1136C–D); ibid. 37 (1296A); ibid. 67 (1397B–C, 1401D); also ibid. 20 (1241B), describing the interrelation of "practical philosophy" (πρακτικὴ φιλοσοφία), "natural contemplation" (φυσικὴ θεωρία), and "theological mystagogy" (θεολογικὴ μυσταγωγία). In *Amb. Jo.* 21 (1245D–1248A), the four Gospels are said to symbolize faith (Matt.), practical contemplation (Mark), natural contemplation (Luke), and theological contemplation (John). In *Q. Thal.* 3 and 52 (CCSG 7:55, 419), Maximus reduces the three principal disciplines to two, pairing "practical philosophy" and "contemplative mystagogy" (θεωρητικὴ μυσταγωγία).

[41] For a superb analysis of classic Greco-Roman models of the "philosophical life" lying behind patristic and monastic tradition, see John Cooper, *Pursuits of Wisdom: Six Ways of Life in Ancient Philosophy from Socrates to Plotinus* (Princeton: Princeton University Press, 2012).

[42] *Q. Thal.* 27 (CCSG 7:193–5).

This is no strictly phased or sequenced progress of experience and knowledge, as if one could transcend praxis by contemplation, and contemplation by *theologia*. On the contrary, through their mutual co-inherence and perpetual cross-fertilization, the three protocols of ethical, natural, and theological *philosophia* assure for Maximus that the quest for virtue and wisdom, the "passover" (διάβασις) to deification, fully fuses the horizons of life in the body and the quest for transcendence. *Ambiguum* 10, by far the longest in the collection, is a kind of tutorial on the interrelation between the three dimensions of true *philosophia*. The text itself is far from a straightforward roadmap or instructional guide. Andrew Louth calls it an exercise in "lateral" rather than linear thinking, in which Maximus strings together diverse reflections on spiritual *diabasis* which, appearing superficially random, gradually converge and integrate.[43] Perhaps a better image would thus be that of an upward interpretive "spiral" into which Maximus desires to catch up his readers. As is so often the case in his writing, themes hang together associatively and allusively, but not in pure logical sequence, since he desires his reader patiently to discern with him the complex and the subtle interconnections between them. What we have in *Ambiguum* 10, then, is Maximus' own exercise in natural and scriptural contemplation, an exemplification of sanctified intuition.

*Ambiguum* 10 comments on a passage from Gregory Nazianzen's eulogy on Athanasius of Alexandria that describes the transit beyond "this cloud or veil of flesh" to deification through "genuine philosophizing" (τὸ γνησίως φιλοσοφῆσαι).[44] Maximus insists from the outset that in this process there is no leaving behind moral and ascetical struggle with the "cloud and veil" of the flesh for allegedly higher pursuits. Practical reason (λόγος), which elsewhere he calls prudence (φρόνησις), the very "act and manifestation of wisdom,"[45] directs and modulates the body's movements and impulses, while contemplation (θεωρία) opens the mind to illumination and spiritual insight (γνῶσις).[46] The operative

---

[43] Louth, *Maximus the Confessor*, 94, 95.

[44] *Or.* 21.2 (SC 270:112–14), in *Amb. Jo.* 10 (PG 91:1105C–D).

[45] *Myst.* 5 (CCSG 69:25–6, 28); cf. *Car.* 2.26 (PG 90:992B–C), referring prudence to the practical (πρακτική), and knowledge to the contemplative (θεωρητική) life.

[46] *Amb. Jo.* 10 (PG 91:1105C 1108C). For analysis see Carlos Steel, "Maximus Confessor on *Theory* and *Praxis*: A Commentary on *Ambigua ad Johannem* VI (10) 1–19," in Thomas Bénatouïl and Mauro Bonazzi, eds., *Theoria, Praxis, and the Contemplative Life after Plato and Aristotle* (Leiden: Brill, 2012), 229–57.

word is *wisdom*, which comes through experience, to be sure, but also through tireless imitation of the biblical saints. Rather than simply outlining the constitutive elements of ethical, natural, and theological philosophy, Maximus thereupon sets forth the literary equivalent of an iconostasis, a series of evocative profiles of biblical saints who either exemplified or symbolized these disciplines. Moses appears in his traditional image as the consummately virtuous and contemplative prophet who both pioneered the exodus through the "sea" of sensible temptations and, on Sinai, penetrated the mysterious darkness of the divine presence.[47] Joshua, David, Elijah, Elisha, Anna and Samuel, Melchizedek, Abraham and other figures are profiled not in a strictly chronological order, but only as each conveys an image of spiritual *diabasis*. Reapplying Origen's principle of "transposition" (μετάληψις), the internalizing of biblical narratives and characters, he recommends each believer to become, by imitation, a "spiritual" Melchizedek or David or Moses.[48]

Above all these friezes, however, Maximus exalts the tableau of the transfiguration, in which Peter, James, and John ascended Tabor to envision the luminous face and garments of Christ. Here is the consummate *diabasis*, since the apostles crossed over to behold, in a foretaste of his overwhelming glory, the Word who is the primary object, the beginning and end, of all ethical, natural, and theological philosophy. In this privileged moment on Mt. Tabor, *oikonomia*, God's extraverted revelation in creation and sacred history, and *theologia*, the sublime mystery of the internal life of the Trinity, intersect in the transfigured but still incarnate Christ. I shall say more later about the profound symbolic significance of the transfiguration in Maximus' thought, but the point here is that there is no advance in Christian *philosophia* apart from the personal theophany of the Logos, who reaches out to the believer commensurate with the believer's own striving for intimacy with the Logos through the practice of virtue, through seasoned contemplation, and through the rigors associated with theology proper.

Maximus' writing prior to the monothelete controversy is dominated by the pursuit and articulation of this three-dimensional *philosophia*.

---

[47] *Amb. Jo.* 10 (PG 91:1117A–C; cf. 1148A–1149C); cf. *Th. Oec.* 1.85 (PG 90:1120A).
[48] *Amb. Jo.* 10. (PG 91:1144A–B). The opposite is to become biblical villains spiritually (*Q. Thal.* 23, CCSG 7:151–3). Cf. Origen, *Comm. in Johannem* 20.10 (GCS 10:337, ll. 30–2).

He distinctly echoes Evagrius's terse assertion that "Christianity is the teaching of Christ our Savior, consisting of the practical, the natural, and the theological."[49] Maximus seeks not simply to write "about" these disciplines but *from within* them, exemplifying asceticism, contemplation, and the mystical quest of *theologia* through his writing itself (as we saw earlier in his ascetical kenosis as an author, and in his demonstration of contemplation in *Ambiguum* 10). This *philosophia* is altogether integral to Maximus' principal works of spiritual doctrine: the *Dialogue on the Ascetical Life, Chapters on Love, Chapters on Theologia and Oikonomia, Commentary on the Lord's Prayer, Questions and Responses for Thalassius, Questions and Uncertainties, Commentary on Psalm 59,* and *Questions and Responses for Theopemptus.* It also occupies him constantly throughout his *Ambigua.* Its fuller implications will be elicited in later chapters as we explore the deep connections between Maximus' cosmology, Christology, and asceticism. Though in his early monastic career he could not have anticipated the direction his life and writing would take in the struggle against imperial monotheletism, we can hardly imagine Maximus' later, painstakingly precise discourses on technical matters of Christology apart from the foundation laid in this very *philosophia.* When, for example, in *Opusculum* 7 (*c.*642) he addresses Marinus, a Cypriot deacon, about the emerging error of monenergism and monotheletism, and begins to explicate the full humanity of Christ as including a natural human will, he first dwells at length on how Marinus's exceptional virtue and acquired wisdom have already qualified him to grasp the mysteries of the constitution of Christ.[50]

## MAXIMUS AS INTERPRETER: THE TRANSFIGURED AND TRANSFIGURING WORD

Maximus was at heart an *interpreter.* One could say that, of course, about many patristic writers who would likely have chosen to be considered foremost as expositors of sacred revelation rather than as dogmatic theologians. But this is true *a fortiori* of Maximus, who postured himself as an unremitting interpreter of Scripture and of canonical Christian traditions of doctrine and asceticism. Vittorio

---

[49] *Practicus* 1 (SC 171:498).          [50] *Opusc.* 7 (PG 91:69B–72B).

Croce has traced his theological method itself according to the coordinates of "tradition" and "research,"[51] as Maximus pursued the *sensus plenior* of revelation and sought to elicit ever more fully and precisely the substance of Scripture and of the accrued interpretive wisdom of his cherished predecessors.

Understanding Maximus as an interpreter, however, entails far more than mapping the methodology of his exegesis of Scripture and tradition. Like Origen, Gregory Nazianzen, Gregory of Nyssa, and Dionysius the Areopagite, Maximus is a *hermeneutical theologian*, for whom the premier consideration in interpretation is the conditions under which divine revelation to humanity is even possible in the first place. His interpretive work starts from the principle of the absolute freedom and initiative of Christ the Logos to reveal himself—or better yet to "incarnate" or "embody" himself—in all the forms he so desires. Interpretation, in turn, is an extended, multidimensional participation in the polymorphous epiphany of the Word in Scripture, in the fabric of creation, and preeminently in historical *flesh*—and yet also prospectively in the devout interpreter's own insight and attendant virtue. In the distant background here is Origen's doctrine of the "aspects" (ἐπίνοιαι) of Christ, indicating his prerogative, as the premier agent of divine self-revelation, to assume diverse forms (as Wisdom, Word, Light, etc.) and thereby to accommodate himself to the manifold intellectual and perceptual capacities of created beings.[52] Origen, moreover, had inaugurated the notion of the Logos mysteriously *embodying* himself in the media of his revelation of the Father, be it in the *logoi* of created things or in the words and meanings of Scripture. Maximus, however, took this idea to new heights by portraying any and all manifestations of the Logos as immediately tributary to the recapitulative purpose of his historical incarnation in Jesus of Nazareth. It is the Logos *as Christ* who initiates the terms of his own appearance (and hiddenness) and who, while using various media of revelation in the invisible and visible creation, is not himself constrained by those media. Indeed, just as he permeates the spiritual universe with his wisdom, he can personally penetrate the veil of matter or text or flesh as he so pleases.

---

[51] *Tradizione e ricerca: Il metodo teologico di san Massimo il Confessore* (Milan: Vita e Pensiero, 1974).

[52] See Origen's *Comm. in Johannem* 1.118–292 (GCS 10:24–51).

## The Transfiguration as Paradigm

Maximus maps the conditions of divine revelation in select passages in his writings. A pivotal one, in my estimation, is his exposition of the transfiguration of Christ. For him the transfiguration is a prism through which the sublime, blinding light of revelation is refracted in manifold colors, shining on all who would dare to approach the Revealer and participate, according to their capacity, in his uncircumscribable glory. It is striking that unlike the Cappadocians and Dionysius, who gave privileged place to the Sinai Theophany in Exodus, with its details of Moses's intimate encounter with God from the "cleft in the rock" (Exod. 33:22), as the supreme biblical narrative for exploring the dynamics of divine revelation, Maximus instead follows Origen in giving primacy to the transfiguration. Not that he intends to slight the Sinai Theophany; quite the contrary he honors its significance.[53] But the transfiguration, as a theophany, has the advantage, first, of having grounded revelation in *theologia*, the relation of Father and Son, and second, of doing so precisely in the context of the Son's incarnation. *Theologia* and *oikonomia* dramatically intersect in the transfiguration. As Maximus states in his *Commentary on the Lord's Prayer*, the Logos incarnate "teaches *theologia*."[54] In his incarnate mission he has opened access to the mystery of the Trinity, the reality beyond all realities which has nonetheless given rise to *our* reality as created beings. The transfiguration, then, is a unique mode of divine "body language" insofar as Christ's luminous face, flesh, and even garments communicate God's glory without him ever uttering a word. But can sacred *text*, another material medium indwelled by the Logos, accomplish the same?

First let us examine just how Maximus views the transfiguration as a resplendent icon of the dynamics of revelation. In a separate study I have appealed to the phenomenologist and theologian Jean-Luc Marion's rich notion of "saturated phenomena" as instructive for analyzing Maximus' perspective on the transfiguration.[55] A saturated phenomenon is, by

---

[53] See *Amb. Jo.* 10 (PG 91:1117B–C).     [54] *Or. dom.* (CCSG 23:31).

[55] "The Interpretive Dance: Concealment, Disclosure, and Deferral of Meaning in Maximus the Confessor's Hermeneutical Theology," in Maxim Vasiljević, ed., *Knowing the Purpose of Creation through the Resurrection: Proceedings of the Symposium on St. Maximus the Confessor, Belgrade, October 18–21, 2012* (Alhambra, CA: Sebastian Press, 2013) (hereafter Vasiljević), 253–9. Unfortunately the publisher mistakenly printed this essay without its footnotes, but a fuller version will appear as "The Transfiguration of Jesus Christ as 'Saturated Phenomenon' and as Key to the Dynamics of Biblical Revelation in St. Maximus the Confessor," in Seraphim Danckaert, Matthew Baker, and Mark

Marion's scrupulous description, so overwhelmingly "given," so thoroughly engaging of "intuition," that it defies any "intentional" human subjectivity and so also, by its "excess," undermines conceptualization, and in fact opens out onto an infinite "horizon" of apprehensions and provisional appropriations.[56] To call it a miracle or wonder would not be adequate, since such terminology is merely relative to the gamut of intentional sensate experience. A saturated phenomenon simply *is*, and is unconstrained by any inherent necessity to solicit perception or conceptualization. One among other of the cases of Marion's saturated phenomena is the "icon" or "face" of another,[57] a theme also famously and trenchantly developed by Emmanuel Levinas. The other's face has its own epiphany, its own "visage" (as opposed to façade) independent of *my* willed attention to it or perceptual attempt to capture it. As Marion suggests, "the face arises—a counter-intentionality that does not manifest itself in becoming visible but in addressing its look to me."[58] Or as Levinas would have it, the face of the other puts a moral question to my existence and speaks precisely in its overwhelming silence.[59]

In Maximus' theological exegesis of Tabor, the prime focal point is precisely the transfigured *face* of Christ. "The face of the Logos, which radiated like the sun, is the inaccessibility ($\kappa\rho\upsilon\varphi\iota\acute{o}\tau\eta\varsigma$) that characterizes his essence, upon which it is impossible to gaze by an interpretation of thoughts, just as neither can one gaze upon the brightness of the sun even if someone has entirely purified his or her optical ability."[60]

---

Mourachian, eds., *What is the Bible? The Patristic Doctrine of Scripture* (Minneapolis: Augsburg Fortress, forthcoming 2016).

[56] For Marion's exposition of "saturated phenomena," "intentionality," "intuition," and "horizon," see esp. his *Being Given: Toward a Phenomenology of Givenness*, trans. Jeffrey Kosky (Palo Alto: Stanford University Press, 2002), 13, 17, 23–7, 179–247.

[57] See Marion's *In Excess: Studies of Saturated Phenomena*, trans. Robyn Horner and Vincent Berrand (New York: Fordham University Press, 2002), 113–23. The other three principal examples are an overpowering "event," like one's own birth, the givenness of which defies subjective analysis; an "idol," something that totally commands the human gaze, such as a work of art; and the "flesh," the inexorable condition passively experienced by embodied human beings. See Marion, *Being Given*, 225–33; *In Excess*, esp. 30–127.

[58] *In Excess*, 78.

[59] *Totality and Infinity: An Essay on Exteriority*, trans. Alphonso Lingis (Pittsburgh: Duquesne University Press, 1969), 197–204; id., *Otherwise than Being: Or Beyond Essence*, trans. Alphonso Lingis (Pittsburgh: Duquesne University Press, 1998), 89–93.

[60] *QD* 191 (CCSG 10:134, ll. 46–51), trans. Despina Prassas, *St. Maximus the Confessor's Questions and Doubts* (DeKalb, IL: Northern Illinois University Press, 2010), 139 (slightly altered). Cf. Marion, *In Excess*, 115–17, 119ff.

Without uttering a word, Christ's transfigured face instructed the apostles on the mountain by symbolizing his ineffable, unapproachable divinity.[61] "In an undifferentiated, simultaneous moment (ἐν ταυτῷ καὶ ἅμα),"[62] an intensive and eschatological "present" as it were, past and future collapsed into the foreground of the Revealer. Here is what Marion calls the "second degree" saturated phenomenon of revelation or epiphany, where "the Other" grants an icon/face that enfolds or "concentrates" the saturated phenomena of event, idol, and flesh.[63] Revelation would be the "saturation of saturation," and Marion himself proposes Christ's transfiguration as just such a possibility.[64]

Like Dionysius, whose apophaticism Marion extols for its posture of sheer worship,[65] Maximus insists that there is no revelation of the Other's essence, as the divine Other is "beyond essence" (ὑπερουσίος).[66] And yet the Logos, in his transfiguration and always, freely commands the threshold of revelation, and *is* that threshold. The apostles on Tabor beheld precisely the paradox that the Logos "in appearing conceals himself, and in hiding manifests himself."[67] Bereft of God's essence, there is still a gift, a *givenness* to use Marion's term, that Maximus names only by indicating that he who was *without form or beauty* (Isa. 53:2) nonetheless radiated in his transfigured body a beauty *more beautiful than the sons of men* (Ps. 44:3, LXX).[68] This beauty, the Savior's Gaze, is utterly purgative, reducing its captive beholders to hermeneutical ground zero, though also opening up, like Marion's saturated

[61] *Amb. Jo.* 10 (PG 91:1128A).   [62] Ibid. (PG 1160C), trans. Constas I, 255.
[63] *Being Given*, 234–6.
[64] Ibid., 236–8. See also Merold Westphal, "Transfiguration as Saturated Phenomenon," *Journal of Philosophy and Scripture* 1 (2003): 26–35.
[65] *In Excess*, 134–48.
[66] Maximus regularly echoes Dionysius's emphasis on the hyper-essentiality of God: cf. *Th. Oec.* 1.4 (PG 90:1084B–C); *Q. Thal.* 35 (CCSG 7:239), describing the Logos as one who, though beyond essence and Creator of all things, "bore in himself, along with incomprehensible intuitions of his proper divinity, the natural principles (λόγοι) of all phenomenal and intelligible beings." Also ibid. 64 (CCSG 22:237); *Orat. dom.* (CCSG 23:42, 47); and later *Amb. Th.* 1 (CCSG 48:7); ibid. 5 (CCSG 48:20, 21, 22, 23, 26, 27, 29). For a close comparison of the similarities and differences in Maximus' and Dionysius's respective interpretations of the transfiguration, see Ysabel de Andia, "Transfiguration et théologie negative chez Maxime le Confesseur et Denys l'Aréopagite," in Ysabel de Andia, ed., *Denys l'Aréopagite et sa posterité en Orient et en Occident: Actes du Colloque International, Paris, 21–4 septembre 1994* (Paris: Institut d'Études Augustiniennes, 1997), esp. 294–319.
[67] *Amb. Jo.* 10 (PG 91:1129B–C), recalling Dionysius's similar formula in his *Epistula* 3 (PTS 36:159). Cf. also *Amb. Th.* 5 (CCSG 48:22).
[68] *Amb. Jo.* 10 (PG 91:1128A–B).

phenomena, an infinite interpretive or contemplative horizon. That horizon, for Maximus, is the very theatre wherein the Logos trains contemplation and practice through what we will later see is a perpetual "play" of concealment and disclosure.

## The Transfiguring Word in Scripture and Creation

Maximus follows Origen in envisioning the transfigured garments of Christ as symbolic of the Scriptures, rendered translucent not by human perception but by the underlying divinity of the Logos. The transfigured Word signals his own transfiguring power, such that the focus is less on the unique visionary experience of Peter, James, and John than on the factitive nature of the transfiguration. Christ's garments symbolize the material "texts" of both Scripture and creation, which the Logos uses to "realize the mystery of his embodiment"[69] in all things. Improvising on the ancient analogy of the dual divinely-authored "books" of Scripture and creation, Maximus expounds on their deep integration, Scripture being a kind of "cosmos" and creation a "bible." Just as Scripture has its own "heaven, earth, and the things in between" conducive to ethical, natural, and theological philosophy, the universe is itself a harmonious web of symbols, its "letters and syllables" the bodies of created beings. Both books reciprocally disclose the Logos in the *logoi* of things, that is, the "words" (meanings) of Scripture and the "principles" ordering all created existents.[70] Most importantly, the Logos's self-inscription in the two books is of a piece with his larger work of incarnation and deification.[71]

What Maximus describes is served more by an aesthetic than by a purely rational analysis, or better still by von Balthasar's paradigm (partially inspired by Maximus himself) of "theo-dramatic" revelation, since Scripture and creation are the conjoint "scripts" through which the Logos, as both dramaturge and actor, carries forward his creative

---

[69]  Ibid. 7 (1084D).

[70]  Ibid. 10 (1128D–1133A). See also Paul Blowers, "The Analogy of Scripture and Cosmos in Maximus the Confessor," *Studia Patristica* 27, ed. Elizabeth Livingstone (Leuven: Peeters, 1993), 145–9; id., "Entering 'this Sublime and Blessed Amphitheatre': Contemplation of Nature and Interpretation of the Bible in the Patristic Period," in Jitse van der Meer and Scott Mandelbrote, eds., *Interpreting Nature and Scripture: History of a Dialogue in the Abrahamic Religions* (Leiden: Brill, 2009), 148–76.

[71]  *Amb. Jo.* 10 (PG 91:1129D–1132C).

and salvific activity and engrosses the whole universe in his play. There are two passages in his writings that bear this out especially well. The first is a long reflection on the nature of scriptural contemplation (θεωρία γραφική) in *Ambiguum* 37, a sophisticated but rarely cited text that spells out, in formally hermeneutical terms, a method of interpreting Scripture and the created universe reciprocally.[72] The key is Maximus' assumption, carried over from *Ambiguum* 10, that the Bible *is* in some sense a "world," and that it always mirrors the larger *universal* story of creation and redemption. He proposes ten progressive but interrelated modes or predicative categories (Fig. 1) by which the scriptural world can be contemplated (θεωρεῖσθαι) in terms of its complex unity.

By the first five modes, some of which are reminiscent of Aristotle's "categories," Maximus believes it possible to explore *particularities* in biblical revelation, especially as regards the circumstances and individual "characters" (animate and inanimate beings, higher and lower beings) in the cosmic drama being played out across Scripture. The meaning of the movements and dispositions of the characters in this universal cast is not restricted to the conditions of the narratives in which they appear, since they point symbolically beyond their own historical setting. Indeed, "place" and "time" might seem innocent enough, but Maximus understands Scripture as having a whole spiritual topography evinced in the etymologies of local place-names and in the peculiar kinds of locales (heavens and earth, air, sea, inhabited lands, far limits, countries, islands, cities, temples, fields, mountains, etc.) in which sacred events unfolded. "Time" engages the Bible's

Fig. 1.

[72]  Ibid. 37 (1293A–1296D). For a detailed analysis of this text, see Paul Blowers, "The World in the Mirror of Holy Scripture: Maximus the Confessor's Short Hermeneutical Treatise in *Ambiguum ad Joannem* 37," in Paul Blowers, Angela Russell Christman, David Hunter, and Robin Darling Young, eds., *In Dominico Eloquio/In Lordly Eloquence: Essays on Patristic Exegesis in Honor of Robert Louis Wilken* (Grand Rapids: Eerdmans, 2002), 408–26.

complex language of temporality, including not only its tricky use of tenses that mingle past, present, and future but also the terminology of temporal and trans-temporal "ages" (αἰῶνες). "Genus," according to Maximus, ranges between general groupings and particular instantiations of created existents, from the orders of intelligible beings down to inanimate minerals extracted from the earth. It is no triviality, for example, that Scripture meticulously identifies ranks of angels, or distinctive ethnic or tribal groups in Old Testament narratives whose dispositions toward the people of God hold moral or spiritual significance. Scripture can also profile a "persona" (πρόσωπ-ον)—a human being or any other individual creature within a genus—who explicitly or implicitly warrants contemplation. These persons' peculiar "dignity" (ἀξία) or occupation (ἐπιτήδευμα) can be conducive to more nuanced prosopography, depending on whether they appear in their native narratives "laudably" (ἐπαινετῶς) or "culpably" (ψεκτῶς). The classic example here is the multi-guised kings recounted in the Old Testament:

> The gnostic will come to know the significance of all the rest of the kings [in 3 Kgdms., LXX] through the interpretation of their names, or by their geographic location, or by the common tradition which prevails in those lands, or by the particular customs that are pursued among them, or by the sort of antipathy each has toward Israel... For not all the [foreign] kings are always interpreted in the same way or according to one meaning; rather, they are interpreted with a view to their underlying utility (χρείαν) and prophetic potential (τῆς προφητείας τὴν δύναμιν). Indeed, Scripture was able to render the Pharaoh as [a figure of] the Devil when he sought to destroy Israel, but then again as [a figure of] the law of nature when he served Israel according to the dispensation of Joseph... Likewise the King of Tyre is intended to represent the Devil when he waged war on Israel through Sisera, but elsewhere signifies the law of nature when he made peace with David and contributed so much to Solomon for the building of the temple. Each of the kings recounted in Scripture is interpreted in many different meanings according to his underlying prophetic potential.[73]

This "prophetic potential" could well apply to the figural power of virtually everything in the biblical text. As in Origen's exegesis, there is no waste, nothing merely incidental, in Scripture. Maximus' first five categories of scriptural contemplation simply constitute entry

---

[73] *Q. Thal.* 26 (CCSG 7:179–81).

points for the discipline. The vast field of scriptural "realities" ($\pi\rho\acute{a}\gamma\mu$- $a\tau a$) must be patiently scrutinized in order to discern the complex relations— the *con*-figuration—between and among persons, events, and everything else in the Bible.[74]

At the next stage of scriptural contemplation, Maximus deduces that what has been discriminated through the first five categories will be subsumed into the protocols of "ethical, natural, and theological philosophy." In other words, the contemplative interpretation of Scripture, and of the created world mirrored therein, decisively informs the three principal disciplines of the Christian's life. These three, in turn, are further contracted into "present" and "future," or "type" and "truth." This is not a simple pattern of prophetic prefiguration and later fulfillment ($\H{\epsilon}\kappa\beta a\sigma\iota s$); rather, it suggests that all things heretofore revealed by God in the past, which also have effect in the present life of Christians (1 Cor. 10:11), open out onto an unrestricted horizon of future fulfillments or perspectives on their meaning, the congruence, coherence, and "reality" ($\dot{a}\lambda\acute{\eta}\theta\epsilon\iota a$) of which are an eschatological project of the transcendent and immanent Logos himself. Interpretation goes as far as it can, but its limit is the utter freedom of the Logos in setting out the terms of accessibility to himself as the ultimate *telos* of Scripture and creation.

Maximus' contemplative hermeneutic is best understood, I believe, by what David Dawson, drawing on Erich Auerbach and Hans Frei, identifies as "figural" interpretation, whereby meaning comes not in a self-enclosed referentiality of words but in *relations* discerned between and among persons or events in the historical continuum.[75] Maximus, like Origen, has no desire to obliterate the "literal" or historical meaning of the texts. But *historia* in its patristic exegetical usage consisted not in establishing facts of the sacred past but in discerning the narrative coherence of the transcending "story" uniting that past with the present and future in Jesus Christ.[76] Maximus' object is a perennial *sensus plenior*, "the power of the literal meaning in the Spirit, which is always

[74] Scriptural contemplation thus entails the same comparative and discriminatory role ($\tau\grave{o}$ $\sigma\nu\delta\iota a\kappa\rho\acute{\iota}\nu\epsilon\iota\nu$) of reason in the contemplation of the *logoi* of creation (cf. *Amb. Jo.* 7, PG 91:1077C).

[75] See Dawson's *Christian Figural Reading and the Fashioning of Identity* (Berkeley: University of California Press, 2002), 10 11, 83 137.

[76] See Frances Young's rich discussion of $\iota\sigma\tau o\rho\acute{\iota}a$ in *Biblical Exegesis and the Formation of Christian Culture* (Cambridge: Cambridge University Press, 1997), 80, 86–90, 179–82.

abounding into its fullness."[77] Accordingly, all of Scripture's content is tributary to the "fullness" which is the mystery of Jesus Christ—the mystery of Christ's "saturating" or transfiguring power and his ultimate embodiment in all things.

## Contemplative Interpretation as a Play of Intimacy and Elusion

In considering Maximus' hermeneutical focus on Christ the Logos's presence and performance through the revelatory media of Scripture and the created cosmos, a second key text is his commentary on an arresting poetic line from Gregory Nazianzen:

> For the Logos on high plays ($\pi\alpha i\zeta\epsilon\iota$) in all sorts of forms,
>     mingling ($\kappa i\rho\nu\alpha s$) with his world here and there as he so desires.[78]

Maximus finds in Gregory's phrase a provocative description of the same dialectics of disclosure and concealment in the Logos's self-revelation that he highlighted in *Ambiguum* 10 on the transfiguration. Nazianzen's Logos-at-play is a marvelous tutorial both in the Logos's radical transcendence and in his kenotic identification with creation in all aspects of his incarnation. His "play" evokes the sublime "foolishness" of God (1 Cor. 1:25), a term the apostle introduced paradoxically to indicate precisely the *excess* of divine prudence that could never be straightforwardly grasped by creaturely intelligence.[79] Play also bespeaks the "ecstasy" of God, the Creator's *erôs* or yearning in reaching beyond himself to creation with the anticipation of a reciprocal response.[80] Play is also the Logos's salutary teasing of his creatures, his use of the vagaries, instabilities, and travails of mundane existence in order to goad creatures toward enduring, eternal goods.[81] As Maximus explores different possible nuances of Nazianzen's image, it becomes

---

[77]  *Q. Thal.* 17 (CCSG 7:111, ll. 19–21).
[78]  Gregory Nazianzen, *Poemata theologica (moralia)* 1.2.2 (PG 37:624A–625A), quoted in Maximus, *Amb. Jo.* 71 (PG 91:1408C). Various MSS have $\kappa\rho i\nu\alpha s$ ("judging"), but most modern critics view the correct reading as $\kappa i\rho\nu\alpha s$ ("mingling"); see Constas II, 350 (n. 1 on *Amb. Jo.* 71).
[79]  *Amb. Jo.* 71 (PG 91:1409A–D).
[80]  Ibid. (1413A–B), quoting Dionysius the Areopagite, *Div. nom.* 4.12 (PTS 33:158–9). Cf. also *Amb. Jo.* 23 (PG 91:1260B–C), quoting Dionysius, *Div. nom.* 4.14 (PTS 33:160).
[81]  *Amb. Jo.* 71 (1413B–1416A).

obvious that the interpreter's challenge is precisely to "play along" with the Logos-at-play, to be drawn into his game of hide-and-seek.[82]

Indeed, for Maximus interpretation is an ongoing form of sophisticated play, a "dance" with the Logos in the quest for intimacy amid his mysteriously redemptive elusiveness. The dialectics of disclosure and concealment, embodiment and radical transcendence, lies at the heart of all of the Confessor's works of biblical commentary, works that mostly take the form of elucidations of ambiguous or difficult scriptural texts in which the Word seems to perplex or evade the interpreter. Recalling his appropriation of the transfiguration, it is the Logos who perpetually commands the conditions of his self-revelation, graciously enabling Scripture and the created cosmos to become prisms of his transforming and transfixing light.[83] Maximus certainly respected the apophaticism of Gregory of Nyssa, who emphasized how biblical texts, constrained by διάστημα, the ontological chasm between uncreated God and creation, provided no direct access to the divine essence but depended on God's free incursions into the realm of human language.[84] He would also have acknowledged Dionysius the Areopagite's axiom that negotiating the profundity of biblical symbolism was tantamount to plunging into a salutary "darkness."[85] And yet Maximus' chosen analogy for the Bible was not the "abyss" of language, but an orderly "cosmos" inhabited by Christ the living Logos, who sets the conditions not only of revelation itself but also of its interpretation.[86]

---

[82] For detailed analysis of *Amb. Jo.* 71 and the image of the Logos-at-play, see Paul Blowers, "On the 'Play' of Divine Providence in Gregory Nazianzen and Maximus the Confessor," in Christopher Beeley, ed., *Re-Reading Gregory of Nazianzus: Essays on History, Theology, and Culture* (Washington, DC: Catholic University of America Press, 2012), 183–201; and Carlos Steel, "Le jeu du Verbe: À propos de Maxime, *Amb. ad Ioh. LXVII [= Amb. 71]*," in Anton Schoors and Peter van Deun, eds., *Philohistôr: Miscellanea in honorem Caroli Laga septuagenarii* (Leuven: Peeters, 1994), 281–93; Joshua Lollar, *To See into the Life of Things: The Contemplation of Nature in Maximus the Confessor and His Predecessors* (Turnhout: Brepols, 2013), 36–40, 331–2.

[83] See Thomas Cattoi, *Divine Contingency: Theologies of Divine Embodiment in Maximos the Confessor and Tsong Kha Pa* (Piscataway, NJ: Gorgias Press, 2008), 51–4.

[84] On this Cappadocian vision of God's "metadiastemic intrusions" into the diastemic realm so as to empower human language, see Scot Douglass, *Theology of the Gap: Cappadocian Language Theory and the Trinitarian Controversy* (New York: Peter Lang, 2005), esp. 127–91. Cf. also Alden Mosshammer, "'Disclosing but Not Disclosed: Gregory of Nyssa as Deconstructionist," in Hubertus Drobner and Christoph Klock, eds., *Studien zu Gregor von Nyssa und der christliche Spätantike* (Leiden: Brill, 1990), 103–20.

[85] *Myst. theol.* 1.3 (PTS 36:143–4), a teaching that Dionysius ascribes to the apostle Bartholomew.

[86] See esp. *Amb. Jo.* 10 (PG 91:1129A–B).

The interpretive dance with the Logos plays out concretely in Maximus' exegetical practices.[87] First and foremost is the play of polysemy. Given the saturation or overflow of the Logos's gracious self-divulgence, and that he has "mingled himself invisibly with all the [scriptural] figures that were given to ancient people, thereby bringing about the ascent (ἀνάβασις) of those whom he is educating,"[88] the interpreter is faced with a mass of possible legitimate interpretations of any given text. Maximus calls these diverse intuitions (ἐπινοίαι)[89] or attempted readings (ἐπιβολαί),[90] and he often introduces them with phrases conveying varying degrees of confidence and tentativeness: "nay . . . " (ἢ πάλιν), "or rather . . . " (ἢ μᾶλλον), "perhaps . . . " (ἢ τάχα; τυχόν), "by another reading . . . " (κατ᾽ ἄλλον τρόπον).[91] Occasionally he identifies one or another interpretation as "figurative," "tropological," "allegorical," "anagogical," or "mystical," but like Origen he allows for significant fluidity in determining non-literal meanings. Sometimes too, he highlights a certain interpretation as "more insightful" (γνωστικώτερον) or "more sublime" (ὑψηλοτέρως),[92] which is as likely to relate to *oikonomia* as to *theologia*; and like Origen he acknowledges how scriptural Word can accommodate to the inner spiritual disposition of its reader or interpreter.[93] There is not, however, a sustained systematic attempt to graduate his own multiple interpretations, scaling them to various levels of receptivity and maturity.[94] Along the way, Maximus uses a variety of exegetical strategies, most of them inherited from Origen, in order to do justice to the polysemy of biblical texts—especially those raised in the *Questions and Responses for Thalassius, Questions and Uncertainties,*

---

[87] I have treated Maximus' exegesis in detail in Paul Blowers, *Exegesis and Spiritual Pedagogy in Maximus the Confessor: An Investigation of the* Quaestiones ad Thalassium (Notre Dame, IN: University of Notre Dame Press, 1991); id., "The Anagogical Imagination: Maximus the Confessor and the Legacy of Origenian Hermeneutics," in Gilles Dorival and Alain le Boulluec, eds., *Origeniana Sexta: Origène et la Bible/Origen and the Bible. Actes du Colloquium Origenianum Sextum, Chantilly, 30 août—3 septembre 1993* (Leuven: Peeters, 1995), 639–54; and id., "Exegesis of Scripture," OHMC, 253–73.

[88] Q. Thal. 31 (CCSG 7:223).          [89] Amb. Jo. 10 (PG 91:1160D).

[90] Q. Thal. 3 (CCSG 7:55); ibid. 63 (CCSG 22:159).

[91] For examples, see Blowers, *Exegesis and Spiritual Pedagogy*, 191, 232–3, nn. 45–50.

[92] Cf. Q. Thal. 50, 54 (CCSG 7:391, 465); ibid. 63 (CCSG:173). See also Blowers, *Exegesis and Spiritual Pedagogy*, 185–92.

[93] e.g., Q. Thal. 28 (CCSG 7:203); ibid. 44 (p. 299).

[94] e.g. Amb. Jo. 67 (PG 91:1396B–1401B), where Maximus tenders no less than nine possible legitimate meanings of the number *twelve* in the "twelve baskets" left over from Jesus's feeding of the five thousand (Matt. 14:13–21 et par.).

and *Questions and Responses for Theopemptus*—that pose particular interpretive difficulties and solicit deep exploration.[95]

Meanwhile, Maximus admits that interpretation sometimes consists of "good and pious speculations" (καλὰ καὶ εὐσεβῆ θεωρήματα).[96] Drawing on an axiom going back to Philo but more likely mediated to him by Gregory of Nyssa, he warrants reverent "conjecture" (στοχασμός) in certain instances where the Word seems to frustrate interpretation:

> It is not improper, in view of that faculty in us that naturally longs for the knowledge of divine things, to undertake a conjecture about higher truths, as long as two good things from the conjecture present themselves to those who possess genuine reverence for divine realities. For the one who approaches the divine realities conjecturally either attains to intelligible truth and, rejoicing, offers the *sacrifice of praise* (Ps. 49:14, 23, LXX; Heb. 13:15), thanksgiving, to the Giver of the knowledge of what was sought, or he finds that the meaning of the scriptures eludes him, and reveres the divine truths all the more by learning that the acquisition of them exceeds his own ability.[97]

Even in the *Ambigua*, in commenting on Gregory Nazianzen, Maximus occasionally posits a conjecture where Gregory has spoken sublimely.[98] He is not averse, moreover, to "honoring in silence" a mystery that defies even the most intelligent speculation.[99] Maximus probably learned this principle from Nazianzen himself, though certainly the Greek monastic sages had long attested that sober silence on theological mysteries was the healthiest response to overly inquisitive monks.

Interpretive play nonetheless demands boldness. Maximus on occasion follows Dionysius in "daring" (τολμᾶν; παρρησιάζεσθαι) to set forth a particular interpretation.[100] But that same boldness is

[95] On these strategies, see Blowers, *Exegesis and Spiritual Pedagogy*, 196–228; id., "Exegesis of Scripture," *OHMC*, 262–9.

[96] *Q. Thal.* 63 (CCSG 22:165, l. 329).

[97] *Quaestiones ad Thalassium* 55 (CCSG 7:481–3). Philo undertakes "conjecture" in e.g., *De opificio mundi* 72–5 (regarding the divine plural in Gen. 1:26–7); *De decalogo* 18; *De Josepho* 7, 104, 143; *De aeternitate mundi* 2; and in Gregory of Nyssa see esp. *In Canticum Canticorum, Hom.* 1 (GNO 6:37).

[98] *Amb. Jo.* 7 (PG 91:1076A); ibid. 10 (1193B); ibid. 19 (1233D, 1236C–D); ibid. 20 (1240B); ibid. 21 (1244B); ibid. 37 (1293A); ibid. 45 (1352D–1353A); ibid. 71 (1412A).

[99] *Amb. Jo.* 10 (PG 91:1129C, 1165B); ibid. 17 (1228A); ibid. 20 (1241D), *Q. Thal.* Intro. (CCSG 7:37); ibid. 21 (p. 133); ibid. 43 (p. 293); *Amb. Th.* 5 (CCSG 48:31).

[100] See *Amb. Jo.* 71 (PG 91:1412A, 1412B); cf. Dionysius, *Div. nom.* 4.7 (PTS 33:152, l. 10); 4.10 (p. 155, l. 14); 4.19 (p. 163, l. 9).

constrained and conditioned by a more fundamental humility acknowledging dependence on the Logos to open access to his mysteries and allow the interpreter to come within an understanding distance. In one passage Maximus sets forth a kind of interpreter's prayer:

> Come, Logos of God, worthy of all praise, grant us proportionately the revelation of your own words, removing altogether the thickness of any shrouds. Show us, Christ, the beauty of spiritual meanings. Seize our right hand—that is, our intellectual faculty—and *Guide us in the ways of your commandments* (Ps. 118:35, LXX). Lead us into *the place of your wondrous tabernacle, even unto the house of God, with a voice of exaltation and thanksgiving, and with the celebrative sound of one who is keeping festival* (Ps. 41:5, LXX), that we too, by celebrating in praxis and exulting in contemplation, and being found worthy of coming to your ineffable place of feasting, may make sound together with those who are spiritually feasting there, and begin to sing the knowledge of unspeakable truths with the eruptive voices of the mind . . . [101]

We will need to keep in mind Maximus' interpretive playfulness and flexibility when we later consider his rigor for precise and final definitions in formulating christological doctrine. How do we reconcile these very different dispositions in one and the same writer, over and beyond differences of occasion and audience between his earlier and later writings?

## GENRE AND STYLE IN MAXIMUS' LITERARY CORPUS

Maximus wrote in a variety of literary genres, which reveal much about his pedagogical techniques, his attention to antecedent literary models, and his discursive styles, as well as the changing circumstances in which he composed his works.[102] Like Evagrius and certain

---

[101] *Q. Thal.* 48 (CCSG 7:331, ll. 17–29).

[102] For an extended survey, see Peter van Deun, "Maximus the Confessor's Use of Literary Genres," *OHMC*, 274–86. See also Blowers, *Exegesis and Spiritual Pedagogy*, 28–94; Louth, *Maximus the Confessor*, 20–2; Joshua Lollar, Intro. to *Maximus the Confessor: Ambigua to Thomas; Second Letter to Thomas*, CCT 2 (Turnhout: Brepols, 2009), 16–20. For good overall surveys of Maximus' literary corpus, see Jankowiak

other earlier monastic authors, Maximus composed *sententiae*, pithy "chapters" (κεφάλαια) sometimes in "centuries" (sets of one hundred) symbolizing the quest for perfection. Evagrius's ascetical *sententiae*, known to Maximus, scrupulously integrated contemplative and practical teaching, and strategically built toward ever more intensive wisdom and thus difficulty.[103] *Sententiae* were meant to be pondered patiently, even struggled with. Maximus' *sententiae* in the *Chapters on Love*, *Chapters on Theologia and Oikonomia*, *Fifteen Chapters*, and other diverse *Chapters* ascribed to him in the *Philokalia* but perhaps simply inspired by him, followed no strict rule on length. They can treat themes in blocks, but also move freely in and out of motifs the precise connection of which is not necessarily obvious. Maximus notes of his *Chapters* that "not all, I believe, are easily understandable by everyone, but the majority will require much scrutiny (συνεξετάσεως) by many people even though they appear to be very simply expressed."[104] Like Origen and Evagrius, Maximus sought to mimic the tradition of biblical Wisdom, wherein insight was to be granted only after much searching and reflection.

Maximus' other early works appear in diverse genres. I have noted his *Dialogue on the Ascetical Life*, a throwback to the monastic conferences or dialogues which, like his *Chapters*, signals his enduring debt to the charismatic tradition of the desert sages. Two "commentaries" appear. Maximus' *Commentary on Psalm 59* is his only true line-by-line commentary on a biblical text, though its exegetical-pedagogical style matches his *Questions and Responses for Thalassius*.[105] His *Commentary on the Lord's Prayer* is less a commentary, strictly speaking, than an unearthing of the implicit substance of the prayer, which Maximus understands to be a vow of the Son to the Father (its content as

---

and Booth, "A New Date-List," *OHMC*, 28–72; Larchet, *Saint Maxime le Confesseur* (Paris: Cerf, 2003), 27–114.

[103] See Columba Stewart, "Evagrius Ponticus on Monastic Pedagogy," in John Behr, Andrew Louth, and Dimitri E. Conomos, eds., *Abba: The Tradition of Orthodoxy in the West* (Crestwood, NY: St. Vladimir's Seminary Press, 2003), 258–62.

[104] *Car.* Prol. (PG 90:960B), trans. Berthold, 35.

[105] For analysis and a full translation of this work, see Paul Blowers, "A Psalm 'Unto the End': Eschatology and Anthropology in Maximus the Confessor's *Commentary on Psalm 59*," in Brian Daley and Paul Kolbet, eds., *The Harp of Prophecy: Early Christian Interpretation of the Psalms* (Notre Dame, IN: University of Notre Dame Press, 2014), 257–83.

*theologia*) and an exhibition of the great soteriological mysteries of the *oikonomia* divulged by the Son in his incarnation.

A considerable amount of Maximus' early writing falls into the broad genre of question-and-response, a pedagogical genre deeply rooted in Greco-Roman philosophy but having a rich history of its own in early Christian literature, including biblical commentaries. The *Questions and Responses for Thalassius, Questions and Uncertainties*, and *Questions and Responses for Theopemptus*, which all focus mainly on biblical "difficulties" (ἀπορίαι), evidence Maximus' Origenian assumption that scriptural revelation is intrinsically educative and occasionally but intentionally "scandalous" in order to navigate its interpreters toward richer and deeper meanings. Both sets of Maximus' *Ambigua*, the earlier group (6–71) addressed to John of Cyzicus and the later group (1–5) addressed to Thomas, also fall within this genre, and it is clear that for Maximus, *aporiae* in the writings of theological masters like Gregory Nazianzen and Dionysius the Areopagite are of a piece with those from Scripture, since they have already plumbed the depths of the biblical mysteries. Though his actual elucidations in the *Ambigua* are carefully constructed and argued, Maximus confesses his lack of rhetorical skill and his liability to verbosity (τῷ πολυστίχῳ) compared to Gregory's strict economy of words; moreover, he notes that his objective, as with Scripture, is to excavate latent meaning (διάνοια).[106] Predictably, then, Maximus posits multiple legitimate senses of the pregnant statements of his predecessors, as we observed earlier in the extensive *Ambiguum* 10 on divine theophany and in his interpretations of Nazianzen's image of the Logos-at-play in *Ambiguum* 71. The Logos's own pliant "textuality"—his incarnation or self-inscription in multiple material modes—allows for this multiplicity and diversity of nuance in Scripture and so too Scripture's inspired interpreters, those of the "patristic tradition" (ἡ πατρικὴ παράδοσις).[107]

A fairly dramatic change occurs in the tenor of Maximus' writings from the 640s on, when he became ever more publicly embroiled in the monothelete controversy. While some of his theological and polemical *Opuscula* pre-date this crisis, many of the most meticulous ones stem from his deepening involvements in it. The *Opuscula*, as Jean-Claude Larchet notes, actually take different forms: miniature treatises, letters,

---

[106] *Amb. Jo.* Prol. (PG 91:1064D–1065A); cf. *Myst.* prooemium (CCSG 69:5).
[107] *Ep.* 17 (PG 91:581D). See also Croce, *Tradizione e ricerca*, 83–101.

definitions, florilegia, disputation, and summations.[108] The common thread is a painstaking desire for linguistic precision in doctrinal formulations, and an urge toward relatively concise resolutions of complex issues, especially those of Christology. *Opusculum* 1, a letter to the Cypriot priest Marinus, is exemplary in this regard, where Maximus defines the various distinctive phases in human volition in defending the perfect operation of a natural human will in Christ.[109] This attention to rigorously precise definitions should not, however, be seen as antithetical to the more "playful" discourse of Maximus' earlier writings, where he was demonstrably patient of polysemy. Such playfulness was unimaginable apart from a thoroughgoing grounding in trinitarian and christological language, language that was itself semantically dense and demanding of continuous unpacking of its subtleties. For Maximus, this language was already honed and tested within patristic and conciliar tradition, but he did not hesitate to add refinements of his own, to the point that, as we saw in the preceding chapter, his prosecutors accused him of linguistic nitpicking and failure to be accommodating.

Ever since the ninth-century Byzantine encyclopedist Photius decried the Confessor's Greek as prolix and obscure,[110] there have been few serious attempts to analyze, much less defend, his actual style of writing, though his critical editor Carl Laga has lamented the modern caricature of Maximus' style as "artificial, impenetrable, lacking of restraint, and so dissolute that it disheartens even his most enthusiastic supporters."[111] Laga is among the few working to correct this perception and to vindicate the sophistication of Maximus' prose. For example, the Confessor enjoyed occasional word-plays and homophonies—and why not, since the Logos himself is altogether "playful" (*Ambiguum* 71)? Indeed, one of Maximus' most consistent plays on a word was the term *logos* itself, the polyvalence of which proved too strategic not to exploit.[112] It is a habit learned from his

[108] Introduction to Emmanuel Ponsoye, trans., *Maxime le Confesseur: Opuscules théologiques et polémiques* (Paris: Cerf, 1998), 17. Larchet (*Saint Maxime le Confesseur*, 18–108) provides a good survey of the individual *Opuscula*, on the chronology of which he generally follows Sherwood's *Date-List*.

[109] See *Opusc.* 1 (PG 91:9A–37A).     [110] *Bibliotheca*, cod. 192.

[111] "Maximus as a Stylist in *Quaestiones ad Thalassium*," *MC*, 139.

[112] Numerous scholars and translators of Maximus have noted this. Cf. Sherwood, *The Earlier Ambigua of St. Maximus the Confessor and His Refutation of Origenism* (Rome: Herder, 1955), 166; Croce, *Tradizione e ricerca*, 39–40; Aldo Ceresa-Gastaldo, "Tradition et innovation linguistique chez Maxime le Confesseur," *MC*, 130–2; Louth, "St. Maximos' Doctrine of the *logoi* of Creation," in Jane Baun, Averil Cameron, Michael

master Gregory Nazianzen, whose theology of the revealed Word is enriched by distinctions and associations between "the Word of the Father, any word or speech, any reason or rationality, logic, oration, study, Scripture, and definition."[113] In various instances Maximus too deliberately blurred the lines between the divine "Word," the scriptural "word," and the "word" of inspired expositors like Nazianzen.[114] At the beginning of *Ambiguum* 32, he quotes the relevant passage from Nazianzen and writes: "Being wholly inspired by the Word, the great teacher adds to the previous words [from *Oration* 38.2], in accordance with the Word, the word about the Word that the great prophet Isaiah mystically spoke concerning the incarnate Word . . . "[115] In other cases Maximus plays off of the intrinsic relation between the divine Logos, the universal *logos* of creation, the *logoi* of individual creatures, the *logos* which is instructive or interpretive of divine mysteries, and the *logos* of sanctified human "reason" such as discerns these connections.[116] In another case, which I shall detail later, Maximus exploits the different meanings of the term *politeia*, including its associated cosmological, christological, ascetical, ecclesiastical, and even eschatological nuances.[117]

Other stylistic features as well marked Maximus' writing. Laga notes against Photius's charges that Maximus often strove for economy of words, such as in his omission of prepositions in adverbial phrases, often favoring prepositions agglutinated with verbs.[118] The charge of prolixity holds greater weight when we observe Maximus' penchant for enormously long sentences with multiple clauses and clauses-within-clauses, a function of what Laga accurately calls an "intricate, self-correcting and, as it were, self-analyzing style."[119] I already mentioned Maximus' admission in his *Ambigua* to rhetorical deficiency and verbal prolixity in comparison with the master wordsmith, Gregory Nazianzen. And yet Maximos Constas has drawn attention in the *Ambigua* to occasional

---

Edwards, and Markus Vinzent, eds., *Studia Patristica* 48 (Leuven: Peeters, 2010), 77–84; Françoise Vinel, *Maxime le Confesseur: Questions à Thalassios*, SC 529:94.

[113] Andrew Hofer, *Christ in the Life and Teaching of Gregory of Nazianzus* (Oxford: Oxford University Press, 2013), 13. See his larger discussion, ibid., 11–54.

[114] As Constas observes (I, xiii–xv), Maximus believes that Gregory's words, as an inspired interpreter, are tantamount to the Word's own words; see esp. *Amb. Th.* Prol. (CCSG 48:4).

[115] *Amb. Jo.* 32 (PG 91:1281B–C), trans. Constas II, 53. My thanks to Maximos Constas for pointing this passage out to me.

[116] Cf. *Amb. Jo.* 59 (PG 91:1384B–D); *Myst.* 17 (CCSG 69:46).

[117] See pp. 131–4 in this volume.      [118] "Maximus as a Stylist," 142–3.

[119] Ibid., 146.

exhibitions of rhetorical flare, such as Maximus' invective against cynics of "itching ears and tongues" who maligned Gregory's good words, and who acted like racehorses that, "even before the races and the blast of the trumpet, prick up their ears and stamp their feet on the ground, scraping it with their hooves, rousing themselves for the race, and not infrequently breaking away from the gate and bolting forward before they have felt the sting of the starting whip."[120] Maximus certainly also applied the rhetorical commonplace of accusing theological calumniators precisely of being *rhetorical* charlatans.[121]

Meanwhile, Maximus was also capable of occasional demonstrations of literary elegance of his own. Quite apart from the aphoristic style of his *Chapters*, in the *Questions and Responses for Thalassius* he occasionally erupts into elegant elaborations on the spiritual life, such as a long passage describing the interrelated phases of the mystery of deification. Rather than a mere paratactic string of definitions, the text uses anastrophe to build and aspire upward toward the heights of the mystery of the salvation that the prophets themselves *searched out and investigated* (1 Peter 1:9–11). This poetic glossary of deification is worth quoting in full:

> Properly speaking, the *salvation of souls* is the *end of faith* (1 Peter 1:9).
>
> The *end of faith* is, in turn, the true revelation of that in which one has faith.
>
> The true *revelation* of that in which one has faith is, in turn, the ineffable penetration of what has been entrusted proportionate to each believer's faith.
>
> The *penetration of what has been entrusted* consists, in turn, in the ascent of believers to their proper beginning as defined by their end (ἀρχὴν κατὰ τὸ τέλος).
>
> The *ascent* of believers to their proper beginning as defined by their end is, in turn, the fulfillment of their desire.
>
> The *fulfillment of their desire* is, in turn, the ever-moving repose of desirers in relation to the object of their desire.
>
> The *ever-moving repose* of desirers in relation to their object of desire is, in turn, the uninterrupted and continuous enjoyment of the object of desire.

---

[120] *Amb. Jo.* 13 (PG 91:1209D–1212A), trans. Constas I, 553–5. My thanks again to Constas for directing me to this exemplary text.

[121] e.g. ibid. 42 (1345C).

The *uninterrupted and continuous enjoyment of the object of desire* consists, in turn, in the participation in supernatural divine realities. The *participation in supernatural divine realities* is, in turn, the assimilation of participants to that in which they are participating.

The *assimilation of believers to that in which they are participating* is, in turn, the operative identity of the participants with the participated, which is possible through their acquired likeness to it.

The *operative identity of the participants with the participated*, possible through acquired likeness, consists, in turn, in the deification of those who are worthy of it.

*Deification* in turn, by a descriptive account, is the circumference and terminus of all times and ages, and of the things within those times and ages.

The *circumference and terminus of times and ages*, and of everything in them, are, in turn, the continuous union, in those being saved, of their pure and proper beginning to their proper and pure end.

The *continuous union between pure beginning and end* in those being saved is, in turn, the exodus of the superior of the elements—measured as of the essence by that beginning and end—from the constraints of nature.

The *exodus from what is defined by beginning and end* is, in turn, the immediate, infinitely infinite, almighty, and supremely powerful activity of God in those he finds worthy of this projected exodus of what is superior from the constraints of nature.

The *immediate, infinitely infinite, almighty, and supremely powerful activity of God* is, in turn, the unutterable and supremely ineffable pleasure and joy of those in whom God acts, based on an unspeakable union transcending human intelligence. It is absolutely impossible for the human mind or reason to acquire a sense or expression of this pleasure and joy within the nature of created beings.[122]


MAXIMUS SCHOLASTICUS?

At the beginning of this chapter, I remarked on Averil Cameron's vivid profile of Maximus as a proto-scholastic theologian whose literary corpus addressed the need to stabilize the Byzantine Christian cultural cosmos during the turbulent seventh century. Cameron's portrait of Maximus as a proto-scholastic is most compelling when framed against

---

[122] *Q. Thal.* 59 (CCSG 22:53–5, ll. 122–59) (emphasis added).

the backdrop of a select group of his writings, including especially his *Ambigua to John* and some of his *Questions and Responses for Thalassius*, in which he essays enormous, interconnected issues of cosmology, Christology, and eschatology, and sets out the contours of his theological *philosophia*. It befits as well certain of Maximus' theological and polemical *Opuscula*, which develop various doctrinal themes with painstaking linguistic, philosophical, and theological precision. Cameron's profile also suits his little-known *Computus Ecclesiasticus*, a work in the genre of Byzantine chronography, which sought to provide Christianity's sacred history, particularly liturgically-celebrated events like Pascha, with a comprehensive chronology extending all the way back to the creation of the world.[123] Clearly the scholastic profile suits Maximus' expertise as an organizer of dyothelete florilegia for the Lateran Council of 649, and his repeated appeals, during his imperial prosecution, to the integrity of the tradition bearing the Nicene and Chalcedonian faith.[124]

Superficially, the image of Maximus as a conservative scholastic seems improbable. How could his work contribute to securing Byzantine culture when, at least in the extended monenergist/monothelete controversy, he maintained such a blatantly adversarial and destabilizing posture toward the authority of the emperor and the imperial patriarchate? And yet the documentation of both the Lateran Council of 649 and the Council of Constantinople in 680–1 reveals how pro- and anti-monothelete campaigns alike laid claim to scriptural, patristic, and conciliar tradition and commonly recognized the indispensability of doctrinal consensus to the security of an Empire standing under God's judgment—a judgment already visibly impending in the exposure of imperial territories to a massive foreign invader. In this respect, then, Maximus' dissidence, together with that of scores of other Greek dyothelete monks, could be interpreted as a religio-cultural loyalism—though the powerful political sting of that dissidence cannot be underplayed.

Cameron's scholastic profile hardly does justice, however, to Maximus as a spiritual pedagogue deeply rooted in a monastic tradition of charismatic wisdom, or as a self-deprecating ascetical and

---

[123] Text in PG 19:1217–80.

[124] Maximus' deference to patristic and conciliar tradition is well-treated in secondary studies. See esp. Croce, *Tradizione e ricerca*; Jaroslav Pelikan, "'Council or Father or Scripture:' The Concept of Authority in the Theology of Maximus the Confessor," in David Neiman and Margaret Schatkin, eds., *The Heritage of the Early Church: Essays in Honor of Georges Florovsky* (Rome: Pontificium Institutum Orientalium, 1973), 277–88.

contemplative *philosophos*, or as a sometimes "playful" interpreter of Scripture and the Fathers who delighted in their polyvalent language and was willing to put forward "conjectures" in the quest for spiritual insight. It is fair enough, I would argue, to read Maximus as a proto-scholastic through the lens of a later Byzantine scholasticism that he did not live long enough to see in its full fruition. This descriptor, however, will not suffice as an exhaustive profile of Maximus' achievement in the religio-cultural dynamics of seventh-century Byzantium. Nor, I suggest, will the very much opposite portrait of Maximus recently put forward by Polymnia Athanassiadi. By her account he was one of the few authentic bearers of the great tradition of Hellenic culture in his time, a genuine Platonic mystic and "cosmic optimist" who strongly cut against the grain of the increasing intellectual intolerance of Byzantium in late antiquity.[125] Such a highly romanticized portrait fully fails to account for Maximus' own capacity for conceptual severity, theological exactness, and linguistic rigor on those linchpins of theology and Christology which he deemed worthy of uncompromising interpretive precision.

---

[125] Polymnia Athanassiadi, *Vers la pensée unique: La montée de l'intolérance dans l'antiquité tardive* (Paris: Les Belles Lettres, 2010), 126–32.

# Part II

# The Cosmic Landscapes of
# Maximus' Theology

# 3

## Creation as the Drama of Divine Freedom and Resourcefulness

In this and the two following chapters, my purpose is to sketch the "cosmic landscapes" of Maximus' theology, and to propose that in the context of the turbulent seventh century in Byzantium, he projected a vision of the world that was "cosmopolitan" in a highly theologically-qualified sense. For Maximus, the Christian Gospel gave witness to a universe being transfigured, to an emerging cosmic and eschatological *politeia* embracing all of spiritual and material creation, of which Jesus Christ was both the pioneer and the perfecter in his incarnation.[1] The properly christological dimension of this theme I will resume in more detail in Chapter 4. In this chapter I wish to examine the cosmological framework of this *politeia*, this ordered "way of being" *in Christ*,[2] that Maximus ultimately projected for *all* creatures in their diverse stations and fields of movement within the cosmos.

At the outset I would note my debt to the work of Hans Urs von Balthasar, who, in exploring the intricate web of dialectical themes and syntheses that constitute Maximus' christocentric *Weltbild*,[3] did not simply measure Maximus' universe by the cosmological and metaphysical bequests of Neoplatonism and Aristotelianism, no matter the significance of those philosophical idioms to his doctrine

---

[1] See *Amb. Th.* 5 (CCSG 48:32). Cf. *Amb. Jo.* 7 (PG 91:1097C), speaking of Christ having inaugurated a "newer mode" ($\kappa\alpha\iota\nu\sigma\tau\acute{\epsilon}\rho\sigma\varsigma$ $\tau\rho\acute{\sigma}\pi\sigma\varsigma$) of human nature.

[2] *Myst.* 24 (CCSG 69:61, l. 975).

[3] *Kosmische Liturgie: Das Weltbild Maximus' des Bekenners*, 3rd edn. (Einsiedeln: Johannes Verlag, 1988); trans. Brian Daley, *Cosmic Liturgy: The Universe according to Maximus the Confessor* (San Francisco: Ignatius Press, 2003).

of creation.[4] Instead, von Balthasar recognized that for Maximus, as for others earlier in the Greek patristic tradition, the goal was less to construct a philosophical cosmology per se than to articulate a vision of the panoramic *theo-drama* of divine action in which creation and redemption form a seamless plot unveiling the triune Creator's unbridled freedom and love. At the heart of that drama, moreover, was the true play-within-the-play, the "fiat of Jesus" as François-Marie Léthel aptly calls it,[5] Maximus' carefully constructed tableau of the work of Christ in his incarnation and passion constituting not only the climactic but also the *original* expression of God's plan to realize his creative and salvific purposes.


MAXIMUS' NEO-IRENAEAN PERSPECTIVE

While heavy attention has been given to Maximus' cosmology as a correction of Origenism (to which I shall return shortly) or as an appropriation and adjustment of the metaphysics of Dionysius the Areopagite, I would suggest that, at an even more basic level, it is a sophisticated expansion on key insights of the Confessor's distant predecessor Irenaeus of Lyons, which becomes clearer as Irenaeus's doctrine of creation has itself come into sharper focus in recent scholarship. Irenaeus's own theo-dramatic perspective, as recognized by von Balthasar and others,[6] found new traction and reworking in Maximus' theology of creation.

Irenaeus's signature principle is the "recapitulation" ($\dot{\alpha}\nu\alpha\kappa\epsilon\varphi\alpha\lambda\alpha\acute{\iota}\omega\sigma\iota\varsigma$) of creation in Jesus Christ, for which he was heavily indebted to Paul's

---

[4] For the properly philosophical (esp. Neoplatonic) background of Maximus' doctrine of creation, see Torstein Tollefsen, *The Christocentric Cosmology of St. Maximus the Confessor* (Oxford: Oxford University Press, 2008).

[5] *Théologie de l'agonie du Christ: La liberté humaine du Fils de Dieu et son importance sotériologique mises en lumière par saint Maxime le Confesseur* (Paris: Beauchesne, 1979), 86–99.

[6] See von Balthasar's treatment of Irenaeus in *The Glory of the Lord: A Theological Aesthetics*, 7 vols., trans. Erasmo Leiva-Merikakis et al. (San Francisco: Ignatius Press, 1983–91), 2:31–94; id., *Theo-Drama: Theological Dramatic Theory*, 5 vols., trans. Graham Harrison (San Francisco: Ignatius Press, 1988–98), 2:140–9, 216–19; 4:244–8; also Kevin Tortorelli, "Balthasar and the Theodramatic Interpretation of St. Irenaeus," *Downside Review* 111 (1993): 117–26.

christological reflection in Ephesians 1:3–14 (esp. 1:10).[7] Recapitulation meant that only in the incarnation did the Creator truly fulfill his plan for creation. In Christ, the past and future of sacred history—of *all* the history of creation—collapsed into a perfect singularity of purpose. John Behr has demonstrated, however, that Irenaeus does not just set out a linear chronological progression of episodes constituting "salvation history" (creation, fall, incarnation, redemption); rather, seemingly counterintuitively, he posits the solution before the ostensible problem.[8] The Creator's *original* plan for the world was to reveal himself in Jesus Christ. Creation was not the "beginning" per se but was itself a staging-point toward gradually disclosing the fullness of the mystery of the incarnation and cross. "For insofar as [the Creator] preexisted as the one who saves, it was necessary that what would be saved should also come into existence, in order that the Savior should not exist in vain."[9] The real "beginning" (ἀρχή) in Genesis 1:1, as Origen and numerous patristic writers after Irenaeus argued, was Jesus Christ himself.[10] As Irenaeus further states in a key passage,

> no one, either in heaven or on earth or under the earth, was able to open *the book* of the Father *or to behold it* except the *Lamb who was slain*, who redeemed us by his blood (Rev. 5:3, 9, 12), and who, when *the Word became flesh* (John 1:14), received all power from the very God who made all things by his Word and adorned them by his Wisdom—this so that, just as the Word of God had sovereignty in the heavens, so also he might enjoy sovereignty on earth insofar as he was a righteous man *who committed no sin nor was found with guile upon his lips* (1 Peter 2:22); and that he might have preeminence over the things that are under the earth since he became *firstborn from the dead* (Col. 1:18); and that all things, as we already said, might behold their King; and that the Father's light might land upon the flesh of our Lord, and come to us from his resplendent flesh, so that humanity might acquire incorruptibility, being surrounded by the Father's light.[11]

---

[7] Cf. *Adv. haer.* 1.10.1 (SC 264:156); 4.38.1 (SC 100:946); 5:20.2 (SC 153:260), referencing Eph. 1:10. See also Jacques Fantino, *La théologie d'Irénée: Lecture des Écritures en réponse à l'exégèse gnostique—Une approche trinitaire* (Paris: Cerf, 1994), 240–58.

[8] John Behr, *The Mystery of Christ: Life in Death* (Crestwood, NY: St. Vladimir's Seminary Press, 2006), 77–86.

[9] *Adv. haer.* 3.22.3 (SC 211:438).

[10] See Paul Blowers, *Drama of the Divine Economy: Creator and Creation in Early Christian Theology and Piety* (Oxford: Oxford University Press, 2012), 140–5.

[11] *Adv. haer.* 4.20.2 (SC 100:628–30).

In the passage immediately following, Irenaeus further reiterates that the Son, or Logos, was present together with the Spirit, or Wisdom, and the Father prior to creation.[12] The mystery of Jesus Christ, to be divulged in its eschatological fullness as the very rationale of creation, was grounded within the preexistent counsel of the Trinity. "Viewed in the light of Christ, beginning with the Savior," Behr observes in Irenaeus,

> creation and salvation are not two distinct actions, but the continual process of God's activity in his handiwork, bringing the creature, when he allows himself to be skillfully fashioned, to the stature of the Savior, by whom and for whom all creation has come into being. This process... includes human apostasy, the acquisition of the knowledge of good and evil, the experience of sin and death.[13]

Irenaeus means, not that the Creator predestined Adam to sin, but that, in the primordial light of the flesh and cross of Jesus Christ, the Creator's sacrificial love for the creation, Adamic sin has been exposed as the tragic underbelly of the endless renewal of creation en route to its consummation.

In Maximus this theo-dramatic perspective is cast afresh. Cosmology, as cumulative reflection on the origins, structure, and destiny of the world, revolves around Christology. In Maximus as in Irenaeus, the notion of divine *economy* (οἰκονομία), while retaining its traditional meaning of divine providential government of the cosmos,[14] takes on the sense of the Creator's resolute "strategy" in revealing Jesus Christ and salvation (and deification) in him.[15] It has a strongly dramatic tone, in the spirit of what Irenaeus called the

---

[12]  Ibid. 4.20.3 (SC 100:632).

[13]  *The Mystery of Christ*, 86. See also Behr's fuller exposition of Irenaeus's doctrine of recapitulation in his *Irenaeus of Lyons: Identifying Christianity* (Oxford: Oxford University Press, 2013), 121–203.

[14]  For the distinct but interconnected senses of *oikonomia* in Irenaeus, see Fantino, *La théologie d'Irénée*, 94–8.

[15]  e.g. *Amb Jo*. 7 (PG 91:1092D–1093A), describing the "God who does whatever is necessary for our salvation" (ὁ τὴν ἡμετέραν σωτηρίαν οἰ κονομῶν Θεὸς), trans. Constas I, 121; also ibid. (1093C):... τὴν οἰ κονομουμένην ἡμῶν σοφῶς παρὰ τοῦ Θεοῦ σωτηρίαν; ibid. 8 (PG 91:1104A):... κατὰ θείαν ψῆφον τὴν σοφῶς τὴν ἡμῶν σωτηρίαν οἰκονομοῦσαν... For the traditional notion of *oikonomia* as God's providential government or stewardship of creation, see e.g. *Amb. Jo*. 10 (PG 91:1149B); ibid. 15 (PG 91:1217A). Maximus can also routinely use the term as virtually synonymous with the incarnation itself: cf. *Amb. Jo*. 27 (PG 91:1269D); ibid. 42 (1317D); ibid. 56 (1380B); *Amb. Th*. 5 (CCSG 48:25, l. 118).

"plot" (ὑπόθεσις; *argumentum*) running through the complexity of scriptural revelation.[16]

The christocentric plot of creation is nowhere more lucid in Maximus' corpus than in two classic passages, the first of which directly ties the meaning of all creation (and Scripture) to Christ's cross, burial, and resurrection.

> The mystery of the incarnation of the Logos holds the power of all the hidden *logoi* and figures of Scripture as well as the knowledge of visible and intelligible creatures. Whoever knows the mystery of the cross and the tomb knows the *logoi* of these creatures. And whoever has been initiated in the ineffable power of the resurrection knows the purpose for which God originally made all things.[17]

As Cornelia Tsakiridou insightfully comments on this text, the one who contemplates the world in the "iconic" light of Christ's death, burial, and resurrection—the very heart of the incarnational mystery—is brought to an epistemic standstill; and there is no going forward conceptually or theologically without coming to grips with the divine sacrifice underlying the fabric of the cosmos.[18]

In the other text, *Questions and Responses for Thalassius* 60, Thalassius has asked who "foreknew" Christ as a "pure and spotless lamb . . . manifested at the end of time" (1 Peter 1:20). Maximus answers, on Paul's authority in Colossians 1:26, that Scripture (and here, by extension 1 Peter 1:19–20) uses the term "Christ" of the whole "mystery of Christ," namely, his composite person, which perfectly united uncreated and created natures, and which constitutes the very rationale for the creation of the world:

> For it was fitting for the Creator of the universe, who by the economy of his incarnation became what by nature he was not, to preserve without change both what he himself was by nature and what he became in his incarnation. For naturally we must not consider any change at all in God, nor conceive any movement in him. Being changed properly

---

[16] e.g. *Adv. haer.* 1.8.1; 1.9.4 (SC 264:112, 150), using the negative example of the false *hypothesis* of Scripture fashioned by Gnostic interpreters, which clearly stands in stark contrast with the true *hypothesis* embodied in the Rule of Faith. See also Robert Grant, *Irenaeus of Lyons* (London: Routledge, 1997), 47–9, indicating the close and important relation of the *hypothesis* of Scripture and the divine *oikonomia*; also Behr, *Irenaeus of Lyons*, 78–9, 105 6, 112 14, 116, 117, 118, 121, 144 5, 207.

[17] *Th. Oec.* 1.66 (PG 90:1108A–B).

[18] Cornelia Tsakiridou, *Icons in Time, Persons in Eternity: Orthodox Theology and the Aesthetics of the Christian Image* (Farnham: Ashgate, 2013), 179–80.

pertains to movable creatures. This is the great and hidden mystery, at once the blessed end for which all things are ordained. It is the divine purpose conceived before the beginning of created beings. In defining it we would say that this mystery is the preconceived goal for which everything exists, but which itself exists on account of nothing. With a clear view to this end, God created the essences of created beings, and such is, properly speaking, the terminus of his providence and of the things under his providential care. Inasmuch as it leads to God, it is the recapitulation of the things he has created. It is the mystery which circumscribes all the ages, and which reveals the grand plan of God (cf. Eph. 1:10–11), a super-infinite plan infinitely preexisting the ages. The Logos, by essence God, became a messenger of this plan (cf. Isa. 9:5, LXX) when he became a man and, if I may rightly say so, established himself as the innermost depth of the Father's goodness while also displaying in himself the very goal for which his creatures manifestly received the beginning of their existence.

Because of Christ—or rather, the whole mystery of Christ—all the ages of time and the beings within those ages have received their beginning and end in Christ. For the union between a limit of the ages and limitlessness, between measure and immeasurability, between finitude and infinity, between Creator and creation, between rest and motion, was conceived before the ages. This union has been manifested in Christ at the end of time, and in itself brings God's foreknowledge to fulfillment, in order that naturally mobile creatures might secure themselves around God's total and essential immobility, desisting altogether from their movement toward themselves and toward each other. The union has been manifested so that they might also acquire, by experience, an active knowledge of him in whom they were made worthy to find their stability and to have abiding unchangeably in them the enjoyment of this knowledge.[19]

On the basis of this text, some scholars have posed to Maximus questions that became famous in medieval debates between Thomists and Scotists over whether the incarnation was logically necessary to the original plan of creation (Scotus) or instead the expression of God's freedom to use incarnation, as opposed to other options, to redeem humanity from its lapse into sin (Aquinas). Jean-Claude Larchet suggests that in his own purview, Maximus had three principal options open to him: (1) that the incarnation was indissolubly linked to humanity's fall, which the Creator foresaw before he created the world; (2) that the Creator predetermined

[19] *Q. Thal. 60* (CCSG 7:75–7), trans. Blowers and Wilken, 124–6.

Adamic sin as a necessary precondition for bestowing good in the incarnation; and (3) that the incarnation would have occurred even had humanity not lapsed.[20] Larchet rightly dismisses the second option as totally foreign to Maximus. The third alternative has been the interpretation of Maximus' position in a significant segment of later scholarship.[21] It is congenial with a larger Byzantine/Orthodox tradition in which the mystery of deification (θέωσις)—related to but teleologically distinct from redemption from sin—is grounded, both protologically and eschatologically, in the incarnation. Besides his lofty statement about the incarnation as key to creation in *Questions and Responses for Thalassius* 60 quoted earlier, Maximus asserts a complementarity of the "ages of incarnation" and "ages of deification," though in his eschatological frame of reference these ages actually overlap.[22] He also unequivocally states (*Amb. Jo.* 36) that the incarnation completes a creaturely communion with God "far more marvelous than the first," the first as in Adam's original, limited state.[23] Larchet meanwhile believes that Maximus deliberated on how precisely to frame the rationale of the incarnation vis-à-vis the plan of creation. Maximus seems to entertain the theoretical prospect that the recapitulation of God's purpose in creation was already a *natural* possibility of the human creature as the mediating link in creation (*Amb. Jo.* 41[24]), apart from the incarnation of the New Adam; but elsewhere (especially in the *Q. Thal.*) he commits to the absolute primacy of the incarnation as the *original* plan for recapitulating all things and fulfilling the mystery of deification.[25] The two would not necessarily be thoroughly incompatible. The first scenario presupposes still that created human nature, as called to its strategic role in creation, nonetheless depends on the prior and still gracious "incarnation" of the Logos in the *logoi* of nature. The second scenario, however, demands the incarnation proper in Jesus of Nazareth as the completion of the divine mission to see humanity (and creation as a whole) to its providential end.

---

[20] *La divinisation de l'homme*, 84–105, esp. 87ff.

[21] See the modern studies noted by Larchet (ibid. 87–9, nn. 16–20).

[22] *Q. Thal.* 22 (CCSG 7:137–43). See also Paul Blowers, "Realized Eschatology in Maximus the Confessor, *Ad Thalassium* 22," in Elizabeth Livingstone, ed., *Studia Patristica* 32 (Leuven: Peeters, 1997), 258–63.

[23] *Amb. Jo.* 36 (PG 91:1289B–D), using Gregory Nazianzen's phrase, *Or.* 38.13 (SC 358:134); cf. also Irenaeus, *Adv. haer.* 4.38.1 (CCSG 100:942–8).

[24] Specifically the passage in PG 91:1305A–1308C.

[25] *La divinisation de l'homme*, 92–105.

In affirming the incarnation as the original rationale for God's creation of the cosmos, Maximus is not proposing, any more than Irenaeus, that the Creator intended some mechanical ontological mutation in creaturely nature, such as Adolf von Harnack alleged in his criticism of "physical redemption" in the Greek Fathers.[26] Nor does Maximus, any more than Irenaeus, propose to relate divine *incarnation* exclusively to the goal of deification, and the *passion* of Christ solely to the goal of remedying sin. They are of a piece. In *Ambiguum* 7, again citing Colossians 1:26 (*the mystery hidden for ages*), Maximus makes clear that the incarnational mystery of deification addresses both Adam's natural limitations as creature and his sinful abuse of his natural faculties. Adam was both an inchoate being, needing completion or perfection, and a sinner needing redemptive grace. Thus Christ simultaneously recapitulated the old Adam and inaugurated the New Adam, a "newer mode" (καινοτέρος τρόπος) of creaturely being.[27]

For Maximus, as for Irenaeus, protology must always be qualified not only by Christology but also by teleology or eschatology, from which perspective all creation and history appear as the outworking of the Creator's pure freedom and resourcefulness. On the one hand, creation is the stage on which the drama of divine freedom and resourcefulness is played out; on the other hand, all created natures are themselves *dramatis personae* thoroughly implicated in that drama. Maximus, as we shall later see, does not allow Christ himself to be treated merely as a *deus ex machina* introduced at the most strategic or climactic moment in this unfolding drama. Rather, the activity of Christ as the Logos and Wisdom of God saturates the drama from beginning to end. He is the central character whose appearance is also constantly qualified by his elusiveness. Most mysteriously, his appearance in flesh and on a cross is what holds the primary key to understanding his role and presence in the beginning and end of the world. Maximus thus not only renews a Wisdom Christology, he relates to it a Wisdom cosmology and anthropology.

The problem with posing hypothetical scholastic questions or scenarios to Maximus, or to Irenaeus for that matter, is that these

---

[26] *History of Dogma*, 7 vols., trans. Neil Buchanan (Boston: Roberts Brothers, 1897), 2:239–43.

[27] *Amb. Jo.* 7 (PG 91:1097B–D); cf. *Q. Thal.* 54 (CCSG 7:459).

can obscure their realist, mimetic reading of Scripture and lead us to compartmentalize what they themselves, in their imitation of biblical narrative, held seamlessly together. For Irenaeus, Adam represents the whole of creation in its initial goodness but vulnerability, and in its orientation toward future maturation, completion, and glorious transformation. Maximus spends even less time than Irenaeus reflecting on Adam in prelapsarian paradise and pining after its recovery, and in Chapter 6, I will explore in more detail the implications of Maximus' views on the impact of Adam's sin and on humanity's "historical" condition as informing his theological anthropology. Here, I would simply emphasize how humanity, as microcosm, dramatizes and epitomizes the challenge set before all of creation. For Maximus, all creatures, by their very materiality, maintain a measure of chaos or instability (τὸ ἄτακτον) needing constantly to be reordered by the Creator.[28] Salvation, then, comes as an unceasing work of divine Wisdom stabilizing this chaos and using it as the raw material of an ever new creation. Maximus' cosmology as a whole is a sustained demonstration of the embodiments of this Wisdom—a Wisdom that is transcendent, immanent, but most importantly free, active, resilient, resourceful.[29] The Creator's whole creative and salvific work is like a "sacred tent and everything in it [is] a representation, figure, and imitation of Wisdom."[30]

## COSMIC DIVERSITY ASPIRING TO UNITY

*Ambiguum* 7, Maximus' single most substantial reflection on the beginning and end of creation, is actually his commentary on a curious statement of Gregory Nazianzen in his *Oration 14, On the Love of the Poor*:

> What is this wisdom that concerns me? And what is this great mystery? Or is it God's will that we, who are a portion of God that has flowed down from above, not become exalted and lifted up on account of this

---

[28] *Amb. Jo.* 8 (PG 91:1101D–1105B).
[29] On the divine Wisdom (= Christ = the Son), see esp. ibid. 7 (1081D); ibid. 26 (1268A); ibid. 31 (1277D); ibid. 41 (1313B); ibid. 42 (1329C–D); ibid. 50 (1369A); ibid. 71 (1408C–1409B); *Car.* 3.22, 27 (PG 90:1024A, 1025A).
[30] *Th. Oec.* 1.88 (PG 90:1120C), trans. Berthold, 145.

dignity, and so despise our Creator? Or is it not rather that, in our struggle and battle with the body, we should always look to him, so that this very weakness that has been yoked to us might be an education concerning our dignity?[31]

Maximus' subsequent exposition of these lines constitutes his definitive counter to Origenist protology and eschatology. He ostensibly targets a specific but elusive group (recusant Origenist monks perhaps) who still propagated Origen's speculations on the beginning and end of the world. According to this cosmic myth, which Origen candidly admitted was hypothetical, preexistent spiritual beings (νόες), connatural with God and dwelling in perfect unity with him, breached that unity when, through satiety (κόρος) or over-indulgence in the good that they enjoyed, they became negligent and fell away, at which point the Creator placed them in bodies in order to chasten them. Nazianzen's words about "a portion of God that has flowed down from above" were apparently taken as justifying this theory of a primordial fall. Maximus is quick to caricature his opponents' thesis as a flawed construction in which spiritual beings were already at rest (στάσις) before their deviant movement (κίνησις), which led to their actual origination (γένεσις) as materially embodied creatures. In response, Maximus insists that created beings could never have begun in a state of perfect security or rest. Creatures, from their very inception, move progressively toward an *unprecedented* stability, a goal or end (τέλος) which is God himself, who alone actualizes the potential encoded in their respective natural principles (λόγοι), and who eschatologically satisfies creatures' passivity (πάθος) and driving desire (ἔφεσις).[32] That creatures have yet to reach their appointed *telos* is, in Maximus' judgment, scripturally confirmed.[33]

[31] Gregory Nazianzen, *Oration* 14.7 (PG 35: 865B–C); in Maximus, *Amb. Jo.* 7 (PG 91:1068D–1069A), trans. Constas I, 75.

[32] *Amb. Jo.* 7 (PG 91:1069A–1077B). The principal features of Maximus' correction of Origenist cosmology and metaphysically were mapped long ago by Sherwood, *The Earlier Ambigua.* For more recent analyses, see Pascal Mueller-Jourdan, "The Foundation of Origenist Metaphysics," *OHMC*, 149–63; Adam Cooper, "Spiritual Anthropology in *Ambiguum* 7," ibid., 360–77.

[33] He cites in order (1) Deut. 12:9: *For you have not as yet come to the rest and the inheritance that the Lord your God gives you*; (2) Ps. 16:15, LXX: *Crying out, I will be satisfied when your glory appears*; (3) Phil. 3:11: *That if possible I may attain the resurrection of the dead. Not that I have already obtained this or am already perfect, but I press on to make it my own because Christ Jesus has made me his own*; (4) Heb.

Here, in sum, is Maximus' vision of the universe as a divinely pre-meditated, panoramic diversity of spiritual and material creatures together aspiring toward a new unity and integrity made possible only through Jesus Christ. Each individual creature has its unique status and vocation, its proper "natural principle" (λόγος φύσεως) and "mode of existence" (τρόπος ὑπάρξεως),[34] an irreducible hypostatic distinctiveness or particularity, and an intrinsic interconnectedness with all other created beings.[35] Indeed, a striking feature of Maximus' ontology is his balancing of the dimensions of the universal and the particular, and his consistent preservation of particularity and difference (διάφορα).[36] Maximus interprets the Dionysian "hierarchies" with an emphasis less on their scaled ontological structure per se than on their instrumentality for conveying the intimate presence of the Logos even to the least of created beings. Another image deployed by Maximus of the orderly cosmos and its subservience to the Logos's self-revelation, an image also in Dionysius, is the wheel whose spokes or radii are the *logoi* of beings that bind even the most remote creatures back to the Logos as center of the universe.

> It is he who encloses in himself all beings by the unique, simple, and infinitely wise power of his goodness. As the center of straight lines that radiate from him he does not allow by his unique, simple, and single cause and power that the principles of beings become disjoined at the periphery but rather he circumscribes their extension in a circle and brings back to himself the distinctive elements of beings which he himself brought into existence.[37]

Still another image is the "harmonious web" (ἐναρμόνιον ὕφασμα) of the universe as a "book" (βίβλιον) in which the Logos has not only inscribed "words" (i.e. the *logoi* of beings) but also inscribed himself

---

4:10: *For whoever enters into God's rest also ceases from his labors as God did from his*; and (5) Matt. 11:28: *Come to me all you who labor and are heavy laden and I will give you rest.*

[34] On the *logoi* respective to different creatures, see *Amb. Jo.* 7 (PG 91:1080A–B). The distinction between *logos* and *tropos* is pervasive in Maximus' cosmology.

[35] On this interconnectedness, see *Amb. Jo.* 41 (PG 91:1312C–D).

[36] Besides *Amb. Jo.* 7 and 41, see esp. ibid. 10 (PG 91:1188D–1189B, 1192A); *Q. Thal.* 48 (CCSG 7:341). On Maximus' robust embrace of difference and differentiation in the cosmos, see Tollefsen, *Christocentric Cosmology*, 97–106; Melchisedec Törönen, *Union and Distinction in the Thought of St. Maximus the Confessor* (Oxford: Oxford University Press, 2007), 86–91.

[37] *Myst.* 1 (CCSG 69:13, ll. 189–93), trans. Berthold, 187; cf. *Th. Oec.* 2.4 (PG 90:1125D–1128A); Dionysius, *Div. nom.* 2.5 (PTS 33:129); ibid. 5.6 (p. 185). On this image, see also Törönen, *Union and Distinction*, 39–41.

in order to draw those who read (contemplate) the book toward him
as the true meaning of the book as a whole and in its parts.[38]

Maximus' intricate doctrine of the *logoi* of beings frames the
multiple manifestations and embodiments of Christ the Logos, and
furnishes a kind of grid or map of the theatre of the cosmos and of the
diverse creatures that are its *dramatis personae*. Maximus adopts
from Dionysius the definition of the *logoi* as God's very intentions
($\theta\epsilon\lambda\acute{\eta}\mu\alpha\tau\alpha$) for his creatures,[39] and while, in creatures' own purview,
the *logoi* are protologically fixed within the Logos,[40] they signal, in an
eschatological perspective, the freedom and virtuosity of the Logos to
work through his creatures in effecting the mystery of deification.

The *logoi* seem, then, to be divine "energies,"[41] either God's "uncreated energies" or at least the "*creative* energies" of the Creator.[42]
Vasilios Karayiannis is correct that for Maximus, the *logoi* themselves
are "uncreated" insofar as the uncreated energies *inhere in* them.[43]
Nikolaos Loudovikos adds that the distinction of the *logoi* from the
uncreated energies is principally epistemological, whereas their identification bespeaks more basically "the activity of divine will being
carried out in its uncreated energies."[44] The precise ontological status
of the *logoi* must thus be carefully nuanced. As Thunberg observes,

> Are the *logoi* transcendent or immanent, are they created or uncreated?
> The answer must be a double one. On the one hand Maximus affirms

---

[38] *Amb. Jo.* 10 (PG 91:1128D–1129A).

[39] Ibid. 7 (PG 91:1085A); *Q. Thal.* 13 (CCSG 7:95); Dionysius, *Div. nom.* 5.8 (PTS
33:188).

[40] *Amb. Jo.* 7 (PG 91:1081A).

[41] Ibid. 22 (PG 91:1257A–B). In his *Le monde et l'église selon Maxime le Confesseur*
(Paris: Beauchesne, 1973), 60–1, Alain Riou sees Maximus as equating the *logoi* and
the energies. On the *logoi* as distinct but deeply related to the uncreated energies, see
Vasilios Karayiannis, *Maxime le Confesseur: Essence et énergies de Dieu* (Paris:
Beauchesne, 1993), 201–10; Tollefsen, *Christocentric Cosmology*, 169–89; also Lars
Thunberg, *Man and the Cosmos: The Vision of St. Maximus the Confessor* (Crestwood,
NY: St. Vladimir's Seminary Press, 1985), 137–40.

[42] Tollefsen, *Christocentric Cosmology*, 170–1; cf. Vladimir Lossky, *The Mystical
Theology of the Eastern Church* (Cambridge: James Clarke, 1957), 95, 98.

[43] "The Distinction between Essence and Energy according to Maximus the Confessor," in Constantinos Athanasopoulos and Christoph Schneider, eds., *Divine
Essence and Divine Energies: Ecumenical Reflections on the Presence of God in Eastern
Orthodoxy* (Cambridge: James Clarke, 2013), 251. This is closer to Maximus' precise
language in *Amb. Jo.* 22 (PG 91:1157A).

[44] *A Eucharistic Ontology: Maximus the Confessor's Eschatological Ontology of
Being as Dialogical Reciprocity*, trans. Elizabeth Theokritoff (Brookline, MA: Holy
Cross Orthodox Press, 2010), 100.

that the *logoi* are preexistent in God. On the other hand, he also says that God brought them to their realization in concrete creation, according to the general law of the continual presence of God and of the Logos. In a certain way they are, thus, *both transcendent and immanent.* Yet, this immanence does not invite us to conclude that they are created. As immanent they represent, and are, the presence of the divine intention and principle of every single nature and species ... As realized in the existence of things, they materialize in the created order. Yet they are certainly not themselves created or part of that created order in the sense that they are bound by its material appearance or actual realization.[45]

But from a theo-dramatic perspective, I would argue, the *logoi* altogether constitute also the Logos's "script" in the cosmic drama of his self-revelation. In the last chapter I noted Maximus' penchant for playing on the variant-but-interrelated nuances of *logos/logoi*. On the one hand, the *logoi* are, much like Augustine's *rationes seminales*, principles or signatures of a creature's essence and nature, teleological "codes" that project creatures toward their fulfillment in the divine plan ($\beta o\nu\lambda\acute{\eta}$). On the other hand, they project the dynamic character of the relation between Creator and creation. There is a further sense in Maximus that the *logoi* constitute the benedictory "word" of divine Wisdom in and on creation.

> From all eternity, [the Creator] contained within himself the preexisting *logoi* of created beings. When, in his goodwill, he formed out of nothing the substance of the visible and invisible worlds, he did so on the basis of these *logoi*. By his *word (logos) and his wisdom he created* (Wis. 9:1–2) and continues to create *all things*—universals as well as particulars—at the appropriate time.[46]

In the *logoi*, Christ the Creator-Logos has already *pre-evangelized*, as it were, the whole of creation, and together they recite the Creator's providence and judgment and attest to the depth of his identification with the creation. As such, the *logoi* are necessarily objects of the sustained contemplation ($\theta\epsilon\omega\rho\acute{\iota}\alpha$), or sanctified intuition, that induces in rational creatures a vision of the deeper rhythms and harmonies of creation. On the level of moral and ascetical development, meanwhile, Maximus' preeminent concern is the cosmic struggle of created beings

---

[45] *Man and the Cosmos*, 138.
[46] *Amb. Jo.* 7 (PG 91:1080A), trans. Constas I, 95–7.

(notably rational beings) to align their existential "modes" (τρόποι) with the *logoi* of their nature and thereby find their true rhythm, orientation, and freedom.

## FROM AESTHETICS TO DRAMATICS IN MAXIMUS' COSMOLOGY AND ESCHATOLOGY

Within the groundbreaking modern scholarship on Maximus, it is to von Balthasar's credit to have recognized and amplified the fact that he was not just a scholastic logician obsessed with precise doctrinal definitions, but an aesthetical and "theo-dramatic" theologian concerned for the *form* of the triune God's self-revelation in creation, history, and Scripture. While it would be a stretch to claim that there is a highly conceptually developed theological aesthetics in Maximus, there are clear resonances in his doctrines of creation and revelation of the transformative power of Beauty alongside the other divine transcendentals of Goodness and Truth. His aesthetics is a lively composite of various thematic strands and emphases.[47]

One of these, studied in depth by Torstein Tollefsen,[48] is the cosmological exemplarism inherited broadly from the Christian Platonist tradition extending back to Origen and Clement and redirected in the work of the Cappadocians and Dionysius. Altogether, the *logoi*, as preconceived in the Logos, are the divine forms representing the ideal or potential state of creation. Maximus reaffirms the notion, familiar from Gregory of Nyssa and Augustine, of the "simultaneous" plan of creation projected by the Creator like an Artisan or Architect before he actualized and governed the creation in time and space: "God, as he alone knew how, completed the primary principles of creatures and the universal essences of beings once for all (ἅπαξ)."[49] This exemplarist view of creation as developing according to a primordial

---

[47] An excellent entry into Maximus' theological aesthetics is Tsakiridou, *Icons in Time, Persons in Eternity*, 167–92.

[48] *Christocentric Cosmology*, 21–63.

[49] *Q. Thal.* 2 (CCSG 7:51), trans. Blowers and Wilken, 99–100. See also the discussion in Blowers, *Drama of the Divine Economy*, 159–66.

archetype conveys "beauty" in terms of economy, harmony, and proportionality—identifiable features in Hellenic-Byzantine aesthetics as well as in earlier patristic interpretation of the divine work of creation, which emphasized beauty's teleological aspect, its aspiration toward the final perfection of form. One is reminded of Basil of Caesarea's emphasis on the Creator as an Artisan who, beholding his work, reiterated his primordial blessing of creation as good or "beautiful" (καλόν; Gen. 1:4, 8, 10, 12, 18, 21, 25, 31), a beauty that is "brought to perfection according to the logos of art and that contributes to the usefulness of its end (πρὸς τὴν τοῦ τέλους εὐχρηστίαν)."[50] Such beauty is not reflexive but points beyond itself to the eschatological glory of the cosmos's original Creator.

This teleological or eschatological dimension of Beauty proved decisive for Maximus in making adjustments to the Platonic notion of Beauty as the mimesis of transcendent forms. He was aided by the nuanced perspective on Beauty in the apophatic theologies of Gregory of Nyssa and Dionysius the Areopagite, for whom all beauty in created nature is utterly relativized by the ineffable, infinite Beauty of the triune Creator. Dionysius, while resisting Beauty as a definition of the divine essence, still affirmed that insofar as God was the *source* of all beauty, named "beauty" (τὸ κάλλος) for "calling" (καλοῦν) all creatures back to itself, Beauty effectively indicated God's dignity as Cause and End of all things, as well as his character as the Beloved, the object of all creaturely desire.[51]

In *Ambiguum* 7 Maximus elaborates on this eschatological dimension of divine Beauty in the context of demonstrating how rational creatures can move progressively only toward that which is beautiful and desirable *in and of itself*, that which lies absolutely beyond them since by nature they are neither self-originating, self-moved, nor ends-in-themselves.[52] Specifically he rebukes his opponents (Origenists) on two counts: first, for suggesting that preexistent spiritual beings were able to be distracted from ultimate Beauty—a distraction that could conceivably recur *ad infinitum*; and second, for purporting that spiritual beings were able but unwilling to focus on ultimate Beauty, thereby implying that ultimate Beauty could only be experienced by first engaging with its opposite

---

[50] *Hom. in Hexaemeron* 3.10 (GCS NF 2:55, ll. 7 10).

[51] *Div. nom.* 4.7 (PTS 33:151).

[52] *Amb. Jo.* 7 (PG 91:1069B–1073B), with quotations of Gregory Nazianzen, *Or.* 38.7 (PG 36:317C) and *Or.* 45 (PG 36:628A).

(evil). But ultimate Beauty, as eschatologically deferred, has never been experienced by creatures.[53]

Divine Beauty, moreover, is not a matter of possession but of attraction and of a mysterious elusiveness that draws the creature ever toward it "ecstatically." Maximus owed much on this point to Gregory of Nyssa, who insists that such Beauty can only be enjoyed through spiritually refined "seeing" or contemplation, and that the more purified one's seeing, the more assimilated one becomes to this Beauty. Over time, one "becomes" not only what one wills by free choice but also what one *sees*, "stretching your springtime splendor out to match the everlastingness of your life."[54] Famously, Gregory imagined that only the Creator himself, by gracious condescension, could penetrate the radical gap (διάστημα) between uncreated and created natures, and, without annihilating that gap, paradoxically sate creatures' desire for transcendent Beauty precisely by arousing it, launching them in a ceaseless striving or "epectasy" (ἐπέκτασις).[55] With certain adjustments, Maximus affirms Nyssen's vision of creatures' perpetual progress.[56] This continuing epectasy not only draws out of the creature the latent, protological beauty of its own nature but also opens it to an endless eschatological horizon of transformation and deification, an "ever-moving rest" in the Creator's Beauty and stability.[57]

Maximus' theological aesthetics, both in its teleological and ecstatic dimensions, plays a profound role, no doubt, in the development of his cosmology, but it does not stand in conceptual isolation. It is subservient to his larger project of expounding the christocentric *oikonomia* in ways that honor the canons of apophatic trinitarian theology but that also remain mimetically faithful to the dramatic realism of scriptural

---

[53] *Amb. Jo.* 7 (PG 91:1069B–1072A).

[54] See *Hom. in Canticum Canticorum* 4 (GNO 6:103–7).

[55] e.g. *De vita Moysis* lib. 2 (GNO 7/1:110–20); *Hom. in Canticum Canticorum* 6 (GNO 6:174–5); ibid. 8 (pp. 245–6).

[56] See Paul Blowers, "Maximus the Confessor, Gregory of Nyssa, and the Concept of 'Perpetual Progress,'" *Vigiliae Christianae* 46 (1992): 151–71. Of special interest is *Q. Thal.* 17 (CCSG 7:111–15), which clearly draws from Gregory's *De vita Moysis*. Most striking is the fact that Nyssen's term ἐπέκτασις, a neologism based on the Pauline participle ἐπεκτεινόμενος (Phil. 3:13) and only used once by Gregory (*Hom. in Cant.* 6, GNO 6:174, l. 15), is picked up by Maximus (*Opusc.* 1, PG 91:228B).

[57] Maximus speaks both of "ever-moving rest" (ἀεικίνητος στάσις) (*Amb. Jo.* 67, PG 91:1401A; *Q. Thal.* 59, CCSG 22:53, ll. 131–2) and "stationary identical movement" (στάσιμος ταυτοκινησία) in relation to the Divine (*Q. Thal.* 65, CCSG 22:285, l. 546).

revelation. In his immense trilogy, von Balthasar cites Maximus much more abundantly in his *Theo-Drama* series than in his *Aesthetics* series (*The Glory of the Lord*), and for good reason. In Maximus, Beauty is revealed not simply as isomorphic conformity to the *logoi*, but as *in graceful motion* in the contingencies of history, and so too as insinuating itself into the tension between the *logoi*, fixed in the all-provident Logos, and the *tropoi* or existential modalities of created beings as they strive to validate their respective *logoi*. Beauty unveils itself not solely in a serene contemplative vision uplifting the mind beyond the fray of materiality, but through the dynamics of tragedy, resilience, freedom, and hope that inevitably factor into the creaturely quest for deification.

Let us return to Maximus' *tour de force* in *Ambiguum 7*. Here he notes that in *Oration* 14, on which he is commenting, Gregory Nazianzen had been interested to address, not cosmology per se, but the miseries attending bodily life.[58] "Theoretical" cosmology must strive for insight ($\theta\epsilon\omega\rho\acute{\iota}\alpha$) into the real world, the world teetering between vanity and the hope of transfiguration, and within it the drama of the Creator-Logos reordering the world from chaos and inaugurating the new creation. The dialectics whereby the Logos is understood always to be rescuing creation from chaos or nothingness, while also using that chaos or vanity as the raw material of a new creation, comes into focus in Maximus' commentary in *Ambiguum 8* on another phrase from Gregory's same oration: "But whether the affliction that [the infirm] suffer comes from God is not clear so long as matter bears with it chaos ($\tau\grave{o}$ $\mathring{\alpha}\tau\alpha\kappa\tau o\nu$), as in a flowing stream ($\mathring{\omega}\sigma\pi\epsilon\rho$ $\mathring{\epsilon}\nu$ $\mathring{\rho}\epsilon\acute{\upsilon}\mu\alpha\tau\iota$)."[59] The phrase brings to a head issues of theodicy and of the function of rehabilitative suffering in a teleological perspective, and Maximus picks up on the salient Cappadocian theme of the divine discipline or *paideia* operative through bodily experience. Bodily life, he posits, is an active/passive dialectic of "bearing and being borne along" ($\varphi\acute{\epsilon}\rho o\upsilon\sigma\acute{\alpha}$ $\tau\epsilon$ $\kappa\alpha\grave{\iota}$ $\varphi\epsilon\rho o\upsilon\mu\acute{\epsilon}\nu\eta$) in a flowing stream that, while having an undercurrent of chaos and attrition, nonetheless moves relentlessly forward under divine providence.[60]

---

[58] *Amb. Jo.* 7 (PG 91:1089D–1092A). *Amb. Jo.* 6 and 8 also deal with the liabilities of bodily existence.

[59] Gregory Nazianzen, *Or.* 14.30 (PG 35: 897B); Maximus, *Amb. Jo.* 8 (PG 91:1101Dff.).

[60] On "bearing and being borne along," see *Amb. Jo.* 8 (PG 91:1105B); ibid. 17 (1228C); ibid. 42 (1348D); ibid. 71 (1416B); *Q. Thal.* 64 (CCSG 22:191, l. 67). I have examined this theme in Paul Blowers, "Bodily Inequality, Material Chaos, and the

At the core of this cosmic drama of embodied life, however, is the Logos-Christ himself "playing," maneuvering, piloting his creatures through the vagaries of corporeality in virtue of his own assumption of the flesh and appropriation (οἰκείωσις) of creaturely finitude. With this sublime analogy of the Logos-at-play, Maximus wagers that his "game" (παίγνιον) is one of "projecting intermediate things, poising them equidistant between extremes on account of their flowing and pliable state."[61] These "intermediate things" are the visible created things (and circumstances) that envelop and effectively constitute human life, to which the Logos alone grants stability amid the flux of history:

> This is also a paradox: that stability (στάσις) is seen as constantly flowing and being borne away, an ever-moving flow providentially purposed by God for the improvement (βελτιώσεως) of the beings governed within his economy, enabling those who are disciplined (παιδαγωγούμενους) through this stable flux to be wise, to hope always for transition to a better place, and to have faith in being deified by grace as the goal of this mystery by inclining steadfastly toward God.[62]

Maximus further explains that the "extremes" between which the Logos stabilizes creatures are the substance (cf. Heb. 11:1) of those unseen *future* benefits yet to be manifest for humanity, the very same things that God *originally* effected according to his good purpose (σκοπός) and plan (λόγος).[63] In a striking appeal to Ecclesiastes 1:9,[64] Maximus avers that the Preacher is referring, not to the vanity of historical existence, but to the "first things" (τὰ πρῶτα) and "last things" (τὰ τελευταῖα), the fact that what has been established protologically in God's providence is what will unfold eschatologically.[65] In Maximus' more familiar language, the Logos-Christ *is* in his own right the "beginning" (ἀρχή), "middle" (μεσότης), and "end" (τέλος), the permeating reality of the *oikonomia* who assures the fulfillment of the Creator's purposes.[66]

---

Ethics of Equalization in Maximus the Confessor," in Frances Young, Mark Edwards, and Paul Parvis, eds., *Studia Patristica* 42 (Leuven: Peeters Press, 2006), 51–6.

[61] *Amb. Jo.* 71 (PG 91:1412B).      [62] Ibid. (1412B–C).

[63] Ibid. (1412C–D).

[64] *What is that which has happened? It is that which will happen! And what is that which has been done? It is that which will be done. And there is nothing novel under the sun* (NETS).

[65] *Amb. Jo.* 71 (PG 91:1412D).

[66] *Q. Thal.* 19 (CCSG 7:119); ibid. 22 (CCSG 7:139); cf. Dionysius, *Div. nom.* 5.8 (PTS 33:187).

In yet another provocative image of the Logos's immanent activity in the cosmos, based on figural readings of John the Baptist "leaping" in Elizabeth's womb (Luke 1:41ff.) and David "leaping" at the sight of the Ark (2 Kgdms. 6:16, LXX), Maximus depicts the Logos's hidden activity with humanity in the "womb" ($\mu\acute{\eta}\tau\rho\alpha$) of material creation.

> For it is true—though it may be a jarring and usual thing to say—that both man and the Word of God, the Creator and Master of the universe, exist in a kind of womb, owing to the present condition of our life. In this sense-perceptible world, just as if he were enclosed in a womb, the Word of God appears only obscurely, and only to those who have the spirit of John the Baptist. Human beings, on the other hand, gazing through the womb of the material world, catch but a glimpse of the Word who is concealed within beings (and this, again, only if they are endowed with John's spiritual gifts). For when compared to the ineffable glory and splendor of the age to come, and to the kind of life that awaits us there, this present life differs in no way from a womb swathed in darkness, in which, for the sake of us who were infantile in mind, the infinitely perfect Word of God, who loves God, became an infant.[67]

This image, like that of the Logos-at-play in *Ambiguum* 71, is "playful," and again Maximus explicitly connects it with the Logos's incarnational kenosis. All of the Logos's embodiments, or penetrations of the material world, are *strategies*—either in anticipation of, or in light of, his own experience of incarnation—to quicken and advance his creatures in their quest for deification.

## A DRAMA OF FREEDOM AND DESIRE

In the more systematic forms of Origenism that had taken various shapes in certain Eastern monastic communities from the fourth through the sixth centuries, the plot of the cosmic drama was the struggle of embodied rational creatures ($\tau\grave{\alpha}$ $\lambda o\gamma\iota\kappa\acute{\alpha}$) to resume their noetic dignity as spiritual beings ($\nu\acute{o}\epsilon_S$) amid the constraints and testings experienced in soul and body. The ultimate goal was *apokatastasis*, literally the recovery of *stasis*, the spiritual repose in God that was

---

[67] *Amb. Jo.* 6 (PG 91:1068A–B), trans. Constas I, 71–3.

primordially enjoyed by the *henad*, or pure unity, of spiritual beings. We have seen how Maximus disparaged this myth as misdirected and used it as a foil for his own paradigm of creation as a progressive project of the Creator-Logos (Christ) piloting the cosmos from beginning (ἀρχή) to an unprecedented and transcending end (τέλος). And yet Maximus was not, any more than Origen or Evagrius, preoccupied purely with macro-narratives or grand cosmological schemes. Sacred revelation itself, after all, was focused on the many sub-plots in the cosmic drama, the sobering sagas of angels, peoples, nations, particular persons in contingent circumstances, and the triumphs and tragedies of their respective spiritual journeys. As we observed in Chapter 2, Maximus even produced an interpretive model precisely to engage the diversity of characters in Scripture's complex narratives so as carefully to discern their significance in the larger mystery of the *oikonomia* recapitulated in and by the Logos.[68]

And yet the actual suspense of the drama of creatures' progress toward their appointed *telos* in Maximus (and in Gregory of Nyssa) shares much in common with Origen's cosmology: the challenge before *logika*, creatures of reason and conscience, to use their freedom virtuously, and to realize the fullness of their nature (leading to deification) as encoded in the *logoi* with which they have been gifted. But like the will itself, this freedom is complex. It entails a configuration of faculties of reason, volition, *and desire* that must be habitually reintegrated, reoriented, and pressed to and beyond their capacities.

Philosophically, this freedom is conceived through a carefully nuanced dialectics of activity and passivity. In Maximus' metaphysics of creaturely motion, which exhibits clear if mediated Aristotelian influence,[69] every rational creature, for its own well-being, has an underlying passivity (τὸ πάθος; τὸ πάσχειν) to the superior activity (ἐνέργεια) of the Creator-Logos.[70] As certain Aristotle scholars have emphasized, "passivity" in the Stagirite's philosophy does not denote sheer inactivity but

<hr/>

[68] *Amb. Jo.* 37, discussed on pp. 83–5 in this volume.
[69] On the Aristotelian component in Maximus, see esp. Philipp Gabriel Renczes, *Agir de Dieu et liberté de l'homme: Recherches sur l'anthropologie théologique de saint Maxime le Confesseur* (Paris: Les Éditions du Cerf, 2003); David Bradshaw, *Aristotle between East and West* (Cambridge: Cambridge University Press, 2007), 188–207; Claudio Moreschini, "Sulla presenza e la funzione dell'aristotelismo in Massimo il Confessore," *KOINΩNIA* 28–9 (2004–5): 105–24; and Marius Portaru, "Classical Philosophical Influences: Platonism and Aristotelianism," *OHMC*, 127–48.
[70] *Amb. Jo.* 7 (PG 91:1073B–C).

*the positive capacity to be moved*, the potential for something that can be accomplished by the active agent.[71] For Maximus too, passivity is connected with potentiality and the Creator's gracious power to actualize it,[72] and given the strong teleological vector of his thought, his notion of the basic creaturely passivity to divine activity is informed by the expectation that eschatological deification will itself be a form of sublime passivity.[73] Aristotle had claimed, moreover, that rational beings distinguished themselves from irrational by their capability of resisting the external mover, mitigating the transition from potency to actuality by their own exercise of "desire (ὄρεξις) or choice (προαίρεσις)."[74] This has positive meaning for Maximus as well. Rational creatures must *learn* authentic freedom by conforming their personal choice (προαίρεσις) and "inclination" (γνώμη) to the "natural will" (θέλημα φυσική) and "appetency" (ὄρεξις) for God with which God endowed them—a leitmotif with significant ramifications for Maximus' Christology, anthropology, and ethics. Just as the Logos is providentially active within creatures in the realization of their potential, they too must in turn become active in appropriating and cultivating their freedom, all within the larger *oikonomia* of the triune God and his plan to deify the whole of creation. Maximus provides a rich synopsis in *Questions and Responses for Thalassius* 2:

> God, as he alone knew how, completed the primary principles of creatures and the universal essences of beings once for all. Yet he is still at work, not only preserving these creatures in their very existence (τὸ εἶναι) but effecting the formation, progress, and sustenance of the individual parts that are potential within them. Even now in his providence he is bringing about the assimilation of particulars to universals until he might unite creatures' own voluntary inclination (αὐθαίρετον ὁρμήν) to the more universal natural principle of rational being through the movement of these particular creatures toward well-being (τὸ εὖ εἶναι), and make them harmonious and self-moving in relation to one another and to the whole universe. In this way there shall be no

---

[71] See Helen Lang, *The Order of Nature in Aristotle's Physics: Place and the Elements* (Cambridge: Cambridge University Press, 1998), esp. 47–9. Lang speaks of the "active orientation of potency toward actuality" in Aristotle, and cites William Charlton's notion of the "passive powers" in Aristotle, since "passivity" really means "to be affected" or "to be moved," quite distinct from "to be passive" in colloquial usage.

[72] Maximus notes how creatures long for the gift *of being moved*, like an image that focuses solely on its archetype or something stamped which can only desire the impress of the stamp that fits it (*Amb. Jo.* 7, PG 91:1076B–C; cf. ibid. 10, 1180A).

[73] See Larchet, *La divinisation de l'homme*, 540–5.

[74] *Metaphysica* 1048A.

intentional divergence (γνωμικὴν διαφοράν) between universals and particulars. Rather, one and the same principle (λόγος) shall be observable throughout the universe, admitting of no differentiation by the individual modes (τρόποις) according to which created beings are predicated, and displaying the grace of God effective to deify the universe. It is on the basis of this grace that the divine Logos, when he became man, said, *My Father is working even now, and I am working* (John 5:17). The Father approves this work, the Son properly carries it out, and the Holy Spirit essentially completes both the Father's approval of it all and the Son's execution of it, in order that the God in Trinity might be *through all and in all things* (Eph. 4:6), contemplated as the whole reality proportionately in each individual creature as it is deemed worthy by grace, and in the universe altogether, just as the soul naturally indwells both the whole of the body and each individual part without diminishing itself.[75]

The training of "right reason" (ὀρθὸς λόγος) on creatures' part is critical, no doubt, to this process of learning true freedom,[76] but the most dramatic struggle is the conditioning of will and desire, at the level both of the microcosm of the individual hypostasis and the macrocosm of universal creation. Maximus calls this the "gnomic surrender" (ἐκχώρησις γνωμική),[77] creatures' sustained deliverance to God of their self-interested will, or γνώμη—a term with a history all its own in the Confessor's theology. In his relatively late technical definition of human will from the 640s, *gnômê* is not really a volitional stage, but the "deep-seated desire for those things that are within our power, whence arises choice" (ὄρεξις ἐνδιάθετος τῶν ἐφ᾽ ἡμῖν, ἐξ ἧς ἡ προαίρεσις), or else "a disposition toward what is in our power, over which we have appetitively deliberated" (διάθεσις ἐπὶ ἐφ᾽ ἡμῖν ὀρεκτικῶς βουλευθεῖσι).[78] Most simply put, gnomic will is free will as we rational creatures actually experience it, comprising deliberation and subsequent choice over the proper course of action toward a perceived good. Gnomic will, while morally neutral in its own right, effectively has no baseline or "original innocence" since it found itself precisely in Adam's fall,[79] and he fell at the instant he was created. Gnomic will is therefore volition

---

[75] *Q. Thal.* 2 (CCSG 7:51), trans. Blowers and Wilken, 99–101; cf. ibid. 54 (CCSG 7:451); *Amb. Jo.* 7 (PG 91:1084A–B); *Myst.* 1 (CCSG 69:11).
[76] e.g. *Amb. Jo.* 7 (PG 91:1085D–1088A); *Car.* 1.92 (PG 90:981B); *Or. dom.* (CCSG 23:43, 46, 47).
[77] *Amb. Jo.* 7 (PG 91:1076B–C).      [78] *Opusc.* 1 (PG 91:17C).
[79] *Amb. Jo.* 8 (PG 91:1104A).

already implicated in discerning worthy moral ends and striving to attain them. Maximus eventually would reject its presence in Christ precisely because *gnômê* could connote vacillation and a lack of moral clarity or resolve.

The appetitive and self-interested dimension of *gnômê* problematized it, since it set personal desire (ὄρεξις) in tension with the rule of reason and the mind. And yet Maximus did not dismiss it simply as an unfortunate aberration. Indeed, *gnômê* epitomizes the ambiguity of historical existence. As von Balthasar aptly observes, gnomic decision-making "is limited by the double bind of being forced by one's created condition to make a choice, in order to realize one's being, and yet of having to choose something whose implications one does not fully understand."[80] *Gnômê* thus endures as the agent of moral experience and conditioning in the context of interactions and relations with other created beings.[81] *Gnômê* is necessary for the mind to negotiate, as it were, with the baser faculties of the soul, including the drives of raw desire (ἐπιθυμία) and fervor (θυμός), not just so that reason may rule them but that these baser drives can be integrated and transformed in the context of moral and spiritual progress.

I will return to *gnômê* in later sections of this study, but in my judgment, Maximus preserved its positive aspect, especially in his earlier writings, because, again, it bespoke the existential and experiential dimension of creaturely desire and will. This raises the crucial question: Is *gnômê* intrinsic to creaturely "nature" as such, or rather a self-invented desire or an "acquired" disposition of the will? Maximus calls it *endiathetos*, which can mean "innate" but probably only implies "deep-seated." The question is not resolved by looking at it protologically, since, as noted above, *gnômê* was never innocent of self-interest. *Gnômê* must be interpreted dialectically like creaturely possibility itself. Even if it does not qualify as a natural faculty in the strict sense, it becomes a "resource" of the passible creature in its postlapsarian life. As with Origen and Gregory of Nyssa, freedom has to be constantly reeducated under the guidance of divine providence and judgment, and it is the gnomic will, not the natural will, that needs training in order for the rational creature to attain moral virtuosity. Only later, when the issue of Christ's own human volition

---

[80] *Cosmic Liturgy*, 265.     [81] *Opusc.* 16 (PG 91:193B–C).

comes to the forefront, does Maximus describe *gnômê* more pejora-
tively, as merely a "mode" or "quality" of desiring and willing easily
given to deviance.[82]

An interrelated sub-plot in Maximus' cosmic drama of freedom
was the reorientation of *erôs*, the soul's non-rational love, together
with the soul's passible faculties, which play a vital role in connection
with volitional freedom and the cultivation of virtue. But I reserve this
theme for later discussion, in Chapter 8, where I will explore the
mystery of love and desire in Maximus' vision of the moral and
spiritual life.

## DISTANCE, RECIPROCITY, AND THE OPENNESS OF CREATED NATURE TO DEIFICATION

Over and beyond its metaphysical implications, the Dionysian–
Maximian image of a mutual erotic ecstasy of Creator and creation
framed the drama of the interplay between the uncreated Creator and
the created universe. The Creator's ecstatic movement was manifest, *in
the beginning* (Gen. 1:1), in the act of creating the world *ex nihilo*
according to the archetypal *logoi*. Already here, creation is an act of
divine condescension or kenosis, since the Logos's "incarnation" in the
*logoi* is itself a humbling movement toward the contingent world,[83]
establishing the conditions for reciprocal communion between God and
the cosmos.

Creation *ex nihilo* was a long-debated issue in patristic interpretation, some of it focused on whether the "nothing" from which God
made the cosmos was (1) a vacuum or nonentity out of which God
miraculously and omnipotently produced matter; (2) created matter
in its formless or chaotic state (Gen. 1:2); or (3) matter created already
with incipient form and open to refashioning by the Creator.[84]
Gregory of Nyssa, however, in answering those who insisted that
matter must have originated *outside* God's own being, warned that
such might fuel convictions akin to the Manichaean doctrine of

---

[82] See pp. 164–5 in this volume.
[83] Thunberg, *Microcosm and Mediator*, 81–3.
[84] See Blowers, *Drama of the Divine Economy*, 167–78.

matter as a principle *contrary to* God. Nyssen proposed, in turn, that matter had existence only "from God," insofar as matter had no reality apart from the qualities bestowed on it by God.[85] Dionysius in his turn reads the issue in a strongly apophatic key. The Creator, who is himself honored as "non-being" (τὸ ἀνούσιον)—which is really an "excess of being" (οὐσίας ὑπερβολή)—allows what is formless and non-existent (τὸ μὴ ὄν) a relative participation in his Good even before granting it existence.[86] To equate creation *ex nihilo* with creation *ex Deo* is to acknowledge—worshipfully so—that the God whose "being" is unspeakable, who is "no-thing" among others,[87] has sourced material and spiritual essences as a *pure gift* of love. This God, as Jean-Luc Marion has interpreted Dionysius and Maximus, demands to be acknowledged, not as an idolatrous "Object" of human metaphysical discourses aspiring to comprehend it, but as a "Subject" whose "distance" from creatures invites sheer praise and the embrace of creaturely identity.[88] This distance is, writes Marion, "the positive movement of the Ab-solute, which, through its being set in distance, is ecstatically disappropriated from Itself in order that man might receive himself ecstatically in difference."[89]

Maximus, again following Dionysius, posits that creation *ex nihilo* means foremost that the Creator brought his creatures into being from himself (ἐκ θεοῦ)[90] as "no-thing" among others. For he is

> the sole intelligence of intelligent beings and intelligible things, the meaning behind those who speak and what is spoken, the life of those who live and those who receive life, who is and who becomes for all beings, through whom everything is and becomes but who by himself never is nor becomes in any way anything that ever is or becomes in any manner. In this way he can in no way be associated by nature with any being and thus because of his superbeing is fittingly referred to as nonbeing. For since it is necessary that we understand correctly the difference between God and creatures,

[85] Cf. *Hexaemeron* 7 (GNO 4/1:15–16); *De hominis opificio* 23 (PG 44:209C); ibid. 24 (212D–213C); *De anima et resurrectione* (PG 46:124B–D); cf. Basil, *Hom. in hex.* 1.8 (GCS NF 2:15).

[86] *Div. nom.* 4.3 (PTS 33:146); ibid. 4.7 (PTS 33:152).

[87] Ibid. 5.10 (PTS 33:189); ibid. 7.3 (PTS 33:198).

[88] Nikolaos Loudovikos has, however, criticized Marion's phenomenological approach as overly, even idealistically dismissive of ontology and metaphysics vis-à-vis the divine gift of being. See his *A Eucharistic Ontology*, 7, 38.

[89] *The Idol and Distance: Five Studies*, trans. Thomas Carlson (New York: Fordham University Press, 2001), 139–95, quoted at 153.

[90] *Amb. Jo.* 7 (PG 91:1080A–B).

then the affirmation of superbeing must be the negation of beings, and the affirmation of beings must be the negation of superbeing. In fact both names, being and nonbeing, are to be reverently applied to him although not at all properly. In one sense they are both proper to him, one affirming the being of God as cause of being, the other completely denying, the other completely denying in him the being which all being have, based on his preeminence as cause.[91]

One hears echoes of Dionysius's dictum that "[God] is all things in all things (cf. 1 Cor. 15:28) and he is no thing among things,"[92] and that there is, worthy of praise, "a being-creating procession of the thearchic Source of being into the whole realm of beings."[93] This apophatic interpretation of creation *ex nihilo* does not cancel other meanings, such as God bringing order from the nothingness of formless matter. Rather, it establishes the premise that creation is a *pure gift* out of the "saturating" generosity (to use Marion's terminology) of the unknowable, superessential Creator.

In interpreting Dionysius and Maximus alike, Marion has furthermore averred that the "distance" between unknowable God and human subjects, or between Creator and creation, is a positive absence, a "withdrawal" granting a "space" for creatures to participate in the "mystery of alterity."[94] "Distance brings about separation in order that love should receive all the more intimately the mystery of love. Alterity grows as much as union—solely in distance, anterior and perennial, permanent and primordial."[95]

In Maximus' own terms, this "distance" is the non-negotiable hiatus, or διάστημα, separating Creator and creatures-*ex-nihilo* like an ontological and epistemic fault line. Maximus assumed much from Gregory of Nyssa's articulation of *diastêma* both as the chasm separating the uncreated Trinity from creation, and as the spatio-temporal dimensionality of mutable creation such as also restricts the scope of human knowledge and language.[96] But this same distance—and

---

[91] *Myst.* prooemium (CCSG 69:9, ll. 10–19), trans. Berthold, 185. Cf. *Th. Oec.* 1.4 (PG 90:1084B–C).

[92] *Div. nom.* 7.3 (PTS 33:198). See also Marion's comments on this text in *In Excess*, 140–1.

[93] *Div. nom.* 5.1 (PTS 33:180).    [94] *The Idol and Distance*, 140, 162 et passim.

[95] Ibid., 156.

[96] Maximus declares God as "adiastemic" (ἀδιάστατον) in *Amb. Jo.* 17 (PG 91:1232B); cf. *Myst.* 5 (CCSG 69:25). On *diastêma* as designating spatio-temporal extension, see *Amb. Jo.* 10 (PG 91:1157A); ibid. 15 (1217C); ibid. 17 (1132A); ibid. 41

Maximus often uses the term *diastasis*[97] in conjunction with *diastêma*—is a space, a *horizon*, for participation and communion, ultimately inducing deification but without that frontier ever being fully traversed. Marion is correct that creaturely difference, otherness, is already a pure gift in its own right. Or as von Balthasar puts it, "being different from God," for Maximus, "is [already] a way of imitating him."[98] Indeed, the image (εἰκών) of God (Gen. 1:26–7) in human beings still presupposes this difference, otherwise there would be no space for ongoing assimilation (ὁμοίωσις) to God.[99]

Besides the theological and cosmological conditions of the reciprocity of Creator and creation, Maximus crucially integrates its anthropological and christological dimensions as well, especially in *Ambiguum* 41. Here he sets out five graduated polarities or divisions (διαιρέσεις) respecting created existence (see Figure 2).[100]

Maximus designates the first as the non-negotiable diastemic/diastatic division which defies human knowledge. The other four have to do with the Creator's "orderly arrangement" (διακόσμησις) of the universe, within reach of human contemplation. While the first three divisions in this scheme seem altogether "natural" and the last two appear pertinent more to the postlapsarian state of creation, this is

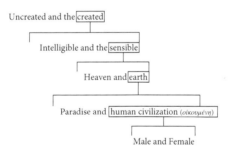

Fig. 2.

(1305C, 1308A); ibid. 42 (1345B, 1348D); ibid. 67 (1397B). On Gregory of Nyssa's multifaceted notion of *diástema*, see esp. Paulos Gregorios, *Cosmic Man: The Divine Presence—The Theology of St. Gregory of Nyssa* (New York: Paragon House, 1988), 67–99.

[97] *Th. Oec.* 1.5 (PG 90:1085A); *Amb Jo.* 41 (PG 91:1305A).

[98] *Cosmic Liturgy*, 87.

[99] For Maximus' distinction between the divine "image" and "likeness" in Gen. 1:26–7, see *Amb. Jo.* 7 (PG 91:1084A); *QD* III, 1 (CCSG 10:170); *Th. Oec.* 1.13 (PG 90:1088B–C); *Q. Thal.* 53 (CCSG 7:435).

[100] *Amb. Jo.* 41 (PG 91:1304D–1305A); see also *Q. Thal.* 48 (CCSG 7:333–5).

another case of Maximus' seamless cosmological perspective. All the
divisions are salutary insofar as they are providentially enjoined. But
Maximus focuses, in fact, more on the *mediation* of these divisions than
the divisions themselves. Humanity mediates them all because of being
a "microcosm," both as a natural "link" (συνδεσμός) between the last
four binaries and as having the vocation actively to mediate all five
binaries through the disciplines of moral, spiritual, and ecclesial life.[101]
Human mediation is meaningless, however, apart from the context of
the supreme mediation of all these binaries in the person and work of
Jesus Christ. The presupposition of all mediation is the simultaneous
two-way movement, within Christ's composite person, of kenotic descent, as Son of God, and recapitulative ascent, as the New Adam
inaugurating a new creation. This eschatologically "simultaneous"
work of Christ will be addressed in more detail in the next chapter.

Crucially for Maximus, the universe is both structurally and existentially directed toward a reciprocal communion between Creator and
creation that demands a redefinition of "being" itself. Marion is correct
that the apophatic posture of Dionysius and Maximus discourages any
ontology or metaphysics that would dare to circumscribe the mystery of
creation conceptually. And yet both writers invested in metaphysics as
expedient to contemplating and expounding the intelligibility of the
world and of creatures' vocations within it. Maximus' reflection on
"natures" and "person" (ὑπόστασις) in Jesus Christ proved instrumental
for his understanding of universal and particular being, and of
the possibility of created nature participating in God. *Ambiguum* 41,
highlighted earlier, is actually Maximus' commentary on Nazianzen's
phrase, "The natures are innovated (καινοτομοῦνται), and God becomes
man."[102] Later in *Ambiguum* 5 he assesses Gregory's additional claim,
from the same oration, that in becoming human, the Savior "innovated
(καινοτομήσας) the laws of natural birth."[103] While fiercely guarding the
inviolability of uncreated and created natures in their own right, Maximus explains that the "innovation" of nature pertains to the new, deified
"mode" (τρόπος) or "regimen" (πολιτεία) of created nature pioneered by

[101] *Amb. Jo.* 41 (PG 91:1305B–C). Cf. Gregory of Nyssa, *Contra Eunomium* 1.270–2
(GNO 1:105–6). Doru Costache ("Seeking Out the Antecedents of the Maximian
Theory of Everything") makes a compelling case that Gregory Nazianzen (*Or.* 38) is
a more important source for *Amb. Jo.* 41 than Gregory of Nyssa.
[102] *Or.* 39.13 (SC 358:164), as in Maximus, *Amb. Jo.* 41 (PG 91:1304D).
[103] *Or.* 39.13 (SC 358:176, l. 8), as in Maximus, *Amb. Th.* 5 (CCSG 48:22, ll. 67–8).
Cf. *Amb. Jo.* 31 (PG 91:1273D–1276D).

Christ.[104] In *Ambiguum* 42, however, he intimates how this break-through applies to *all* of created nature, not just humanity. Christ's innovation is of a piece with the innovations in the behavioral *mode* of natural creatures manifested in the many miracles already recounted in the Old Testament, like elderly women giving birth to children and seas parting in order to provide fugitives safe passage and to drown their pursuers.[105] The ultimate miracle, however, is the inauguration of a *deified* mode of the natures of rational creatures, since deification signifies a boundless eschatological horizon of transformation.

While Maximus asserts that natures as such cannot be innovated, only their existential modes ($\tau\rho\acute{o}\pi\omega\iota$) or performances, there is nonetheless, with respect to created nature ($\varphi\acute{u}\sigma\iota s$), an underlying dynamism. Thus he may equate nature with "essence" ($o\mathring{u}\sigma\acute{\iota}a$) to emphasize ontological stability in beings;[106] but nature as such bespeaks a (universal) essence tending toward hypostatic or particular instantiation. Nature is the theatre of the actualization of movement. As von Balthasar, Nikolaos Loudovikos, Torstein Tollefsen, and Christoph Schneider[107] have all rightly emphasized, moreover, Maximus does not entertain a state of *pura natura* devoid of participation in grace, since nature is already a gift, a grace.[108] Vladimir Lossky doubtless has Maximus in mind when he writes:

> The Eastern tradition knows nothing of "pure nature" to which grace is added as a supernatural gift. For it, there is no natural or "normal" state, since grace is implied in the act of creation itself. The eternal determinations of the "divine Counsel," the divine ideas cannot really be made to correspond with the "essences" of things which are postulated in the so-called natural philosophy of Aristotle and of every other philosopher whose

---

[104] See pp. 201–3 at nn. 111–12 in this volume.

[105] *Amb. Jo.* 42 (PG 91:1341D–1345A, esp. 1344D). See also Irénée-Henri Dalmais, "L'innovation des natures d'après S. Maxime le Confesseur (à propos de *Ambiguum* 42)," *Studia Patristica* 15, ed. Elizabeth Livingstone (Berlin: Akademie-Verlag, 1984), 285–90.

[106] e.g. *Opusc.* 14 (PG 91:149B); ibid. 23 (260D–261A). See also Tollefsen, *Christocentric Cosmology*, 95–104.

[107] See Schneider, "The Transformation of Eros: Reflections on Desire in Jacques Lacan," in Adrian Pabst and Christoph Schneider, eds., *Encounter between Eastern Orthodoxy and Radical Orthodoxy: Transfiguring the World through the Word* (Farnham: Ashgate, 2009), 272: "There is no dichotomy between nature and grace in St. Maximus. Nature is already shot through with grace and primordially designed to find completion and fulfilment in a perpetual striving and progress toward God."

[108] von Balthasar, *Cosmic Liturgy*, 190; Loudovikos, *A Eucharistic Ontology*, 10; also Tollefsen, *Christocentric Cosmology*, 122. See also pp. 201–3 in this volume.

experience reaches only to nature in its fallen state. "Pure nature," for
Eastern theology, would thus be a philosophical fiction corresponding
neither to the original state of creation, nor to its present condition which
is "against nature," nor to the state of deification which belongs to the age to
come. The world, created in order that it might be deified, is dynamic,
tending always toward its final end, predestined in the "thought-wills"
[= *logoi*].[109]

Nature for Maximus is "a capacity, a plan (λόγος), a field and system of
motion," and given its goal-directedness, the boundary between "natural"
and acquired "moral" goodness or beauty is fluid.[110] Teleologically—and
here Maximus closely follows Gregory of Nyssa—nature is the resource
out of which the hypostasis is able, through a grace that pushes out its
frontiers, to move toward deification with ever new virtuosity and
creativity, but always in the context of communion both with God and
with fellow creatures. As Loudovikos observes of Maximus, "nature as
gift is already and always personal, already and always reciprocity; nature
is an eschatological, dialogical becoming and not just a frozen 'given.' Out
of the above context [of reciprocity] nature (along with person) can turn
out to be death, but within it, *nature can be freedom*."[111]

Such an approach to nature and its intrinsic openness to deification is
no purely abstract metaphysical construction. By now it should be clear
that Maximus always maintains attention to the way this openness
unfolds at the personal or hypostatic level as an existential drama in
which the Logos-Christ is multifariously and "playfully" involved. The
particular creature's reciprocal dance or play is, conversely, an entry
into the new *tropos* or *politeia* of which Christ is already the forerunner
by virtue of his incarnation. Its moral, spiritual, and ecclesial-
sacramental dimensions will be taken up in subsequent chapters.


## A "COSMO-POLITEIAN" VISION

We long from Maximus for an overt deliberation on how he saw his
cosmology and *Weltbild* directly addressing the context of Byzantine
imperial and ecclesiastical culture in the seventh century. We have
none, and therefore must cautiously draw inferences, even if they risk

[109] *The Mystical Theology of the Eastern Church*, 101.
[110] von Balthasar, *Cosmic Liturgy*, 146, 147.
[111] Loudovikos, *A Eucharistic Ontology*, 10. See also pp. 188, 317 in this volume.

superficiality. For comparative purposes, however, we may acquire some help from Maximus' contemporary, the Byzantine poet laureate George of Pisidia, who drew on Greek cosmology and the biblical creation narrative in the interest of articulating an imperial cosmology. One of George's epics, the *Hexaemeron* (*c.*630), combines classical rhetorical and literary conventions, knowledge of pagan natural philosophy with spirited criticism thereof, apophatic-doxological discourse revering the biblical Creator, and imagery from the six-day creation story (Gen. 1) in a panegyric extolling the virtual "recreation" of the world through the grandiose military and political exploits of the Emperor Heraclius. George seeks to reinforce Christianity's cultural victory and domestication of the Greek intellectual tradition, and he undertakes a serious theological vindication of the Christian cosmogony and worldview, but his cosmology is culminated by a strong political eschatology. Whereas Christ's wooden cross defeated the forces of chaos once for all, Heraclius's wooden spear put down the Persians, instating a glorious new imperial stability. Heraclius, in the image of Christ, is the "cosmic deliverer" (κοσμορύστης).

George's vision is "cosmopolitan" in the sense of rallying the panoply of resources of his Greco-Byzantine culture to retell the cosmic story as political myth, with Constantinople as its new center of gravity. For Maximus, as we have seen, the only true resource for the transfiguration of creation is created nature itself, endowed with its own dramatic "script," the *logoi* of all things, being authored and enacted by the Logos-Christ through his multiple embodiments, and most decisively through his incarnation, death, resurrection, and glorification—all as the final recapitulation of God's creative purposes. The new mode, or *tropos*, of creaturely being that Christ has opened up applies not just to angels and humans but to all creatures, even if Maximus' primary focus is on rational creatures as the principal *dramatis personae* along with the Logos in the still-unfolding drama of the cosmos.

Maximus' vision is "cosmopolitan" in the sense that all creatures, seen and unseen, are called to participate in the new, unprecedented *politeia* of Jesus Christ. Maximus uses this terminology in expounding Dionysius's controversial idea of a single "theandric activity" (θεανδρικὴ ἐνέργεια) observable in how Christ actually conducted his life (πολιτευσάμενος) on earth.[112] "A way of life (πολιτεία)," says Maximus,

---

[112] *Amb. Th.* 5 (CCSG 48:29, ll. 204–5; 30, ll. 211–12), commenting on Dionysius, *Ep.* 4 (PTS 36:161).

"is life lived according to the law of nature," and since Christ was in two natures, he concurrently observed the laws proper to each. His *politeia* was new "not simply because it is strange and astounding to those on earth, and without precedent in the nature of beings, but because it constitutes the form of the new energy as newly lived out by him."[113] Beyond its properly christological significance, however, the new "theandric activity" represents to Maximus the Creator-Christ's prerogative in opening up new possibilities for created nature. Christ's lived *politeia* presupposes his authority to work through the "law of nature" on behalf of all creatures. As Maximus indicates elsewhere, Christ the Logos alone authors and integrates the "three laws" of *nature, Scripture, and grace* in the history of his dealing with his creatures,[114] so that the true fulfillment of the law of nature is already implicated with the fulfillment of the other two in the *politeia* of each and every creature.[115] As we saw in the previous chapter, this is how Maximus proposes that we read Scripture, with an eye to the complex interactions of particular creatures who altogether unveil the salvific rule of the Logos-Christ.[116]

We need not look here for any overtly political meaning of this *politeia*. In early Christian usage, *politeia* typically denoted the Christian way of life or moral-spiritual regimen. It could indicate Christian moral discipline over against pagan, or the rigorous vocation of the monastic life.[117] Dionysius said that Christ had "fashioned the way of life" (πεπολιτευμένος) of the "new theandric energy" in his incarnation,[118] and that Scripture had revealed the "divinely delivered and theo-mimetic regimens of life" (θεοπαραδότους καὶ θεομιμήτους πολιτείας) appropriate to Christ's disciples.[119] Colm Luibheid translates this phrase "god-given and god-imitating communities," which Paul Rorem further sees as referring to the biblical Acts of the Apostles and their testimony to the apostolic churches.[120] This rendering would

---

[113] Ibid. (CCSG 48:32–3, ll. 260–6), trans. Constas I, 55.

[114] Cf. *Q. Thal.* 19 (CCSG 7:119, ll. 7–30); ibid. 39 (p. 259, ll. 14–45).

[115] I take *politeia* to be a cosmologically, christologically, and ascetically amplified synonym for Maximus' much more common phrase the "existential mode" (τρόπος ὑπάρξεως) of a creature.

[116] *Amb. Jo.* 37, discussed on pp. 83–5 in this volume.

[117] See G. E. H. Lampe, ed., *A Patristic Greek Lexicon*, s.v. πολιτεία (Oxford: Oxford University Press, 1961), 1113–14.

[118] *Ep.* 4 (PTS 36:161).     [119] *Eccl. hier.* 3.3.4 (PTS 36:83).

[120] *Pseudo-Dionysius: The Complete Works*, Classics of Western Spirituality (New York: Paulist Press, 1987), 214 and n. 78 (Rorem has supplied the notes for Luibheid's translation).

seem better to translate πολιτεύματα than πολιτείας, though the latter can certainly carry communal overtones. Dionysius's notion of theomimesis, however, is cosmic as well as ecclesial, as it applies to all beings from the Seraphim in the celestial hierarchy down to the lowliest neophyte in the Church.[121] In Maximus' cosmic Christology, built on the foundation of the particular *politeia* of Jesus in the Gospels as well as on his universality as the Logos-Christ, the term could now apply to all creatures as interconnected "citizens" of the cosmic ecclesia, aspiring denizens of the new creation, summoned to play out their diverse roles in a theatre bridging heaven and earth, a theatre not constrained or circumscribed by the boundaries of empire.[122] In the Church, meanwhile, the Christian *politeia*, symbolized in the *Corner Gate* of Jerusalem (2 Chron. 26:9), is the gate at which "the insightful mind builds, like strong and noble towers, the fortresses of the divine doctrine of the incarnation, composed of the *stones* of different concepts, along with virtuous conduct to secure the fulfillment of the commandments."[123]

I do not wish to suggest, then, that this "cosmo-politeian" perspective rises to the level of an anti-imperial ideology deployed by Maximus to motivate the monastic dissent against the Empire in the monothelete crisis from the 640s on. But one can scarcely deny that it induced a sober "triumphalism from within," and the "theoretical" (θεωρητική, i.e. spiritually *visionary*) inspiration for an ascetical regimen which, altogether bound up with dogmatic and devotional allegiance to Christ the true Pantocrator, empowered conspiratorial actions that overtly challenged imperial presumptions. Christ's "rule" (ἀρχή), says Maximus, was embodied in the cross he hoisted on his shoulders, a cross that "afterward he gave . . . to another to bear, indicating through these things that whoever is entrusted with governing must first lead those who are governed, by complying with all the rules of government (for only thus will his own rulings be acceptable), and then he can issue directives to those who have been entrusted to him to perform the same things."[124] We might be tempted here to assume that Maximus is

---

[121] Cf. *Cael. hier.* 7.2 (PTS 36:29); *Eccl. hier.* 2.3.6 (PTS 36:77). On this theomimesis in Dionysius, see also Alexander Golitzin, *Mystagogy: A Monastic Reading of Dionysius Areopagita* (Collegeville, MN: Liturgical Press/Cistercian Publications, 2013), 186–8.

[122] See *LA* (CCSG 40:121), encouraging Christians to embrace their "citizenship" (πολίτευμα) in heaven while still on earth.

[123] *Q. Thal.* 48 (CCSG 7:339–41, ll. 165–72).

[124] *Amb. Jo.* 32 (PG 91:1284B).

referring to the rule of Christ devolving onto an emperor or patriarch. His image of Christ with the cross hoisted on his shoulders is altogether reminiscent of the celebrated sixth-century Christ Militant mosaic in the Archiepiscopal Chapel in Ravenna. The mosaic depicts the Savior bearing his cross like a military standard or weapon and treading on beasts who represent evil powers in the world that threaten empire and church. But Maximus clarifies that he is really speaking of all who imitate Jesus's own rule in the form of ascetical praxis and *apatheia*. For the crucified Christ solicits all human beings, who already bear "christoformity" (ἡ χριστοειδὴς κατάστασις) within them, also to govern their lives in a *cruciform* way.[125] The transfiguration of the cosmos first takes shape as a revolution that Christ inaugurates from within the moral and spiritual life of rational creatures. Any political ramifications of this christoform and cruciform *politeia* would necessarily be wholly derivative of the upheaval that Christ himself has erupted in the world from top to bottom.

---

[125]  Ibid. (1285A); and on this "christoformity," see also ibid. 38 (1300A).

# 4

## Maximus' Cosmic Christology: Flesh Transfiguring the World

Always, and in all things, the Logos, who is God, desires to realize the mystery of his embodiment.

—Maximus, *Ambiguum ad Johannem 7*

### A CHALCEDONIAN "LOGIC"?

Assessing the full development of Maximus' doctrine of Christ, from early writings where dogmatic Christology was not always front and center, to later works of the monothelete controversy in which it dominated, scholars have looked for an organizing principle to make sense of the whole and to demonstrate the centrality of Christology in his thought. A sizeable body of scholarship has supported the thesis, as propounded by von Balthasar and Thunberg among others, that the Council of Chalcedon (451), with its canonical definition of Jesus Christ as one person in two unconfused natures, provided Maximus with a "logic" of union and distinction that applied broadly across his doctrine.[1] Melchisedec Törönen has offered a rare but serious challenge to this consensus. "It is like taking a photograph of a landscape while focusing on a nearby signpost: important as the signpost is, it blurs the view of the landscape."[2]

---

[1] e.g. von Balthasar, *Cosmic Liturgy*, 207–8; Thunberg, *Microcosm and Mediator*, 21–48, 426–7, 430–1; id., *Man and the Cosmos*, 64, 66, 71–2, 143; Louth, *Maximus the Confessor*, 49–51; Tollefsen, *Christocentric Cosmology*, 100, 200–14.

[2] *Union and Distinction*, 2.

Törönen's criticism has merit. After all, how can we hold Maximus to a single "Chalcedonian" template when his train of thought often closely tracks with his cherished pre-Chalcedonian Christian sources, especially the Cappadocian Fathers, and when he so obviously makes use of non-Christian (namely Neoplatonic and Aristotelian) sources in his logic and metaphysics?[3] It is especially problematic to insist on a strictly Chalcedonian logic in early works where his christological thinking is so intricately and organically tied up with multifarious cosmological, anthropological, and spiritual-doctrinal issues, and where he shows some sympathy with the concerns of miaphysites about the integrity of Christ's concrete person. On the other hand, the Confessor's devotion to Chalcedon does indeed often bleed through, such as when he reads Dionysius the Areopagite as indisputably faithful to Chalcedonian Christology,[4] or when he applies various qualifiers from the Chalcedonian definition (e.g. "unconfused," ἀσύγχυτος) to the overall inviolability of uncreated and created natures as a matter of cosmological principle.[5] There is little question, moreover, that Chalcedon helps to frame the "reciprocity" between Creator and creation discussed in the previous chapter.[6] But I find more compelling Cyril O'Regan's suggestion that for Maximus, Chalcedon still protects the genuine *mystery* of Jesus Christ, that its definition is a "semantic density that far from closing off investigation actually encourages it," like a "dense knot, both visionary and interpretive, that demands unravelling."[7] Only later, in the heat of the debate over wills in Christ, does Maximus appear relatively more scholastic about a Chalcedonian model of union and distinction.

Recalling Vittorio Croce's characterization of Maximus' theological method operating according to the dual coordinates of "tradition" and "research,"[8] this tradition as such is both broader and older than Chalcedon. Maximus draws heavily from Irenaeus's doctrine of recapitulation, for example, not because it provides a proto-Chalcedonian

---

[3] See ibid., 11–43 on Maximus' indebtedness to logical "tools" drawn from Neoplatonism.

[4] *Amb. Th.* 5 is exemplary here.

[5] e.g., *Amb. Jo.* 7 (PG 91:1077C); ibid. 10 (1176C, 1189A); ibid. 21 (1245A); *Myst.* 1 (CCSG 69:11).

[6] See also Thunberg, *Man and the Cosmos*, 71–91.

[7] "Von Balthasar and Thick Retrieval: Post-Chalcedonian Symphonic Theology," *Gregorianum* 77 (1996): 246–7.

[8] Referenced in this volume on p. 78 and n. 51.

definition of Christ's person but because it is a proven model that effectively interconnects Christology with creation, anthropology, and cosmic redemption. Even more basically, we do well to remember Maximus' devotion to the fecundity and inexhaustibility of sacred Scripture, the "literal" (i.e. *theologically* literal) meaning of which, he says, "is always abounding into its fullness."[9] The saturating power of revelation defies the Church's ability to encapsulate it, even in dogmatic definitions produced by ecumenical councils. Chalcedon was crucial to Maximus, not as possessing absolute conceptual or linguistic finality, but as doing a fundamental justice to the complexion of the mystery of Christ as the mystery of the world.

We have frequented christological themes in the previous two chapters, but the goal of this chapter is to set out an enhanced portrait of the "cosmic Christology" of Maximus that integrates his earlier and later writings and provides vital connecting tissue for his theology as a whole. Indeed, Maximus' fierce pro-Chalcedonian defense of the two wills of Christ in the monothelete crisis, which led at last to his imperial punishment, cannot be understood apart from the accumulated constellation of doctrinal insights with which it was bound up. Without this truly *cosmic* perspective, that defense could all too easily appear like a last sophistic hurrah or scholastic pedantry at the culmination of a debate on mere christological technicalities.

## THE ESCHATOLOGICALLY SIMULTANEOUS "INCARNATIONS" OF CHRIST THE LOGOS

Incarnation and embodiment are complex concepts in Maximus. A good place to begin is with his reassertion of the ancient notion, coming from the second-century *Shepherd of Hermas* and echoed by numerous intervening patristic thinkers, that the Creator "contains" or "encloses" the world but is not himself contained or enclosed.[10] For Maximus, this idea expresses not only the ontological transcendence of the Creator, but also his active circumscription of creation

---

[9] *Q. Thal.* 17 (CCSG 7:111).
[10] *Th. Oec.* 1.6 (PG 90:1085A–B). For other patristic reiterations of this notion, see Blowers, *Drama of the Divine Economy*, 79–80, n. 42.

and its history,[11] and so too his freedom to *penetrate* his creation
whenever, wherever, and however he so wills. The Creator both
fiercely upholds the integrity of created nature and renders it permeable to his gracious interventions. Furthermore, as we have previously
observed, divine incarnation or embodiment is already intrinsic, in
Maximus' neo-Irenaean perspective, to the plan and actualization of
creation, both in the sense that the Creator-Logos has condescended
to embody himself in the preexistent *logoi* of all creatures, and in the
sense that the Logos—as *Christ and Savior*—is charged to bear in the
flesh the hope and future of the world, the mystery of deification.
As Maximus reiterates in *Ambiguum* 42:

> For all the divine mysteries are surpassed by the mystery of Christ, and
> this mystery is definitive of every conceivable perfection in all things
> either present or to come, and it exists above and beyond every limit
> and boundary. Now this mystery teaches us that the body of God the
> Word—which was taken from us and which is consubstantial with us,
> and which was united to Him in a union according to hypostasis when
> he assumed flesh and perfectly became man—is the same body with
> which he ascended into the heavens, *far above all rule and authority and
> power and dominion, and above every name that is named, not only in
> this age but also in that which is to come* (Eph. 1:21), so that now and for
> infinite ages He is seated together with God the Father, *having passed
> through* all *the heavens* (Heb. 4:14) and *surpassing all* (Eph. 4:10) things,
> and he shall come again to refashion and transform the universe, and
> for the salvation of our souls and bodies, just as we have believed and
> believe and will continue to believe forever.[12]

Meanwhile Maximus' provocative statement at the heading of this
chapter—"Always, and in all things, the Logos, who is God, desires
to realize the mystery of his embodiment (ἐνσωματώσεως τὸ
μυστήριον)"[13]—is essentially shorthand for the *mysterium Christi* as
a whole in his theology. The statement is both *protological*, tying
embodiment to the Creator's original will in creation, and *eschatological*,

---

[11] *Th. Oec.* 1.10 (PG 90:1085D–1088A): "God is the beginning, middle, and end of
beings in that he is active and not passive, as are all others, which we so name. For he
is beginning as Creator (δημιουργός), middle as Provider (προνοητής), and end as
Goal (τέλος), for it is said, *From him and through him and for him are all beings*
(Rom. 11:36)" (trans. Berthold, 130).

[12] *Amb. Jo.* 42 (PG 91:1332C–D), trans. Constas II, 155. Cf. *Q. Thal.* 60 (CCSG
22:75–7).

[13] *Amb. Jo.* 7 (PG 91:1084C–D).

anticipating the consummation when God will be *all in all* (1 Cor. 15:28). Comparing Maximus with Irenaeus, as I did in the preceding chapter, the primeval act of creation is not simply the temporal beginning of the divine *oikonomia* but even more basically a staging point on the way to revealing the fullness of the Word and Wisdom of God, Jesus Christ. In this perspective, creation and salvation are ongoing, seamlessly interconnected aspects of the single divine initiative, or *energeia*, God's urge to share his glory with an "other." Embodiment, in turn, is the Creator's primary strategy to preserve, renew, and transfigure that created other, drawing it into the ever more intimate communion with himself that is deification. God's embodiment has to do with transgressing and "inhabiting" the very diastemic space that he has opened for the created other. It has to do with the Creator's kenotic pledge, his commitment to penetrate corporeality in all its diversity, complexity, and tragedy, and to dignify the role of materiality and historical concreteness in his Kingdom.

God's embodiment is larger, but not qualitatively greater, than his enfleshment in Jesus of Nazareth. I have touched in earlier chapters on the conjoint "incarnations" of the Logos in the *logoi* (words, letters, figures, meanings) of Scripture and the *logoi* (constitutive principles) of creation. Maximus holds together Scripture and creation as mutual, even interchangeable, economies of the material self-manifestation of the Logos. And yet he looks precisely to the Transfiguration, a crucial event in the ministry of the *historically incarnate* Word, as key to envisioning his other incarnations.[14] Already, as incarnate, Christ is a "type and symbol of himself" since his flesh uniquely conveys his divine glory, his hidden infinity.[15] As transfigured, then, he is an all the more intensive symbol of himself, as his blinding face/flesh signals his ineffable divinity while his radiant garments signify his glory concealed within the material Scriptures and within the fabric of creation.[16] He is a symbol of himself because his transfiguration is a gestured, embodied, theophanic demonstration of his fiat, his prerogative as Word and Wisdom of God to work through any means he so wills to reveal and to share his glory. Effectively Maximus redeems Origen's depiction of

---

[14] See my earlier discussion of the significance of the transfiguration for Maximus, pp. 79–82 in this volume.

[15] *Amb. Jo.* 10 (PG 91:1165D–1168A).

[16] Ibid. 10 (PG 91:1128A–C). See also Riou, *Le monde et l'église*, 108–9; Törönen, *Union and Distinction*, 5; Lollar, *To See into the Life of Things*, 255–62. This description of the transfigured Lord as a "symbol of himself" became a point of interpretive conflict centuries later in the hesychast controversy (see pp. 304–5 in this volume).

the symbolic dimension of the transfiguration by privileging even more profoundly the incarnational sacramentality of the symbol itself.

For Maximus, moreover, the different embodiments or incarnations of the Logos are, in an eschatological perspective, *simultaneous*. This is especially clear in *Questions and Responses for Thalassius* 22, where he reflects on the Creator's wise division of "ages" (αἰῶνες) of incarnation and deification. The former refers broadly to those ages "intended for the outworking of the mystery of God's embodiment" and "predetermined in God's purpose for the realization of his becoming human," which have already *come upon us* (1 Cor. 10:11) and reached their term in the incarnation of Christ. The latter refer to the new and future ages in which God *will show the immeasurable riches of his goodness to us* (Eph. 2:7).[17] But Maximus, astute to the complexity of biblical language about times and ages, understands that in the perspective of what scholars now call Paul's "realized eschatology," which defies pure chronological sequence, there is overlap between history and eternity.[18] It may be epistemologically helpful to distinguish *consecutive* ages of incarnation and deification, but Maximus is actually suggesting that the incarnation of Christ, far from putting a chronological end to a series of ages that are now destined simply to give way to a new series, is the final goal of the totality of time, since he is *simultaneously* the "beginning (ἀρχή), middle (μεσότης), and end (τέλος) of all the ages, past and future," and now we only know him as the end-come-upon-us "in potency through faith."[19] Maximus presumes that the ages of the "mystery of divine embodiment" began at creation and continue even after Christ's advent since the Creator is always working to deify the creation until the final consummation of the world. The ages of deification, moreover, cannot be relegated purely to a trans-temporal eternity since deification has been the operative goal of divine embodiment and creativity from the beginning.

In sum, time and eternity have converged in Jesus Christ, and in him the fullness of divine embodiment and the fullness of creaturely deification have arrived, and the Church now dwells in the relative "meantime" until the full effects of Christ's recapitulative work are

[17] *Q. Thal.* 22 (CCSG 7:137–9), trans. Blowers and Wilken, 115–18.
[18] Maximus specifies that these are "'ages' not as we normally conceive them" (*Q. Thal.* 22, CCSG 7:137, ll. 23–7). See also Paul Blowers, "Realized Eschatology in Maximus the Confessor, *Ad Thalassium* 22," in Elizabeth Livingstone, ed., *Studia Patristica* 32 (Leuven: Peeters, 1997), 258–63.
[19] *Q. Thal.* 22 (CCSG 7:139), trans. Blowers and Wilken, 117.

revealed. Thus Maximus can speak of the Logos's continuing embodiment sacramentally in the Church and in the saints. A major theme of his spiritual theology is the "incarnation" of Christ in the virtues of the Christian, a sign that the mystery of divine embodiment and deification plays out sacramentally in the fruition of personal faith and the *imitatio Christi*.[20] For Maximus, then, the "body" of the divine Word is a complex theological construction, the intersection of all the Logos's different incarnations, of which Jesus Christ is indubitably definitive.[21]

## JESUS OF NAZARETH: UNIVERSALITY AND PARTICULARITY

I hasten to re-emphasize that Maximus' Christology is not simply reducible to a methodical defense of Chalcedon, since it connects with so many other themes besides the internal convergence of divinity and humanity in Christ. It is helpful to see the Confessor's developing Christology as a "thick" logic with concurrent and intersecting tracks: natures and hypostasis (person), universals and particulars, macrocosm and microcosm. I will have more to say in the next section about the enormous issue of natures and hypostasis. But first I will say a word about his blending of "universality" and "particularity" in a cosmic-christological context.

Von Balthasar, Tollefsen, and Törönen have especially enhanced this dimension of Maximus' thought.[22] "Universal being, for Maximus," von Balthasar writes, "is in no sense simply the (higher-ranked) ground

[20] On this theme of Christ's incarnation in the Christian's virtues, see *Amb. Jo.* 7 (PG 91:1081D); *Amb. Th.* Prol. (CCSG 48:3); *Or. dom.* (CCSG 23:59); *Car.* 4.76 (PG 90:1068A); *Q. Thal.* Intro. (CCSG 7:23); ibid. 22 (p. 143); ibid. 40 (p. 273); ibid. 41 (p. 281); ibid. 61 (CCSG 22:105). On virtue as the 'flesh' of the Logos, see *Q. Thal.* 33 (CCSG 7:239–41); 40 (p. 273); cf. Evagrius, *Ad Monachos* 118–20. On the Logos's 'proportional' indwelling of the virtuous (1 Cor. 9:22), see *Q. Thal.* 47 (CCSG 7:325). See also Luis Joshua Salés, "Divine Incarnation through the Virtues: The Central Soteriological Role of Maximos the Confessor's Aretology," *St. Vladimir's Theological Quarterly* 58 (2014): 159–76.
[21] See Cooper's magisterial study, *The Body in Maximus the Confessor*, esp. 36–48, 117–64.
[22] Von Balthasar, *Cosmic Liturgy*, 154–65; Tollefsen, *Christocentric Cosmology*, passim.

of particular being, as it would be for Neoplatonic thinking, but it is equally its effect, its result. Its changeless stability (διαμονή) is not self-sufficiency but is also something supported from below, *something always newly brought into being (γένεσις) from particularity.*"[23] Indeed, the unity of the cosmos in Jesus Christ is not simply a transcendent universal pattern ontologically "downloaded" into particular created beings, and into the parts within those beings, but a movement "from below" among those differentiated beings/parts to achieve new integrity and solidarity such as enriches the whole universe. Maximus describes this as the ongoing "work" of the Creator in John 5:17:

> Even now in his providence [the Creator] is bringing about the assimilation of particulars to universals until he might unite creatures' own voluntary inclination to the more universal natural principle of rational being through the movement of these particular creatures toward well-being (τὸ εὖ εἶναι), and make them harmonious and self-moving in relation to one another and to the whole universe.[24]

Here as ever, Christ leads the way. It is no coincidence that in discussing the polarities in the universe bridged or reconciled by Christ (uncreated and created; intelligible and sensible; heaven and earth; paradise and inhabited earth; and male and female), Maximus describes Christ's mediation of them *from below*, beginning with male and female.[25] Leaving aside for now the question of whether sexual division was original to universal human nature or superadded in God's prevision of the Adamic fall, the point here is that Christ's reconciliation of sexual distinction is no abstraction in Maximus' thinking. The person of the Creator-Logos kenotically interacted with the (particular) historical person of the Virgin Mary to enable his human birth apart from sexual passion, thus overcoming the moral alienation between male and female precipitated by sexual desire and pleasure.[26]

Maximus' depiction of Christ's other cosmic mediations is squarely grounded in the Gospel accounts of Jesus's ministry and acts. He revels in the fact that a particular (albeit thoroughly deified) human being—

[23] *Cosmic Liturgy*, 159, 238 (emphasis added).
[24] *Q. Thal.* 2 (CCSG 7:51); the fuller text is quoted on pp. 121–2 in this volume.
[25] *Amb. Jo.* 41 (PG 91:1309A–B, 1313C–D).
[26] On the soteriological dynamics of Jesus's virginal conception and birth, cf. *Or. Dom.* (CCSG 23:35–6); *Amb. Jo.* 31 (PG 91:1276A–B); *Amb. Th.* 5 (CCSG 48:26); *Opusc.* 20 (PG 91:240B).

"my Jesus, who is God and the sole cause of all things"[27]—can, out of a particular historical and cultural location, bear the weight of the very plan of creation and the full mystery of creation's redemption and deification. Christ mediates the divide between "paradise and inhabited earth"—that is, between creatures' innocent state and the postlapsarian condition in which humanity struggles to civilize and govern itself—by his sanctifying human demeanor and his breakthrough to paradise with the thief at his death (Luke 23:43). And this, together with Christ's bodily appearance among his disciples after his resurrection, effectively erased any empirical distinction between paradise and inhabited earth.[28] Maximus does not dwell at length on this mediation. The modern interpreter might want to see here an idealized "return to paradise," but it points, like the mediation between male and female, rather to the *present* inauguration of the new creation as an existential reality.[29]

Christ's third and fourth mediations, again from below, consist in his ascension into heaven (Luke 24:51; Acts 1:9) and even through the intelligible hierarchies. Entering the heavens in his transformed earthly body, he reconciles heaven and earth. The fact that he ascends as the perfect human being, with soul and body thoroughly bonded, demonstrates his fusion of sensible and intelligible realms and his authentication of the primary universal principle (λόγος) integrating all creation.[30] Certainly there is the sense here that Christ is working to restore humanity to its "original" vocation in creation as a bridge between sensible (material) and intelligible (spiritual) reality. And yet this cannot simply be the reversion to a lost primal glory—not if we take seriously Maximus' realism about the fall of Adam, who never really actualized this human vocation since he instantly squandered

---

[27] *Amb. Jo.* 31 (PG 91:1276D–1277A), trans. Constas II, 43.

[28] *Amb. Jo.* 41 (PG 91:1309B); *Q. Thal.* 48 (CCSG 7:333–5).

[29] For suggestive interpretation of Paradise and the οἰκουμένη here, see Doru Costache, "Going Upward with Everything You Are: The Unifying Ladder of St. Maximus the Confessor" (in Romanian), in Basarab Nicolescu and Magda Stavinschi, eds., *Science and Orthodoxy: A Necessary Dialogue* (Bucharest: Curtea Veche, 2006), 135–44, at 140–3; Eng. trans. by author, available at <https://www.academia.edu/ 1077440/The_Unifying_Ladder_of_St_Maximus_the_Confessor_Going_Upwards_ with_Everything_You_Are>. See also Thunberg, *Microcosm and Mediator*, 381–91, who notes the decisive reference to Christ's death as the means of entry into paradise, recalling a longstanding patristic tradition connecting his entry into paradise with his descent into hell.

[30] *Amb. Jo.* 41 (PG 91:1309B–C).

his sensate nature. Christ's work is an eschatological achievement from within the Adamic history, completing the Old Adam as he realizes the New Adam.

Christ's fifth mediation is when, at the term of his ascension, he sums up "the whole plan (βουλή) of God the Father for us" and presents his new eschatologically transfigured humanity *before the face of God* (Heb. 9:24), an enthronement that seals the union-in-distinction of uncreated and created natures. As he describes it, the incarnate and glorified Word has effectively re-embodied creation through his intense intimacy with it:

> with us and for us he encompassed the extremes of the whole creation through the means, as his own parts, and he joined them around himself, each with the other, tightly and indissolubly... since like us he possesses a body, sense perception, soul, and intellect, to which (as his own parts), he associated individually the extreme that was thoroughly akin to each one of them (i.e. his parts), ... and he recapitulated in himself (cf. Eph. 1:10), in a manner appropriate to God, all things, showing that the whole creation is one, as if it were another human being, completed by the mutual coming together of all its members.[31]

These five mediations focus especially on the high points of the Logos's incarnate ministry, from his virgin birth to his death, resurrection, ascension, and session in heaven. But there is much in between these events in the Gospel narratives, and Maximus finds constant signals in these too of Christ's Lordship in the cosmos and his fresh creative and redemptive activity. His temptations in the wilderness, for example, were but a single episode in a universal war against the spiritual forces of evil that attended his earthly work. Since the evil powers were hiding, as it were, behind the universal law of nature in its present condition (i.e. the law as accommodating sexuality and bodily passibility), and since they knew Jesus as a passible human being, they bombarded him from the outset until, after a lifelong resistance, he put to death the "powers and principalities" (Col. 2:15) on his cross.[32] Over and beyond his divine impeccability, he *used his natural human passibility* as an individual human being to conquer vice and to give a new orientation to universal creaturely *pathos*, "healing the passibility associated with

---

[31] Ibid. (PG 91:1309C–1312B; quoted at 1312A), trans. Constas II, 113–15. For the analogy of creation as *makranthrôpos*, see also *Myst.* 7 (CCSG 69:33–6).
[32] *Q. Thal.* 21 (CCSG 7:127–33).

pleasure" by his divinized free choice (κατὰ προαίρεσιν) rather than by mere deliberation (γνώμη).[33]

By his teaching in parables (Matt. 13:34), Jesus acted as the incarnate Logos who "thickens" himself (πανύχεται) by indwelling at once the differences among created beings and the complexities of human language. For he accommodated himself not only to the *logoi* of beings but also the *logoi* that are words, sounds, syllables, so as to render the world intelligible. Through the precision of his parables he granted access to unspeakable mysteries. Here too we see his salutary combination of particularity and universality, since, by hiding himself in the *logoi* (principles/words) Christ "is obliquely signified in proportion to each visible thing, as if through certain letters, being whole in whole things while simultaneously remaining utterly complete and fully present, whole, and without diminishment in each particular thing."[34] As Logos, he is the saturating meaning of all things, and wields the power to overwhelm language by transgressing the *diastêma* that delimits human communication and knowledge; but, to recall Maximus' paradox from *Ambiguum* 71, the Word operates "playfully" from "on high" (αἰπύς) precisely through his weakness from below.[35]

In his miracles, Jesus performed actions of an individual human being, but he did so "divinely" (θεϊκῶς) just as he also did divine things "humanly" (ἀνθρωπικῶς) or "carnally" (σαρκικῶς) within his composite person.[36] And yet these wonders often revealed his creative and redemptive resourcefulness beyond the momentary marvel, such as when he walked on water (Matt. 14:26) and demonstrated his power not just to light upon an unstable substance but also to command the element of water itself, "innovating" its universal nature by a particular act on particular water in a particular historical episode on the Sea of Galilee.[37] The drama of Jesus's earthly ministry is for Maximus

[33] Ibid. (pp. 129–33, ll. 36–107); ibid. 42 (p. 285, ll. 18–28). On this theme, see Blowers, "Gentiles of the Soul: Maximus the Confessor on the Substructure and Transformation of the Human Passions," *Journal of Early Christian Studies* 4 (1996): 69; also Demetrios Bathrellos, "The Temptations of Christ according to St. Maximus the Confessor," in Young et al., eds., *Studia Patristica* 42, 45–50.

[34] *Amb. Jo.* 33 (PG 91:1285C–1288A; quoted at 1285D).

[35] Ibid. 71 (1408C–1409C); see also pp. 86–7 in this volume.

[36] *Amb. Th.* 5 (CCSG 48:29–30); *Ep.* 19 (PG 91:592D–593A); *Opusc.* 7 (PG 91:84C); cf. *Disp. Pyrr.* (PG 91:308D–309A).

[37] See *Amb. Th.* 5 (CCSG 48:23). Maximus here is drawing on Dionysius's allusions to Jesus's water-walking miracle (*Div. nom.* 2.9, PTS 33:133; *Ep.* 4, PTS 36:160–1).

thoroughly shot through with cosmic implications and repercussions.[38] His every work is a gesture toward recapitulating the universe, since the Logos's incarnation in Jesus of Nazareth is the culmination and perfection of all his "embodiments." Jesus begins the end, the final integration (union-in-difference) of all things and inauguration of a "new creation." I will resume analysis of the fuller cosmic repercussions of Jesus's acts in Chapter 7.

## PENETRATING THE MYSTERY OF THE COMPOSITE PERSON OF JESUS CHRIST

Maximus' Christ has been described as the *universale concretum*, "concrete universal" or "concrete and particular universal," and for good reason, as we have just seen.[39] The origin and destiny not just of individuals and hypostases but also of entire natures, spiritual and material, rational and non-rational, hinge on the singular person of Jesus Christ. This, however, raises definitive issues of Christ's peculiar *physiologia*, hypostasis, and concrete activity, issues to which Maximus devoted meticulous attention. The heart of his Christology is the "composite person" (ὑπόστασις σύνθετος) of Christ, a doctrine crucial not simply because it is Maximus' vital contribution to the interpretation of Chalcedon and the foundation for his fatal defense of the dual wills of Christ in the monothelete debates, but also because it is the abiding center of gravity of both his early and later Christology, and certainly one of the centers of gravity of his theology as a whole.

### Jesus Christ and the Trinity

Maximus worked out his Christology long after the trinitarian disputes of an earlier era had subsided, and he largely remained content with the aggregate achievement of the Cappadocian Fathers (especially the two Gregories) on trinitarian doctrine. Yet he grounded his teaching about

[38] See Chapter 7, pp. 228–30 in this volume.
[39] Von Balthasar applies the phrase to Maximus' Christology in *Theo-Logic*, vol. 2: *Truth of God*, trans. Adrian Walker (San Francisco: Ignatius Press, 2004), 188–91, at 190; see also David Yeago, "Jesus of Nazareth and Cosmic Redemption: The Relevance of St. Maximus the Confessor," *Modern Theology* 12 (1996): 163–93, at 177ff.

Christ's composite person squarely on the principle that the whole Trinity was invested in the incarnation of the Son. Maximus develops this point most forcefully in a soteriological key, as when, in his *Commentary on the Lord's Prayer*, he avers that the Word incarnate came to "teach *theologia*," to manifest *in flesh* the mystery of the Trinity.[40] As the Prayer is for Maximus a virtual "vow" of Jesus to the Father and an intimation of the tri-unity of God, his *Commentary* becomes a tutorial in how the saving and deifying benefits of the incarnation are an outworking of the whole Trinity.

> For the whole Father and the whole Holy Spirit were essentially and perfectly in the whole Son, even the incarnate Son, without themselves being incarnate; rather, the Father was present by approving the incarnation, while the Holy Spirit cooperated with the Son who carried it out, since the Logos remained with his own intelligence and life, contained in essence ($\kappa\alpha\tau'$ $o\dot{v}\sigma\acute{\iota}\alpha\nu$) by no one but the Father and the Spirit, while in his own person ($\kappa\alpha\theta'$ $\dot{v}\pi\acute{o}\sigma\tau\alpha\sigma\iota\nu$) uniting with the flesh out of his love for humanity.[41]

A similar phrase appears in *Questions and Responses for Thalassius* 2 where Maximus explains what the incarnate Logos meant when he said, "My Father is working even now, and I am working" (John 5:17):

> The Father approves this work, the Son properly carries it out, and the Holy Spirit essentially completes both the Father's approval of it all and the Son's execution of it, in order that the God in Trinity might be *through all and in all things* (Eph. 4:6).[42]

The kenosis of the Son in the incarnation is the perfect intersection between *theologia* and *oikonomia*, immanent Trinity and "economic" Trinity—and, by extension, apophatic and kataphatic language. Jesus Christ bears the inner-trinitarian life and *energeia* in his own person, and thus Maximus was pressed to elucidate the simultaneous identity

---

[40] *Or. dom.* (CCSG 23:31–2, ll. 87–9). Maximus also cites Paul's description of Jesus as "mediator between God and human beings" (1 Tim. 2:5), suggesting that "through his flesh he manifested the Father of whom humanity was ignorant, while through the Spirit leading those humans whom he had reconciled in himself to the Father" (ibid., p. 30, ll. 71–4).

[41] Ibid. (pp. 31–3, ll. 89–92).

[42] Q *Thal.* 2 (CCSG 7:51, ll. 23–6), trans. Blowers and Wilken, 100–1. Cf. also ibid. 60 (CCSG 22: 79, ll. 94–105). On these kinds of trinitarian enhancements, see Felix Heinzer, "L'explication trinitaire de l'économie chez Maxime le Confesseur," *MC*, 160–72.

and alterity within the divine Triad as a corollary of clarifying natures and hypostasis in Jesus. Here I must be brief, and am happy to defer to Pierre Piret's excellent study of the interface of Trinity and Christology in Maximus.[43] Three points are crucial, however. First, the Trinity to which the incarnate Christ is creatures' access is a perfect Unity-as-Trinity. The Triad of divine Persons, as Maximus insists in explaining Gregory Nazianzen in his *Theological Orations*, is neither ontologically nor temporally "after" the Monad but *is* the Monad.[44] Specifically in the case of the Son's generation from the Father, there is no disparity between the Father as the subject of the generation and the Son as its object, since the generation only bespeaks the ontologically *simultaneous* (ἄμα) relation between Father and Son.[45] Second, alterity in the Trinity bespeaks only the hypostases, or else the "mode" (τρόπος) proper to each of the three Persons, not the *logos* of their common essence.[46] Still, the *interrelation* of three Persons irreducibly *is* the divine essence or nature, lest that interrelation be ascribed exclusively to the Persons' sharing of activity (ἐνέργεια) in the economy. Third, the divine hypostasis (Person) of the Son is the true hypostasis of Jesus Christ, otherwise it would be possible to interpret the "composite hypostasis" as a combination of dual hypostases (and subjectivities) paired with the two divine and human natures—a view that pro-Chalcedonians well before Maximus' time had repudiated as Nestorian and destructive of Christ's personal agency. Maximus, meanwhile, defended the full humanity of Jesus as fiercely as he guarded the "asymmetry" of his composite person.

## Natures and Person in Christ

The constitution of the person of Jesus Christ is an immense theme in Maximus, so again I must be concise and will forgo surveying earlier

---

[43] *Le Christ et la Trinité selon Maxime le Confesseur* (Paris: Beauchesne, 1983).

[44] *Amb. Th.* 1 (CCSG 48:7); cf. *Or. dom.* (CCSG 23:53–54, ll. 441–67). See also Piret, *Le Christ et la Trinité*, 64–70.

[45] *Amb. Jo.* 24 (PG 91:1261B–1264B).

[46] On identity and alterity in the Trinity, see *Opusc.* 13 (PG 91:145A–149A), and the commentary on this text in Piret, *Le Christ et la Trinité*, 105–55. For the trinitarian application of the *logos–tropos* distinction, see *Myst.* 23 (CCSG 69:53); *Amb. Jo.* 67 (PG 91:1400D–1401A); *Amb. Th.* 1 (CCSG 48:7), as identified by Sherwood, *The Earlier Ambigua*, 164–5.

developments in Chalcedonian Christology, the seventh-century context of which I discussed in Chapter 1.[47] From the outset we are faced with Maximus' own engagement of inherited terms like "nature" (φύσις) and "person" (ὑπόστασις), terms with tortuous histories in philosophical and christological usage, terms that Christian thinkers long before had tried to negotiate between their abstract and concrete nuances. Maximus aspired to consistency and clarity all the while maintaining that precision was imperative both for christological *and soteriological* reasons. Such precision also had to operate under the discipline of a healthy apophaticism in attempting to articulate how the superessential divine essence or nature could unite with a man. What kind of human nature, let alone individual human being, could bear such a union?

In describing how Christ's composite hypostasis was internally constituted of divine and human natures, Maximus saw himself in a line of Chalcedonian protagonists working to negotiate a way beyond extremes, including that of Severus of Antioch's alleged miaphysite diminution of Christ's humanity, "Mani's fantasy" (undermining divine embodiment altogether), "Apollinaris's confusion (σύγχυσις)" of Christ's natures, "Eutyches's essential fusion (συνουσίωσις)" of them, and Nestorius's "turning the distinction of essences into a disparity of persons."[48] Reductionistic caricatures were a part of the polemical culture of the time and, though inevitable, unfortunately mask the fact that occasionally

[47] On Christology immediately before and after Chalcedon and the "Neo-Chalcedonian" thesis, see esp. Charles Moeller, "Le Chalcédonisme et le néo-Chalcédonisme en Orient de 451 à le fin du VIe siècle," in Aloys Grillmeier and Heinrich Bacht, eds., *Das Konzil von Chalkedon: Geschichte und Gewart* (Würzburg: Echter-Verlag, 1951), 637–720; Aloys Grillmeier, *Christ in Christian Tradition*, vol. 1, 2nd edn., trans. John Bowden (Atlanta: John Knox Press, 1975), 414–557; ibid., vol. 2, part 2, trans. John Cawte and Pauline Allen (Louisville: Westminster John Knox Press, 1995), 21–523; Patrick Gray, *The Defense of Chalcedon in the East (451–553)* (Leiden: Brill, 1979). For a revised view of "Neo-Chalcedonianism," see Karl-Heinz Uthemann, "Der Neuchalkedonismus als Vorbereitung des Monotheletismus: Ein Beitrag zum eigentlichen Anliegen des Neuchalkedonismus," in Elizabeth Livingstone, ed., *Studia Patristica* 29 (Leuven: Peeters, 1997), 373–413. On Maximus' own Christology in context, see esp. Demetrios Bathrellos, *The Byzantine Christ: Person, Nature, and Will in the Christology of St. Maximus the Confessor* (Oxford: Oxford University Press, 2004), 9–98; Hovorun, *Will, Action and Freedom*, 5–102; Guido Bausenhart, *In Allem uns gleich ausser der Sunde: Studien zum Beitrag Maximos' des Bekenners zur altchristlichen Christologie* (Mainz: Matthias Grünewald, 1995); and Felix Heinzer, *Gottes Sohn als Mensch: Die Struktur des Menschseins Christi bei Maximus Confessor* (Fribourg: Éditions Universitaires, 1980).
[48] *Opusc.* 3 (PG 91:49B–C, 56C–D).

there was some identifiable common ground with the concerns of anti-Chalcedonians.

For example, in his early writing Maximus pursued a constructive rendering of Cyril of Alexandria's teaching on the "one incarnate nature of God the Logos,"[49] a phrase endorsed in the *Pact of Union* (633),[50] but also one that Severus of Antioch and his miaphysite disciples had used to uphold the concrete unity of Christ and to rescue Cyril from pro-Chalcedonian interpretations. For Cyril himself, the "one nature" applied specifically to the *incarnate* Word, the Logos once he had assumed flesh and constituted a single embodied reality, a single hypostasis,[51] "the single subject of the incarnation event."[52] But Cyril had also affirmed the appropriateness of "two natures" language to describe the ontologically prior difference between God and man, Logos and flesh, "from which" (ἐξ) the unity that is Jesus Christ was formed.[53] Severans maintained that this duality of natures (= duality of hypostases) was thoroughly dissolved with the union.[54] Maximus certainly did not. Asserting that the duality (and difference) of natures endured without confusion after the union, he writes: "It is clear that, just as whoever denies that Christ is 'one incarnate nature of God the Logos' based on the hypostatic union (διὰ τὴν καθ᾽ ὑπόστασιν ἕνωσιν) does not believe that the union has even come about, so far as that phrase of our most holy Father and teacher Cyril is correctly interpreted, so too whoever does not confess that there are two natures from which (ἐξ ὧν) Christ is constituted *after* the union is unable to affirm that the difference of the two natures was preserved."[55] This statement is striking because, first, it indicates Maximus' early sympathy with the Cyrilline equation, properly nuanced, of one nature and one person in Christ; and second,

---

[49] See Cyril, *Ep.* 45 (= *Ep. 1 ad Succensum*) (PG 77:232D); *Ep.* 46 (= *Ep. 2 ad Succensum*) (PG 77:241A).

[50] See pp. 44–6 in this volume.

[51] "One nature" = "one hypostasis" is explicit in Cyril, *Apol. contra Theodoretem* (PG 76:401A).

[52] John McGuckin, *Saint Cyril of Alexandria and the Christological Controversy: Its History, Theology, and Texts* (Crestwood, NY: St. Vladimir's Seminary Press, 2004), 208–9.

[53] *Ep.* 45 (PG 77:232D): ἐκ δύο φύσεων. Scholars differ on whether for Cyril this duality obtained even after the incarnation. McGuckin (*Saint Cyril of Alexandria and the Christological Controversy*, 355, n. 6) says no. Others say yes. See Hans van Loon, *The Dyophysite Christology of Cyril of Alexandria* (Leiden: Brill, 2009), 554–6.

[54] e.g. Severus, *Ep.* 15 (PO 2/2:210).

[55] *Ep.* 18 (PG 91:588B). Emphasis added in my translation. Cf. *Ep.* 12 (472A), where Maximus quotes Cyril as defending the distinction of natures after the union.

because he acknowledges the legitimacy of calling it a union "from" the natures when Chalcedon had expressed only a single person "in" two natures.

Another phrase endorsed by the *Pact of Union* was Dionysius's "one theandric energy" (μία θεανδρικὴ ἐνέργεια), or "*new* (καινή) theandric energy" in the Areopagite's actual words, on which Maximus insisted.[56] This formula, which for Maximus had precedence in Cyril's "one connatural energy" (μία συγγενὴς ἐνέργεια),[57] did not nullify dual divine and human energies in Christ; rather, it was a circumlocution (περί-φρασις) intended to express the *novel* insinuation of divine and human energies/wills operating to one and the same purpose.[58] It bespoke the "mode of exchange of the natural properties inherent in the ineffable union,"[59] and thus was another way of expressing how Christ did human things divinely and divine things humanly. Frederick Lauritzen, moreover, argues rather convincingly from *Ambiguum 5* that Maximus adopted a Proclean usage to explain the "new theandric energy," one that paired infinite divine *dynamis* with finite human *energeia* as eliciting the integrity of Christ's activity.[60]

Maximus' sympathy with Cyril's and Dionysius's language is understandable in the light of the anti-Nestorian urgency, on the part of miaphysites and "Neo-Chalcedonians" alike, to avoid positing a separate *human* hypostasis in Christ such as would polarize his unitary subjectivity and agency. But what, then, becomes of Christ's human *nature* in the hypostatic union? Aloys Grillmeier summarizes the post-Chalcedonian dilemma of the precise origin or location of the one hypostasis, "Christ":

> The formal "concept" of the *hypostasis* was not yet located in the one Logos-subject. The one Christ was presented as a complex totality, seen from the end-point of the incarnation and its result, in the unmingledness

---

[56] *Announcement* (Πληροφορία), Art. 6 (Allen, *Sophronius*, 170–2), based on Dionysius, *Ep.* 4 (PTS 36:161); also Maximus, *Amb. Jo.* 5 (PG 91:1057A–B).
[57] *Comm. in Johannem* 73 (PG 73:577C–D), cited by Maximus in *Opusc.* 8 (PG 91:100B, 101A) and *Opusc.* 7 (88A). Maximus understood Cyril to be describing the intimacy of the Logos and his flesh in the work of Christ.
[58] *Amb. Th.* 5 (CCSG 48:29–30); *Opusc.* 7 (PG 91:84D–85A); *Opusc.* 8 (100C); *Disp. Pyrr.* (PG 91:348A).
[59] *Amb. Th.* 5 (CCSG 48.32, ll. 267–9).
[60] "Pagan Energies in Maximus the Confessor: The Influence of Proclus in *Ad Thomam* 5," *Greek, Roman, and Byzantine Studies* 52 (2012): 226–39. The especially relevant passages are *Amb. Th.* 5 (CCSG 48:23, ll. 73–84; 25, ll. 127–33).

of the two natures and of the properties of each, which, however, have come together in one person and in one *hypostasis*. The Fathers knew that the whole event of union had as its starting-point the perfect Logos and Son in the pre-existence. Nevertheless the concept of the "one *hypostasis*" was not applied to this, but to the final form of him who had assumed flesh and in the "one *hypostasis*" let the two natures be recognized. From this view of the one concrete *hypostasis* in the end-result (*apotelesma*, as Leontius of Byzantium said) the theologians laboriously attempted to change to the predicative placing of the "one *hypostasis*" in the pre-existent Logos, in order to determine from there how the humanity of Christ is to be integrated into this pre-existent uniqueness. Thus where precisely is the *hypostasis* realized? What does *hypostasis* mean when it is already there in the pre-existent Logos and nevertheless has to integrate into itself a second complete existence, which is also *physis* (nature) or *ousia* (essence), even if in historical finitude? Why is it also not a *hypostasis*?[61]

Here Maximus ostensibly gained crucial help from the sixth-century author Leontius of Jerusalem (whom some scholars identify with "Leontius of Byzantium"[62]), who had grappled with a lively Nestorian source that strictly endorsed two natures, two hypostases, and even two "personas" (πρόσωπα) in Christ.[63] Leontius reverted to the older language of the Logos "becoming" flesh in order to preclude a separate hypostasis or *prosôpon* in Christ, insofar as "Christ" designates a single "I" (ἐγώ).[64] Specifically he described the pre-existent hypostasis of the Logos having "en-hypostasized" (ἐνυπέστησε) the human nature of Jesus when he became flesh in the last times,[65] an idea also explicit in Leontius of Byzantium,[66] meaning *not* that the Logos absorbed a human hypostasis but that he granted Jesus's human

---

[61] *Christ in Christian Tradition*, 2/2: 277–8.
[62] Friedrich Loofs was the first to equate them. See Grillmeier, *Christ in Christian Tradition*, 2/2: 185ff., 271ff. Bathrellos (*The Byzantine Christ*, 39–54) distinguishes the two Leontii, as does Piret (*Le Christ et la Trinité*, 124–5); cf. earlier Marcel Richard, "Léonce de Jérusalem et Léonce de Byzance," *Mélanges de science religieuse* 1 (1944): 35–88.
[63] See Luisa Abramowski, "Ein nestorianischer Traktat bei Leontius von Jerusalem," in René Lavenant, ed., *Symposium Syriacum 1980* (Rome: Pontificum Institutum Orientalium Studiorum, 1983), 43–55.
[64] *Adversus Nestorianos* 2.48 (PG 86:1601A).        [65] Ibid. 5.28 (PG 86:1748D).
[66] *Elypsis* (*Adv. argumenta Severi*) (PG 86:1944C), noting how the humanity of Christ did not preexist his incarnation, but "has its being in the Logos" (ἐν τῷ Λογῷ ὑποστῆναι).

nature personal existence.[67] Did not the Logos possess the divine prerogative to *compose* and sustain the composite person of Christ? In addition, Leontius suggested that the human nature in the Logos's composite or "synthetic" hypostasis was an *individual human nature* (φύσις ἰδική) with its own properties (ἰδιόματα),[68] an idea that taxed the presentation of the hypostatic integrity of Christ[69] but in Leontius's judgment safeguarded the genuineness of Christ's humanity in answer to the Nestorian challenge. As well, Christ's individual human nature in the hypostatic union was not universal human nature in its current condition but an already thoroughly *deified* humanity,[70] a notion that would seem to facilitate the Logos's creation of a composite ("theandric") hypostasis while also problematizing *Christ's* identification with postlapsarian human nature.

Be that as it may, Maximus capitalized on certain key insights of Leontius, who had effectively exploited the inevitable flexibility of *hypostasis* in christological usage. Bathrellos observes that Maximus acquired from the two Leontii a balance of "asymmetrical" and "symmetrical" perspectives on the constitution of Christ.[71] The more top-heavy, asymmetrical perspective appears, for example, in Maximus' claim that

> the Logos of God, perfect in the nature and essence in which he is identical and consubstantial with the Father and the Spirit, while remaining different from them in hypostasis (ὑπόστασις) and person (πρόσωπον) in a way that preserved prosopic difference without confusion, and being incarnated from the Holy Spirit and the holy Theotokos and ever-Virgin Mary, was made thoroughly human. He became perfect man, clearly by assuming flesh endowed with a rational and intellectual soul, flesh that received both its nature and its hypostasis in him—received that is, both its being (τὸ εἶναι) and its subsisting (τὸ ὑφεστᾶναι) simultaneously (ἅμα) at

[67] On the proper meaning of "enhypostatic," see Brian Daley, "A Richer Union: Leontius of Byzantium and the Relationship of Human and Divine in Christ," in Elizabeth Livingstone, ed., *Studia Patristica* 24 (Leuven: Peeters, 1993), 241–3. Cf. Grillmeier, *Christ in Christian Tradition* 2/2: 193–8.

[68] *Adversus Nestorianos* 1.20 (PG 86:1485C–D); ibid. 2.1 (1528D–1532A, esp. 1529C). See also Heinzer, *Gottes Sohn als Mensch*, 70–116, on this important Leontian principle of the *Einzelnatur* of the human Christ as a key influence on Maximus.

[69] This because Maximus also wants to posit that the *idiomata* are only an expression of the *enhypostasis*, as noted by Grillmeier, *Christ in Christian Tradition* 2/2: 292 and n. 88.

[70] I.e. deified in its perfect union with the Logos (*Adv. Nest.* 5.1, PG 86:1721C), though Leontius concedes that as flesh there is a divinization of Christ not complete until after his resurrection (ibid. 4.37, 1712A).

[71] *The Byzantine Christ*, 48–9.

the very conception of the Logos, as effected by the Word himself instead of by human seed. For, simply willing it, he was found to be the seed of his own incarnation, and became synthetic (σύνθετος) in his hypostasis but was simple and uncompounded in his natures.[72]

We must track the subtleties of Maximus' language of *hypostasis* here. This is the hypostasis of the Son/Logos, who became flesh and in so doing gave ontologically simultaneous natural and *personal* being (= τὸ ἐνυπόστατον) to Jesus Christ but not a separate personhood. The Logos, moreover, became subject to human birth but in so doing paradoxically created the "synthetic" or composite hypostasis that was Jesus Christ. Later in this passage and elsewhere too, Maximus appropriates Leontius's language of "Christ" as a synthesis, the end-product (ἀποτέλεσμα) composed "from two natures" (ἐκ δύο φύσεων) as from two "parts" (μέρη) or "poles" (ἄκρα) that maintained their difference but together realized a perfect hypostatic union.[73]

Here we can see the more "symmetrical" side of Maximus' doctrine of Christ's composite hypostasis, the integrity of both his divine and human natures even after their union—the decisive key in Maximus' larger cosmological emphasis on the reciprocal union-in-distinction of uncreated and created natures. He approves of affirming not only that Christ's hypostasis was composed "from" two natures (Cyril, the Leontii, et al.) and "in" two natures (Chalcedon), but also that it *was* the two natures, a point on which he seems to have followed Leontius of Byzantium's lead in propounding the absolute irreducibility of the relation of natures, and of natures and hypostasis, in Christ.[74] The signature formula on the natures "from which is Christ"—"in which is Christ"—"which is Christ"—already appears in Maximus' earlier writings, including both sets of *Ambigua*, in two of his *Epistles*, in *Opuscula* from the 640s, and even in some documents from his trials.[75]

---

[72] *Ep.* 15 (PG 91:553C–556A). On Christ's hypostasis as a "synthesis" of his natures in Leontius of Jerusalem, see *Adv. Nest.* Prol. (PG 86:1401A); also Grillmeier, *Christ in Christian Tradition* 2/2: 283, 287.

[73] *Ep.* 15 (PG 91:556A–557D); also *Ep.* 12 (492D–493A): "a single synthetic hypostasis is achieved (ἀποτετελέσθαι) from them [the two natures]."

[74] See Leontius Byz., *Capita contra Severum* 6 (PG 86:1904A), identified by Bathrellos, *The Byzantine Christ*, 108, n. 48. Piret credits Maximus himself with coining this formula (*Le Christ et la Trinité*, 204).

[75] *Amb. Jo.* 27 (PG 91:1269C); *Amb. Th.* 5 (CCSG 48:26); *Ep.* 15 (PG 91:573A); *Ep.* 12 (488C, 500B–C); *Opusc.* 6 (PG 91:68A, D); *Opusc.* 19 (224A); *Opusc.* 1 (36C); *Opusc.* 9 (117C–D, 121A–B); *Relatio motionis* 7 (Allen and Neil, 62); *Disputatio*

Maximus resonates all of Leontius's aversion to a hybridized Christ as suggested by strict miaphysites, and to a Nestorian Christ of merged hypostases united only by a moral union. But the Leontian connection, turning Maximus toward a much more technical ontological analysis of Christ's constitution, profoundly enriched his Christology and helped prepare him for the rigors of the debate over Christ's wills in the monothelete controversy.[76]

Numerous modern studies of Maximus have investigated both the fine points and the broader ramifications of his doctrine of the composite person of Christ. Much attention has focused on whether "person" ultimately has a certain priority to "nature" in the maturation of his Christology. Eastern Orthodox "Personalist" theologians like John Zizioulas and Christos Yannaras have inclined this way, with sympathy from others who see Maximus as representing the ultimate Christian victory over Greek philosophical ontology, in which "nature" invariably carried the sense of ontic "necessity" and of dangerously abstract notions of divinity and humanity.[77] I shall take this up in later chapters,[78] but some initial observations are in order. First, it is thoroughly understandable that modern theologians gravitate to Maximus' rich notion of the composite *person* of Christ as having a privileged role in his Christology and in his theology as a whole. Christ's theandric person is not only the intersection of *theologia* and *oikonomia*, and of uncreated and created nature, but also the fulcrum of Maximus' entire doctrine of salvation and deification. Second, however, is the fact that in his meticulous treatment of the constitution of Christ, he points precisely to the ontological simultaneity of natures and person without privileging one over the other, though it would be proper still to say that Christ's person has priority to his *human* nature insofar as the Logos himself gave rise to Jesus's unique humanity, which has no existence apart from him.[79]

---

*Bizyae* (Allen and Neil, 84). See Piret's extensive commentary on these texts in *Le Christ et la Trinité*, 203–39; also Bathrellos, *The Byzantine Christ*, 108–10.

[76] See Brian Daley, "Maximus the Confessor, Leontius of Byzantium, and the Late Aristotelian Metaphysics of the Person," in Vasiljević, 55–70.

[77] Cf. Zizioulas, *Being as Communion: Studies in Personhood and the Church* (Crestwood, NY: St. Vladimir's Seminary Press, 1985), 27–49; Christos Yannaras, *Person and Eros*, trans. Norman Russell (Brookline, MA: Holy Cross Orthodox Press, 2008), 5–70.

[78] See pp. 205–6, 316–18 in this volume.

[79] See Bathrellos, *The Byzantine Christ*, 110–11.

Third, if there is a Christian overhaul of Greek ontological language operative here, it would seem to entail as much the notion of "nature" as of "person," insofar as the ineffable divine nature, beyond all essence ($\dot{v}\pi\epsilon\rho o\nu\sigma\acute{\iota}os$), has opened up, out of the tri-hypostatic life of the Trinity, and directly through Jesus Christ, whose composite person *is* the union of two natures, a new *tropos* of human nature. And by gracious extension, Christ has renovated the *tropoi* of all other created natures in their dynamic openness to the transformative power of the Creator, even if humans are his prime beneficiaries.[80]

Another critical question arising from Maximus' meticulous teaching on the constitution of Christ—one to which I shall return in Chapter 7— is the extent of Christ's identification with *fallen* humanity, since his human nature in the composite hypostasis was an individual, inherently deified nature.[81] Maximus has a strong affinity for Hebrews 4:15 (Christ as *tempted in every way like we are, save without sin*)[82] and he draws heavily on Gregory Nazianzen's explorations into the depth of Christ's kenosis and appropriation ($o\dot{\iota}\kappa\epsilon\acute{\iota}\omega\sigma\iota s$) of the human condition. A critical test, as we shall soon see, was the consideration of whether Christ exercised human volition in its stunted, "gnomic" state, or solely as a capacity of his (perfect) human nature.

## The Battle over Wills

Before the 640s, Maximus could scarcely have imagined how crucially his disquisitions on the precise constitution of the person of Christ would serve him in the intensifying monenergist–monothelete conflict, which

[80] See pp. 128–9 in this volume; also Tollefsen, *Christocentric Cosmology*, 132–4; Törönen, *Union and Distinction*, 55–9.
[81] See esp. *Amb. Th.* 5 (CCSG 48:21): "The combination of these [i.e. his kenosis without compromising his deity and his genuine assumption of flesh] established the constitution of his human nature both 'above mankind' ($\dot{v}\pi\grave{\epsilon}\rho\ \dot{a}\nu\theta\rho\acute{\omega}\pi ovs$)—for he was divinely conceived without the participation of a man—and 'after the manner of men,' in a human way, for he was born 'according to the law of conception,' and thus 'the One who is beyond being came into being by taking upon himself the being of humans'" (trans. Constas I, 35). Maximus here is quoting combined passages from Gregory Nazianzen and Dionysius. See also Larchet's extensive discussion of Maximus' doctrine of Christ's deified humanity in *La divinisation de l'homme*, 275–362.
[82] e.g. *Q. Thal.* 21 (CCSG 7:127); ibid. 22 (p. 139); ibid. 61 (CCSG 22:87); ibid. 64 (p. 195); *Amb. Jo.* 42 (PG 91:1316D); *Amb. Th.* 2 (CCSG 48:9); ibid. 5 (p. 20); *Ep. secunda ad Thomam* (CCSG 48:43); cf. *Opusc.* 4 (PG 91:57D–60A). See also Bausenhart, *In Allem uns gleich außer der Sünde*, 121–8.

tested the technical substance of his Christology in a sustained refiner's fire of imperial and ecumenical-ecclesiastical proportions.[83] But beyond the politics of this controversy, Maximus' defense of the dual wills of Christ is an extraordinary case study in the profound role of a single biblical pericope—the agony of Christ in Gethsemane (Matt. 26:36–42 *et par.*)—in shaping a historic doctrinal commitment of the Church. In retrospect, it is also the singularly most impressive example of how Maximus grounded his Christology in the Gospel narratives of Jesus's life. An exacting theological exegesis of this narrative was imperative, not just for properly christological purposes, but also because one whole dimension of the mystery of deification was the Savior's remaking of human volition and his "liberation" of human freedom. Long after Paul, but centuries before Paul's "New Perspective" interpreters began to rediscover how the Apostle's own "participatory Christology" soteriologically valorized the concrete obedience and faithfulness of Jesus to the will of the Father,[84] Maximus asserted that the composite person of Jesus Christ was the very theatre in which was staged the ultimate concert of divine and human wills. Here unfolded, from Galilee to Gethsemane to Golgotha, the "play within the play" of the cosmic drama of divine and creaturely freedom.

Maximus' doctrinal position on the divine and human wills of Christ is more striking if we track it as a vital developing theme in his theology rather than as purely a reaction to controversy. Let us recall from Chapter 3 his key distinction between "gnomic" will (γνώμη), a function of the inclination and deliberation of creatures in their individual moral trajectories, and the ontologically more basic "natural will" (θέλημα φυσική) that aims all rational creatures toward their true *telos*.[85] In his early works of moral and spiritual doctrine, gnomic will was a recurrent theme. Even at this stage in his thinking, *gnômê*, a term of amazing versatility in classical Greek usage,[86] as well

---

[83] See pp. 42–54 in this volume.

[84] See esp. Richard Hays, *The Faith of Jesus Christ: The Narrative Substructure of Galatians 3:1–4*, 2nd edn. (Grand Rapids: Eerdmans, 2002), xxix–xxxiii.

[85] See pp. 121–4 in this volume.

[86] See Peter Karavites, "*Gnome's* Nuances: From Its Beginning to the End of the Fifth Century," *Classical Bulletin* 66 (1990): 9–34. Karavites himself notes the wide gamut of meanings in classical poets and writers: e.g. the "judgment" or acquired perspective informing action; categorically *bad* judgment; reasoned opinion; intention; decision; mind (or mindedness). Cf. also Bronwen Neil, "Divine Providence and the Gnomic Will before Maximus," *OHMC*, 235–49.

as in its biblical and patristic usage,[87] had certain pejorative connotations, for it represented humanity's reinvention of freedom in and after the Adamic fall,[88] and was not so easily distinguished from self-interest. And yet it also fit into Maximus' fierce moral realism. The gnomic will, and the personal horizon of moral choice ($\pi\rho o\alpha i\rho\epsilon\sigma\iota s$) with which it was closely associated,[89] were also the media through which true freedom had to be relearned in humanity's stunted condition. Indeed, *gnômê* factored into the realization of virtue because it represented an individual's acquired moral *experience*.

According to Maximus, Christ's own exercise or "use" of *gnômê* appeared most spectacularly in his passion, where he kept his *gnômê* impassible and imperturbable, not allowing it at all to vacillate contrary to nature.[90] By the voluntary character of his suffering, Christ broke the pattern of human nature warring against itself, so also "reconciling us through himself to the Father and to one another such that we no longer exercise *gnômê* in opposition to the principle of our nature ($\tau\hat{\omega}$ $\lambda\acute{o}\gamma\hat{\omega}$ $\tau\hat{\eta}s$ $\phi\acute{\upsilon}\sigma\epsilon\omega s$), being as constant in our *gnômê* as in our very nature itself."[91] The incarnate Christ himself, Maximus affirms, inaugurated the "transformation and change in deliberative will and in free choice" ($\gamma\nu\omega\mu\iota\kappa\grave{\eta}\nu$ $\tau\epsilon$ $\kappa\alpha\grave{\iota}$ $\pi\rho o\alpha\iota\rho\epsilon\tau\iota\kappa\grave{\eta}\nu$ $\mu\epsilon\tau\alpha\beta o\lambda\grave{\eta}\nu$ $\kappa\alpha\grave{\iota}$ $\dot{\alpha}\lambda\lambda o\acute{\iota}\omega\sigma\iota\nu$) that will factor into the eschatological consummation of creation.[92] The clear implication is that Christ alone, in his perfect and deified humanity, could actively repair the deviation of gnomic will from natural volition, healing the penchant of *gnômê* to vacillate and deliberate in its moral inclinations by thoroughly and finally conforming it to the natural will.

This all changed in the monothelete crisis, as the christological and soteriological focus moved squarely to the precise constitution and

[87] In *Disp. Pyrr.* (PG 91:312B–C), Maximus claims to have identified 28 different meanings of $\gamma\nu\acute{\omega}\mu\eta$ in Scripture and the Fathers. Perhaps its most prolific Greek patristic usage before Maximus was in John Chrysostom (more than 800 times), for whom it is a "mindset" or a (moral) disposition of the soul, according to Ray Laird, "*Gnomê* in John Chrysostom," *OHMC*, 194–211. See also Bronwen Neil, "Divine Providence and the Gnomic Will before Maximus," *OHMC*, 235–49.
[88] On Adam's "gnomic" fall, see *Amb. Jo.* 8 (PG 91:1104A). Human fallenness is sustained "gnomically" ($\gamma\nu\omega\mu\iota\kappa\hat{\omega}s$) or by $\gamma\nu\acute{\omega}\mu\eta$: e.g. *Q. Thal.* 1 (CCSG 7:47); ibid. 21 (pp. 127–9); ibid. 61 (CCSG 22:101).
[89] Maximus also early on attributed a perfect $\pi\rho o\alpha i\rho\epsilon\sigma\iota s$ to Christ: e.g. *Q. Thal.* 21 (CCSG 7:127); ibid 42 (pp. 285–7).
[90] *Or. dom.* (CCSG 23:34, ll. 136–9). For further analysis, see pp. 234–40 in this volume.
[91] Ibid. (CCSG 23:35, ll. 149–53). [92] *Exp. Ps. 59* (CCSG 23:3, ll. 11–12).

operation of Christ's volition, especially as dramatized in Gethsemane. In the transitional period of the early 630s before the crisis broke wide open, Maximus had approved the *Psephos* of Patriarch Sergius, which for the sake of consensus discouraged enumerating the operations or wills in Christ, pronouncing simply that "our Lord Jesus Christ, true God, performs both the divine and the human activities," and that "the intellectually ensouled flesh of the Lord never separately and of its own initiative (ἐξ οἰκείας ὁρμῆς) made its own natural movement at variance with the approval of God the Word united to it hypostatically."[93] Maximus was apparently satisfied that the *Psephos* extolled the Son of God's voluntary kenosis in the flesh, with no need further to specify the exact dynamics of his volition after becoming incarnate.[94]

The Emperor Heraclius's *Ekthesis* (638), which straightforwardly condemned the possibility of two *contrary* wills (δύο ἐναντία θελήματα) and enunciated "*one will* (ἕν θέλημα) of our Lord Jesus Christ,"[95] effectively threw down the gauntlet for Maximus' painstaking response, his fine-tuned dyothelete definitions spread across a series of christological *Opuscula* and in his transcribed public debate with the deposed Patriarch Pyrrhus. If there is justification to calling the Confessor a proto-scholastic, it is here, where he spares no detail in working out a model of the interplay of divine and human freedoms in Christ. Despite his initial trust of imperial bids for consensus, Maximus determined that the monothelete logic turned Jesus into the passive subject of a *tour de force* of divine *energeia* and will, in which case he had to show, from the ground up, how human will (minus its "gnomic" mode, as we shall see) functioned in Christ and how that will was "different" but not intrinsically "opposed" to the divine will. The added anthropological benefit of this demonstration, of course, was an insight into how will is intended "naturally" to operate in all human beings.

"Will" did not mean, as it often connotes today, the mere resolve to act on the basis of immediate or protracted judgment, moral or otherwise. Drawing on Aristotle, the Stoics, and even more on the Christian writer Nemesius of Emesa's substantial treatise *On Human Nature*, Maximus understood human volition as a whole physio-psychological process including endowed faculties, composite stages,

[93] *Psephos*, as summarized in Sergius, *Ep. 1 ad Honorium* (Allen, *Sophronius of Jerusalem*, 188, 189, 190, 191).

[94] See *Ep.* 19 (PG 91:592B–593A). For analysis, see Léthel, *Théologie de l'agonie du Christ*, 60–4.

[95] *Ekthesis*, Greek text with trans. by Allen, *Sophronius of Jerusalem*, 214, 215.

and material action toward projected ends.[96] Collating key passages from *Opusculum* 1 and from the *Disputation with Pyrrhus*,[97] we can reconstruct an outline of its phases (see Figure 3).

According to this scheme, the will, as an endowment of human *nature*, arises from the full intellectual *and affective* matrix in which it is hard to distinguish strictly between faculty and function, and in which reason and desire are deeply interwoven. "Will" ($\theta\acute{\epsilon}\lambda\eta\sigma\iota\varsigma$) as such was a term rarely used in classical sources, where volition was more a matter of rationalized desire and a fairly pure function of the mind. Richard Sorabji argues that both Augustine and Maximus were instrumental in cultivating a uniquely Christian notion of the will as an independent faculty, though he also suggests that Maximus' *thelêsis*, defined (with Clement of Alexandria) as "a faculty desirous of what is in accordance with nature" ($\delta\acute{\upsilon}\nu\alpha\mu\iota\varsigma$ $\tau o\hat{\upsilon}$ $\kappa\alpha\tau\grave{\alpha}$ $\varphi\acute{\upsilon}\sigma\iota\nu$ $\ddot{o}\nu\tau o\varsigma$ $\mathring{o}\rho\epsilon\kappa\tau\iota\kappa\acute{\eta}$),[98] closely paralleled the Stoics' *oikeiôsis*, one's attachment to one's own nature (and so also to the *telos* of that nature).[99] Demetrios Bathrellos has appropriately emphasized, moreover, that the instinctive and non-rational appetitive elements of human nature, not just the mental ones, factored positively into Maximus' definition.[100] Appetite and impulse launch the will, as it were, albeit under the orienting power of intellect and reason.

Indeed, in Maximus' richly reworked notion of "nature," the will, with its constituent resources, is "naturally" projected toward a transfiguring state of deification in which divine grace is both intrinsically

[96] On Maximus' doctrine of the will and its sources, see René-Antoine Gauthier, "Saint Maxime le Confesseur et la psychologie de l'acte humaine," *Recherches de théologie ancienne et medievale* 21 (1954): 51–100 (esp. for connections with Aristotle and the Stoics); Irénée-Henri Dalmais, "Le vocabulaire des activités intellectuelles, voluntaires et spirituelles dans l'anthropologie de Saint Maxime le Confesseur," in *Mélanges offerts à M.-D. Chenu* (Paris: Vrin, 1967), 189–202; Jean-Luc Marion, "Le deux volontés du Christ selon Maxime le Confesseur," *Résurrection* 41 (1972): 48–66; John Madden, "The Authenticity of Early Definitions of Will," *MC*, 61–79; Thunberg, *Microcosm and Mediator*, 208–26; Bathrellos, *The Byzantine Christ*, 117–29; David Bradshaw, "St. Maximus the Confessor on the Will," in Vasiljević, 143–80.
[97] *Opusc.* 1 (PG 91:12C–24A); *Disp. Pyrr.* (PG 91:293B–C).
[98] *Opusc.* 1 (PG 91:12C); ibid. 26 (276C).
[99] *Emotion and Peace of Mind: From Stoic Agitation to Christian Temptation* (Oxford: Oxford University Press, 2000), pp. 337–40; id., "The Concept of the Will from Plato to Maximus the Confessor," in Thomas Pink and M. W. F. Stone, eds., *The Will and Human Action: From Antiquity to the Present Day* (London: Routledge, 2004), 20–2.
[100] *The Byzantine Christ*, 125–6.

| NATURAL "WILL" (θέλημα / θέλησις) | "A faculty desirous of what is according to nature" (δύναμις τοῦ κατὰ φύσιν ὄντος ὀρετική); "rational and vital desire" (ὄρεξις λογικὴ καὶ ζωτική); or "appetitive mind" (νοῦς ὀρεκτικός) |
|---|---|

| Component Phases of the Will | |
|---|---|
| "wish" (βούλησις) | "Imaginative appetency"(ὄρεξις φανταστική) connecting both reason and imagination, and aimed at those ends that are "within our power and not within our power"(τὰ ἐφ' ἡμῖν καὶ οὐκ ἐφ' ἡμῖν). |
| "inquiry" (ζήτησις)<br><br>"consideration" (σκέψις)<br><br>"deliberation" (βουλή or βούλησις) | This cluster of phases (adapted from Aristotle)involves reason, induced by the soul's natural desire, inquiring and scoping things out in the direction of a projected end (τέλος). βούλησις, as "appetitive inquiry" (ὄρεξις ζητική) is the culminating phase, at which point the soul is deliberating on the *means* to the end; but this deliberation is still absolutely distinct from "choice" (προαίρεσις) itself. |
| "judgment" (κρίσις) | Reason's final determination (or even discernment), after all deliberation, of the proper means to an end; it clearly parallels "consent" (συγκατάθεσις) in Stoic volitional theory. |
| ["inclination," γνώμη] | Though Maximus does not formally include γνώμη as a stage of willing in its own right, he does adjacently define it as the "deep-seated appetency" (ὄρεξις ἐνδιάθετος) for that which is within our power, "whence springs choice (προαίρεσις);" or also as "a disposition (διάθεσις) toward what is in our power, on which we have appetitively deliberated (ὀρεκτικῶς βουλευθεῖσι)." |
| "choice" (προαίρεσις) | As in Nemesius (*De natura hominis* 33), this is "deliberating appetency" (ὄρεξις βουλετική), and is a composite of appetite (ὄρεξις), deliberation (βουλή), and judgment (κρίσις). It is the ultimate intersection of reason with underlying desire, committing the soul to a course of action. Maximus at times comes close to equating προαίρεσις and γνώμη (PG 91:28D), as προαίρεσις is the actualization of the "disposition" that is γνώμη. |
| "impulsion" (ὁρμή) | A key Stoic notion used in various ways by Maximus without a strictly uniform technical meaning, it goes along with "movement" (κίνησις) and signals the overall *urge* that, with the mind's consent, moves the soul from wish, through choice, to action. |
| "use" (χρῆσις)<br>(action, execution) | The meaning of "use" has to be inferred from other deployments of χρῆσις in Maximus' writings, e.g. "using" the passible drives (desire and temper) and other psychic faculties for good or ill (Gauthier). It could also adapt the Stoic idea of "using things," i.e. the external manifestation of the internal moral "use" (or judgment) of the "thoughts" of things, as leads to the use of the "things" themselves. "Use" prompts action and is virtually equatable with it (Thunberg). |

Fig. 3.

and extrinsically operative. Jesus Christ had recapitulated this volitional process to its very perfection, and Maximus looked to Scripture's own authoritative witness, the Gethsemane prayer, which was especially effective since it exhibited at once Christ's human fear of death and his resolute obedience to the Father's will. The monothelete reading of this narrative focused on the divine will ultimately overriding and thus supplanting a human will in Christ in the economy of divine kenosis. Especially disturbing for Maximus was the monotheletes' appeal to Gregory Nazianzen to support their case. Gregory understood Christ's words in John 6:38—*For I have come down from heaven, not to do my own will, but the will of him who sent me*—as uttered by the Son incarnate, the Savior whose (human) will was already "wholly deified" (θεωθὲν ὅλον), not a "mere man" with a will like ours that resists God. The Son was specifically referencing the *divine* will that he perfectly shared with the Father, and he did the same in the Gethsemane prayer— *Father, if it be possible, let this cup pass from me; nevertheless, not as I will, but as thou wilt* (Matt. 26:39).[101] Gregory thus rendered these key statements in a trinitarian rather than a properly christological register. Monotheletes nevertheless inferred that Gregory was actually denying a human will in Christ.[102] Countering their interpretation of Jesus in Gethsemane and their appeal to Nazianzen as an authority, Maximus both vindicated and moved beyond his theological hero. Without explicitly rejecting the possibility of reading Jesus's prayer in a trinitarian key like Gregory, he pursued a strictly christological reading, confident that Gregory was himself a dyothelete for whom the Savior's *human* will was "wholly deified."[103] Marcel Doucet is absolutely correct that "in the Savior, for Gregory, there is an *alterity* of divine will and of his divinized [human] will but *no contrariety* in the object shared respectively by each will."[104] Maximus understood Gregory thus.[105] He even mentions how certain monothelete opponents drew on alternative manuscripts of Gregory that allegedly read θεόθεν ὅλον ("wholly from God") rather than θεωθὲν ὅλον ("wholly deified"), obviously hoping to prove an exclusively divine will and to accuse dyotheletes like Maximus of a quasi-Nestorian belief that Christ and the saints were united to God merely by a relational union, a union of (dual) hypostases.[106]

But Maximus still had to articulate his own christological interpretation of Jesus's prayer, which meant reconciling the emotional

---

[101] *Or.* 30.12 (= *Or. theol.* 4.12) (SC 250:248–50).
[102] Léthel sees the monothelete appeal to be justified on the fact that Gregory had indeed denied a human will in Christ (*Théologie de l'agonie du Christ*, 31, 32, 34–5). But Gregory had not done so, as pointed out by Marcel Doucet, "Est-ce que le monothélisme a fait autant d'illustrés victimes? Réflexions sur un ouvrage de F.-M. Léthel," *Science et esprit* 35 (1983): 54–7.
[103] For Maximus' references to Gregory in *Or.* 30.12, see *Opusc.* 4 (PG 91:61A–B); ibid. 20 (233B–236B); ibid. 6 (65B); ibid. 7 (81C).
[104] "Est-ce que le monothelisme . . . ?" 55.      [105] *Opusc.* 7 (PG 91:81C).
[106] Ibid. 20 (PG 91:233B–236B).

resistance (fear of death) and volitional resolve that it combined.[107] In his first substantial analysis of the agony of Gethsemane in *Opusculum* 6 (*c*.640), Maximus propounded the principle that the *difference* of human and divine wills in Christ did not intrinsically amount to their *opposition*, and that from beginning to end Christ's human will was marked by perfect harmony (συμφυΐα) and concurrence (σύννευσις) with his divine will.[108] In *Opusculum* 7 (*c*.642), *Opuscula* 16 and 3 (both post-643), and the *Disputation with Pyrrhus*, however, he explored more keenly the element of resistance in Jesus's prayer, and so also the salvific role of Jesus's human constitution both ontologically and morally, though I shall develop this theme in more detail in Chapter 7. For Maximus, Christ was proactively demonstrating his natural human will in Gethsemane, obediently handing it over to the divine will. His resistance to the cup of suffering was a function of his equally natural instinct to fear death, but this too he deliberately and openly displayed so that, by subjugating his innate passions to his (deified) human will, he might embolden and retrain the passions of believers facing suffering and death.[109]

The real struggle in Gethsemane for Maximus was not, then, between Christ's human and divine wills (as his deified human will was "naturally" disposed to obedience) but *within* his human volition itself, in the complexity of its relation to his deep-seated desires and aversions.

> Either, as man, he had a natural will, and for our sake, under the terms of the *oikonomia*, willingly pleaded to be spared from death, and again, because he perfectly concurred with the Father, *was urged to confront it* (ὥρμα κατ' αὐτοῦ), or else, as man, he did not have a natural will...[110]

Von Balthasar translates the italicized phrase "went against his own will," referring the pronoun αὐτοῦ to Christ's human will itself, in evidence of the fact that the divine will became the will of the singular

---

[107] For background on patristic interpretation of the Gethsemane prayer, see Bathrellos, *The Byzantine Christ*, 140–7; also Kevin Madigan, "Ancient and High-Medieval Interpretations of Jesus in Gethsemane: Some Reflections on Tradition and Continuity in Christian Thought," *Harvard Theological Review* 88 (1995): 157–73.

[108] *Opusc.* 6 (PG 91:65A–68D); cf. ibid. 7 (81D); ibid. 16 (193A); *Disp. Pyrr.* (PG 91:292A–B).

[109] See *Opusc.* 7 (PG 91:80C–81C); ibid. 3 (48B–C); *Disp. Pyrr.* (PG 91:297B–300A). See also pp. 238–9 in this volume.

[110] *Opusc.* 7 (PG 91:81B) (emphasis added in my translation).

"I" of the composite hypostasis.[111] Doucet is correct, however, that this αὐτοῦ refers to death.[112] In fact this reading is confirmed later in the same work when Maximus reiterates that Christ demonstrated human apprehension at the specter of death precisely so that "he might toughen [our nature] and impel it bravely against it—against death, I mean."[113] Maximus' point is precisely that the human will of Christ roused itself obediently to confront death. The use of the verb ὥρμα, moreover, accentuates the role of impulse (ὁρμή), the upsurge from the depths of his *affective* self in perfect desire and love for the Father, in the fulfillment of his human will. Von Balthasar is right to see Gethsemane as Maximus' dramatic crux of the interplay of divine and human freedoms in Christ, with the former having the primary initiative in the incarnational kenosis; but Doucet has justifiably criticized von Balthasar for insufficiently recognizing Maximus' emphasis on the internal dynamics of Jesus's human obedience. The asymmetrical and symmetrical dimensions of Maximus' Christology must always be held together.

Especially problematic in retrospect, however, is Maximus' ultimate denial of "gnomic" human will in Christ after having affirmed this in his early works. His logic seems straightforward enough. In his debate with Pyrrhus, he no longer defined *gnômê* as a deliberative stage or even faculty within human volition but instead deemed it a "quality of willing" (ποιὰ θέλησις), "a mode (τρόπος) of use [of the will], not a principle of nature."[114] Maximus appealed, then, to Dionysius's principle of a "new theandric energy," which the Confessor redefined as a new *qualitative rather than quantitative mode* of willing, "the new and ineffable mode (τρόπον) of the manifestation of Christ's [dual] natural energies, through the ineffable manner of the fitting 'circumincession' (περιχωρήσεως) of Christ's natures in relation to each other."[115]

In a changing semantic landscape, *gnômê* now specifically evoked the fallen mode or disposition of the will in which hesitation about worthy

---

[111] *Cosmic Liturgy*, 268.

[112] "La volonté humaine du Christ, spécialement en son agonie: Maxime le Confesseur, interprète de l'Écriture," *Science et esprit* 37 (1985): 135–6 and n. 75.

[113] *Opusc.* 7 (PG 91:84C): πρὸς ὁρμὴν ἀνδρικῶς τὴν κατ᾽ αὐτοῦ, φημὶ τοῦ θανάτου, στομώσῃ τε καὶ διεγείρῃ.

[114] *Disp. Pyrr.* (PG 91:308C–D).

[115] Ibid. (PG 91:345D). On Maximus' doctrine of circumincession (περιχώρησις), see also Larchet, *La divinisation de l'homme*, 333–46; Thunberg, *Microcosm and Mediator*, 21–36.

ends had to be unlearned, as it were, in the quest for virtue. There could not have been the least such vacillation or indecision in the sinless Christ's determination to do the will of the Father, so Christ had no *gnômê*.[116] Pondering alternatives was not an "option" for him—not because of an ontological necessity imposed on his natural human will, such as would obliterate its voluntary character, and blaspheme God's own natural freedom from inner compulsion[117]—but because true freedom is not reducible merely to decision or choice.[118] Recalling Figure 3, it is at last the "use" ($\chi\rho\hat{\eta}\sigma\iota\varsigma$) of the whole panoply of natural engrained faculties (rational, appetitive, etc.) that enables action, and this same use in its deified mode ($\theta\epsilon\ddot{\iota}\kappa\hat{\omega}\varsigma$) in Christ, liberated creatures to embrace their *telos*: being ($\tau\grave{o}\ \epsilon\hat{\iota}\nu\alpha\iota$), yes, but also a "well-being" ($\tau\grave{o}\ \epsilon\hat{\upsilon}\ \epsilon\hat{\iota}\nu\alpha\iota$) through the synergy of grace and free will, and ultimate transfiguration in a graced state of "eternal well-being" ($\tau\grave{o}\ \dot{\alpha}\epsilon\grave{\iota}\ \epsilon\hat{\upsilon}\ \epsilon\hat{\iota}\nu\alpha\iota$).[119]

It will remain for us to investigate in Chapter 7 whether Maximus' christologically justified denial of *gnômê* in the Savior came at too high a soteriological price. How could Christ liberate rational creatures from gnomic vacillation, or better yet reorient *gnômê* to stable choosing of the good, if he did not experience it in his own right? Even if Maximus honestly hoped to avert not only monotheletism but also its opposite extreme, the Nestorian view that Christ was a union of two hypostases and thus two *gnômai*, what of the depth of Christ's kenosis into the weakened condition of human volition, his own *learning of obedience through suffering* (Heb. 5:8), and submission to the process of being *perfected* (Heb. 2:10; 5:9; 7:28)? Does Maximus' cosmic Christology do exegetical justice to the redemptive suspense of the biblical narrative of Gethsemane? Can the concrete drama of Gethsemane bear the weight of Maximus' vision of cosmic reconciliation and transfiguration? Certainly he believed it could, but not, as we shall eventually see, apart from its interconnection with the full paschal ministry of Christ, from his birth to his ascension and glorification.

---

[116] *Disp. Pyrr.* (PG 91:308C–309A).      [117] Ibid. (PG 91:293C–295A).

[118] See Ian McFarland, "'Willing is Not Choosing': Some Anthropological Implications of Dyothelite Christology," *International Journal of Systematic Theology* 9 (2007): 3–23.

[119] For this trio of ontological benefactions, see *Amb. Jo.* 7 (PG 91:1073C, 1084B); ibid. 10 (1116B–C, 1204D); ibid. 42 (1325B–C, 1329A–B, 1348D); and esp. ibid. 65 (1392A–C); also *Th. Oec.* 1.56 (PG 90: 1104C). Cf. also Gregory Nazianzen, *Or.* 38.3 (SC 358:108).

# 5

## The Church and Its Liturgy as Threshold of the New Creation

In the cosmic landscapes of Maximus the Confessor's thought, the Church holds a strategically crucial place, even though he treats its reality in depth only in a single work, the *Mystagogia*, which includes his substantial commentary on the Divine Liturgy. The Church for him is the sanctified space in which the "cosmic liturgy" of praise and worship is perennially lifted up, but that space transcends the earth since its chorus embraces also the heavenly hierarchies, indeed all the orders (τάξεις) above and below, macrocosmic and microcosmic, whole and parts, that reflect and resound the majestic theophany of the triune Creator who permeates the universe in order to ingather all creatures to himself. In turn, Maximus' ecclesiology is less a straightforward account of the Church's institutional and sacramental features[1] than a nuanced contemplation (θεωρία) of the Church's role in the cosmic drama of the transfiguration of all things in Jesus Christ. Like the creation as a whole, and especially like human nature, the Church for Maximus is both a theatre of that drama and a character within it. It is both a location, a staging point as it were, and an animate body acting out its role in synergy with divine grace. What began in creation and climaxed in the incarnation of Jesus

---

[1] So Cooper, *The Body in St. Maximus the Confessor*, 165, 166: "In no single work does Maximus present what we might recognize as a systematic doctrine of the Church," and his vision of the Church is strongly "liturgico-centric." See, however, Andrew Louth, "The Ecclesiology of Saint Maximus the Confessor," *International Journal for the Study of the Christian Church* 4 (2004): 109–20; id., "The Views of St. Maximus the Confessor on the Institutional Church," in Vasiljević, 347–55; also George Berthold, "The Church as *Mysterion*: Unity and Diversity according to Maximus the Confessor," *Patristic and Byzantine Review* 6 (1987): 20–9.

Christ now finds its eschatological denouement in the foreground which is the Church, the threshold of the new creation. Maximus' ecclesiology is therefore profoundly *participatory*, since penetrating the deifying mystery of Jesus Christ, and of his Body the Church, can only begin from within the ecclesial context itself, where Word, ritual, mystagogy, sacrament, ministry, confession, catechesis, and the ascetical quest for Christian virtue all converge in and through the Spirit.

## THE HISTORICAL AND LITERARY SETTING OF MAXIMUS' TEACHING ON CHURCH, LITURGY, AND SACRAMENT

### Maximus at the Crossroads of Monastic and Ecclesiastical Worship

Phil Booth, who positions Maximus, together with Sophronius and John Moschus, at the helm of seventh-century Byzantine monastic dissent, argues that this movement hardened its political resistance to imperially-sponsored monotheletism by giving Chalcedonian orthodoxy a patently more ecclesiastical and sacramental cast. By Booth's account, Maximus underwent a profound change from an earlier, deeply ascetical piety wherein devotion to Christ did not hinge on Eucharistic observance and devotion to the Church was "internalized" and "spiritualized," to an ecclesiocentric and sacramental piety signaled foremost in the *Mystagogia*. In producing a commentary on the Church and liturgy which also integrated ascetical discourse, Maximus the monk invaded the domain of bishops, or rather sought to fortify it with a comprehensive vision of Church, cosmos, and humanity that could withstand both the rise of Islam and the attempts of secular rulers to unite the empire on fallacious doctrinal grounds.[2]

Booth accurately and vividly represents Maximus' interweaving of ecclesial-sacramental and ascetical discourses in the *Mystagogia*, and his dignifying of clerics, monks, and laity alike in the ascetical and liturgical communion of the Church.[3] But he has exaggerated the shift in the Confessor's devotional ethos and the novelty of his mystagogical achievement. To posit that Maximus in his early ascetical writings

---

[2] Booth, *Crisis of Empire*, 170–85.     [3] Ibid., 173, 176–80, 182–3.

"expounds a traditional monastic vision, in which the Eucharist does not feature,"[4] is both an argument from silence and an oversimplification of the piety he inherited from Eastern monastic communities where, in fact, the Eucharistic *synaxis* had played an increasingly vital role well before Maximus' time.[5] Booth's claim that, in the relatively early *Commentary on the Lord's Prayer*, he had "spiritualized" the Eucharist, because he interpreted the *bread from heaven* (John 6) metaphorically as the intelligible food of the Logos himself,[6] imposes an artificial wedge between the symbolic and the sacramental, and between material type and spiritual reality, the very things Maximus fiercely sought to hold together. To feed on sacred Word and on sacred bread were already of a piece. Maximus certainly spoke the Origenian–Evagrian language of ascetical and contemplative striving after transcendent food, but his rich notion of the multiple incarnations of Christ, supremely in flesh but also in other material forms (the *logoi* of creation, scriptural text, sacramental bread, the institution of the Church, the embodied virtues of Christians) had always precluded any evaporation of the material into the spiritual. There were indeed certain non- or anti-sacramental monastic initiatives in the East, most famously the so-called Messalian or Euchite ascetics, who styled themselves masters of an asceticism of pure prayer;[7] but Maximus not only had no association with them, he explicitly repudiated them and echoed the concerns of earlier anti-Messalian writers like Mark the Monk and Pseudo-Macarius.[8]

---

[4]　Ibid., 171.

[5]　See the extensive documentary and archaeological evidence produced by Joseph Patrich, *Sabas, Leader of Palestinian Monasticism: A Comparative Study in Eastern Monasticism, Fourth to Seventh Centuries* (Washington, DC: Dumbarton Oaks, 1995), 239–54; also H. Ashley Hall, "The Role of the Eucharist in the Lives of the Desert Fathers," in Frances Young, Michael Edwards, and Paul Parvis, eds., *Studia Patristica* 39 (Leuven: Peeters, 2006), 367–72. That monks in some places participated in the Eucharist less often than non-monastic laypersons was mainly not ideological but circumstantial: e.g., the unavailability of priests routinely to administer it; and the fears of monks attending public Eucharists that crowds would force them into ordination to the priesthood.

[6]　*Or. dom.* (CCSG 23:34, ll. 128–34; 59, ll. 549–57; *Th. Oec.* 2.56 (PG 90:1149A–B), as noted by Booth, *Crisis of Empire*, 171–3.

[7]　Booth (*Crisis of Empire*, 15–22) also notes the second wave of Origenist monks whose spiritualizing tendencies were recounted in Cyril of Scythopolis's *Life of Sabas* and other sources. Booth is assuming Maximus' Palestinian rather than Constantinopolitan monastic provenance, enabling him to be under their influence.

[8]　See *Q. Thal.* 6 (CCSG 7:69–71), where Maximus' position on the efficacy of baptism for post-baptismal sin clearly echoes Mark the Monk's anti-Messalian treatise

Booth's argument for the novelty of Maximus' *Mystagogia*, which he considers the pinnacle of his whole corpus, is based on a stark contrast with one of the Confessor's own sources, Dionysius the Areopagite, whose liturgical and sacramental commentary in the *Ecclesiastical Hierarchy* Booth mistakenly lumps with the "products of bishops," guardians of hierarchy in the Church.[9] Accordingly, unlike Dionysius with his consciousness of ranks into which the monks have been appropriately fitted, Maximus' *Mystagogia* not only integrated asceticism and liturgy but also democratized the spiritual journey of the faithful by paralleling the active life ($\pi\rho\hat{a}\xi\iota\varsigma$), to which all Christians are called, and the contemplative life ($\theta\epsilon\omega\rho\acute{\iota}a$) of monastics, in pursuit of "the same enlightenment—realized both in the eucharist and in the *eschaton*."[10] Booth concludes: "Alienated from the East because of foreign incursion, and in parallel with Moschus in the same period, Maximus abandoned the traditional monastic ambivalence to the structures of the Church and set out a new vision that reconciled the ascetic and the sacramental lives, presenting an orthodox Church in which all members were united around and dependent upon the eucharist."[11]

In fact, however, one of Maximus' original inspirations for this blended ascetical–liturgical–sacramental mystagogy was none other than Dionysius himself. Alexander Golitzin has persuasively demonstrated that the Areopagite's own mystagogy was deeply influenced by early Syrian *ascetical* tradition, and even (positively and negatively) by the Origenist tradition of Evagrius.[12] Von Balthasar too surmised that Maximus in his *Mystagogia* was consciously synthesizing the monastic-gnostic "cult" or worship from Evagrius with the ecclesial-liturgical cult of Dionysius.[13] In a remarkable text that Golitzin considers perhaps the *locus classicus* of his entire corpus, Dionysius correlates the internal perceptual and intellectual faculties of the soul with the external material elements of the liturgy (candles, incense, etc., and most importantly the Eucharist) that transport the soul and body toward God:

> It would not be possible for the human intellect ($vo\hat{\iota}$) to be ordered with that immaterial imitation of the heavenly minds [i.e., the angels] unless it were to use the material guide that is proper to it, reckoning the visible

---

*On Baptism*, questions 1 and 4 (PG 65:985A, 992D). On the resonances of Pseudo-Macarius in Maximus' baptismal theology, see Plested, *The Macarian Legacy*, 230–2.

[9] *Crisis of Empire*, 173.      [10] Ibid., 182–3.      [11] Ibid., 184.
[12] *Mystagogy: A Monastic Reading of Dionysius Areopagita*, 20–4, 305–63.
[13] *Cosmic Liturgy*, 314–26.

beauties as reflections of the invisible splendor, the perceptible fragrances as impressions of the intelligible distributions, the material lights an icon of the immaterial gift of light, the sacred and extensive teaching [of the Scriptures] [an image] of the intellect's intelligible fulfillment, the exterior ranks of clergy [an image] of the harmonious and ordered state (ἕξεως) [of the intellect] which is set in order for divine things, and [our partaking] of the most divine Eucharist [an icon] of our participation in Jesus Christ.[14]

As Golitzin observes, the liturgy is a grand symbol, "which for [Dionysius] means always a kind of incarnation, a 'real presence' of God and heaven coming to us in and through the material forms and objects—bread and wine, oil and water—which we have received from the teachings of Christ and the traditions of the Apostles."[15] Dionysius's novel contribution to mystagogy, he adds, was to coordinate between the "inner" and "outer" hierarchies both of the soul and of the Church, a theme on which he found help from the prolific anti-Messalian homilist Pseudo-Macarius and a Syrian ascetical tradition anxious to hold monks and ascetics accountable to the Church's liturgical and sacramental disciplines.[16]

Precisely from the Dionysian corpus, *pace* Booth, Maximus learned to embrace the Divine Liturgy as a rich and multifaceted symbolic vector toward deifying assimilation to God in which asceticism—especially purification and the "imitation of God" (θεομίμησις)—was thoroughly integrated,[17] for all the ranks, clerical and lay alike (monastics being the preeminent laypersons), each in its proper order in relation to the Eucharistic altar, the throne of God. Dionysius's chosen pseudonym as a disciple of Paul, and his consistent reference to his venerable mentor Hierotheos, bespeak his own asceticism, his urgency to submit to an elder's authority and to be seen as an "imitator of God" through the Church and its liturgy.[18]

Committing his mystagogy to writing required posing as an initiate himself and not simply as a mystagogue demonstrating superior

---

[14]  *Cael. hier.* 1.3 (PTS 36:8–9, l. 19–9, l. 6), Golitzin's own translation, *Mystagogy*, 16 (bracketed additions are his).

[15]  *Mystagogy*, 16.          [16]  Ibid., 20–4.

[17]  On purification, see e.g. *Eccl. hier.* 5.1.3 (PTS 36:101); *Cael. hier.* 10.3; 13.4 (PTS 36:41, 48–9); and on imitation of the Divine, e.g. *Cael. hier.* 3.2 (PTS 36:18); ibid. 7.2 (p. 28); also Golitzin's analysis, *Mystagogy*, 186–91.

[18]  On the rationale of the Areopagite's pseudonym, see most recently Charles Stang, *Apophasis and Pseudonymity in Dionysius the Areopagite: "No Longer I"* (Oxford: Oxford University Press, 2012).

comprehension of the revelatory hierarchies. Golitzin even suggests, and plausibly so, that Dionysius's pose as a privileged disciple was a ploy designed to "de-gauss" apocryphal and esoteric writings that were distracting Syrian monks, and that he actually intended his corpus for a wide audience.[19] Maximus opened his *Mystagogia* by indicating his dependence on "a certain grand old man ($\gamma\epsilon\rho\dot\omega\nu$)," an unidentified monastic sage (Sophronius perhaps) to whom he held himself accountable as he embarked on an instruction about Church and liturgy primarily but not exclusively for monks. This figure was not Dionysius himself, whose *Ecclesiastical Hierarchy* Maximus explicitly mentions as a source for his own work.[20] Rather than duplicating Dionysius or pretending to match his superior spiritual insight, Maximus says he wants to provide a follow-up, a kind of catechesis on the Church and liturgy intended to deepen believers' habitus ($\xi\xi\iota\varsigma$) of desire for divine truths through continuing interpretation ($\xi\kappa\theta\epsilon\sigma\iota\varsigma$) and exercise ($\gamma\upsilon\mu\nu\alpha\sigma\iota\alpha$) of the Areopagite's insights.[21] Maximus' anonymous "grand old man," meanwhile, had already paved the way forward for monks to engage in just such a project.

## Maximus as a Commentator on the Liturgy and Sacraments

Liturgy never receded from its original and essential role in shaping Christian religious identity by ritualizing and dramatizing the divine *oikonomia*. From the fourth century on, as liturgy became more elaborate and comprehensive, and was enriched as well by the influence of monastic worship, its role in spiritual formation became more complicated but no less crucial. Maximus' *Mystagogia* and Dionysius's *Ecclesiastical Hierarchy* stood within a trajectory of liturgical commentary rooted in the older mystagogical sermons and catecheses of fourth- and fifth-century authors like Ambrose of Milan, Cyril of Jerusalem, John Chrysostom, and Theodore of Mopsuestia, all of them bishops initiating the faithful in the deeper mysteries of liturgy and the sacraments.[22] This makes it all the more striking that, as non-bishops, Dionysius and

---

[19] *Mystagogy*, 12–13.

[20] See *Myst.* prooemium (CCSG 69:6); also Nikolaou, "Zur Identität des $\mu\alpha\kappa\dot\alpha\rho\iota\sigma\varsigma$ $\gamma\dot\epsilon\rho\omega\nu$ in der *Mystagogia*," 407–18.

[21] *Myst.* prooemium (CCSG 69:6–7).

[22] On these earlier sources see Enrico Mazza, *Mystagogy: A Theology of Liturgy in the Patristic Age*, trans. Matthew O'Connell (New York: Pueblo, 1989).

Maximus also aimed their mystagogy broadly, even if Maximus' primary audience was monastic. And yet both he and Dionysius postured themselves as disciples rather than illuminati. Later Byzantine liturgical commentators included bishops (Germanus of Constantinople, eighth century; Nicholas of Andida, eleventh century) and monk-bishops (Nicholas Cabasilas, *c.*1320–90; Symeon of Thessaloniki, 1381–1429).

A fundamental question in considering Maximus as a liturgical commentator is precisely which liturgy was his subject in the *Mystagogia*. The presumption for years was that it was the Divine Liturgy in Constantinople, especially if this was his original home; and our historical imagination is certainly tempted to assume that Maximus sees Justinian's spectacular Basilica of Hagia Sophia when he reflects on the architectural ambiance of the liturgy. And yet the Confessor is notoriously silent on various aspects of the seventh-century Byzantine rite as reconstructed from limited sources. Among his omissions is the anaphora, the very nucleus of the Eucharistic liturgy, though his silence about it is doubtless intentional, as we shall see further on. Bryan Spinks suggests that in the *Mystagogia* "the commentary is so vague that it could be any [Eastern] rite," and thinks it plausible that Maximus was interpreting a Palestinian liturgy,[23] though the thesis that he was commenting on the Constantinopolitan liturgy has also been vigorously reasserted.[24]

Maximus' distinctiveness as a commentator on the liturgy surfaces especially by contrasting his work with Dionysius's. Not just the differences but the commonalities are crucial. For both writers, liturgy arises from an apophaticism that paradoxically energizes doxology. It is from the utterly ineffable God that generous and deifying light proceeds down through the celestial and terrestrial orders of beings and through the symbolic and sacramental protocols of the liturgy. In his preface to the *Mystagogia*, Maximus obliges himself to a strict Dionysian apophaticism before segueing into his liturgical commentary proper:

> But let God be the guide of our words and our concepts, the sole intelligence of intelligent beings and intelligent things, the meaning

---

[23] *Do This in Remembrance of Me: The Eucharist from the Early Church to the Present Day* (London: SCM Press, 2013), 124–5.

[24] See Robert Taft, "Is the Liturgy Described in the *Mystagogia* of Maximus Confessor Byzantine, Palestinian or Neither?" *Bollettino della Badia Greca di Grottaferrata*, 3rd series 8 (2011): 223–70; Tamara Grdzelidze, "Liturgical Space in the Writings of Maximus the Confessor," in Maurice Wiles and E. J. Yarnold, eds., *Studia Patristia* 37 (Leuven: Peeters, 2001), 499–504; earlier René Bornert, *Les commentaires byzantins de la divine liturgie du VIIe au XVe siècle* (Paris: Institut Français d'Études Byzantines, 1966), 105–6.

behind those who speak and of what is spoken, the life of those who live and those who receive life, who is and who becomes all for all beings, through whom everything is and becomes but who by himself never is nor becomes in any way anything that ever is or becomes in any manner. In this way he can in no way be associated by nature with any being and thus because of his superbeing is more fittingly referred to as nonbeing. For since it is necessary that we understand correctly the difference between God and creatures, then the affirmation ($\theta\acute{\epsilon}\sigma\iota\nu$) of superbeing ($\tau o\hat{\upsilon}\ \acute{\upsilon}\pi\epsilon\rho\acute{o}\nu\tau o s$) must be the negation ($\grave{\alpha}\varphi\alpha\acute{\iota}\rho\epsilon\sigma\iota\nu$) of beings, and the affirmation of beings must be the negation of superbeing. In fact both names, being and nonbeing, are to be reverently applied to him although not at all properly. In one sense they are both proper to him, one affirming the being of God as cause of beings the other completely denying in him the being which all beings have, based on his preeminence as cause. On the other hand, neither is proper to him because neither represents in any way an affirmation of the essence of the being under discussion as its substance or nature. For nothing whatsoever, whether being or nonbeing, is linked to him as a cause; no being or what is called being, no nonbeing or what is called nonbeing, is properly close to him. He has in fact a simple existence, unknowable and inaccessible to all and altogether beyond understanding which transcends all affirmation ($\kappa\alpha\tau\alpha\varphi\acute{\alpha}\sigma\epsilon\omega s$) and negation ($\grave{\alpha}\pi o\varphi\acute{\alpha}\sigma\epsilon\omega s$).[25]

Here I would recall Jean-Luc Marion's observation, that in the apophaticism of Dionysius and Maximus, the absolute inaccessibility of God is God's own gracious withdrawal, or "ecstatic disappropriation," granting space for created beings, in their radical otherness from God, to move toward union.[26] Praise and worship are intrinsic, then, to the *ecstatic appropriation* of this deifying grace on the part of creatures. Through worship (in all its modes) they become what they are eschatologically called to be.

The paradoxical converse side of this divine inaccessibility, in both Dionysius and Maximus, is the fact that liturgy is still a *theophany* insofar as concealment *and disclosure* are simultaneously operative. The Sinai Theophany played a paradigmatic role in Dionysius's vision of the worshiping Church because it depicted a people called and gathered to a holy place, to mysteries in which they were allowed

---

[25] *Myst.* prooemium (CCSG 69:9–10, ll. 103–26), trans. Berthold, 185–6.
[26] *The Idol and Distance: Five Studies*, trans. Thomas Carlson (New York: Fordham University Press, 2001), esp. 140, 153, 156, 162. See also pp. 125–6 in this volume.

only partially and proportionately to participate, mysteries mediated by a "hierarch" (Moses), in a numinous tableau attended by lights, sounds, and smoke.[27]

Though Dionysius is certainly attentive to the flow of liturgy, its various movements, cadences, and climaxes, what stands out is the *synchronicity* of the liturgy as a kaleidoscopic icon of divine transcendence and approach, of the ingathering of the whole company of heaven and earth, and of the fruition of celestial and ecclesiastical hierarchies.[28]

By contrast, Maximus' *Mystagogia* focuses more intently on the liturgical theophany as a *diachronic* rehearsal of the mystery of the incarnation of Jesus Christ, with the bishop/hierarch as himself the Christ-figure piloting the way through the various sequences toward the supreme eschatological mystery of the Eucharist. His premier entry into the church symbolizes Christ's advent on earth, and his seating on the episcopal throne symbolizes Christ's ascension into heaven and session at the Father's right hand.[29] The bishop's entering the church *with the people* simulates Christ's conversion of the faithless to faith and godly life.[30] Yet we are also reminded that Christ himself, as Word, indwells the liturgy in his own (kenotic) descent at the public reading of the Gospel text.[31] The bishop's descent from his throne after the Gospel reading, and his dismissal of the catechumens whereupon the church's doors are closed, signal the completion of Christ's first dispensation and the imminence of his second coming, so that only the worthy are allowed to advance into the Eucharistic *synaxis*, the "nuptial chamber of Christ."[32]

Whereas in Dionysius, the sacraments stand preeminently at the top of the three descending ecclesiastical hierarchies,[33] Maximus portrays them primarily as eschatologically-oriented climaxes in the dramatic

[27] *Myst. theol.* 1.3 (PTS 36:143–4); *Cael. hier.* 4.3 (PTS 36:22); *Eccl. hier.* 5.1.2 (PTS 36:104–5). See also Golitzin, *Mystagogy*, 227–38, who details the resonances of the Sinai Theophany within the liturgy according to Dionysius.

[28] Golitzin (*Mystagogy*, 294–8) persuasively shows that for Dionysius, all things and all people in the liturgy are *icons* imaging "that specific 'procession' of God which re-established us in communion with him and so with the angels: the Incarnation of Jesus Christ" (p. 295).

[29] *Myst.* 8 (CCSG 69:37).       [30] Ibid. 9 (CCSG 69:38–9).
[31] Ibid. 13 (CCSG 69:41–2).       [32] Ibid. 14–16 (CCSG 69:43–5).
[33] *Eccl. hier.* 5.1.1–3 (PTS 36:104–6). The hierarchies are (1) the sacraments; (2) the sacred ministers, or clergy; and (3) the initiates (monastics, lay faithful, catechumens, penitents).

replaying of the economy of salvation in the lives of believers in a still-unfolding "history."[34] Though he mentions baptism in the *Mystagogia* only in brief reference to its efficacy for divine adoption,[35] Maximus elsewhere frames it as participation in the birth into "well-being" ($\tau\grave{o}$ $\epsilon\mathring{v}$ $\epsilon\mathring{i}\nu\alpha\iota$) already inaugurated in Christ's own baptism.[36] Baptism plants in believers the potential for deification to be eschatologically actualized and perfected.[37] The Eucharist is the eschatological sacrament par excellence, collapsing sacred past, present, and future, and also merging earth and heaven in the glorious celebration of the paschal mystery of Jesus Christ.[38] To this I shall return later.

Irénée-Henri Dalmais, an esteemed scholar of the Confessor's liturgical theology, averred that Maximus favored "the dialectic of preparation-fulfillment to the antithesis of figure-reality,"[39] an opinion Dalmais may well have formed from comparing him with Dionysius. Certainly Maximus' strongly eschatological frame of reference enhances the suspense, within liturgy and sacrament, of a deferred disclosure of the full saturating effects of the mystery of Jesus Christ. I would resist, however, an exaggerated distinction between a more "typological" (horizontal-historical) approach in Maximus and a more "symbolistic" (vertical-hierarchical) one in Dionysius. Such a distinction cannot be forced upon either writer's liturgical—or scriptural—interpretation without oversimplification. When Dionysius or Maximus speaks of "symbols" and "types," whether in Scripture or in the liturgy, it is not as if either, in his refined Christian–Platonic hermeneutical idiom, ultimately evaporates the "inferior" material symbol into its "superior" spiritual

---

[34] In his *The Eucharistic Communion and the World* (London: T. & T. Clark, 2011), 89, John Zizioulas writes, "Maximus the Confessor, in an extremely interesting corrective, without appearing to disagree with Dionysius, transfers the whole subject of imagery in the Divine Liturgy from the historical plane to the eschatological. So while Dionysius regards the Divine Liturgy as an image of the heavenly Liturgy, Maximus alters his position by interpreting it as imaging the Kingdom which is to come." I would agree, but not that this is a corrective or alteration of Dionysius, since for Maximus the symbolic and eschatological axes already fully intersect.

[35] *Myst.* 24 (CCSG 69:66).

[36] *Amb. Jo.* 42 (PG 91:1316A–1325C). This points forward as well to the ultimate new birth, into "eternal well-being" ($\tau\grave{o}$ $\mathring{a}\epsilon\grave{\iota}$ $\epsilon\mathring{v}$ $\epsilon\mathring{i}\nu\alpha\iota$) inaugurated in Christ's resurrection.

[37] *Q. Thal.* 6 (CCSG 7:69–71). On Maximus' fuller theology of baptism, see also Larchet, *La divinisation de l'homme*, 409–24.

[38] See *Myst.* 24 (CCSG 69:58–9).

[39] "La manifestation du Logos dans l'homme et dans l'Église: Typologie anthropologique et typologie écclesiale d'après *Qu. Thal.* 60 et la *Mystagogie*," MC, 21.

referent. Scriptural and liturgical symbols point "upward," yes, but also "forward" to where history and eternity overlap. The axis of the liturgy is therefore an oblique one, toward an ascending horizon in which the full fertility of these symbols comes gradually to light. Maximus may not have articulated what liturgists today call "liturgical time," but his "realized" eschatology cheated the boundary between the *saeculum* and the age to come.[40]

## THE CHURCH AS THEATRE OF THE COSMIC LITURGY

### Ecclesial Staging of the Liturgical Drama of Salvation and Deification

In the early sections of the *Mystagogia*, Maximus dwells at length on different levels of contemplation (θεωρία) of the reality of the Church. He begins with the Church as an icon of God himself before considering the analogical and anagogical significance of the architectural dimensions of a basilica. As sanctuary (ἱερατεῖον) and nave (ναός) it is an image of the created cosmos in its intelligible and sensible parts. But the whole point of foregrounding this polarity is to accentuate the underlying ontological unity:

> [The church building] is one in reality (μία κατὰ τὴν ὑπόστασιν) without being divided into its parts due to the mutual difference between those parts. Rather, it frees these very parts, in their relation to the one purpose of the church, from their nominal difference. It exhibits to each of the parts that they are the same thing, and reveals that one is to the other in turn what each one is for itself. So the nave is the sanctuary *in potency* by being consecrated for the purposes of mystagogy, and in turn the sanctuary is the nave *in actuality* by maintaining the very basis of this mystagogy, which is inseparable from it. The church remains one and the same on account of both [sanctuary and nave].[41]

The same holds true, by analogy, for the intelligible and sensible parts of creation. *Difference is not division*, a principle Maximus applied

---

[40] See Blowers, "Realized Eschatology in Maximus the Confessor," 258–63.

[41] *Myst.* 2 (CCSG 69:15, ll. 215–25), with emphasis added in translation. See also the analysis of this passage in Riou, *Le monde et l'église*, 149–50; and Törönen, *Union and Distinction*, 149–50.

most famously to the wills of Christ. The intelligible and sensible parts of the universe penetrate each other without confusion, and there is an irreducible relation between the whole and the parts, just as in the Church.[42] More than a simple architectural typology, as Pascal Mueller-Jourdan has shown, Maximus' attention to spatiality or "place" (τόπος) interchangeably in his cosmology and ecclesiology bespeaks his deeper concern for ontological circumscription, bodily boundaries, continuity and order, wholeness and individuation, and the positioning of created beings/members/parts vis-à-vis their inherent *logoi*, each other, and the infinite Creator.[43] There remains throughout the *Mystagogia*, moreover, Maximus' overarching concern to project a unity ever enriched by diversity. All these things are underlying conditions for the cosmic liturgy, the "service" (λειτουργία) of creatures to the Creator which is at once their natural fulfillment (participation in God) and their moral and spiritual vocation.[44]

In a series of subsequent analogies in the *Mystagogia*, all supportive of his vision of the cosmic liturgy, Maximus describes how the Church is an image of the sensible cosmos considered on its own terms (sanctuary as heaven; nave as earth); also of a human being (sanctuary as mind; nave as body); also of the soul alone (sanctuary as its intellectual power for contemplation; nave as its animating power for praxis).[45] Next he draws analogies between Scripture and a human being (New Testament as mind and Old Testament as body; or spiritual sense as mind and literal sense as body); and finally between a human being and the cosmos (soul as intelligible world, body as sensible world).[46] I would recall that in *Ambiguum* 10 Maximus also extensively develops the analogy between Scripture and the cosmos.[47] In each analogy, the binaries (spiritual and material; intelligible and sensible; invisible and visible; internal and external; etc.) indicate a proportional and structural unity constituting altogether the stage, as

---

[42] *Myst.* 2 (CCSG 69:16–17).

[43] See Pascal Mueller-Jourdan, *Typologie spatio-temporelle de l'Ecclesia byzantine: La* Mystagogie *de Maxime le Confesseur dans la culture philosophique de l'antiquité tardive* (Leiden: Brill, 2005), 38–62, 113–14, 127–31, 137–43, 150–69. Mueller-Jourdan interprets the *Mystagogia* here in the light of Maximus' extensive reflection in *Amb. Jo.* 10 (PG 91:1080B–1181B) on "place" (τόπος), "position" (θέσις), and other Aristotelian categories.

[44] See Thomas Cattoi's excellent overview, "Liturgy as Cosmic Transformation," *OHMC*, 414–35.

[45] *Myst.* 3–5 (CCSG 69:17–31).     [46] Ibid. 6–7 (pp. 31–6).

[47] See *Amb. Jo.* 10 (PG 91:1128D–1133A); see also pp. 82–3 in this volume.

it were, on which the drama of the cosmic liturgy plays out. This whole arrangement, or *oikonomia*, to which all the Church's ritual and sacramental capacities are intrinsically fitted, serves the *diabasis*, or "passover," of creatures to deification and new creation.[48] For Maximus, then, the Church is the foreground in which this trans-formative drama unfolds in its teleological intensity. "If any of these three human beings—the cosmos, holy Scripture, and the one who is just like us—desires to maintain a life and purpose pleasing and acceptable to God, let her or him do what is best and most honorable of all,"[49] that is, in all her or his spiritual and ascetical disciplines. Given his antecedent analogies, why does Maximus not include the Church too as one of these "human beings" or players in the cosmic liturgy? Doubtless it is because the Church, with its liturgy, is the focusing and nurturing context of them all.

## Ecclesial Theo-Mimesis: Mystagogy and Asceticism

In what is actually Maximus' very first analogy, the premier contem-plative foray attributed to his "grand old man" in the *Mystagogia*, the Church, "by imitation and type," is an icon of God himself, or more specifically of God's *energeia*.[50] The image actually begins from the perspective of the unity of diverse created beings in God:

> Maintaining around himself, as cause, beginning, and end all beings which are by nature distant from one another, he makes them converge in each other by the singular force of their relationship to him as origin. Through this force he leads all beings to a common and unconfused identity of movement and existence, no one being originally in revolt against any other or separated from him by a difference of nature or of movement, but all things combine with all others in an unconfused way by the singular indissoluble relation to and protection of the one beginning and cause.[51]

More to the point ecclesiologically, he continues:

> the holy Church of God will be shown to be working for us the same effects as God, in the same way as the image reflects its archetype. For

---

[48] On the rich notion of *diabasis*, see Blowers, *Exegesis and Spiritual Pedagogy*, 95–183.

[49] *Myst.* 7 (CCSG 69:35, ll. 576–9).   [50] Ibid. 1 (p. 10).

[51] Ibid. 1 (p. 11, ll. 135–9), trans. Berthold, 186 (altered).

numerous and of almost infinite number are the men, women, and children who are distinct from one another and vastly different by birth and appearance, by nationality and language, by ways of life and ages, by inclinations (γνώμαις) and skills, by manners and habits, by occupations, by breadth of knowledge, and still again by reputations, fortunes, characteristics, and connections. All are born into the Church and through it are reborn and recreated in the Spirit. To all in equal measure it gives and bestows one divine form and designation, to be Christ's and to bear his name. In accordance with faith it gives to all a single, simple, whole, and indivisible solidarity (σχέσιν) which does not allow us to consider the existence of the myriad differences among them, even if those do exist, because of the universal relationship and union of all things with [the Church].[52]

Later in the *Mystagogia*, Maximus reiterates this eschatological image of the Church:

the holy Church . . . is the figure and image of God inasmuch as through it he effects in his infinite power and wisdom an unconfused unity from the various essences of beings, attaching them to himself as their highest point, and this operates according to the grace of faith for the faithful, joining them all to each other in one form according to a single grace and calling of faith, the active and virtuous ones in a single identity of will (γνώμης ταυτότητα), the contemplative and gnostic ones in an unbroken and undivided concord as well.[53]

Like Dionysius, Maximus understands the imitation of God to be a crucial revelatory and eschatological dynamic at the core of both the created cosmos and the Church. "The aim of theological mystagogy is to establish one by grace in a state of being like God and equal to God, as much as this is possible."[54] For Dionysius theo-mimesis (θεομίμησις) correlates with his well-developed doctrine of hierarchies,[55] while for Maximus it inheres in his all-embracing notion of the constitutive principles (λόγοι) and modes (τρόποι) of created beings. For both there is an unmistakable ontological groundwork. All creatures, in virtue of their inherent *logoi*, reflect the Creator, though humanity specially enjoys the divine image (εἰκών) as gift and vocation. Thence

---

[52] Ibid. (pp. 12–13, ll. 163–78), trans. Berthold, 187 (altered).
[53] Ibid. 24 (pp. 59–60, ll. 950–9), trans. Berthold, 208.
[54] *Amb. Jo.* 20 (PG 91:1241C), trans. Constas I, 419
[55] On the definition and operation of "hierarchy," see esp. *Cael. hier.* 3.1–3 (PTS 36:17–20); also René Roques's foundational *L'univers dionysien: Structure hiérarchi-que du monde selon Pseudo-Denys* (Paris: Aubier, 1954; reprinted Paris: Cerf, 1983).

opens up the existential horizon of *likeness* (ὁμοίωσις) implied with the image (Gen. 1:26–7), which Maximus, following earlier authorities, identifies as the teleological dynamic of *assimilation* to God,[56] a process inseparable from the worship and communion of the Church. It is a cosmic process because, as in Dionysius, *all* creatures, through the generous radiation of divine illumination, are being "recalled" and "uplifted" proportionately to an archetypal perfection that is nonetheless eschatological and only partially realized here below, where lower creatures must imitate higher ones as each in its proper order aspires to divine likeness.[57] The aesthetics of the procession (πρόοδος) of divine glory/illumination and of the creaturely return or assimilative conversion (ἐπιστροφή) to God are as unmistakable in Maximus as they are in Dionysius, though in Maximus the *dramatic* character of the theophany operative in the Church and its liturgy is even more pronounced. The Beauty of the theophany unfolds not only as the economy and proportionality of the divine revelation to which the faithful respond in kind, but as the suspense and build-up to the mystery of deification.[58] The Church moves forward and pioneers the ingathering of all creation in a doxological and Eucharistic chorus.

The Church's liturgy, then, is the ritual protocol of this worshipful return of all creation to the triune Creator. It is a mystagogical gift offered back to the God who is Mystagogue, who in his Word initiates all creatures in the mysteries concerning their ultimate transformation. Describing the symbolism of the nave and holy of holies, Maximus states that the nave is "potentially" the holy of holies insofar as it is "sanctified by the offering up of mystagogy (ἀναφορᾷ τῆς μυσταγωγίας) to its proper end," while the holy of holies is "in actuality the nave by containing the principle of utterly uninterrupted mystagogy (τῆς ἀδιαστάτου μυσταγωγίας ἀρχήν), a principle that remains one and the same in its two parts."[59] By this Maximus

---

[56] For Maximus' distinction of "image" and "likeness," see p. 127, n. 99, in this volume.

[57] Cf. Dionysius, *Div. nom.* 1.2–3 (PTS 33:110–12); ibid. 4.1–2 (pp. 143–6); *Cael. hier.* 1.2–3 (PTS 36:7–9); ibid. 3.1–3 (pp. 17–20); ibid. 4.1–2 (pp. 20–1); *Eccl. hier.* 1.1–3 (PTS 36:63–6); ibid. 5.1.4 (pp. 106–7); Maximus, *Car.* 3.33 (PG 90:1028B); ibid. 3.80 (1041B); ibid. 3.94 (1045B); *Amb. Io.* 20 (PG 91:1240C–D).

[58] See Irénée-Henri Dalmais, "Mystère liturgique et divinisation dans la *Mystagogie de saint Maxime le Confesseur*," in Jacques Fontaine and Charles Kannengiesser, eds., *Epektasis: Mélanges patristiques offerts au Cardinal Jean Daniélou* (Paris: Beauchesne, 1972), 55–62.

[59] *Myst.* 2 (CCSG 69:15, ll. 221–5).

qualifies his doctrine of the reciprocal relation between the empirical and noetic levels of reality in the Church, the cosmos, and human nature, in all of which the lower imitates the higher. The pure mystagogy of the holy of holies—namely, the Eucharistic mystery—is *already* the eschatological perfection of the mystagogy operative in the public sights, sounds, words, and motions within the nave. Conversely, the nave has the potential not just to mirror but to *become* the sanctuary, the dwelling place of divine glory—presumably to the extent that its mystagogical rituals and actions also embody the Eucharistic presence of Christ conducive to his "incarnation" in the lives and virtues of the faithful.

The mystagogy operative in the Church's liturgy and sacraments functions through the twin disciplines, so familiar in Maximus and his major predecessors, of contemplation ($\theta\epsilon\omega\rho\iota\alpha$) and ascetical performance ($\pi\rho\hat{\alpha}\xi\iota\varsigma$). In its ecclesial and liturgical context, this contemplation, as a spiritual discipline, differs little from its function in the reverential gaze on created nature or in the interpretation of Scripture.[60] It is a deep, intuitive insight into the visible object or symbol, a seeing through to its *logos* (so also to the Logos-Christ as author), accomplished gradually and patiently and always in tandem with diligent practice of the virtues. Contemplation does not "overcome" the object or symbol since that object or symbol is the material locus of a reality (divine Truth and Goodness[61]) that is present and approachable but, in its eschatological fullness, deferred. As René Bornert and others have observed, every figure ($\tau\upsilon\pi o\varsigma$), image ($\epsilon\iota\kappa\omega\nu$), or symbol ($\sigma\upsilon\mu\beta o\lambda o\nu$) in liturgy, in Scripture, or in creation, is for Maximus a representation not of an absent but of a mysteriously present reality ($\dot{\alpha}\lambda\eta\theta\epsilon\iota\alpha$).[62] The reality

---

[60] Ibid. (CCSG 69:16–17); ibid. 7 (CCSG 69:35–6). Bornert (*Les commentaires byzantines*, 92) correctly observes that "As with Origen, liturgical mystagogy is for Maximus less an initiation in the mystery of the liturgy than an introduction to the mystery [of Christ] based on the liturgy." He also rightly notes (p. 90) that Maximus actually uses the language of "contemplation" ($\theta\epsilon\omega\rho\iota\alpha$) much more than "mystagogy" per se. On the parallel between liturgical and scriptural contemplation, see Bornert, *Les commentaires byzantines*, 93–7.

[61] *Myst.* 5 (CCSG 69:22).

[62] See Bornert's analysis of Maximus' language of symbolism in *Les commentaires byzantines*, 110–23; cf. Irénée-Henri Dalmais, "Théologie de l'église et mystère liturgique dans la *Mystagogie* de S. Maxime le Confesseur," in Elizabeth Livingstone, ed., *Studia Patristica* 13 (Berlin: Akademie-Verlag, 1975), 146–8; Balthasar, *Cosmic Liturgy*, 324–5; Larchet, *La divinisation de l'homme*, 404–7, 426–30; Thunberg, *Man and the Cosmos*, 151–9.

signified is not exhausted by its immanence in the signifier, but the latter still graciously offers a "real" presence to its contemplating subjects. This contemplative "seeing" is a *becoming*. Before actually treating the contemplation of the liturgy, Maximus details the restorative change of soul and body attending this sanctified intuition. The five pairings of mind and reason, wisdom and prudence, contemplation and praxis, knowledge and virtue, sustained knowledge and faith, respectively vectored toward divine Truth and Goodness, are like strings of the lyre of the soul attuned to the worship of God and reuniting the self to Christ:

> Jesus my God and Savior, who is completed by me who am saved, brings me back to himself, who is always filled to overflowing with plenitude and who can never be exhausted. He restores me in a marvelous way to myself, or rather to God from whom I received being and toward whom I am directed, long desirous of attaining well-being (τὸ εὖ εἶναι). Whoever has been enabled to know this by experience (ἐκ τοῦ παθεῖν), already *has recognized*, by palpable experience (πεῖραν) of his own *dignity*, how *there is rendered to the image what is made in the image*, how *the archetype is honored*, what is *the power of the mystery* of our salvation, *for what Christ died*, and finally how we can remain in him and he in us (John 15:4).[63]

Reminiscent of Origen's *Logosmystik*, Christ himself is the Mystagogue and Pedagogue. God leads by the hand (χειραγωγοῦντος) his faithful ones,[64] guiding them in liturgy and sacrament to the "restoration" which is also a transfiguration through the overflow of divine grace unleashed in the Word's multiple incarnations.

As for the asceticism of mystagogy, Maximus assumes, as with contemplation, that its formation through liturgy does not differ from its formation in other contexts. It is still a matter of moral reasoning grounded in prudence allied with wisdom, and of the perfected alignment of "prudence, action, and virtue," or of "potency (δύναμις), habitus (ἕξις), and act (ἐνέργεια)."[65] Praxis and contemplation, virtue and knowledge, cross-fertilize each other in the advance toward

---

[63] *Myst.* 5. (CCSG 69:21–4, quoted at ll. 354–65), trans. Berthold, 192 (altered). Maximus cites here (in italics) Gregory Nazianzen, *Or.* 1.4 (SC 247:76–8). The restoration of human nature to itself is also one of the "seven mysteries" of salvation and deification in *Or. dom.* (CCSG 23:34–5); cf. also *Q. Thal.* 35 (CCSG 7:241).

[64] *Myst.* 22 (CCSG 69:49). Loudovikos explores this theme in *A Eucharistic Ontology*, 132–9.

[65] *Myst.* 5 (CCSG 69:25–6).

deification, the most sublime experience (πεῖρα; τὸ πάσχειν) and peace of God; and as Maximus is quick to add, this is an *ecclesial* experience through and through:

> It is in [God's] blessed and most holy embrace that is accomplished this awesome mystery of a union transcending mind and reason by which God becomes one flesh and one spirit with the Church and thus with the soul, and the soul with God. O Christ, how shall I marvel at your goodness? I shall not presume to sing praise because I have not enough strength to marvel in a worthy manner. For, *they shall be two in one flesh*, says the divine Apostle; *this is a great mystery, I speak of Christ and the Church* (Eph. 5:32). And he adds, *The one who cleaves to the Lord is one spirit* (1 Cor. 6:17).[66]

In his extended commentary on the elements of the Divine Liturgy, Maximus in turn demonstrates how each dramatic action advances the faithful contemplatively and ascetically in their *diabasis* to deification:[67]

- The first entrance (of priests and people) as departure from the corruption of the world to a haven of sublime and progressive contemplation.
- The public readings from Scripture as counsels in asceticism and virtue.
- The sacred chants as incitements of ecstatic desire (ἔρως) for God.
- The reading of the Gospel as Christ communicating a final contemplative vision of the *logoi* of things, followed by the bishop's descent from his cathedra, symbolic of the second coming of Christ to punish the wicked and ingather the faithful.
- The closing of the royal doors (into the holy of holies) and dismissal of the catechumens as a transition to more intense judgment of the faithful and yet also their invitation into the "nuptial chamber of Christ" for the ineffable mystery of the Eucharist.
- The Great Entrance in the Eucharistic liturgy as initiation in the secret plan (βουλή) of God for creatures' salvation, and an invitation to the eschatological Eucharist with Christ (Matt. 26:29).
- The holy kiss as a signal of the harmony and singular mind of those becoming intimate with the divine Word.

---

[66] Ibid. (CCSG 69:26–30, quoted at ll. 464–73), trans. Berthold, 194.
[67] The figurative and symbolic descriptions that follow here in summary are drawn from *Myst.* 8–24 (CCSG 69:36–59).

- The recitation of the Creed as the eternally enduring "mystical thanksgiving" for the "principles and modes" (*logoi* and *tropoi*) by which we are saved.

- The Trisagion ("Thrice-Holy" hymn) as an anticipated sharing in the worship of the angelic and intelligible powers of heaven as they move eternally around God.

- The Lord's Prayer (an epiclesis of the Father) as the "personal" (ἐνυπόστατος) and "real" (ἐνυπάρκτος) adoption by the grace of the Holy Spirit of those whose virtues radiate the "divine beauty of goodness."

- The collective "One is Holy," among the hymns concluding the "mystical hierurgy" and transitioning into communion, as the transcendent "gathering and union" of those initiated in the divine simplicity and enjoying the vision of divine glory with the angels.

- The communion/distribution of the Eucharistic *mystêrion* as "transmuting into itself" those who worthily commune, and "revealing them as assimilated by grace and participation to the causal [divine] Good," which is tantamount to deification.


## THE EUCHARIST AND NEW CREATION

### The Cosmic and Ontological Dimensions of Eucharistic Communion with Christ

Though Maximus actually writes relatively little on the Eucharist itself, it is central for him in the drama of the divine economy of creation, redemption, and deification. Indeed, it is the center of gravity of the cosmic liturgy. But his Eucharistic doctrine, the deep roots of which go all the way back to Ignatius of Antioch, Justin Martyr, and Irenaeus of Lyons,[68] is more implicit than explicit, and is couched in his larger incarnational soteriology and eschatology, especially his teaching on the multiple incarnations of Christ the Logos. Scholars have regrettably polarized Maximus' treatment of the

---

[68] Cf. Ignatius, *Ep. ad Smyrnaeos* 6, 20; *Ep. ad Romanos* 7; *Ep. ad Philadelphos* 3–4; Justin, *1 Apologia* 66; and Irenaeus, *Adv. haer.* 5.2.3. All these texts display a strong primary connection between the incarnation proper and Christ's embodiment in the Eucharistic elements.

Eucharist between "symbolistic" and "realistic" interpretations, as if these were irreconcilable, or else they have found little if any reference to the Eucharist's sacrificial dimension in Maximus.[69] Such categorizations, however, force the issue of his allegiance to distinct patterns that scholars have tagged in the history of Eucharistic theology and the doctrine of the Real Presence. Meanwhile, contemporary treatments of symbolism are also not satisfying for understanding Maximus' perspective. As Christoph Schneider writes:

> it is important to keep in mind that Maximus' symbol is not that of the modern, secularized aesthetic experience in which the range of possible meanings is viewed as merely contextually and culturally conditioned. Rather, the multiple meanings of the symbol fulfil a mystagogical function. Under the conditions of the Fall, God is no longer recognized as the centre and ultimate *telos* of all creation, so that creation has lost its original, unconfused unity. Through liturgy, the diachronically and synchronically fragmented creation is led (back) to the one truth of Christ. The relationship between the symbol and that which it signifies is "epiphanic," as the reality which it renders accessible is itself present in the symbol. Consequently, semiotics and ontology are inextricably intertwined. To "interpret" and to "understand" a liturgical symbol is not just a hermeneutic and cognitive activity. Rather, it enables the believer to *participate* in the divine mysteries, that is, in the salvific events of Christ's life, death, and resurrection.[70]

The true beginning (and ending) point for Maximus' Eucharistic teaching is the larger theophanic mystery of divine embodiment,[71] which determines, through the definitive perspective of the recapitulative incarnation of God in Jesus Christ, the conditions of all communion between Creator and creatures. Thus it is imperative to dig deep again into the Confessor's christocentric cosmology and eschatology, for communion is not simply, *pace* John Zizioulas, a communication of life between *persons*, but is grounded in created *nature* itself. To his credit, Zizioulas has drawn much attention to the cosmic and eschatological dimensions of the Eucharist in Maximus and the Greek Fathers. But his emphasis on the "eucharistic or priestly function of man, [who] reconnects created nature to infinite existence, and thus liberates it from slavery to necessity by letting it

---

[69] As noted by Thunberg, *Man and the Cosmos*, 149–59; cf. Loudovikos, *A Eucharistic Ontology*, 13–15.
[70] Schneider, "The Transformation of Eros," 282–3.
[71] Recalling again *Amb. Jo.* 7 (PG 91:1084C–D).

develop its potentialities to the maximum" since nature itself "possesses neither personhood nor communion [but] 'groans and is in travail' (Rom. 8:22),"[72] risks eclipsing the prior High Priesthood of Christ the Word already operative in the very fabric of all created nature. For according to Maximus, Christ graced it for communion when he pre-evangelized the cosmos in the immanent *logoi* of nature. The Gospel of Christ—the full harvest of his creative and salvific acts—is a "priesthood" (ἱερωσύνη) in its own right,[73] dramatized in the Divine Liturgy but already pervading creation's stage in anticipation of the new creation.

Nikolaos Loudovikos has in fact extrapolated from Maximus an entire "Eucharistic ontology" and metaphysics of communion. Its roots lie in the "loving self-multiplication of the Lamb, who becomes, as a gift, 'all things to all men' (1 Cor. 9:22) corresponding to the unique personal character and otherness of each of the participants."[74] The Eucharistic gift at bottom is the gift of creaturely being itself, which, through the exchange of gifts of Creator and creatures,[75] and crucially through the overflow of divine generosity (Eph. 2:4),[76] becomes ever richer and deeper, in the direction of creatures' "well-being" and ultimate "eternal well-being," an unceasing eschatological communion. In *Ambiguum* 48, which Loudovikos rightly highlights, Maximus portrays the Word as the Paschal Lamb who feeds the many higher and lower parts of his body to those who—"according to ability, order (1 Cor. 15:23), and the grace of the Spirit given him or her"[77]—benefit from those parts in their perfect individuation and diversification.

> For example, the head shall be partaken of by whosoever possesses faith, a faith whose rational principles of theology (θεολογίας λόγους) are entirely free from indemonstrable first principles, for it is on the basis of such faith that the whole body of the virtues and knowledge is *knit together and grows with a (spiritual) growth* (Col. 2:19). The ears shall be

---

[72] *Being as Communion*, 118; also id., *Communion and Otherness: Further Studies in Personhood and the Church* (New York: T. & T. Clark, 2006), 55–68. On nature and necessity in Zizioulas's reading of Maximus, see also my remarks on pp. 205–6, 316–17 in this volume.

[73] Cf. QD 7 (CCSG 10:6–7); *Myst.* 13 (CCSG 69:41–2). See also Cooper, *The Body in St. Maximus the Confessor*, 169–77.

[74] Loudovikos, *A Eucharistic Ontology*, 30–7 (quoted at 36–7).

[75] Ibid., 37–41.     [76] See *Amb. Jo.* 48 (PG 91:1361D–1364A).

[77] Ibid. (1364B).

partaken of by whosoever spiritually receives the divine words (λόγους) with knowledge, and because of these words becomes in actual deeds submissive and "obedient to God unto death (Phil. 2:8). The eyes shall be partaken of by whosoever beholds creation spiritually, and blamelessly gathers together all the principles (λόγους) pertaining to sensation and intellect for the singular fulfillment of the glory of God. The breast shall be partaken of by whosoever has filled his heart with theological contemplations, like the great Evangelist John (cf. John 13:25; 21:20) . . .

. . . of the lower members of the Word let him partake chastely who stands in the strength of his reason when confronting matter, and who together with his soul keeps his flesh perfectly undefiled, and who by means of the virtues completely forms within it the whole Word who became flesh. Of the thighs let him partake who has reason set in authority over the passionate part of the soul, and who has completely uprooted its propensity toward matter. Of the knees let him partake who providentially bends down in compassion to those who have fallen and are weak in faith, thereby imitating the gracious condescension to us of the Word . . .[78]

In *Ambiguum* 48, Maximus clearly conflates but hardly confuses the Johannine images of Christ as Word incarnate, Lamb, and spiritual food (manna/bread from heaven). In any one role the Logos is playing all his roles, and gives himself, without diminution, to all his beneficiaries, through the *logoi* in which he is "enfleshed." The Eucharistic overtones, meanwhile, are unmistakable. The Word consumed (whether through virtue, contemplation, or the sacramental meal itself) is always also the Paschal Lamb, and Maximus warns against partaking of his body overconfidently or illicitly (cf. 1 Cor. 11:17–34).[79] He further instructs Thalassius and his Libyan monks that no creature could fully consume Christ's body or exhaust communion with him, for while one may commune through his "flesh and blood" (the *logoi* of sensible and intelligible realities[80]), "not a bone of him shall be broken" (Exod. 12:46; John 19:36), since his bones are the utterly ineffable *logoi* of his divinity, "or the unknown power itself that sustains nature unto eternal well-being through deification."[81]

Maximus' broadened doctrine of "Eucharistic" communion thus does not undermine its properly paschal dimension but locates it at every level in the intricate web of created being. Communion with

---

[78] Ibid. (1364C–1365A), trans. Constas II, 217–19.　　[79] Ibid. (1364B).
[80] Q. *Thal.* 35 (CCSG 7:239–41).　　[81] Ibid. (quoted at ll. 43–4).

Christ through the *logoi* accesses the faithful to the drama at play in the bosom of the world, a world that is eminently purposeful and yet perennially vulnerable, liable to the chaos (τὸ ἄτακτον) that inheres in materiality.[82] Vital communion within and among created beings—generated, nurtured, and perfected by the Logos-Christ in his providence and judgment—is the vocation of the cosmos as a whole and of each particular creature within it. The *logoi* themselves, as Loudovikos stresses, "are by no means impervious entities closed to communication, but on the contrary exist only in relationship, in a communion with each other which unifies the divisions which may appear to exist in creation."[83] Ontologically, they bind together universals and particulars, induce "dialogical reciprocity," and move creatures "ecstatically" beyond self-interest toward the self-giving characteristic of the new creation.[84] But even more basically, as I noted in Chapter 3, the *logoi* are the staging-points through which the Logos is graciously and actively *working still* (John 5:17) with the Father to this end.[85] The durability but also "flexibility" of the *logoi*, and their permeability to the live activity of the Logos, are a function of the seamlessness of the divine operation of creation and redemption, and of the freedom of the Creator always to open up new horizons of deifying communion for and with his creatures.

To contemporary eyes, this vision of communion may appear far too ascetical and "gnosiological" to do justice to the unique sacramentality of the Eucharistic rite itself. Loudovikos rightly emphasizes, however, that for Maximus the peculiar "knowledge" granted through communion with Christ the Word is more akin to biblical representations of knowledge as vital participation.[86] And as Maximus would have recognized from the Cappadocian Fathers, contemplating the *logoi* of creation, and of the Logos's providence and judgment, is not a detached spiritual exercise exclusive to monastics but an altogether *ecclesial* protocol,[87] since the Church is the threshold of the new creation. Whether through the *logoi* or, most intensely, through the Eucharistic elements, the Logos is "transmuting into himself through the Spirit" (μεταποιῶν πρὸς ἑαυτὸν τῷ Πνεύματι) those who partake

---

[82] *Amb. Jo.* 8 (PG 91:1101D–1105B); see also pp. 117–18 in this volume.

[83] *A Eucharistic Ontology*, 123.      [84] Ibid., 123–94, 199–206.

[85] *Q. Thal.* 2 (CCSG 7:51); see also pp. 121–2 in this volume.

[86] *A Eucharistic Ontology*, 101–2. On Maximus' broadened definition of "communion," see also Larchet, *La divinisation de l'homme*, 424–6.

[87] See Blowers, *Drama of the Divine Economy*, 322–8.

of him,[88] just as the ritual distribution (μετάδοσις) of the bread and wine is a "transmuting into itself" (μεταποιοῦσα πρὸς ἑαυτήν) of those who worthily commune.[89]

Such "worthiness" presupposes a whole economy of formation and transformation of the faithful which preserves the otherness of Giver and receiver, their perpetual reciprocity,[90] the sheer gratuity of the Gift, and yet the summons to the receiver to be assimilated in every way possible to the Giver and to the Gift.[91]

## Presence and Mystery: Maximus' Evocative Silence on the Anaphora

What seems superficially to be a glaring omission in Maximus' commentary on the Divine Liturgy in the *Mystagogia* is his silence on the very heart of the Eucharistic rite, the anaphora, or ritual prayer combining elements of thanksgiving, offering, remembrance, invocation, and consecration. Numerous scholars have tried to explain this. One theory is that the anaphora in Maximus' time was uttered inaudibly and that he was respecting the *disciplina arcana*, or rule of secrecy.[92] Another is that he prescinded from it because he was not himself an ordained priest.[93] Still another is that Maximus was

---

[88] *Amb. Jo.* 48 (PG 91:1365C).  [89] *Myst.* 21 (CCSG 69:48).

[90] On this reciprocity, see notably *Amb. Jo.* 10 (PG 91:1113B–C): "For they say that God and man are paradigms (παραδείγματα) of each other, so that as much as man, enabled by love, has divinized himself for God, to that same extent God is humanized for man by His love for mankind; and as much as man has manifested God who is invisible by nature through the virtues, to that same extent man is rapt by God in mind to the unknowable" (trans. Constas II, 165).

[91] See Thunberg, who, considering what "worthy" reception entails, emphasizes the grace of adoption through assimilation (*Myst.* 23), and concludes that "the *likeness* which is referred to here is in the first place that of the sacrament to the divine reality, and secondarily that of the receiver in relation to what is received, thanks to his degree of receptiveness. If that is correct, what Maximus wants to say is that *the incarnational likeness of the sacrament receives the responsive likeness of the communicant into itself and transforms it into the likeness of human deification*" (*Man and the Cosmos*, 171–3).

[92] Bornert, *Les commentaires byzantins*, 107–8; Berthold, *Maximus Confessor*, 222, n. 110; Spinks, *Do This in Remembrance of Me*, 128; cf. Törönen, *Union and Distinction*, 150.

[93] Thunberg, *Man and the Cosmos*, 114, 152, 157–8; Riou, *Le monde et l'église*, 165, n. 37. For still other explanations, see J. P. Williams, *Denying Divinity: Apophasis in the Patristic Christian and Soto Zen Buddhist Traditions* (Oxford: Oxford University Press, 2000), 102–4.

making good on his promise not to repeat the insights of Dionysius,[94] though the Areopagite himself had commented only indirectly on the anaphora, referencing the priests' extolling of the "divine operations" (θεουργίαι) in the economy of salvation, most decisively the incarnation itself.[95]

These are not necessarily irrelevant or mutually exclusive explanations but they are hardly satisfying given the Confessor's meticulous attention to the deep structure of the liturgy. *This is a theologically intentional silence.* As Oliver Davies remarks of Christian apophaticism, "it is shaped within particular liturgical communities who are called to give verbal expression to a specific intervention of God in history. Apophasis in this sense articulates the human response to a divine communicative presence, and it is burdened as much by an excess of presence as it is by an endemic sense of absence."[96] Maximus had learned from the Bible, from the Cappadocian Gregories, and especially from Dionysius that silence can be the most profound language of praise. As the human being is a "mystical church," the worshiping mind is its altar, at which she or he "summons the silence, abounding in hymns in the innermost sanctuary, of the unseen and unknown but overwhelming call (μεγαλοφωνίας) of the Divine, through another silence that speaks and is many-voiced."[97] Presumably those "voices" of silence could express the pure sense of being at a loss to penetrate an ineffable mystery,[98] or be an inversion of ebullient praise in the

---

[94] Hans-Joachim Schulz, *The Byzantine Liturgy: Symbolic Structure and Faith Expression*, trans. Matthew O'Connell (New York: Pueblo, 1986), 46–7.

[95] *Eccl. hier.* 3.3.11 (PTS 36:90–2).

[96] "Toward a Theological Poetics of Silence," in Oliver Davies and Denys Turner, eds., *Silence and the Word: Negative Theology and Incarnation* (Cambridge: Cambridge University Press, 2002), 201.

[97] *Myst.* 4 (CCSG 69:19, ll. 278–81). In ibid. 23 (CCSG 69:54–5, ll. 877–82), Maximus quotes the passage from Dionysius (*Div. nom.* 4.22, PTS 33:169–70) in which the phrase "the silence in the innermost sanctuary" originally appears. See also Q. *Thal.* 48 (CCSG 7:331), where, embarking on an interpretation of a scriptural *aporia*, Maximus prays to the Logos to be "found worthy of coming to your ineffable place of feasting," in order to "make sound together with those who are spiritually feasting there, and begin to sing the knowledge of unspeakable truths with the *eruptive voices of the mind* (ἀσιγήτοις νοῦ φωναῖς) . . ."

[98] For instances of "honoring in silence" a mystery of the faith, see Q. *Thal.* Intro. (CCSG 7:37); ibid. 43 (CCSG 7:293); *Amb. Jo.* 20 (PG 91:1241B); *Amb. Th.* 5 (CCSG 48:31). See also *Th. Oec.* 1.83: "It is precarious to attempt to speak the ineffable in verbal discourse, for this type of language is twofold and manifold in utterance. It is safest to contemplate without words and only in the soul the One Who Is . . ." (PG 90:1117B), trans. Berthold, 144 (slightly altered).

experience of the mystery, or elicit a speechless and ecstatic love (ἔρως) for the triune God, or uphold an apophaticism that complements and conditions the kataphatic language pervasive in liturgy.

But that Maximus, intending as he says to follow up on Dionysius's insights, is even more silent than the Areopagite on the anaphora, is hardly accidental. Since Dionysius had reserved his remarks to the *kataphatic* aspect of the anaphora, the eulogizing of God's works of creation and redemption that was common in the prefaces and post-Sanctus sections of Eastern anaphoras, it makes good sense that Maximus complements him by maintaining *apophatic* silence and talking around the anaphora, as it were. With its anamnetic and consecratory rites, and its epiclesis of the Holy Spirit, the anaphora included the most intense encounter with God in the whole liturgy. It was (always) a fresh epiphany. Just before the anaphora, this intimacy was signaled in the kiss of peace,[99] as well as in the closing of the Royal Doors, when the faithful entered the "nuptial chamber" (νυμφών) of Christ[100]— images that for Maximus likely recalled Song of Songs 1:1–4 and Gregory of Nyssa's interpretation of these verses in terms of progressive mystical identification with the Logos-Bridegroom.[101] In the Dionysian–Maximian dialectics of disclosure and concealment, the anaphora, as the nucleus of the Eucharist, effectively poised the faithful between the "saturating" presence of the incarnate Word (the Word who aspires *always* to be incarnate in *all* created things[102]) and the infinitely inaccessible essence of the Trinity—an inaccessibility experienced as "absence" but in no way constricting God's own freedom to be present in the celebration. On this point I would take issue with Christos Yannaras's otherwise compelling argument that for Dionysius and Maximus, the ecstasy of the divine person "outside-of-nature" and the reciprocal human ecstasy toward God's nature had their "final" realization in the Eucharist.[103] It is the subtle difference, I suggest, between an ecstasy *from* the divine nature accomplished by the Son's person and an ecstasy *of* the

---

[99] Cf. *Myst.* 17 (CCSG 69:46), where "the worthy receive intimacy (οἰκείωσιν οἱ ἄξιοι δέχονται) with the divine Word" through the kiss of peace; also ibid. 23 (p. 52), indicating how the kiss unites them spiritually to the Logos himself.

[100] Ibid. 15 (CCSG 69:44–5).

[101] See *Hom. in Cant.* 1 (GNO 6:14–42), though Gregory himself does not specifically interpret these verses in Eucharistic terms.

[102] *Amb. Jo.* 7 (PG 91:1084C-D).

[103] See *Person and Eros*, trans. Norman Russell (Brookline, MA: Holy Cross Orthodox Press, 2008), 126–8, 150–3.

divine nature in the Son's Person. Maximus, like Dionysius, believed that this ecstasy still allowed God to "remain within himself."[104] The divine Word/Son enjoyed the prerogative to be "naturally" present in person, even while the divine nature itself remained uncircumscribable. The weight of the saturating presence is the drawing nigh of the divine nature, even if the divine "superessence" (ὑπερουσία) commensurately recedes.

Between saturating divine presence and experienced absence, therefore, the anaphora commanded an appropriate posture of silence. Remembering that Maximus poses himself in the *Mystagogia* as an initiate or disciple, not a doyen, his silence on the anaphora is understandable and still very much within the spirit of the Areopagite. Alain Riou goes a step further, suggesting that for the Confessor, "the true anaphora of Christ, with its configuring anamnesis and eschatological epiclesis, is completed only in martyrdom itself: in this apophatic anaphora, the Christian and the Church receive in communion and consummate in silence the mystery of paschal transparency."[105]

Hans-Joachim Shulz, however, has prudently advised that we pay close attention to Maximus' dramatic build-up to the anaphora in his commentary, such as might give us more forthright hints as to why he then circumvents it. The Confessor's discourse noticeably changes as he approaches it. The language of figure and symbol does not disappear, but there is increasing reference to the mystery now made real in the church's midst, signaled in the Great Entrance as

> the beginning and prelude of the new teaching (καινῆς διδασκαλίας) to be delivered in heaven concerning the plan of God for us and the revelation of the mystery of our salvation concealed in the innermost sanctuary of divine secrecy. For the Word of God said to his disciples, *I shall not drink from the fruit of the vine until that day when I drink it anew with you in my Father's Kingdom* (Matt. 26:29).[106]

This new instruction enables the worthy to achieve full knowledge of the *logoi* of sensible and intelligible realities, whereupon the Logos leads them up to genuine *theologia* (encounter with the Trinity) at the end of their spiritual journey (διάβασις).[107] As Shulz notes, this "new teaching" can only reference the anaphora,[108] at which point the Church finds

---

[104] See Dionysius, *Div. nom.* 4.13 (PTS 33:158–9), quoted by Maximus in *Amb. Jo.* 71 (PG 91:1413A–B).
[105] *Le monde et l'église*, 165.    [106] *Myst.* 16 (CCSG 69:45, ll. 721–8).
[107] Ibid. 23 (p. 52).    [108] *The Byzantine Liturgy*, 47.

itself liturgically leaving the dimension of expectation and forthwith entering, sacramentally, the dimension of final fulfillment.

## The Church's Eucharist as Eschatological Denouement

Despite his silence on the anamnesis and the words of institution, Maximus quotes Jesus from the Last Supper—*I shall not drink from the fruit of the vine until that day when I drink it anew with you in my Father's Kingdom* (Matt. 26:29).[109] This is but an accentuation of the eschatological momentum of the Eucharistic liturgy. The Church proceeds with Christ behind closed doors, which are nonetheless, paradoxically, the open doors of eschatological paradise. When, after the reading of the Gospel, the bishop *qua* Christ descends from his cathedra,[110] this is nothing less than the second coming. "All that follows belongs to the life of the future kingdom of Heaven. It is the eschaton made present: union of all with God as he is."[111] Indeed, the Eucharist is the pure liturgical dramatization of the "realized" eschatology that runs throughout Maximus' theology, in which the "ages" of divine embodiment and of creaturely deification are not purely chronologically consecutive but overlap according to the singularity of the Creator's ultimate purpose in and beyond time.[112] Zizioulas remarks,

> The "end" constitutes the "reason" for which both the past and the present "subsist," according to Saint Maximus; and in consequence the "future age which does not end" becomes . . . not an effect, as happens in time as we know it after the Fall, but the *cause* of all past and present events. Consequently, remembrance of this "endless" future is not only possible but also ontologically definitive in the realm of the Eucharist as icon of the Kingdom.[113]

Geoffrey Wainwright has noted this strongly eschatological orientation of the Eucharist in Maximus, but also his silence on the *meal*

---

[109] *Myst.* 16 (CCSG 69:45, ll. 725–8).     [110] Ibid. 14 (p. 43).
[111] Törönen, *Union and Distinction*, 151; cf. Zizioulas, *The Eucharistic Communion and the World*, 48–50; Geoffrey Wainwright, *Eucharist and Eschatology*, 2nd edn. (New York: Oxford University Press, 1981), 73, 90, 117, 126, 153.
[112] *Q. Thal.* 22 (CCSG 7:137–43).
[113] *The Eucharistic Communion and the World*, 59–60. Zizioulas is commenting here on the fact that in the anaphoras of the Divine Liturgy, there is a "remembrance" of the *future* event of the Second Coming.

aspect.[114] The most Maximus does is quote Jesus's promise to celebrate the meal with his disciples in his future Kingdom. But here again, as with the anaphora itself, his silence is telling. In the present celebration of the Eucharistic liturgy, the faithful are already with Christ in the heavenly meal, the ambiance and circumstances of which transcend conceptualization and imagination. The Church shares in Christ's priesthood of the new creation and, through Eucharistic worship, helps to draw all of reconciled creation into the eternal feast, the universal communion among creatures and between creatures and Christ—the perfection of self-giving love and the supreme "distribution of gifts," as Loudovikos calls it.[115] Even if Maximus does not specifically designate the bread and wine in an Irenaean manner as the "first-fruits" of creation offered to God (for the sake of a new covenant and new creation),[116] it is unthinkable that he did not know this interpretation and may well have assumed its validity. But Irenaeus had also connected these "first-fruits" with Christ's own sacrificed body and blood, and Maximus definitely privileged a compatible view. The "incarnate"—enfleshed (in all its forms), crucified, risen, and now glorified—body of Christ, he believes, is the true first-fruits of the new creation,[117] and therefore the prime food for the eschatological repast. An observation of Wainwright is especially relevant to Maximus: the manner by which Christ can be both the Host (Giver) of the eschatologically-charged Eucharistic banquet and its food (Gift) remains a pure mystery for the Church in the historical meanwhile.[118]

As we leave Maximus' ecclesiology to take up other key themes, I would emphasize that lingering always in the background of his deep integration of Christology, cosmology, Eucharist, ecclesiology, and eschatology is the enduring principle, arising from Irenaeus and famously echoed in Athanasius and the Cappadocian Fathers, that the divine incarnational descent is purposed to the ascent of creation to God, which is deification. The fulcrum of Maximus' vision is Jesus Christ and his recapitulation (ἀνακεφαλαίωσις) and transfiguration of all things. And yet there is a kind of derivative primacy in the other angles of Maximus' kaleidoscopic approach. Cosmologically, this is the story of all creation

---

[114] *Eucharist and Eschatology*, 49.
[115] *A Eucharistic Ontology*, 199–200.
[116] See Irenaeus, *Adv. haer.* 4.17.5 (SC 100:590–2).
[117] *Amb. Jo.* 7 (PG 91:1097B); ibid. 31 (1280C–D); ibid. 32 (1281A–B).
[118] Wainwright, *Eucharist and Eschatology*, 107.

and its destiny. The Eucharist brings that story into focus as a cosmic liturgy with Christ as subject (Host) and object. Ecclesiologically, the Church, through the Spirit, shares Christ's priesthood of creation and, as one of his continuing embodiments in the world, works toward the ingathering not only of "all flesh" but of "all things" into the mystery of deification. Eschatology—both "realized" and futurist—presents the whole economy as a christocentric project "from the end." Here as elsewhere we see how Maximus' finesse as a theologian was the intricate insinuation of these motifs, the subtlety with which he constructed and nurtured the connecting tissues between them.

# Part III

# Maximus' Vision for the
# Transfigured Creation

# 6

---

## Protology and Teleology in Maximus' Interpretation of Human Nature, Human Fallenness, and Human Hope

With this chapter and the two that follow, we turn more directly to the *oikonomia*, the intensifying drama of salvation and deification as creative operations of the triune God, and to Maximus' eschatological vision for the transfiguring of creation. In so doing we hardly leave behind the "cosmic landscapes" that I have sketched in the preceding three chapters, especially as we approach Maximus' anthropology and moral psychology. Indeed, Maximus' anthropology is a kind of lattice-work of intersecting cosmological, christological, eschatological, and ascetical themes. Human beings are constituted not to be independent moral agents ultimately saved from their abused freedom, but to be mutually-bonded priests of creation who participate "creatively" and constructively with Christ in the divine project of transfiguring the entire cosmos.

In context, we understand Greek patristic theological anthropology much differently—and, I believe, more accurately—if we divest ourselves of habitual stereotypes about the sequence of action in Genesis 1–3, including the tendency to read the story as a simple linear pattern of cause and effect, or as an uncomplicated plot recounting humanity's incipient perfection, transgression, and rehabilitation. Most patristic authors East and West read the early chapters of Genesis as a "thick" narrative inviting speculation into the precise character of human origins and the primal sin but already thoroughly shot through with the Christian Gospel of renewal and transformation. In the perspective deriving originally from Irenaeus, these chapters previewed, in summary dramatic form, the history of the world as the Creator's work-in-progress. For most patristic interpreters, these chapters were prophetic, teeming with insights into the destiny of creation and especially of the human race, and signaling the strategies of the Creator not only to make good on his plan for creation but to open up all new possibilities for human thriving out of the apparent disastrousness of Adam's lapse.[1]

Even if he does not explicitly articulate the notion of creation as an act of divine kenosis in the manner of some contemporary theologians,[2] Maximus implies that creation was a function of God's condescension, and not just a demonstration of divine sovereignty or creative power, insofar as the Creator already anticipated the tragic as well as salutary consequences of creating, and granting freedom to, an "other." Already in premeditating his work in the *logoi*, God invested *redemptive* as well as creative grace in his project. Creation, in time and space, was therefore abounding from the outset in dramatic suspense. As I noted in Chapter 3 considering Maximus' cosmology, the paradigm of *theo-drama*, which Hans Urs von Balthasar elaborated in part based on his extensive work on Maximus, is an exceedingly useful framework for interpreting the Confessor's re-imagining of the economy of creation and salvation. The crux of the dilemma is not simply whether the Creator's prescience of the Adamic fall or his justice *pre* and *post facto* will be vindicated, but whether, having anticipated and comprehended creatures' deviance, the Creator will use every contingency in creation's history to advance his purposes and to resolve those contingencies into the mystery of deification so as to "do a new thing" (Isa. 43:19). Maximus has little concern for a philosophically-styled theodicy, and would have us concentrate foremost on the unfolding drama commencing when the preconceived, simultaneous, potential creation became actualized.

## THE HUMAN CREATURE: A THEO-DRAMATIC WORK-IN-PROGRESS

Before considering the existential conditions of "paradise" and the primeval Adamic fall in Maximus' thought, there is the underlying

---

[1] See Blowers, *Drama of the Divine Economy*, 101–87; Peter Bouteneff, *Beginnings: Ancient Christian Readings of the Biblical Creation Narratives* (Grand Rapids, MI: Baker Academic, 2008), 55–168.

[2] e.g. John Polkinghorne, ed., *The Work of Love: Creation as Kenosis* (Grand Rapids, MI: Eerdmans, 2001).

issue of the precise *ontological* status of creation, and especially human nature, before and after the lapse. Patristic authors who believed that Adam had misused his freedom were wittingly or unwittingly pressed back onto the question of how a creature fashioned in the divine image (εἰκών) and ontologically predisposed toward the divine likeness (ὁμοίωσις) could squander such a gift unless there was a latent flaw that surfaced when the freedom was actualized. Maximus, maintaining a rather strict *a posteriori* perspective on Adam's transgression, never systematically addressed this issue and presupposed the Cappadocians' absolute insistence that the Creator produced no moral evil in created nature and that rational creatures alone, in Gregory of Nyssa's words, "invented" vice.[3]

But there were other Cappadocian insights on human protology that Maximus revered as well, and that provided springboards for developing his own anthropogenetic ideas. What emerges, in turn, is a carefully worked-out drama of the dynamism and openness of human nature and of the resourcefulness of the Creator who is always free to draw from created nature new possibilities of transformation. Engaging especially the two Cappadocian Gregories, Maximus integrated four salient themes in his own retelling of the story of paradise, the fall, and the consequences of the fall for the human race: (1) a careful dialectical nuancing of human "nature" (φύσις) in its own right; (2) a related and more developed dialectics of the passibility (τὸ πάθος) of human nature considered from before and after the lapse in Genesis 1–3; (3) speculation on the character of the Adamic fall itself; and (4) an overarching *teleological* or eschatological perspective that governed and even redefined protology, the doctrine of origins.

## The Dialectics of Human "Nature"

Already in Chapter 3 I briefly examined some of Maximus' ideas on created nature, which is as much the horizon as it is the matrix and plan (*logos*) of creaturely becoming.[4] In his interpretive playfulness, however,

---

[3] *De virginitate* 12 (GNO 8/1:298–9). Cf. Athanasius's earlier claim that humanity "conceived" (ἐπενόησε) evil when it had no ontological status in creation (*Contra gentes* 7) and that humans are the "inventors of evil" (εὑρεταὶ τῆς κακίας) (*De incarnatione* 5), ed. Robert Thomson (Oxford: Oxford University Press, 1971), 18, 146.

[4] See pp. 129–30 in this volume.

the Confessor exploits the polyvalence of *physis* and does not always signal the specific meaning the term carries when he uses it. In its basic sense "nature" is synonymous with common "essence" (οὐσία),[5] the utter stability of a single nature, together with its "essential activity" (οὐσιώδης ἐνέργεια) and predisposition (ἕξις),[6] as undergirded by the Logos who authors and orders the universe of created natures in their salutary diversity. And yet Maximus resists a notion of *pura natura* nested in the laurels of its ontological security. Each being's "principle of nature" (λόγος φύσεως), the staging point of the Logos's own immanent operation within it, summons that being into the fray, as it were, of existing, and into a peculiar mode (τρόπος) of motion and actualization. Nature is an essence drawn into a "history" of interrelation and inter-action with other natures in the living mosaic that is creation—what I earlier termed Maximus' "cosmo-politeian" vision.[7] In a letter to Thalassius, Maximus calls nature the mediating factor which negotiates humanity between God and "the world," guiding human beings from merely "carnal" existence in this world to the deifying reality of God.[8]

The special dignity of *essential* human nature and its position as a composite "microcosm" of the macrocosm of creation is a central theme of Maximus' theological anthropology that has been thoroughly fore-grounded in the work of Lars Thunberg and others, so I shall not revisit it in detail here. With it Maximus establishes the strategic position and unique mediatory role of human nature in the divine economy.[9] The bond between soul and body lies at the core of human nature and is indicative of the "image of God" (Gen. 1:26–7); and it is a magnet or rallying point for the solidarity of all corporeal creatures, as we find in a salient statement from *Ambiguum 7*:

> It is as if Gregory [Nazianzen] were saying that God in his goodness made man as a union of soul and body, so that the soul which was given to him, being rational and intellectual—because it is created in the very *image* of its Creator—should, on the one hand, by means of its desire and the whole power of its total love, cling closely to God through knowledge, and, growing in *likeness to God*, be divinized; and, on the other hand, through its mindful care of what is lower, in accordance with the commandment to *love one's neighbor as oneself* (Matt. 22:39), it should make prudent use of

---

[5] e.g. *Opusc.* 14 (PG 91:149B); ibid. 23 (264C).
[6] e.g. *Amb. Th.* 5 (CCSG 48:31).      [7] See pp. 130–4 in this volume.
[8] *Ep.* 9 (PG 91:445C–448B).
[9] See esp. *Myst.* 7 (CCSG 69:33–6); *Amb. Jo.* 41 (PG 91: 1305A–1308C); *Ep.* 6 (PG 91:429D). For analysis, see Thunberg, *Microcosm and Mediator*, esp. 95–330.

its body, with a view to ordering it to the mind through the virtues, and acquaint it with God as its fellow servant, itself mediating to the body the indwelling presence of its Creator, making God himself—who bound together the body and the soul—the body's own unbreakable bond of immortality. The aim is "what God is to the soul, the soul might become to the body,"[10] and that the Creator of all might be proven to be One, *and through humanity might come to reside in all beings in a manner appropriate to each, so that the many, though separated from each other in nature, might be drawn together into a unity as they converge around the one human nature.* When this happens, *God will be all things in everything* (1 Cor. 15:28), encompassing all things and making them subsist in himself, for beings will no longer possess independent motion or fail to share in God's presence, and it is with respect to this sharing that we are, and are called, *gods* (John 10:35), *children of God* (John 1:12), the *body*, and *members of God* (Eph. 1:23; 5:20), and it follows, "portions of God,"[11] and other such things, in the progressive ascent of the divine plan to its final end.[12]

Here Maximus has deeply insinuated *vocation* into the human essence, or nature. Human nature's integrity is preserved and extended not only by the soul's internal work of forming and loving its immediate "neighbor" and "fellow servant"—the body—but also by external agapic communion with other individual persons/neighbors/bodies who equally share that nature,[13] and by the benefit of human integrity and solidarity thereby accorded to non-human natures in creation. Framed in terms of a familiar triad in Maximus, it is fruitless to imagine natural human "being" (τὸ εἶναι) apart from the state of moral and ecclesial "well-being" (τὸ εὖ εἶναι) and the eschatological state of "eternal well-being" (τὸ ἀεὶ εὖ εἶναι) to be enjoyed by all transfigured creatures.

Maximus, however, also sometimes speaks of human "nature" with a more pejorative nuance when referencing the postlapsarian condition

---

[10]  Gregory Nazianzen, *Or.* 2.17 (PG 35:428A).

[11]  Ibid. 14.7 (PG 35:865C), the text on which Maximus is commenting at length in *Amb. Jo.* 7.

[12]  *Amb. Jo.* 7 (PG 91:1092B–C), trans. Constas I, 119–21 (emphasis added). On the ontological coexistence of soul and body as constitutive for human nature, see also ibid. (1100A–B); ibid. 42 (1321D–1341C). As in Gregory of Nyssa (*Hom. opif.* 28–9, PG 44:229B–240B), this was a core argument against the Origenist doctrine of preexistence of souls.

[13]  On the *natural* equality of human persons, or hypostases, as the basis for indiscriminate love of all, see *Car.* 1.71 (PG 90:976B–C); ibid. 2.30 (993B).

($\kappa\alpha\tau\acute{\alpha}\sigma\tau\alpha\sigma\iota\varsigma$)[14] or circumstance ($\pi\epsilon\rho\acute{\iota}\sigma\tau\alpha\sigma\iota\varsigma$)[15] of corporeal creation, the nature on its own terms and in its *weakness* ($\dot{\alpha}\sigma\theta\acute{\epsilon}\nu\epsilon\iota\alpha$, 2 Cor. 12:9)[16] apart from indwelling grace, asserting itself as though it were independent of the Creator and groping for a mode by which to perpetuate itself. As we observed earlier, Maximus echoes the view of Athanasius and Gregory Nazianzen that a certain ontological poverty or residual chaos ($\tau\grave{o}$ $\ddot{\alpha}\tau\alpha\kappa\tau o\nu$)—wholly distinct from moral evil—already inheres in material and corporeal nature, rendering it susceptible to misappropriation by the rational, moral beings who inhabit bodies.[17] Altogether, this weak condition of created nature is comprehended in the Pauline image of creation's subjection to vanity and corruption (Rom. 8:20ff.).[18]

Predictably the depiction of human nature as persisting in a compromised or "stunted" ($\kappa o\lambda o\beta o\upsilon\mu\acute{\epsilon}\nu\eta$)[19] mode is most in evidence where Maximus reflects on the precise consequences of the Adamic fall. These include the provisional constraints or "law" now imposed on humanity in the form of the irrational, passible side of human nature left to its own devices;[20] the inexorable bouncing back-and-forth between pain and pleasure in human experience;[21] and the relentless forward advance of sexually-generated procreation wherein life becomes a matter of biological survival rather than of flourishing according to humanity's authentic nature and origin ($\gamma\acute{\epsilon}\nu\epsilon\sigma\iota\varsigma$).[22] Thus, as Joshua Lollar has justly emphasized, Maximus' negative description of "nature" most often shows up in his ascetical doctrine, whereas his positive definition is continually reiterated in his teaching on the contemplation of "nature" as reality pre-ordered to the will of God.[23]

Failure to take account of Maximus' dialectical approach to human nature can lead to serious confusion in interpreting his anthropology

[14] On this current condition ($\kappa\alpha\tau\acute{\alpha}\sigma\tau\alpha\sigma\iota\varsigma$), see *Amb. Jo.* 6 (PG 91:1068A); ibid. 50 (1368C).

[15] Ibid. 6 (PG 91:1068B); ibid. 45 (1353C); ibid. 53 (1373A).

[16] *Car.* 2.39 (PG 90:997A); *Amb. Jo.* 7 (PG 91:1069A, 1091A–B); ibid. 8 (1104D, 1105A–B); *Amb. Th.* 4 (CCSG 48:17).

[17] *Amb. Jo.* 8 (PG 91:1101D–1105B). See also pp. 109, 117, 204 in this volume.

[18] *Amb. Jo.* 8 (PG 91:1104B). On the background of patristic interpretation of Rom. 8:19–23, see Blowers, *Drama of the Divine Economy*, 212–22.

[19] *Q. Thal.* 65 (CCSG 22:279, l. 454).

[20] e.g. ibid. 21 (CCSG 7:127–9); ibid. 62 (CCSG 22:131).

[21] Ibid. 61 (CCSG 22:89–91). See also Christoph Schönborn's important study, "Plaisir et douleur dans l'analyse de S. Maxime, d'après les *Quaestiones ad Thalassium*," *MC*, 273–84.

[22] See esp. *Q. Thal.* 21 (CCSG 7:127–3).

[23] Lollar, *To See into the Life of Things*, 205–6, 250–1, 257–60, 301, 306–17.

and cosmology alike. For example, the Orthodox Personalist theologian John Zizioulas obscures the issue, I believe, by taking Maximus' second, more pejorative nuance as the more basic. Nature is what perennially constrains hypostasis, or person, and ontologically "the conflict remains deep and unredeemable."[24] But nature in this sense is primarily *biological* nature binding persons to the "ontological necessity" of passion, individual drive to survive, and "natural death."[25] Zizioulas meanwhile cites Maximus to the effect that the "*logos* of nature" (λόγος φύσεως) is "not nature as such but nature *personalized.*" He further defends his thesis:

> Not emphasizing this may lead to two fundamental misunderstandings of Maximus' theology: (a) that the Fall and sin, including death, are simply the result of a deviation from a previous natural state of existence; and (b) that the authentic form of existence amounts to conformity to nature as such (nature being an ultimate ontological notion). The "logos of nature" points to nature as it is hypostasized in a person; it is the particularization of nature. In other words, to exist "according to the logos of nature" means to hypostatize your nature in true and authentic personhood, to make the general (nature) exist in a state of otherness and particularity for ever. The "logos of nature" is not to "naturalize" the person but to "personalize" nature by turning it from general to particular, by introducing otherness into its very "being".[26]

In Zizioulas's favor, here, is Maximus' fierce realism about embodied human life and his reticence to speculate "behind" the fall to a "natural" state of human existence in which personal human freedom was not in play. On the other hand, the "*logoi* of nature" maintain the stability and integrity of created nature(s) or essence(s) as preordained within the Logos, and the potentiality of creatures that the Logos is leading to perfection. Already before the fall, within the divine plan, created nature is utterly "personalized" by the indwelling Logos-Christ, who in his creative freedom "flexes" the *logoi* so as to enable creatures not only to survive their fallen condition but to thrive in it and beyond it as "new creatures." In this positive vision of things, "nature" and "person" are ontologically *simultaneous*, as are the principles of the universal (τὸ γενικόν) and the particular (τὸ μερικόν). Person (ὑπόστασις) does not trump nature as though liberating it from nature's ontological oppression. Zizioulas spurns "philological" as opposed to theological

<hr/>

[24] Zizioulas, *Communion and Otherness*, 55–62.
[25] Zizioulas, *Being as Communion*, 50–3.
[26] Zizioulas, *Communion and Otherness*, 65.

interpretations of human nature in Maximus,[27] but in so doing he does not satisfactorily honor the plasticity of the Confessor's usage of *physis* and his hermeneutical playfulness in negotiating the suspense of whether and how the all-resourceful Creator will eschatologically subjugate humanity's provisional "nature"—or rather, its provisional condition or mode (τρόπος) of nature—to the "nature" projected toward a supernatural, deified mode of being.[28] Indeed, one of Maximus' theological preoccupations is to demonstrate how this contingent state of human nature nonetheless works to the Creator's ends. Ever resilient, *essential* nature meanwhile moves creatures forward to fulfill the Creator's will, perennially resisting those who would attempt to pervert its course:

> For such is nature, punishing those who undertake to violate it to the degree that they actually live in unnatural opposition to it, by not allowing them to acquire naturally all of nature's power (δύναμιν), for they have been partially deprived of its very integrity (ἀρτιότητος) and for this they are punished, since it is they themselves who pointlessly and foolishly have procured this lack of existence by inclining toward nonbeing.[29]

## The Dialectics of Human Passibility

Maximus' treatment of human nature comes into even sharper focus in his equally dialectical consideration of the "passibility" (τὸ πάθος) of corporeal natures—that is, their liability to irrational passions, suffering, and ultimate death—a theme already central to Gregory of Nyssa's speculations on paradise, the fall, and the destiny of the human race. In effect, Nyssen had asked: Did humanity invent vice because its bodily nature as such was already weak and passible, or is that weakness and passibility rather a consequence of having voluntarily sinned? In order both to avoid the Origenist doctrine of the soul preexisting the body and a Manichaean tendency to anchor evil in the material body itself, Nyssen had posited that indeed, prelapsarian human nature was created with its passible and appetitive dimension intact, but only Adam's actual vice thrust it into an irrational and

---

[27] Ibid., 65–6.
[28] On the possibility of new, supernatural modes of created natures, see pp. 128–9 in this volume.
[29] *Amb. Jo.* 10 (PG 91:1164C–D), trans. Constas I, 265.

bestial mode. More precisely, in his own revision of the notion, going back to Philo and Origen, of a "double creation" (ideal/potential and actual) of humanity, Gregory proposed three phases: first, the creation of human nature ideally and actually as a perfected whole in the image of God (Gen. 1:26–7);[30] second, but simultaneously, the addition of possibility to that nature in God's foreknowledge of the fall;[31] and third, the allowance, after the fall, for that possibility to materialize in the form of the punitive-but-restorative "tunics of skins" (Gen. 3:21), which indicate the concretized sexual division of male and female, the provisional means of human survival by sexual procreation, and the irrationality of human passions given to refinement in the experiential fire of suffering, illusory pleasure, and ultimate death.[32]

Maximus clearly took serious account of Gregory of Nyssa's dialectics of human possibility. He touches explicitly on it in *Amb. Jo.* 8 when discussing how Adam could possibly have squandered his original dignity in paradise:

> There are two possible explanations of how this came about. One possibility is that God, at the very moment humanity fell, blended our soul together with our body on account of the transgression, and endowed it with the capacity to undergo change, just as he gave the body the capacity to suffer, undergo corruption, and be wholly dissolved—as was evinced when God covered the body with the garments of skins (Gen. 3:21). This explanation accords with the text of Scripture: *And the creature was made subject to corruption, not willingly, but for the sake of him who subjected it in hope* (Rom. 8:20). The other possibility is that from the beginning God, in his foreknowledge, formed the soul in the aforesaid way because he foresaw the coming transgression, so that by suffering and experiencing evil on its own, the soul would come to an awareness of itself and its proper dignity, and even gladly embrace detachment with respect to the body.[33]

Elsewhere in the first of the *Questions and Responses for Thalassius*, where Thalassius has asked whether the cardinal passions are evil in

---

[30] *Hom. opif.* 16 (PG 44:177D–185D). See also Bouteneff, *Beginnings*, 157–66.

[31] *Virg.* 12 (GNO 8/1:297–304); *Hom. opif.* 17–18 (PG 44:188A–196B); *Oratio catechetica* (GNO 3/4:29–30).

[32] For insightful analysis of the "tunics of skins" in Gregory of Nyssa and Maximus, see Panayiotis Nellas, *Deification in Christ: The Nature of the Human Person*, trans. Norman Russell (Crestwood, NY: St. Vladimir's Seminary Press, 1987), 43–91.

[33] *Amb. Jo.* 8 (PG 91:1104A–B), trans. Blowers and Wilken, 76. In ibid. 42 (1324D), Maximus states simply that Adam's creation happened "in a secret manner" (μυστικῶς).

themselves or only become so when they are wrongly "used," Maximus appeals directly to Nyssen:

> These passions, and the rest as well, were not originally created together with human nature, for if they had been they would contribute to the definition of human nature. But following what the eminent Gregory of Nyssa taught,[34] I say that, on account of humanity's fall from perfection, the passions were introduced and attached themselves to the more irrational part of human nature. Then, immediately (ἄμα) after humanity had sinned, the divine and blessed image was displaced by the clear and obvious likeness to unreasoning animals. For since humanity, being shrouded from the dignity of reason, human nature had in fairness to be punished with what humans had deliberately incurred—the marks of irrationality; and humanity had to come wisely to perceive the rational magnanimity of the God who governs it.[35]

Maximus' dependence on Gregory, however, runs much deeper than simply echoing his speculations about human origins and passibility. Already Gregory's interest was less in precise protology than in teleology, in carefully reading historical human experience and destiny back into the story of origins—in imitation of how the story is constructed in the Bible itself. As Rowan Williams has shown from Gregory's dialogue with his sister Macrina *On the Soul and Resurrection*, Nyssen himself struggled dialectically with whether passibility had, in good Platonic fashion, to be excluded *absolutely* from the human essence and divine image, being imposed "from without" (ἔξωθεν),[36] or whether, at the end of the day, the soul's lower passible *faculties*—desire (ἐπιθυμία) and temper (θυμός)—are, along with reason, so vital to the spiritual quest of assimilation to God that they must somehow be recuperated as intrinsic.[37] Even if deviant passions (πάθη) are the risked side effects, the "animal" impulses internally serve, under reason's guide, to propel the mind toward the cultivation of virtues, especially as virtues often entail certain qualities of *affect*. Williams plausibly argues that Gregory

---

[34] See Gregory of Nyssa, *Virg.* 12 (GNO 8/1:297, 24–300, 2); ibid. 18 (pp. 317, l. 10–319, l. 25); *De anima et resurrectione* (PG 46: 49B–68A).

[35] *Q. Thal.* 1 (CCSG 7:47, ll. 5–17), trans. Blowers and Wilken, 97. (The last line of this passage was inadvertently left out of my published translation.)

[36] *De anima et res.* (PG 46:53A–57C).

[37] Rowan Williams, "Macrina's Deathbed Revisited: Gregory of Nyssa on Mind and Passion," in Lionel Wickham and Caroline Bammel, eds., *Christian Faith and Greek Philosophy: Essays in Tribute to George Christopher Stead* (Leiden: Brill, 1993), esp. 229–42.

distinguishes between human "essence" strictly speaking, which is an intelligent animating principle, and human "nature" as that essence tending toward a concrete history in which it is empirically linked with sexuality, passions, and bodily experience.[38]

> The conflict of mind and passion arises only when we are forgetful of their continuity—passion (in the wider sense) sustaining a body which is charged with making sense of itself, coming to 'mean' something, to bear the task of an intelligible communication in the world of what God is like; and reason being incapable of moulding bodily life into meaning without harmony with those impulses which are its own foundations or inchoate forms.[39]

Maximus' own "dialectics of passion," as von Balthasar aptly calls it,[40] follows Gregory most closely in privileging the teleology of human passibility over its protology. The overarching goal is an eschatological vision of the Creator's resourcefulness in revealing and perfecting created nature in all its diversity and intricacy, but also the human creature's progressive existential embrace of the sheer gift (and giftedness) of its complex nature. Maximus, as we shall see further on,[41] capitalizes on the Christianized Stoic notion of virtuous use (χρῆσις) of the instincts and passible drives bequeathed on fallen humanity, and integrates this into his overall doctrine of human free will.

For Maximus, there is already the natural passibility, or passivity, by which contingent creatures are at bottom utterly dependent on the gracious motion of the Creator within them, propelling them toward their proper *telos*. With God as both primary and final cause, Maximus sees, as does Nyssen, a certain benevolent and providential "compulsion" (ἀνάγκη) in the constitution and movement of creatures. Nyssen terms it, in parallel with the Creator's pure freedom, "the necessary order of nature" (ἡ ἀναγκαία τῆς φύσεως τάξις)[42] and "that which is realized to the purposes of God's action necessarily according to the sequence of nature, by a certain order and harmony."[43] Maximus frames this

---

[38] Ibid., 233–5.    [39] Ibid., 240.

[40] *Cosmic Liturgy*, 185–96. See also Claire-Agnès Zirnheld, "Le double visage de la passion: malédiction due au péché et/ou dynamisme de la vie: *Quaestiones ad Thalassium* XXI, XXII et XLII," in Schoors and van Deun, *Philohistôr*, 361–80; Blowers, "Gentiles of the Soul," 57–85; id., "The Dialectics and Therapeutics of Desire," esp. 429–44; Demetrios Bathrellos, "Passions, Ascesis, and the Virtues," *OHMC*, 287–306.

[41] See pp. 269–71 in this volume.    [42] *Hexaemeron* (GNO 4/1:19).

[43] Ibid. (GNO 4/1:23): τὸ ἀναγκαίως κατὰ τὴν ἀκολουθίαν τῆς φύσεως ἐν τάξει τινὶ καὶ ἁρμονίᾳ γινόμενον εἰς θείαν ἐνέργειαν.

"necessity" both in terms of the inviolable permanence of a creature's natural principle,[44] and, from the perspective of creaturely freedom and self-determination (αὐτεξουσία), as its predisposition to its targeted end. The creature's "fixed and unchangeable natural disposition" is such that all expressions of (gnomic) will must be surrendered to its deep orientation to the goal of human nature. "We should long to receive being moved (τὸ κινεῖσθαι λαβεῖν ποθήσωμεν)," or in other words, embrace our natural passivity to the divine activity (ἐνέργεια) within us, like an image conforming to its archetype or an imprint to its stamp.[45]

> This occurs through the grace of the Spirit which has conquered (ἐκνικήσασαν) [the human creature], showing that it has God alone acting within it, so that through all there is only one sole energy, that of God and those worthy of God, or rather of God alone, who in a manner befitting his goodness wholly interpenetrates (περιχωρήσαντος) all who are worthy. For of necessity (ἀνάγκη) all things without exception cease from their willful movement toward something else when the ultimate object of their desire and participation appears before them and is, if I may put it this way, contained in them uncontainably according to the measure of the participation of each.[46]

The point is that human *nature*, as directly moved by God's *energeia*, is constraining not in a primarily negative sense but in the positive sense of saving creatures from a non-teleocentric existence and from slavery to unbridled self-determination. The greatest liberation for creatures is precisely a sanguine passivity or "gnomic surrender" (ἐγχώρησις γνωμική)[47] to the benevolent necessity of God freely working within them.

The dark side of human passibility, however, registers itself only in humanity's postlapsarian state, and emerges precisely in Adam's adventure of moving outside this benevolent necessity to pursue the fateful end of choosing purely according to the whim of his own inclination (γνώμη). As a result, the moral integrity of the passible faculties, desire and temper, gives way to a new liability to detrimental passions, passions that do not simply undermine the rule of sanctified reason but thrust the soul into fragmentation and disintegration. This is the condition of the *tunics of skins* (Gen. 3:21), an ambiguous condition

---

[44] *Amb. Jo.* 31 (PG 91:1280A).    [45] Ibid. 7 (PG 91:1076B–C).
[46] Ibid. (1076C–D), trans. Constas II, 91 (slightly altered).    [47] Ibid. (1076B).

now marked by sexual procreation, the need to use instincts of self-protection and self-preservation, and most especially for Maximus by an imposed "law" of pleasure and pain that contours this provisional state of being.[48]

## THE TRAGEDY OF THE FALL AND HUMAN FALLENNESS

### Adam the Proto-Ascetic and His Inglorious Transgression

Maximus' intense soteriological realism, a function of his mimesis of biblical realism and relative indifference to abstract theories of human protology, strongly qualifies his treatment of the events in Eden. This is because Adam squandered his freedom, and undermined his capacity for *spiritual* pleasure, virtually "at the instant he came into being" (ἅμα τῷ γίνεσθαι),[49] thrusting into the suspenseful historical foreground the ontological mutability and susceptibility of the human creature in staggering contrast with the pure stability of the Creator.

Maximus' Adam-in-paradise is something of a combination of Irenaeus's Adam, an innocent adolescent needing to grow into his freedom, and Gregory of Nyssa's Adam, whose original life in paradise was like that of the angels (ἰσάγγελος).[50] Though Maximus does not, like Gregory, explicitly postulate that prelapsarian humanity would have procreated like the angels, he does aver that it was subject to natural human origination (γένεσις), not the sexually-based generation (γέννησις) characteristic of fallen humanity—a discrepancy rectified by the New Adam's virgin birth.[51] Most importantly, Maximus envisions Adam

---

[48] Ibid. 10 (1157A), describing postlapsarian humanity taking on an "irrational [or brute] form" (ἄλογον μορφήν), doubtless referencing Nyssen's interpretation of the "tunics of skins." Cf. *Q. Thal.* Intro. (CCSG 7:31, ll. 227–39), indicating how fallen humanity *was compared to the irrational beasts and was likened unto them* (Ps. 48:13, LXX).

[49] *Q. Thal.* 61 (CCSG 22:85); *Amb.* 42 (PG 91:1321B). Cf. also *Q. Thal.* 59 (CCSG 22:61), similarly describing Adam as having sinned "at the moment he received existence" (ἅμα τῷ εἶναι). Larchet (*La divinisation de l'homme*, 179–80) correctly observes that there is still an instantaneous historical reality of Adam's paradisiac state before the lapse. His original perfection as a creature was instantiated *in fact*, even if its duration was fleeting.

[50] Cf. Irenaeus, *Epideixis* 12 (PO 12:668); *Adv. haer.* 4.38.1–4 (SC 100:942–60); Gregory of Nyssa, *Hom. opif.* 17 (PG 44:188A–192A).

[51] *Q. Thal.* 21 (CCSG 7:127–9); *Amb. Jo.* 31 (PG 91:1276C); ibid. 42 (1324D).

as a proto-ascetic who sets an example both of despair and of hope for his human progeny. In a rare extended discussion of the prelapsarian Adam in *Ambiguum* 45, commenting on Nazianzen's reflection on the nakedness of the primal human, Maximus notes that Adam shared immortality by grace (κατὰ χάριν), that his body was in a state of metabolic stability ("equilibrium devoid of flux and reflux") and "did not possess the temperament (κρᾶσιν) which 'thickens the flesh and makes it mortal and obtuse.'" Adam lived "a life without artifice (ἀτέχνως)," experiencing no atrophy of his natural condition of good health (εὐεξία) and thus having no need for protective clothing. Most importantly, he had "innate dispassion" (ἐνοῦσα ἀπάθεια) and was thus free from shame.[52]

And yet in character with his heuristic approach to reading Scripture and the Fathers, Maximus takes another angle, positing that Nazianzen may refer rather to humanity in its present state if stripped of the accretions of its fallenness. This would mean cutting away the "irrational fantasies of the passions" and getting back, not just to an original dispassion (which for Maximus would be a sublime stability of the passible faculties) but also to the reality at the core of the primal human, "the unconditioned motion of the whole power of his love for what was above him" (God), "freely chosen movement (αὐθαίρετον κίνησις) to him in love." Free of "circumstantial necessity" (περιστατικὴ ἀνάγκη), Adam before his lapse needed no skills to be wise, possessing a spiritual knowledge (γνῶσις) that already outstripped the contemplation of nature.[53]

It becomes clear at this point that Maximus is reimagining Adam as an ascetic, indeed as our original exemplar in the ascetical life, looking out on a limitless horizon of assimilation to the Creator. Adam may have been naturally gifted and virtuous, but he stood on the threshold of developing his gifts to their fullest. Maximus carries this into one additional reflection on Nazianzen's image of Adam's nakedness, suggesting that it may bespeak his original moral integrity, since by a pure habitus (ἕξις) he already had inculcated the *logoi* of the virtues. The vocation of Adam's posterity, then, is to recuperate this pure asceticism:

it cannot be doubted that those who, by means of a philosophical principle, wish to raise themselves up from the forefather's fall, begin by completely negating the passions, after which they cease busying

---

[52] *Amb. Jo.* 45 (PG 91:1353A–B), trans. Constas II, 195–7. Maximus quotes from Gregory Nazianzen, *Or.* 45.8 (PG 36:633A). On humanity's natural *apatheia* being lost in Adam's fall, see *Q. Thal.* 42 (CCSG 7:285).

[53] *Amb. Jo.* 45 (PG 91:1353B–1356A).

themselves with the principles of technical skills, and finally, peering beyond natural contemplation, they catch a glimpse of immaterial knowledge, which has absolutely no form susceptible to sense perception or any meaning that can be contained by spoken words. Then, just as God in the beginning created the first man, they too will be naked in the simplicity of their knowledge, in their life free of distractions, and in their mortification of the law of the flesh.[54]

Understanding Adam's exemplary ascetical role, however, requires an analysis of the dynamics and consequences of his actual transgression. His ideal state lasting for only an instant, he set in motion a whole process of human disintegration by first estranging the very poles he was intended to unite in created nature,[55] and "cutting human nature to pieces."[56] There is little abstractness here. "Original" sin is concrete vice, and Maximus, like other ascetical theologians in antiquity, inevitably contributed, as we shall see, to longstanding discussion of the primal vice that triggered all the other vices.

Maximus does not labor over the question of how, despite his endowments and glorious condition, Adam could have brought ruination on himself. As mentioned earlier, he deferred to Nyssen, embracing a "reciprocal causality"[57] whereby the consequence of Adamic sin was somehow also its cause. Maximus attributes Adam's lapse most basically to a failure of gnomic will ($\gamma\nu\acute{\omega}\mu\eta$),[58] though he can also call it simply an abuse of freedom or self-determination ($\alpha\mathring{v}\tau\epsilon\xi o\nu\sigma\acute{\iota}\alpha$).[59] Maximus, we must remember, considers gnomic will morally neutral in its own right but capable of directing choice toward either vice or virtue. Because *gnômê* names the "deep-seated desire for those things that are within our power, whence arises choice ($\pi\rho o\alpha\acute{\iota}\rho\epsilon\sigma\iota s$),"[60] it holds great sway in the soul; but its strength is also its flaw, for the implied "deliberation" of gnomic will all too easily devolves into vacillation in relation to what is genuinely good or beautiful. In a split second, it seems, Adam vacillated, distracted himself from his utterly good estate, and "invented" an ulterior and illusory good—the pleasure of the body—as though it were determinative of his ability to thrive in the flesh.[61]

---

[54] Ibid. (1356A–B), trans. Constas II, 201.    [55] Ibid. 41 (1308C).
[56] In *Q. Thal.* Prol. (CCSG 7:33). On the full effects of this disintegration, see Thunberg, *Microcosm and Mediator*, 231–84.
[57] Von Balthasar, *Cosmic Liturgy*, 187.
[58] Cf. *Q. Thal.* 1 (CCSG 7:47); ibid. 61 (CCSG 22:89).
[59] *Amb. Jo.* 7 (PG 91:1092C–D).    [60] *Opusc.* 1 (PG 91:17C).
[61] See esp. *Q. Thal.* 61 (CCSG 22:85).

In patently ascetical terms, Maximus similarly describes Adam's sin as a failure of spiritual vision or natural contemplation, a slavish capitulation to bodily (as opposed to spiritual) senses, and a primal infatuation with eating.[62] Adam "fell into ignorance (ἄγνοιαν) of his [divine] Cause, and, at the advice of the serpent, mistook as god the very thing which God had commanded him to repudiate," thus condemning himself to a "mixed" knowledge inhibiting his ability to see the true good vividly and enduringly:

> The more, then, that man preoccupied himself with a knowledge based exclusively on the experience of sensible things, the more he bound himself with ignorance of God. The more he bound himself with the chain of this ignorance, the more he cleaved to the experience of the sensual enjoyment of material objects of knowledge. The more he indulged himself in this enjoyment, the more he aroused the desire of the self-love which it produces. The more diligently he seized the desire of self-love, the more he invented multiple ways to sustain his pleasure, which is the fruit and object of self-love.[63]

Maximus herein projects two of his strongest images of the Adamic fall and its legacy: as a vicious downward spiral of ignorance, and as a domino effect in which vice spawns vice. He also explicitly identifies self-love as the "original" vice that sprouted all the rest. In Christian antiquity, and especially in the monastic heritage, considerable speculation arose about the truly seminal vice. Origen had famously theorized that pre-existent rational beings fell originally because of *satiety* (κόρος), a virtual "over-indulgence" in the Creator's generosity, leading to negligence and the attrition of spiritual fervency.[64] Gregory of Nyssa, perhaps not wanting to be dogmatic on the point, entertains the idea that *vanity* (κενοδοξία) and its concomitant pleasures started the train of passions.[65] But at long last he targets *envy* (φθόνος)—"the passion that causes evil,

---

[62] *Amb. Jo.* 10 (PG 91:1156C–1157A) expressly identifies Adam's failure of the spiritual sense of sight. For background on the spiritual senses in Maximus, see Frederick Aquino, "Maximus the Confessor," in Sarah Coakley and Paul Gavrilyuk, eds., *The Spiritual Senses: Perceiving God in Western Christianity* (Cambridge: Cambridge University Press, 2011), 104–20. On Adam's transgression in Maximus as a failure of natural contemplation, see also Lollar, *To See into the Life of Things*, 302–6. Gregory of Nyssa likewise indicates that humanity's fall has been a failure of spiritual vision connected with the embrace of "non-existent" evil (*Or. catech.* 7, GNO 3/4:27, l. 15–28, l. 20).

[63] *Q. Thal.* Intro. (CCSG 7:31, ll. 227–50).

[64] See *De principiis* 2.9.2 (GCS 22:165–6).

[65] *Virg.* 4 (GNO 8/1:273, ll. 12–24).

the father of death, the first entrance of sin"—as the kingpin of vices.[66] Maximus instead settles on *self-love* ($\varphi\iota\lambda\alpha\upsilon\tau\iota\alpha$), an aberrant manifestation of the soul's deep-seated desire ($\check{\epsilon}\rho\omega\varsigma$),[67] as the source of sins. It is an insatiable, even narcissistic urge to give pleasure to the body with which the soul has become infatuated,[68] thus deviating from the satisfaction only to be found in spiritual pleasure.

> We who, for the sake of self-love, contend for pleasure and, for the same reason, hasten to flee pain, invent countless sources for the destructive passions. For instance, if we give heed to self-love through pleasure, we give rise to gluttony, arrogance, vainglory, pride, avarice, covetousness, tyranny, haughtiness, vain-boasting, laziness, fury, conceit, vanity, contempt, wantonness, silliness, trickery, prodigality, licentiousness, ostentation, swollen pride, sloth, indifference, mockery, loquacity, untimely chatter, lewd speech, and as many other vices as there are of this kind. If, however, the path of self-love tortures us with pain, we generate anger, envy, hatred, enmity, malice, reproach, slander, sycophancy, grief, hopelessness, despair, false accusations of divine providence, lethargy, negligence, discouragement, despondence, faintheartedness, unseemly sorrow, weeping, dejection, lamentation, jealousy, rivalry, provocation to jealousy, and the rest of the vices that stem from the state of being deprived of pleasure. From the mixture of pleasure and pain that occurs from various causes—namely, from wickedness ($\mu o\chi\theta\eta\rho\iota\alpha\varsigma$), for this is what some call the synthesis of the contrary parts of vice—we engender hypocrisy, pretense, deceit, affectation, flattery, man-pleasing, and the rest of the vices that derive from this compound treachery.[69]

From this passage we can discern that the vices primordially deriving from pleasure are a function of the soul's desiring drive ($\dot{\epsilon}\pi\iota\theta\upsilon\mu\iota\alpha$; $\tau\dot{o}$ $\dot{\epsilon}\pi\iota\theta\upsilon\mu\eta\tau\iota\kappa\dot{o}\nu$), and those deriving from pain a function of its aversive drive ($\theta\upsilon\mu\dot{o}\varsigma$; $\tau\dot{o}$ $\theta\upsilon\mu\iota\kappa\dot{o}\nu$), with some of the vices combining both drives. We can also identify in this alignment of the vices six of the

---

[66] *De vita Moysis lib.* 2 (GNO 7/1:122–3). But very early in his writings (*De virg.* 4, GNO 7/1:273, ll. 19–21), Gregory targets envy as triggering hypocrisy, bitterness, and misanthropy.

[67] *Q. Thal.* Intro. (CCSG 7:31).

[68] *Car.* 2.8 (PG 90:985C), describing self-love as the "mother of passions" ($\mu\alpha\tau\dot{\eta}\rho$ $\tau\hat{\omega}\nu$ $\pi\alpha\theta\hat{\omega}\nu$) and "passion for the body" ($\tau\dot{o}$ $\pi\rho\dot{o}\varsigma$ $\tau\dot{o}$ $\sigma\hat{\omega}\mu\alpha$ $\pi\dot{\alpha}\theta o\varsigma$). Similarly, ibid. 3.8, 57 (1020A–B, 1033C); *Ep.* 2 (PG 91:397C). See also the extensive discussion of $\varphi\iota\lambda\alpha\upsilon\tau\iota\alpha$ in Irénée Hausherr, *Philautie: De la tendresse pour soi à charité selon Maxime le Confesseur* (Rome: Pontificium Institutum Orientalium, 1952), esp. 43–9; Thunberg, *Microcosm and Mediator*, 232–48.

[69] *Q. Thal.* Intro. (CCSG 7:33–5, ll. 272–98).

eight passions that had already appeared in the Evagrian tradition of eight cardinal vices—gluttony (γαστριμαργία), avarice (φιλαργυρία), grief (λύπη), lethargy (ἀκηδία), vainglory (κενοδοξία), and arrogance (ὑπερφανία)—with approximations of Evagrius's other two as well. Maximus' licentiousness (ἀκολασία) approximates Evagrius's fornication (πορνεία), and Maximus' anger (θυμός) approximates Evagrius's wrath (ὀργή). Self-love achieved primacy in Maximus' thinking because of its fertility,[70] its "strategic" position vis-à-vis pleasure and pain, and because, from a teleological perspective, it stood in direct opposition to the ultimately sanctifying and unifying "cosmic virtue" of love (ἀγάπη).

In his ascetical works Maximus seeks to spell out so far as possible the chain of cause and effect in the proliferation of the passions or vices, thus reinforcing in practical teaching the fact that there can be no "original sin" if that means moral evil gaining an ontological foothold or status in created nature. Showing the profound influence of Evagrius and the Cappadocian Fathers, Maximus keeps the focus on the concrete vices, which, because of demonic infestation and the unleashing of myriad wicked or distracting "thoughts" (λογισμοί), allow evil a relative existence through habituation and engrained behaviors.

Maximus clearly distanced himself, then, from an Augustinian doctrine of original sin and maintained, with the Greek patristic consensus, that Adam transmitted the *consequences* of his sin but not the guilt itself.[71] Jean-Claude Larchet has nonetheless insisted that Maximus found common ground with the Western tradition by affirming that sin *qua* "passible nature" inserted itself into the human race after Adam's fall.[72] He points, for example, to the fact that Maximus sometimes speaks of the "laws" of sin, passion, and death as "laws of nature,"[73] that he presupposes "generic sin" (γενικὴ ἁμαρτία) or "ancestral sin" (προγονικὴ ἁμαρτία),[74] and that gnomic will fatefully bound human nature to the chain of evil.[75] I concur with Larchet that Maximus casts a grim portrait;

---

[70] See esp. *Car.* 3.56–7 (PG 90:1033B–C).

[71] Most explicitly in *Q. Thal.* 42 (CCSG 7:285–9), where Maximus distinguishes between the "sin that I caused" (ἡ δι᾽ ἐμὲ ἁμαρτία) and "my sin" (ἡ ἐμὴ ἁμαρτία) or guilt itself. Christ "became" the former (2 Cor. 5:21) but not the latter.

[72] "Ancestral Guilt according to St. Maximus the Confessor: A Bridge between Eastern and Western Conceptions," *Sobornost* 20 (1998): 26–48.

[73] *Amb. Jo.* 31 (PG 91:1276A–B); *Q. Thal.* 21 (CCSG 7:129).

[74] *Q. Thal.* 21 (CCSG 7:127); *LA* (CCSG 40:7, l. 23; 119 ll. 1014–15).

[75] *Q. Thal.* 21 (CCSG 7:127–31).

indeed, he sees postlapsarian humanity in its own right as languishing without hope of liberation.[76] But caution is in order. When the Confessor explains how sin, passion, and death have become "laws of nature," he clarifies that this is purely "circumstantial" (περιστατικός).[77] As in Nyssen, sin has become second nature, as it were.[78] So too "generic sin" refers to the consequential burden laid on humanity in Adam's wake by passion and death, not a *genetic* incapacitation in willing or doing the good. And as we have already observed, the passibility of nature invariably cuts two ways in Maximus' purview. Passion and death are punitive but also redemptive, even transformative. "Gnomic" volition (γνώμη) can indeed bind humans to vice but it can also serve constructively as a means to relearn "natural" willing and the habitual reorientation of the human moral subject toward virtuous ends. Maximus appears never to stray far from the Pauline perspective wherein God has subjected humanity (and all corporeal creation) to futility and corruption—*in hope* (Rom. 8:19–24).

## Sexuality and the Christian Hope

Not surprisingly given his monastic provenance, Maximus considers human sexuality not as a detached theme for anthropological discussion but as already thoroughly couched within the ascetical narrative of paradise, the fall, and the postlapsarian crisis of humankind. Von Balthasar even suggests that "The focal point of the whole question of *pathos* seems, in fact, to be in the phenomenon of sexuality."[79] But if so, it is also a focal point of the healing and reorientation of human passibility. Indeed, it factors into Maximus' consideration of humanity's role in mediating cosmic divisions and the larger *oikonomia* whereby all things are to be reconciled and made new in Jesus Christ. Thus too sexuality turns out to be an important case of how Maximus' teleology or eschatology conditions his reading of human beginnings.

The severity of the alienation of male and female accompanying the fall sets the stage for Maximus' dramatizing creaturely alienation in general. Though he hardly absolves Adam of a primary role in the initial lapse, he subtly demonizes Eve as a seductress who helps the

[76] "Ancestral Guilt according to St. Maximus the Confessor," 30–3, 36–7, 42.
[77] *Q. Thal.* 21 (CCSG 7:129): τῷ περιστατικῷ νόμῳ τῆς φύσεως.
[78] Cf. Gregory of Nyssa, *Hom. de Beatitudinibus* 6 (GNO 7/2:144, l. 26–145, l. 13).
[79] *Cosmic Liturgy*, 196.

serpent do his bidding. In *Amb. Jo.* 7, Eve is certainly the implied harlot when Maximus writes,

> Humanity was created for and to this end [progressive ascent to God]. But our forefather Adam misused his freedom and turned instead to what was inferior, redirecting his desire from what was permissible to what had been forbidden. For it was in his power of self-determination *to be united to the Lord and become one spirit with him, or to join himself to a prostitute and become one body with her* (see 1 Cor. 6:16–17); but deceived he chose to estrange himself from the divine and blessed goal, preferring by his own choice to be a *pile of dust* (see Gen. 2:7) rather than god by grace. Therefore God, who does whatever is necessary for our salvation, in his wisdom and love for humankind, and with the goodness that befits him, affixed the appropriate punishment alongside the irrational movement of our intellectual faculty, where it would not fail to do what was required.[80]

As Doru Costache has demonstrated, Maximus' recognition of Eve's conspiracy was fully consonant with certain representations of her trickery in Byzantine liturgical hymns and preaching of the same era.[81] I would add that such denigration of Eve undoubtedly served also to amplify the contrast between her and the Theotokos as the "New Eve," an epithet already being accorded Mary long before Maximus' time.[82] And yet later, as Costache points out, Maximus also calls Eve a cohabitant or spouse (σύνοικος) of Adam,[83] and though he still disparages her for being the object of Adam's misplaced trust, the softened approach is hardly superfluous, especially since (in his characteristically teleological framework) Maximus desires to uphold, already with the protoplasts, the dignity of marriage as a path to the virtuous life.[84] Indeed, he chastises as quasi-Manichaean those repulsed by the thought that the soul, as image of God, joined with a body, "should coexist with sordid pleasure and bodily secretions," or enter into the estate of marriage.[85]

---

[80] *Amb. Jo.* 7 (PG 91:1092C–1093A), trans. Constas I, 121–3 (altered).

[81] "Living above Gender: Insights from Saint Maximus the Confessor," *Journal of Early Christian Studies* 21 (2013): 263–7.

[82] Already known from Justin Martyr (*Dialogus cum Tryphone* 100), and Irenaeus (*Adv. haer.* 3.22.4; 5.19.1).

[83] *Amb. Jo.* 10 (PG 91:1156D).

[84] See ibid. (1161D), where Moses and Elijah, flanking the transfigured Word, respectively symbolize marriage and celibacy as paths to mystical adoption or deification. See also Costache's analysis, "Living above Gender," 267, 287–8.

[85] *Amb. Jo.* 42 (PG 91:1340B–C). For further analysis of the status of marriage in Maximus, see Adam Cooper, "St. Maximus on the Mystery of Marriage and the Body:

Adam and Eve instantiate the tragedy whereby embodied, sexed creatures, male and female, fell short of the potential of their nature. Presumably they would have reproduced impassibly,[86] dwelling in a state of perfectly-oriented *erôs*.[87] They were predisposed toward reciprocal communion and prospective deification, but succumbed to a bodily self-love that stunted future human existence. Though Maximus upholds sexual procreation after the fall as the Creator's providential means for perpetuating the human race, sexual division becomes the crux of the inescapable syndrome of sensual pleasure (sexual passion) and pain (childbirth) at the heart of this provisional order over which the specter of death prevails. In this context male and female symbolize, internally, the soul's dual thymetic (incensive) and epithymetic (desiring) drives: "male" the ferocity to resist pain, and "female" the urge for pleasure.[88] The modern Christian reader may strain to find a redemptive appraisal of sexual experience in Maximus, but he is intensely cautious. In his view, largely that of the ascetical tradition from which he came, the pleasure and pain associated with sexuality threaten always to take on a life of their own, in a fateful and degenerate spiral whereby men and women strive competitively and egoistically to sustain pleasure and escape pain, and sensually to outsmart, as it were, the essentially remedial modality of sexual procreation. Eschatologically speaking, moreover, sexual pleasure, whatever relative value it might have in conjugal relations, can only give way to the *unprecedented* ecstatic pleasure experienced in the age to come.

Maximus describes the ascetical task of male and female (whether married or celibate) in terms of cosmic "mediation," sketched most lucidly in *Ambiguum* 41 and *Questions and Responses for Thalassius* 48. The division between male and female stands at the bottom of the

---

A Reconsideration," in Vasiljević, 195–221; Kostake Milkov, "Maximus and the Healing of the Sexual Division of Creation," ibid., 427–36.

[86] See *Amb. Jo.* 41 (PG 91:1309A), where Maximus writes of the "possibility" of asexual procreation. Maximus may well have in mind Nyssen's hypothesis of "quasi-angelic" procreation, itself mysterious (*Hom. opif.* 17, PG 44:189C–D).

[87] We can infer this in view of Maximus' high premium on the soul's deep-seated *erôs* as an instrument of deifying desire for God.

[88] *Or. dom.* (CCSG 69·47–8, ll. 341–61). On this point, see also Verna Harrison, "Women in the *Philokalia*?" in Brock Bingaman and Bradley Nassif, eds., *The Philokalia: A Classic Text of Orthodox Spirituality* (New York: Oxford University Press, 2012), 254–9.

*ontological* order of the five polarities of the cosmos,[89] but it is first in the *existential* order, since humanity is "a natural link which by its proper parts mediates between these universal extremes" and is summoned to a sublime ascent by actively negotiating these polarities.[90] The human mediation takes the form of a participation in Christ's supreme mediation of the cosmos. Because Christ, by undergoing human birth (γέννησις) *from a virgin*, free from sexual pleasure (and presumably, for Mary, free from the pain of childbirth), pioneered a new birth that is sacramentally appropriated in baptism, men and women must together begin the task of realizing that "dispassion" (ἀπάθεια) which is, in reality, the *positive* and deifying *use* of the passible faculties.[91] Thus Maximus follows ascetical precedent in encouraging the sublimation of sexual pleasure within marriage,[92] since, as an alternate path of virtuous living alongside celibacy, married persons participate in the existential work of resisting the momentum of corporeal disorder and reconciling human nature to itself. It is imperative to recognize that Maximus, while upholding sexual distinction in paradise, has in mind a concrete existential *alienation* between male and female in the world, the rectification of which is intrinsic to the hope of human—and cosmic—reconciliation.

Maximus meanwhile demonstrates his overriding *teleological* perspective on this human mediation through the sexes in a striking passage where he is applying the oft-used notion of "mean" (μέσον) between "extremes" (τὰ ἄκρα), a logical or cosmological counterpart of his idea of the "middle" (μεσότης) of history between the extremes of "beginning" (ἀρχή) and "end" (τέλος):

> An "extreme" is: *And God said, Let us make humanity according to our image and likeness* (Gen. 1:26). A "mean" is: *And God made humanity, male and female he made them* (Gen. 1:27). Again, an "extreme" is: *In Christ there is neither male nor female* (Gal. 3:21).[93]

Whatever moves midway between "extremes" is unequal or disparate (ἄνισον), says Maximus, in contrast with the "ever-moving repose"

---

[89]  For these five polarities, see Chapter 3, p. 127 (and Figure 2) in this volume.
[90]  *Amb. Jo.* 41 (PG 91:1305B–C).
[91]  On ἀπάθεια, see pp. 279–80 in this volume.
[92]  Cf. *Car.* 2.17 (PG 90:989A–B); ibid. 2.33 (996A–B). Larchet ("Ancestral Guilt," 42) parallels Maximus here with Augustine's thinking on the importance of sublimating *concupiscentia* since it is a viral agent of human sin.
[93]  *Amb. Jo.* 67 (PG 91:1401A–B).

(ἀεικίνητος στάσις) of the extremes themselves.[94] Doru Costache
accurately concludes that "by juxtaposing the trilogy to the three
verses, it becomes clear that Genesis 1:26 refers to the pre-temporal
divine intention concerning humanity (ἀρχή), Genesis 1:27 to our
historically concrete, gendered condition (μεσότης), and Galatians
3:28 to humankind's existential purpose, construed as perfection
(τέλος)."[95]

Von Balthasar finds in Maximus a final sexual "synthesis" in which
sexual difference is thoroughly erased both personally and bodily.
Properly speaking, the actual synthesis applies, through the work of
Christ the New Adam, to the merging of humanity's unspoiled paradisiac state with humanity's present, mortal condition, yielding a
"higher, third condition."[96] But if that is so, it is not clear why the
difference between male and female must absolutely evaporate in the
age to come. Human "mediation" looks toward a final dissolution, not of
sexes as such, but of the alienation between sexes, the legacy of pain
and pleasure, and the drive for survival attending sexual procreation.
Maximus' vision of deification still projects, like Nyssen's, a perpetuation
of the human vocation, a sublime ascending motion "around God" (περὶ
θεόν) that is humanity's eternal sabbatical rest.[97] In this state or aeon,
humans hope and move toward ever new transformations, new ecstasies
of *erôs* reaching for fulfillment, *erôs* now being an instrument of passionate self-giving rather than impassioned self-interest.

## HISTORICAL AMBIGUITY AND
## ESCHATOLOGICAL CLARITY

Maximus' anthropology and soteriology thrive on his deep sense of
the *ambiguity* of historical existence. Humanity, as we have seen,
finds itself caught somewhere between an original-but-unfulfilled
perfection and an unprecedented, hoped for, yet-to-be-realized transfiguration. The Confessor actually relishes this ambiguity as the stage
on which the Creator's theo-dramatic work is set in bold relief. Like a

[94] Ibid. (1401A).    [95] Costache, "Living beyond Gender," 269.
[96] *Cosmic Liturgy*, 203–5.
[97] See Blowers, "Maximus the Confessor, Gregory of Nyssa, and the Concept of
Perpetual Progress."

good play, the plot does not move toward an expeditious resolution; rather, it must thicken and intensify before any clarity is achieved, a clarity thoroughly tempered and textured by the complexities of the drama. I have credited von Balthasar for first reading Maximus in this *theo-dramatic* light,[98] but one of my purposes in this book has been to enhance this perspective more fully than von Balthasar was able to do in his later writings after the final edition of his *Cosmic Liturgy* appeared.

Von Balthasar and Sherwood, from an esteemed generation of Maximus scholarship, observed that in tracing the drama of human history and hope, Maximus dwelled on the old question of whether the "end" (τέλος) is a sheer return to the "beginning" (ἀρχή).[99] Though Origen, with his doctrine of an *apokatastasis*, has often been blamed for equating them, and as sparking a controversy over cosmology and eschatology that Maximus eventually joined, the equation seems more to have been dogma for fundamentalist Origenist ascetics closer to Maximus' than to Origen's time. Origen himself said that "the end is always *like* the beginning" (*semper . . . similis est finis initiis*),[100] and whatever liberties his Latin translator, the monk Rufinus, may have taken to "clarify" him, this is doubtless closer to Origen's own thinking than that of the later zealots who reconceived his cosmology as a monistic resolution of spiritual being into itself. Besides, it was Origen himself who had exploited the plasticity of ἀρχή and interpreted the true "beginning" (Gen. 1:1; John 1:1) or first principle of the universe as God or as Jesus Christ.[101] This view privileged the divine prerogative in creation and shifted the emphasis onto the ongoing work of the provident Creator to rectify the human fall and to make sense of the corporeal diversities and disparities in the world, so that God might subjugate all things into his unity and become "all in all" (1 Cor. 15:28; Eph. 4:6).

Maximus shared common ground with Origen on two key points. First, he agreed that there is a parallel between beginning and end, but, as we saw, he averred that humanity's true and purposeful beginning was barely actualized before Adam lapsed. Hence humanity must

---

[98]  See also pp. 82–3, 102, 114, 117 in this volume.
[99]  See esp. von Balthasar, *Cosmic Liturgy*, 187–8; Sherwood, "Maximus and Origenism: *ΑΡΧΗ ΚΑΙ ΤΕΛΟΣ*," *Berichte zum XI. Internationalen Byzantinisten-Kongress* III, 1 (Münich, 1958), 1–27.
[100]  *De princ.* 1.6.2 (GCS 22:79, l. 22-80, l. 5).
[101]  *Comm. in Johannem* 1.90–124 (GCS 10:20–5).

discover its true origin not by retroversion but by looking ahead hopefully and focusing on the *telos* that lies in the future, and which holds the key to humanity's true beginning.[102] Second, Maximus like Origen understands God or Christ himself as the true and uncircumscribable ἀρχή[103] as well as the *telos*[104] of creaturely existence; indeed, he will more boldly state that Christ is the *beginning* (ἀρχή), *middle* (μεσότης), and *end* (τέλος) alike,[105] providentially enclosing, redeeming, and deifying creatures in their progressive movement and interactions.

That said, Maximus follows the two Cappadocian Gregories in dramatically playing up the suspense wherewith the Creator labors not merely to recover an unfulfilled glory for humanity but to raise humanity, through the experience of the vagaries and vicissitudes of historical existence, to a glory transcending even paradise. As Rowan Williams has described Nyssen's project, the human journey toward the mystery of deification begins more as a struggle already in the making, from out of the "restless" state whereby humanity must grow into itself through the training of desire and choice, cultivating its hidden potential.[106] Gregory Nazianzen, who, as Maximus well knows, dwells at great rhetorical and poetic length on the paradoxes of bodily existence and the specter of suffering that casts a veil of hopelessness over the surface of human existence,[107] also teases out of this somber picture an imaginative redemption of corporeality. As discussed earlier, Maximus developed from Nazianzen the potent image of the Logos-at-play, kenotically insinuating himself into the fray of materiality and corporeality, deftly stealing a revelation of new order and beauty from the jaws of "chaos" (τὸ ἄτακτον).[108]

Like a skillful dramaturge, Maximus focuses his principal attention on the relentless forward movement of the drama. For him, as von Balthasar poignantly puts it, "the bronze doors of the divine home are

---

[102] *Q. Thal.* 59 (CCSG 22:61–5).
[103] *Th. Oec.* 1.69 (PG 90:1108C–D); cf. *Amb. Jo.* 15 (PG 91:1217C–D), calling God both the ἀρχή and the "author of origination" (τῆς γενέσεως γενεσιουργός).
[104] See esp. *Amb. Jo.* 7 (PG 91:1072D–1073C); *Q. Thal.* 60 (CCSG 22:75, ll. 46–8).
[105] *Q. Thal.* 19 (CCSG 7:119, ll. 7–30); ibid. 22 (CCSG 7:139, ll. 60–4).
[106] *The Wound of Knowledge: Christian Spirituality from the New Testament to Saint John of the Cross*, 2nd edn. (Cambridge, MA: Cowley Publications, 1990), 66–7, 73; cf. also Morwenna Ludlow, *Gregory of Nyssa: Ancient and (Post)modern* (Oxford: Oxford University Press, 2007), 121, 127–31.
[107] See esp. *Or.* 14 (PG 35:857A–909C).
[108] On *Amb. Jo.* 71, see pp. 86–7, 118 in this volume.

slammed remorselessly shut at the very start of our existence."[109] We embodied humans find ourselves from the outset caught in the "flowing stream" of the undercurrent of material chaos,[110] "bearing up and being born along" as Maximus often describes it,[111] in a kind of redemptive buffeting that conveys us on the other side to a mysterious, unspeakable—and ecstatic—experience of divine grace. This *telos*, rather than reduplicating prelapsarian paradise, constitutes a new reality, enriched by the events of the historical "middle" played out in countless lives. Maximus tells us that he reads and contemplates the Bible precisely as a mirror on the world in which the interplay and progress of biblical characters of all kinds provide a revelatory *con*-figuration and pre-figuration of the ascetical struggle between truth and falsehood, virtue and vice, that pervades the cosmos.[112] Thus reality here and now must also be read as a complex drama still moving toward a resolution which, though already "finalized" in Jesus Christ, continues to unfold the full effects of his work in the horizon of the Church and the cosmos. Maximus is, in principle, interested in the movements of *all* created beings in his "cosmopoliteian" vision, but humanity takes center stage as the living link in the universe, and remains a work-in-progress—or in his own words, a "workshop containing all things" ($\tau\hat{\omega}\nu$ $\H{o}\lambda\omega\nu$ $\dot{\epsilon}\rho\gamma\alpha\sigma\tau\H{\eta}\rho\iota o\nu$)[113]—through which the triune Creator enduringly manifests his power, grace, and resourcefulness.

How, for Maximus, Christ finalized the creative and redemptive resolution of this drama of existence, and whether it opened up the prospect of *universal* salvation, will be the subject of my next chapter.

---

[109] *Cosmic Liturgy*, 187.    [110] *Amb. Jo.* 8 (PG 91:1101D–1105B).
[111] Ibid. (PG 91:1105B); ibid. 42 (1348D); ibid. 71 (1416B).
[112] Ibid. 37 (1293B–1297A), discussed on pp. 83–5 in this volume.
[113] Ibid. 41 (1305A).

# 7

## Active Passivity: Maximus on the Passion of Jesus Christ

> ... given the notions swirling around it, the cross admits of
> multiple contemplations . . .
>
> —Maximus, *Ambiguum* 32[1]

With this brief line, one wonders if Maximus, wittingly or unwittingly, was understating himself. Patristic teaching East and West on the suffering, death, and resurrection of Jesus Christ did not develop by tidy evolution, or with a singular rationale prevailing as *the* orthodox "doctrine of atonement." How could it when the Bible itself conveyed diverse figures, images, and reasonings concerning divine salvation in general—deliverance, vindication, conquest, mercy, justification, atonement, adoption, transformation, recreation, et al.—and Christ's paschal mystery in particular?

Maximus in his turn learned by experience that the theologian scrambles with this core mystery of the faith to uncover its intrinsic complexity and abiding repercussions in the life, doctrine, and worship of the Church. And in his characteristic theological style, marked by patient and occasionally plodding "research" (ἐξέτασις), often clustered in densely packed *scholia* (extended interpretive reflections like the *Ambigua* and *Questions and Responses for Thalassius*) or *kephalaia* ("chapters"), he did not isolate a soteriology separate from other concerns. Indeed, his ideas of salvation and deification are thoroughly insinuated into other aspects of his teaching. Creation is itself already an act of salvation insofar as it is both a redemption from nothingness

---

[1] PG 91:1281C: ... πολλὰς ὁ σταυρὸς ταῖς περὶ αὐτὸν ἐπινοίαις ἐπιδέχεται θεωρίας ...

and the beginning of the revelation of Jesus Christ—himself "Creator"—
to the world. I have hinted at this theme earlier, but in this chapter I shall
detail more fully how for Maximus, as much as for Irenaeus long before,
the world is already *cruciform*, already marked out for displaying the
triune Creator's love, self-sacrifice, and relentless strategy to bring his
creation to its ultimately transfigured state of "eternal well-being"
through the person and work of Jesus Christ.

   There is a fairly strong consensus in Maximus scholarship that
Christology lies at the core of his thought. A variation on this is the
view that his whole achievement is devoted to spelling out the *sensus
plenior* of the Chalcedonian definition. I am sympathetic with this
perspective but it runs the risk of reading Maximus habitually through
the lens of his later writings concentrated on the wills of Christ, where
he made his greatest mark on the interpretation of Chalcedon, such as
was vindicated (albeit anonymously) at the Council of Constantinople
in 681. The true nucleus of Maximus' oeuvre is what he himself calls the
"mystery of Christ," which, he says, surpasses all mysteries.[2] The New
Testament, he proposes, is referencing the fullness of this mystery every
time it records the simple name of "Christ."[3]

## THE "MYSTERY OF CHRIST"

For Maximus the "mystery of Christ" fuses the purview of his
"cosmic" Christology with the horizon of the Gospels' accounts of
Jesus. Macro-Christology still depends on micro-Christology since
the universal and the particular always and absolutely belong together
and condition each other. In short, we cannot fully fathom the cosmic
Christ without following him to the cross. Maximus puts it succinctly
in an oft-quoted maxim that will launch my analysis in this chapter:

> The mystery of the incarnation of the Logos holds the power of all the
> hidden *logoi* and figures of Scripture as well as the knowledge of visible
> and intelligible creatures. Whoever knows the mystery of the cross and
> the tomb knows the *logoi* of these creatures. And whoever has been
> initiated in the ineffable power of the resurrection knows the purpose
> for which God originally made all things.[4]

---

[2] *Amb. Jo.* 42 (PG 91:1332C–D).        [3] *Q. Thal.* 60 (CCSG 22:73).
[4] *Th. Oec.* 1.66 (PG 90:1108A–B).

Maximus accordingly approaches the mystery of Christ—the mystery of the cosmos—by exploring the whole itinerary of the incarnation and considering the major deeds in Jesus's life and ministry as windows into his larger creative and salvific work. The Confessor frequently uses the phrase "according to the economy" (κατ᾽ οἰκονομίαν)[5] as shorthand for the strategic importance of the incarnation together with all its constitutive elements: Jesus's birth, baptism, temptation, teaching, wonderworking, suffering, death, resurrection, and ascension and glorification.

I touched on these themes earlier in Chapter 4,[6] but it is worth reiterating here that each of these events in Jesus's earthly sojourn is for Maximus a magnitude in its own right, with effects reaching far beyond the immediate circumstances of Jesus's life. When John the Evangelist spoke of Jesus doing *many other things* that could scarcely be contained in books (John 21:25), he indicated that his record of Jesus was only a preliminary register of events of transcending significance, a "forerunner" of the "more perfect Word" (τοῦ τελεωτέρου Λόγου):

> For every word given by God to humanity and written down in this present age is a forerunner of the more perfect Word, which—through that word—is announced to the intellect, spiritually and without writing, and which will be manifested in the age to come, for whereas the written word possesses an indication of the truth in itself, it does not reveal the truth itself, naked and unveiled.[7]

Whatever his differences with Origen, Maximus echoes the great Alexandrian's idea of the Gospel that points to the ultimate spiritual Gospel. Even the events of the Gospels are prophecy of still greater things. As powerful as Christ's incarnational accommodation to creatures has been,

> all the forms and mysteries of divine providence on behalf of humanity in this present age, even though these be of great importance, constitute but a precursor and prefiguration of future things. Thus, when we compare the apprehensible word of the Lord to the more hidden or mystical word that will be granted to the disciples in the coming age . . . we see that it is the forerunner of itself. And this is something that

---

[5] e.g. *Q. Thal.* 29 (CCSG 7:215); ibid. 54 (p. 455); ibid. 59 (CCSG 22:59); ibid. 60 (pp. 73, 79); ibid. 61 (pp. 93, 97); ibid. 64 (p. 237); ibid. 65 (pp. 281–3); *Opusc.* 7 (PG 91:80D, 81A).

[6] See pp. 141–6 in this volume.

[7] *Amb. Jo.* 21 (PG 91:1252B–D), trans. Constas I, 441 (slightly altered).

the Lord indicated indistinctly in himself, in proportion to the capacity of those who receive him, because for the time being the whole world could not contain them (John 21:25).[8]

Each of the events in Jesus's ministry thus has larger salvific and eschatological implications, since "principally, the Savior became human not to suffer but to save."[9] Salvation, in other words, is more than redemption from sin and its consequences; it is the revelation of the incarnational fullness of Christ and the inauguration of a whole new creation.

- His *virginal birth*—human birth but without passion—was a breakthrough to healing sexual procreation ($\gamma \acute{\epsilon}\nu\nu\eta\sigma\iota\varsigma$) of its associated passion and restoring the true creaturely origin ($\gamma \acute{\epsilon}\nu\epsilon\sigma\iota\varsigma$) of humanity.[10] But in doing so Christ was merely starting his work of inaugurating a new, eschatological "mode" ($\tau\rho\acute{o}\pi o\varsigma$) of human existence.

- In his *baptism*, which Maximus closely connected with the grace of the incarnation itself, Jesus preempted the fallen mode of human birth and paved the way of sacramental rebirth and adoption in the Spirit, the believer's own baptismal appropriation of her or his true origin and destiny in Christ.[11]

- With his *temptations* by Satan and the forces of evil, Jesus stepped up to the challenge of usurping the evil powers of this world, who erroneously believed they could seduce him since he was a "mere man" with a *gnomic* (deliberative ≈ indecisive) will, and were ignorant of the fact that he was tempted in every way like us *but without sin* (Heb. 4:15).[12]

- Through his *teaching*, Jesus granted moral and spiritual wisdom for a new kingdom. In his *Dialogue on the Ascetical Life* and especially in the *Chapters on Love*, Maximus depicted Jesus's

---

[8] Ibid. (1256B–C), trans. Constas I, 447 (slightly altered).
[9] *Opusc.* 3 (PG 91:48C): Οὐ γὰρ ἵνα πάθῃ, σώσῃ δὲ, προηγουμένως γέγονεν ἄνθρωπος.
[10] *Amb. Jo.* 42 (PG 91:1316C–1317C); *Q. Thal.* 21 (CCSG 7:127–9). Cf. also *Amb Jo.* 31 (1276A–B); ibid. 41 (1313C–D, 1325A–B).
[11] *Amb. Jo.* 42 (PG 91:1345C–1349A). See also Larchet, *La divinisation de l'homme*, 411–14.
[12] *Q. Thal.* 21 (CCSG 7:131–3); cf. *LA* (CCSG 40:25–7). For analysis, see also Bathrellos, "The Temptations of Christ according to St. Maximus the Confessor," 45–50; Benjamin Heidgerken, "The Christ and the Tempter: Christ's Temptation by the Devil in the Thought of St. Maximus the Confessor and St. Thomas Aquinas" (Ph.D. dissertation, University of Dayton, 2015), 41–229.

teaching on discipleship as summarizing and perfecting the whole of prophetic and apostolic wisdom on the way of righteousness and holiness. But the consummation of it all was his teaching on the mystery of love (*Epistle* 2), the truly *cosmic* virtue in which all the other virtues and the knowledge of God intersect.

- Jesus's *miracles* gestured his benevolent Lordship over the cosmos and had strong eschatological resonances. A premier example was his walking on the water, thereby demonstrating his lordship over the elements of creation.[13]

- The *suffering* or passion of Jesus disclosed the wholly kenotic character of his incarnation (as we shall see), and was dramatized especially in the agony of Gethsemane, where the salvation of creation hinged on the willingness of Christ, under the specter of unspeakable anguish, to conform his human will to the will of the Father.

- The *death* and burial of Jesus, constituting the nadir of the Son's condescension, was the ultimate climax of his incarnation, dramatizing whether and how God could at last defeat evil and death and even *use* death creatively and redemptively to fulfill his purpose for the world. These issues will be discussed further on in this chapter.

- By his *resurrection*, Christ further completed his work as the New Adam, as the "first fruits" of a new creation, leavening the lump of humanity (cf. Rom. 11:16; see 1 Cor. 5:6, 15:23; Gal. 5:9) and drawing those who have suffered with him into the fullness of the resurrection mystery.[14] His resurrection is the bridge to "eternal well-being."[15] The First Sunday of Pascha paves the way to the "New (Octave) Sunday" of the new creation, and the resurrection of human *nature* is complemented by that resurrection which is a deification *by grace* (κατὰ χάριν θέωσις).[16]

- In *ascending* bodily through the heavens, and seating his new humanity on our behalf at the right hand of the Father, Christ completed the ministry of his incarnation proper and healed the division between spiritual and material reality.[17] But also, by his own perpetual embodiment, he confirmed once for all the

---

[13] See *Amb. Th.* 5 (CCSG 48:23).     [14] *Amb. Jo.* 32 (PG 91:1280C–1281B).
[15] Ibid. 42 (1325B–C, 1348D–1349A).     [16] Ibid. 63 (1388C–1389A, 1339B).
[17] Ibid. 41 (1309B–D); *Or. dom.* (CCSG 23:33–5, ll. 116–27).

dignity and purposefulness of bodies and embodiment in the divine economy, and assured the ongoing efficacy of his incarnational grace for those progressing in virtue.[18]

The common thread in all of these achievements is Jesus's (the Son's) obedience or submission to the will of the Father, an obedience unto death, an "active passivity" as I shall call it. Although, in the trinitarian register ($\theta\epsilon o\lambda o\gamma i\alpha$), the Son's unity of will with the Father is presupposed, there is still the sacred drama wherein Jesus must actively learn submission (cf. Heb. 5:8) and so fully open up the receptivity of human nature to the will of God. His "passivity" ($\tau\grave{o}$ $\pi\acute{a}\theta o\varsigma$) to the divine will, his "suffering" of the will of the Father, really consists, as should become clear, not in an unwitting subjection to divine power but in an *active receptivity*, a potentiality aspiring to actuality.[19] Maximus has no interest in forcing an unqualified symmetry of divine and human activity in Christ's composite person; rather, he wants to show how Jesus himself has disclosed and embodied a deified human will, or better yet, how he has perfectly aligned all the faculties contributing to human intention and action.

In what follows, I shall limit the discussion to Maximus' interpretation of the final, decisive events of Jesus's passion proper, the climax of the incarnational drama. I shall focus especially on certain prevailing themes related to Christ's passion that have surfaced broadly in Maximus scholarship, and also offer commentary and clarification with hopes of providing a revised portrait of Maximus' "passiology" of Jesus Christ.[20]

## THEO-DRAMA AND THE COSMIC CRUCIFIX

The Confessor builds on a long antecedent tradition of Greek patristic reflection on the cosmic scope of Christ's death. While this tradition has sometimes been virtually equated with the development of the

---

[18] *Amb. Jo.* 42 (1332C–1333A); cf. ibid. 48 (1364A); *Th. Oec.* 2.32 (PG 90:1140B).

[19] See also pp. 120–1 in this volume, on "active passivity" as an Aristotelian principle reworked by Maximus.

[20] In what follows, I have drawn from my earlier essay "The Passion of Jesus Christ: A Reconsideration," in M. F. Wiles and E. J. Yarnold, eds., *Studia Patristica* 37 (Leuven: Peeters, 2001), 361–77.

*Christus Victor* motif, the principle that Christ's cross constituted the decisive defeat of the cosmic powers of evil and death,[21] there were broad variations and emphases. We have already seen that this tradition registered itself even in Byzantine political theology, especially Maximus' contemporary George of Pisidia,[22] for whom Christ's cross was a defeat of all enemies of the Christian world order. But another emphasis, which had come to expression early on in Irenaeus and later in Athanasius, was that the incarnation and death of Jesus Christ were already immanent in the very plan of creation. From before the world began, incarnation and cross were the Creator's antidote to resurgent chaos or nothingness, and the premeditated demonstration of his extravagant love for the world, thus releasing, in Jesus's passion, and in the Creator's opportune time, the fullness of a grace already hidden away in the depths of creation and sacred history.

Arguably Maximus' most crucial influences in this "staurological" tradition were Irenaeus and Gregory of Nyssa. Irenaeus made the strongest early plea that the Creator projected the cross before creation and time, judging that only to the "Lamb who was slain" did the Father disclose beforehand the secrets of heaven and earth.[23] As I noted in discussing the christocentrism of Maximus' cosmology, he too understood the cross to have been pre-projected within the divine counsel from before the ages. It was none other than the "spotless Lamb"—the incarnate Christ destined to die on a cross—who was "foreknown before the foundation of the world" (1 Peter 1:20) by the triune Creator.[24]

Both Irenaeus and Nyssen, moreover, had advanced the view that the cross, by its very shape or form, extending in four directions, definitively signified God's cosmic plan and rule as well as the universal effects of divine grace. Irenaeus amplified the idea, originating with Justin Martyr, that the Son of God, at his crucifixion, had been affixed crosswise over the world since "he it is who illuminates the height, that is the heavens; and encompasses the deep which is beneath the earth; and stretches and spreads out the length from east to west; and steers across the breadth of north and south; summoning all that are scattered in every quarter to

---

[21] This patristic motif was a major focus of Gustaf Aulén's classic *Christus Victor: A Historical Study of the Three Main Types of the Idea of the Atonement*, trans. A. G. Hebert (New York: Macmillan, 1969), 4–7, 16–60.

[22] See esp George's epic *Hexaemeron*, ll. 1829–37 (PG 92:1574A). See also pp. 15–16 in this volume.

[23] *Adv. haer.* 4.20.2 (SC 100:628–30).

[24] *Q. Thal.* 60 (CCSG 22:73–81). See also pp. 105–6 in this volume.

the knowledge of the Father."[25] Nyssen further enhances this image of the cosmic crucifix, suggesting that, in the "pre-arranged" death of Christ, the four projections of the cross signified his outreach in all directions to the creation, desiring through his death to restore all created beings to himself.[26] Maximus in his turn continues this line of thinking:

> When contemplated in light of its shape (σχῆμα), the cross hints at the power which embraces all things—things above and things below, in both directions—within their proper limits. In light of its composition (σύνθεσιν), it points to essence, providence, and judgment, that is, to their manifestations, by which I mean wisdom, knowledge, and virtue, which belong to the power that governs the universe. Essence and wisdom, as the creative power, are seen in the vertical line; providence and judgment, as the preserving power, are seen in the horizontal; judgment and virtue, as that which destroys evil, and by which what has been created and preserved is joined to its proper governing cause and origin, are seen throughout the whole. As for the properties of the parts, these are seen, on the one hand, through the vertical line, by which the cross signifies that God is always the same, never departing from his own permanence, by virtue of his unshakeable power and immovable abiding. The horizontal line, on the other hand, hints at creation's absolute dependence on God, for apart from him it has no other governing cause or basis of existence.[27]

Especially striking here is how the Creator's *creative* and *preservative* power intersect in the cross. As we have seen before, Maximus thoroughly insinuates creation and salvation in the sacred theo-drama. The cosmic crucifix, moreover, points not simply toward the subjugation of creation to the Creator, but also toward the realization of creation's latent potential for transformation and deification. Not infrequently Maximus hints at the cruciformity of creation. In *Ambiguum* 54, for instance, he calls upon every Christian to become a "Joseph of Arimathea" in spirit, burying the *crucified* body of Christ that symbolizes, among other things, the *logoi* of creation.[28] In *Ambiguum* 53, the penitent thief on the cross, whom believers are also called to embody spiritually, beholds the crucified Logos who suffers with him and simultaneously demonstrates to

---

[25] *Epideixis* 34 (PO 12:685–6). Cf. Justin, *1 Apol.* 60; *Dial. c. Tryphone* 91.
[26] Cf. *Or. catech.* (GNO 3/4:78–81); *Contra Eunomium* 3 (GNO 2:121–2); *Hom.de tridui spatio* (GNO 9:298–303). See also Blowers, *Drama of the Divine Economy*, 265–6.
[27] *Amb. Jo.* 32 (PG 91:1281C–1284A), trans. Constas II, 55–7.
[28] Ibid. 54 (1376C–1377B).

him his cosmic providence and judgment.[29] Again in *Questions and Responses for Thalassius* 53, it is precisely the suffering and dying Logos whose "eyes" convey universal providence and judgment.[30] The point is that the deep structure of creation already expresses the kenosis of the Word, the disclosure of the Creator's self-sacrificial grace as the true meaning of the world and the promise for its future transfiguration.

Nonetheless the criticism has often been leveled that for the Greek Fathers, including Maximus, the passion and death of Christ were relativized by the more instrumental salvific efficacy of the incarnation itself ("physical" redemption[31]), a point to which I shall return later. Modern critics' attempts to insert a wedge between incarnation proper and the cross would nonetheless have struck these patristic thinkers as strange indeed. For them, the work of Christ was a journey through integrally connected events from his nativity to his glorification, grounded in the Son's execution of the Father's will. Von Balthasar revisited the question of whether, for the Greek Fathers, the passion of Christ was just an "epiphenomenon,"[32] "an emergency measure on God's part" or rather "the interior or organic fulfillment of God's original plan, even if its ultimate form in this world is the Cross and the glorifying light of the Holy Spirit that falls on the Cross."[33] Maximus is a key protagonist for the latter, as Cyril O'Regan observes, insofar as the progression of the theo-drama discloses "new and definitive possibilities released into history by Christ's redemptive act" that were putatively unavailable to prelapsarian creation.[34] The Confessor, von Balthasar further suggests, aspires to reenter the purview of the Gospels, where the incarnation is already "ordered to" the cross, and where the pure freedom of Jesus to fulfill the Father's will is situated within the stark narrative of the Son's abandonment (ἐγκατάλειψις)[35] by the Father. This is the theo-dramatic arena of the

---

[29] Ibid. 53 (1372C–D).     [30] *Q. Thal.* 53 (CCSG 7:431).

[31] A criticism identified with Adolf von Harnack and Friedrich Loofs, the reductionism of which was targeted early on by H. E. W. Turner, *The Patristic Doctrine of Redemption: A Study of the Development of Doctrine during the First Five Centuries* (London: Mowbray, 1952), 72–3.

[32] *Mysterium Paschale: The Mystery of Easter*, 2nd edn., trans. Aidan Nichols (Grand Rapids, MI: Eerdmans, 1990), 22.

[33] *The Glory of the Lord: A Theological Aesthetics*, trans. Erasmo Leiva-Merikakis (San Francisco: Ignatius Press, 1982), 1:453.

[34] "Von Balthasar and Thick Retrieval," 243.

[35] *Car.* 4.96 (PG 90.1072B–C), as highlighted by von Balthasar, *Mysterium Paschale*, 78.

divine "necessity" (δεῖ: Mark 8:31; Luke 9:22; 17:25; 22:37; 24:7; 26:44; John 3:14; 20:9), the relentless forward momentum of action within the Gospel accounts that seems to drive Jesus to the cross by a providential inevitability.[36]

## THE AGONY OF CHRIST AND THE LIBERATING OF HUMAN FREEDOM

As explored particularly in the work of François-Marie Léthel, Pierre Piret, and Marcel Doucet, Maximus puts strong soteriological emphasis on the passion of Christ as constituting the drastic reorientation of human will to the will of God—an emphasis that antedates the monothelete controversy but had its consummate expression in writings from that period. His focus throughout is not on the cross alone but on the whole dramatic build-up to the death of Jesus, which, as his final submission to the Father's will, perfects human volition once and for all. From the agony of Gethsemane to the anguish of Golgotha, we vividly behold the paradox whereby the already impeccable human will of Christ must nonetheless *learn obedience through what he suffered* (Heb. 5:8). Jesus's suffering becomes a liberation of freedom itself by healing the rudiments of human will and choice.

Léthel has rightly noted that when Maximus initially (and measuredly) approved the *Psephos* (633) of Patriarch Sergius of Constantinople in the preliminary stages of the monenergist/monothelete controversy,[37] a document that blocked debate on numbering the *energeiai* in Christ, he made no reference at all to the agony of Gethsemane (Matt. 26:36–42 et par.), the pericope destined to become definitive in his defense of the two wills of Christ. Instead, in a letter to Sergius, he lauds the outworking of the divine *energeia* in the overall incarnational kenosis of Christ without

---

[36] On this benevolent "necessity" (δεῖ/ἔδει) in Maximus, *Amb. Jo.* 10 (PG 91:1165D); *Q. Thal.* 60 (CCSG 22:79); ibid. 61 (p. 87); ibid. 64 (p. 197); *Or. dom.* (CCSG 23:37). See also von Balthasar, *Mysterium Paschale*, 14–20. For this notion in Gregory Nazianzen, see Donald Winslow, *The Dynamics of Salvation: A Study in Gregory of Nazianzus* (Philadelphia: Philadelphia Patristic Foundation, 1979), 112–14. Winslow stresses that for Gregory (and the same holds true for Maximus), the "necessity" belongs to the *oikonomia*, and is not an imposition on God's own nature or freedom.

[37] See pp. 44–6, 159 in this volume.

highlighting the passion proper.[38] But in his subsequent christological mini-treatises, *Opusculum* 20 (*c*.640) being a turning-point, he moved beyond Gregory Nazianzen and, in expounding the agony of Christ, attended to Jesus's *human* will in its own right as a theatre of the drama of salvation and of believers' participation in the *tropos* of Christ's new humanity.[39]

In Chapter 4 I discussed the scrupulous christological definitions which Maximus developed in interpreting Jesus's prayer in Gethsemane, especially his insistence that it foregrounded the harmony of divine and human "natural" wills, wills that were *different but not opposed*.[40] And yet over and beyond these precise definitions and the need to ground Christ's human will within the *logos* of his human nature, the narrative of Gethsemane imposed its own exegetical demands. Could technical christological language do full justice to the suspense of the scriptural narrative itself? The graphic realism of Jesus's initial resistance to the specter of suffering, and his *coming to* a point of final resolve in the Gethsemane prayer, begged for an explanation that respected the high drama of the story. Affirming the unmitigated assent of Jesus's already deified human will to the will of the Father (ostensibly Nazianzen's view) did not seem, on the face of it at least, to meet this demand.

Maximus' advantage in his earlier works was to allow for gnomic will in Christ, the capacity to "deliberate" over a moral end, which also presupposed an intrinsic role of desire and even emotion in the process of calculating appropriate action toward that end. It is difficult to imagine the fear of imminent and painful death, combined (as in the martyr) with the resolve to do what is faithful and obedient, apart from the concrete experience of vacillation and trepidation. Indeed, resolve is tempered and honed precisely by the refiner's fire of deliberation and decision-making under duress. The difference for Maximus is that Jesus from beginning to end *used his gnomic will virtuously* and as an instrument for instructing the faithful in obedience, endurance, and perseverance. Christ's own perfect *gnômê* made possible the "gnomic" reconciliation of humanity, which is of a piece with the healing of human nature.

---

[38] *Ep.* 19 (PG 91:592D–593A); and see Léthel, *Théologie de l'agonie du Christ*, 60–4.
[39] See esp. the section in *Opusc.* 20 (PG 91:233B–237C) where Maximus inaugurates his ongoing commentary on the agony of Gethsemane.
[40] See pp. 156–65 in this volume.

He restores [human] nature to itself not only by becoming human, and keeping his gnomic will (γνώμην) impassible (ἀπαθῆ) and imperturbable in the face of nature (πρὸς τὴν φύσιν), and not allowing it, on its own terms, to vacillate contrary to nature (κατὰ φύσιν) in the face of those who crucified him; but he also, for their sake, chose death instead of life, as the voluntary character of his suffering indicates, confirmed by the philanthropic disposition of him who suffered. What is more, he *abolished enmity by nailing to the cross the bond* of sin (cf. Eph. 2:14–16; Col. 2:14) on account of which [human] nature was implacably warring against itself, and by calling *those far* and *those near* (Eph. 2:17)—clearly indicating *those under the law* and *those outside the law* (1 Cor. 9:20; Gal. 4:5). For he manifestly *broke down the wall of hostility,* clearly being *the law of commandments in ordinances,* as *he made two men into one new man, so making peace and reconciling* us through himself to the Father and to one another (Eph. 2:14–16), such that we have a will (γνώμην) no longer opposed to the principle of our nature, a will unchangeable just like our nature.[41]

Here were the makings of an enduring principle of Maximus' soteriology, the view that all the gnomic wills of rational creatures must ultimately be conformed to nature, or more precisely to "natural will" (θέλησις φυσική) predisposed toward God. Though he later retracted it, Maximus claimed that Christ exercised not only *gnômê* but also, in close connection, an immutable "free choice" (προαίρεσις), with a view to healing the passibility associated both with pain and with pleasure (τὸ κατ᾽ ὀδύνην ... [καὶ] ... καθ᾽ ἡδονὴν παθητόν).[42] Christ the New Adam was able to rally the antecedent elements of human will and appetency, enabling the human moral subject to decide for, and commit to, virtuous courses of action.

In early and later works alike, moreover, the Confessor also explored Christ's exemplary *use* (χρῆσις)[43] of the passible faculties and of the natural instincts and "blameless passions" (ἀδιάβλητα πάθη), since the incarnation unveiled Jesus's *passibility without peccability*. In his incarnational kenosis, becoming the "disgrace of humankind" (Ps. 21:7, LXX),[44] a "captive among us captives,"[45] "sin" itself (2 Cor. 5:21),[46] he worked to convert human passibility from the inside out, with a view ultimately to

---

[41] *Or. dom.* (CCSG 23:34–5, ll. 135–53).
[42] *Q. Thal.* 21 (CCSG 7:131, ll. 81–2, 86–8); also ibid. 42 (CCSG 7:285); and the retraction in *Opusc.* 1 (PG 91:29D–32A).
[43] e.g. *Disp. Pyrr.* (PG 91:297B).          [44] *Q. Thal.* 53 (CCSG 7:431).
[45] Ibid. 54 (CCSG 7:455).          [46] Ibid. 42 (CCSG 7:285–9).

making death itself—the ultimate passion—a pure instrument of trans-formation rather than of punishment for sins of passion. Maximus describes vividly in *Questions and Responses for Thalassius* 62 how the Logos incarnate entered the *house* of *wood and stone* (Zech. 5:1–4), interpreted tropologically as "the disposition of each one who loves sin," calloused and hardened, where, having cast out the indwelling Devil, he consumed the passible faculties ("wood" and "stone") of desire (ἐπιθυμία) and temper (θυμός) in his refiner's fire, redirecting them toward virtue and impassibility.[47] As in the passage from the *Commentary on the Lord's Prayer* quoted before, Maximus once more appeals to Ephesians 2:14–17 and Colossians 2:14:

> Or perhaps Scripture calls "stones" the soul's indifference (ῥαθυμία) toward good things when it has no sense of virtue, and "wood" the soul's zeal (προθυμία) for evil things. The Logos, who removes both of these from the heart of the faithful, does not stop *making peace, and reconciling those far away and those near* in one body of virtues, *breaking down the partition* (sin, I mean) which divides them (Eph. 2:14–17). He does not stop cancelling the *bond* of the will (γνώμης) to evil (Col. 2:14), and subjecting the arrogance of the flesh to the law of the Spirit. For I am of the view that Scripture calls the movements of sense *those far away*, since they are by nature distant, and calls the soul's intellectual activities *those near* since they are, by their affinity, not remote from reason. In turn, the Logos, after dissolving the law of the flesh, binds them to one another spiritually through virtuous conduct. For it seems to me that Scripture has called a *partition* (μεσότοιχον, Eph. 2:14) the natural law of the body, while calling a *barrier* (φραγμόν, Eph. 2:14) the attachment to the passions under the law of the flesh, or namely sin. For only the attachment of the natural law (that is, of the passible part (τοῦ παθητοῦ μέρους) of human nature) to the *passions of dishonor* (Rom. 1:26) becomes a *barrier* dividing the body from the soul, and from the reason of the virtues, and preventing the crossover to the flesh via the soul in moral praxis from taking place. But the Logos comes and overturns the law of human nature—that is, the passible part of human nature—and abolishes its attachment to unnatural passions.[48]

In later works from the monothelete crisis, Maximus further explored the internal dynamics of Jesus's emotion of trepidation (δειλία) in connection with his passion. His fear derived, as in all human beings, from the animal drives of inclination (ὁρμή) and aversion (ἀφορμή),

---

[47] Ibid. 62 (CCSG 22:127–9).    [48] Ibid. (CCSG 22:129–31, ll. 225–50).

which are paralleled, in Maximus' moral psychology, by the passible faculties of desire and temper. His human drives being blameless (ἀδιάβλητα), Jesus only had the natural, healthy fear of the destruction of life, not the unnatural mode of that passion, an irrational dread:

> For the natural functions of volition did not operate in the Lord in exactly the same way as they do in us. Rather, he did in truth hunger and thirst, not in the very same mode as we hunger and thirst, but in a way that transcends us since he did so *voluntarily* (ἑκουσίως). So he truly hungered, not like us but *for us* (ὑπὲρ ἡμῶν). On the whole, everything natural in Christ holds together by the self-consistent principle [of nature] and yet operates in a supernatural mode, so that [Christ's human] nature in virtue of its principle, and the economy (οἰκονομία) in virtue of his mode of existence, might each be confirmed.[49]

For Maximus, Christ's fear in a supernatural mode aimed to supplant the dread of death that is a function of self-love and self-interest by embodying a kind of fearful resolve in the face of death that would embolden the faithful.[50] This bespeaks once more the "asymmetrical" element in Maximus' Christology, which privileges the divine initiative in Christ's composite person while nonetheless refusing the reduction of Christ's natural human volition to a mere receiver-mechanism of divine impulses. The paradox of "active passivity," within the drama of God's salvific *oikonomia*, was that Jesus still had to "learn" obedience through suffering (Heb. 5:8), to "submit" to a will that was already his own within his composite hypostasis.

Maximus elucidates this theme in his commentary on Nazianzen's own reflections on Jesus's training through suffering, "a marvelously constructed drama on our behalf" as Gregory had called it:

> It is in this manner, then, as it seems to me, that he who is Lord by nature "honors obedience," and "experiences it by suffering," not simply to preserve what is properly his own, by cleansing all nature of the "meaner element," but so that he who by nature contains all knowledge might also "test our own obedience," and *learn* (Heb. 5:8) that which concerns us by experiencing what is our own, namely, "how much could be demanded of us, and how much we are to be excused," with a view to

[49] *Disp. Pyrr.* (PG 91:297C–300A) (emphasis added in translation). Cf. *Opusc.* 3 (PG 91:48C).
[50] *Opusc.* 7 (PG 91:80D). For discussion of this transcendent mode of Jesus's fear, see also Piret, *Christ et la Trinité*, 281–2.

that perfect submission through which he habitually *leads* to the Father (1 Peter 3:18) those who are saved in him, revealed by the power of grace.[51]

Jesus's kenotic learning-through-suffering is an embodied form of instruction and testing, the implications of which are ontological as well as moral. The incarnate Lord pushes out the frontiers of our human nature, including its passible faculties, inaugurating new "uses" for emotions like the fear of pain or death. It is as if he creates a new repertoire of godly passions that serve the spiritual maturation and deification of believers. "His sufferings ($\pi\alpha\theta\eta\tau\acute{\alpha}$) are wondrous ($\theta\alpha\acute{\upsilon}\mu\alpha\tau\alpha$), for they have been renewed ($\kappa\alpha\iota\nu\iota\zeta\acute{o}\mu\epsilon\nu\alpha$) by the natural divine power of the one who suffered."[52] Such sufferings or passions play a role in the liberation of freedom, the freeing of the will to the embrace of virtue, for if desire and aversion are properly oriented to godly ends, free will is enriched and strengthened (a theme I will take up in the next chapter).

For Maximus, therefore, Jesus's "resistance" to the specter of suffering in Gethsemane is hardly a feigning of anguish; rather it outwardly dramatizes the inner mystery whereby he rallied all his human faculties into the service of his natural human will. Challenging von Balthasar's view that for Maximus the "resistance" in the Garden was overshadowed by Christ's composite person being ultimately in command of the struggle, Marcel Doucet has argued that the real drama unfolded within Christ's humanity itself, the resistance being the pushback of a natural survival instinct against his *natural will* as such.[53] If so, however, this brings back the difficulty of Maximus' denial of *gnomic* will in Christ. For his human natural will was conformed throughout to the divine will, but only the gnomic mode of volition would seem to admit of an existential process for weighing the prospects and consequences of suffering. While in his technical definition of natural will, Maximus had allowed for an element of inner counsel ($\beta o\upsilon\lambda\acute{\eta}$ or $\beta o\acute{\upsilon}\lambda\eta\sigma\iota\varsigma$),[54] this was but one phase in the virtually instantaneous outworking of volition as rational desire. The issue came to the forefront when Pyrrhus suggested in debate that

---

[51] *Amb. Th.* 4 (CCSG 48:17, ll. 91–9), trans. Constas I, 29–31. Maximus quotes from Gregory Nazianzen, *Or.* 30.6 (SC 250:236).

[52] *Amb. Th.* 5 (CCSG 48:29, ll. 196–8), trans. Constas I, 49.

[53] "La volonté humaine du Christ, spécialement en son agonie," 135–6.

[54] *Opusc.* 1 (PG 91:13A–16B); *Disp. Pyrr.* (PG 91:293B–C).

"nature" connotes constraint, undermining true freedom, implying that Jesus would thereby become an automaton.[55]

The other side of this issue was the problem of whether Christ could only bear and renew *universal* human nature and the "natural will" (θέλημα φυσική) common thereto, or else also act as an *individual* human being. Certainly Maximus wanted to claim both for Christ, the "concrete universal." As the New Adam, eschatologically perfected humanity, Christ demonstrates, within the historical particularity of his own life, how a thoroughly deified natural will chooses and acts, perennially and "freely" embracing the will of the Father.[56] Meanwhile the "gnomic" will, actually being a *mode* of willing more than a capacity in its own right, is not rendered evil in itself but simply transcended,[57] since in the eschaton, absent the "mixed" knowledge of good and evil, there will be no deliberation or vacillation toward goodness and beauty. This is but the outcome of Christ's doing *human* things *divinely* (θεϊκῶς).[58]

## THE "WONDROUS EXCHANGE": MAXIMUS ON ATONEMENT

We have seen that Maximus did not make salvation (and deification) contingent on the cross alone but on the whole of Christ's incarnational ministry as purposed before the beginning of the ages. He was profoundly influenced in this regard by Gregory Nazianzen's *Second Oration on the Son* (*Or.* 30) and *Paschal Oration* (*Or.* 45), which depicted the cross precisely as the nadir and climax of the Son's incarnational kenosis.[59] Atonement as such, the internal dynamics of reconciliation, is not something on which Maximus dwells at length, but he does take up three atonement motifs for which Gregory

[55] *Disp. Pyrr.* (PG 91:293B).
[56] For deeper analysis, see Ian McFarland, "'Naturally and by Grace:' Maximus the Confessor on the Operation of the Will," *Scottish Journal of Theology* 58 (2004): 410–33, esp. 422–6.
[57] *Disp. Pyrr.* (PG 91:308C–309A).
[58] Ibid. (308D); *Amb. Th.* 5 (CCSG 48:28–30); also p. 145, and n. 36 in this volume.
[59] See esp. *Amb. Jo.* 45–60; and on Nazianzen's Paschal theology as background, see Winslow, *The Dynamics of Salvation*, 99–119.

of Nyssa is undoubtedly his immediate source.[60] First is the idea of divine deception, whereby the flesh of Christ was like a baited "worm," descending into the deep to hook the Devil, forcing him to release humanity from captivity.[61] Second, and closely related, is the image of Christ's flesh as a "poison" inducing the Devil to vomit out those held captive to death (death itself being the antidote); and third is the depiction of Christ's flesh as a "leaven" causing humanity to rise like a loaf to resurrection life.[62] Meanwhile Maximus avoided any version of atonement by ransom that entailed Christ's flesh or death being a ransom *paid to the Devil* to release captive humanity, as he doubtless knew Nazianzen's rebuke of the logic of the Evil One being owed a debt.[63]

Ultimately Maximus, like Nazianzen, saw the "transaction" of atonement as operative not between God and the Devil but between the Father and the Son, or rather between the Father and sinful humanity through the mediation of the Son. By the "wondrous exchange" (καλὴ ἀντιστροφή), as Maximus calls it, "God is made human for the sake of human deification, and humanity is made God on account of God's hominization."[64] Like Nazianzen, he allows that the incarnation is a ransom (λύτρον) offered to the Father on

---

[60] For a survey of patristic conceptions of atonement as "wondrous exchange," see Hans Urs von Balthasar, *Theo-Drama: Theological Dramatic Theory*, vol. 4, trans. Graham Harrison (San Francisco: Ignatius Press, 1994), 246–54.

[61] *Q. Thal.* 64 (CCSG 22:217–19); cf. Gregory of Nyssa, *Or. catech.* (GNO 3/4:61–2). For Maximus, Christ is worm-like (cf. Ps. 21:7, LXX) in his incarnation itself (being conceived, like the worm, without sexual intercourse); in his baiting of the Devil; and in his going "underground" and emerging again (i.e. his burial and resurrection). For a superb analysis of the patristic background and the pervasiveness of the "fish hook" metaphor, see Maximos (Nicholas) Constas, "The Last Temptation of Satan: Divine Deception in Greek Patristic Interpretations of the Passion Narrative," *Harvard Theological Review* 97 (2004), esp. 143–54, 158–63. On the biblical legitimacy of the *Christus Victor* and "divine deception" motifs, and their recognition both in early Jewish and patristic thought, see Gary Anderson, "The Resurrection of Adam and Eve," in Blowers et al., *In Dominico Eloquio/In Lordly Eloquence*, 3–34. For modern assessments of divine deception and ransom theories of atonement in the Fathers, see Ludlow, *Gregory of Nyssa: Ancient and (Post)modern*, 108–24.

[62] *Or. dom.* (CCSG 23:36); *Amb. Jo.* 31 (PG 91:1280C–D); ibid. 32 (1280C–1281B); cf. Gregory of Nyssa, *Or. catech.* 37 (GNO 3/4:93–8).

[63] See Gregory Nazianzen, *Or.* 45.22 (PG 36:643B). See also Winslow, *The Dynamics of Salvation*, 108–10.

[64] *Amb. Jo.* 7 (PG 91.1004C). ... ποιωῦσαν ... τὸν μὲν θεὸν ἄνθρωπον, διὰ τὴν τοῦ ἀνθρώπου θέωσιν, τὸν δὲ ἄνθρωπον θεόν, διὰ τὴν τοῦ θεοῦ ἐνανθρώπησιν. Larchet suggests that God's "hominization" here refers primarily not to the historical incarnation but rather the Logos's "incarnation" in the believer who is being deified (*La*

behalf of all sinners (cf. Mark 10:25; 1 Tim. 2:6), Christ's suffering for our suffering: "In exchange for our corrosive passions, [Christ] grants (ἀντιδούς) us his life-giving passion as a healing and saving cure for the whole world."[65] Atonement is commensurate, therefore, with the depth of the Son's humiliation and his "appropriation" (οἰκείωσις) of the tragic human condition. In a lengthy exegesis of 2 Corinthians 5:21, he clarifies that Christ "became" consequential sin, the "sin that I caused" (ἁμαρτία δι' ἐμέ), not "my sin" (ἡ ἐμὴ ἁμαρτία) or actual wrongdoing and guilt.[66] He took on passibility, not peccability.[67] Similarly, with reference to Galatians 3:13, Christ "became a curse" by assuming the curse or punishment of death, not the curse of moral sin itself.[68] Even more adventurous is Maximus' claim that Christ appropriated both the punishment (ἐπιτιμία) of deviant passions and the actual ignominy (ἀτιμία) of the *tropos* of human rebellion, in order to destroy it (quoting Nazianzen) "just as a fire consumes wax and the sun consumes ground fog."[69] With Gregory, then, Maximus can legitimately call Christ a "rebel" (ἀνυπότακτος) under the terms of his salvific economy.[70]

Von Balthasar, citing Maximus as an example of "dramatic soteriology," understands the dynamics of atonement in the Confessor as essentially the exchange, in Christ, between infinite divine freedom and a finite, self-enclosed human freedom. The more the Father sacrifices his Son, and the deeper the Son descends to humanity in submitting to the Father's will, the more human freedom is released from suffocating itself and renewed in obedience to God. "If Maximus' portrayal of the reciprocal immanence of finite and infinite freedom seems somehow undramatic, we must remember . . . that the *analogia entis* (the irreducible 'otherness' of created nature) excludes any kind of fusion and confusion in the ever-intensifying reciprocal interpenetration: each increase in 'divinization' on the part of the creature also implies an increase of its own freedom."[71] Christ's agony and passion are thus set

---

*divinisation de l'homme*, 378). But in fact, as he himself acknowledges, those two "incarnations" are effectively inseparable.

[65] *Myst.* 8 (CCSG 69:36–7, quoted at ll. 614–16). Cf. Gregory Nazianzen, *Or.* 1.5 (SC 247:62).

[66] *Q. Thal.* 42 (CCSG 7:285–9).     [67] Ibid. 21 (CCSG 7:129).

[68] Ibid. 52 (CCSG 22:123–5).

[69] *Opusc.* 20 (PG 91:237A–B); and Gregory Nazianzen, *Or.* 30.6 (SC 250:236).

[70] *Opusc.* 4 (PG 91:60B); and Gregory Nazianzen, *Or.* 30.5 (SC 250:234).

[71] *Theo-Drama*, 4:383.

within the cosmic context, a thickening plot that projects the destiny of all creation as hinging on the reciprocal communion of God and humanity and the transformation of humanity "from the ground up" through the labor of Christ's deified human will, the "spiritual drama ... [of] ... the life-and-death struggle of the natures of God and the creature on the stage of the most exalted hypostasis."[72]

By stark contrast, Raymund Schwager, a disciple of René Girard, considers Maximus at length in his distinguished history of Christian theories of redemption, *Der Wunderbare Tausch* ("the Wondrous Exchange"), holding him to a quite different standard of atonement doctrine.[73] Schwager's question for Maximus is: How exactly does Christ vicariously stem the tide of transgenerational vice, the *mimetic* legacy of human rivalry in Girardian terms? One can speculate endlessly about ransoms or about a debt owed to God because of human sin, but at the end of the day redemption is a dilemma of counteracting the downward spiral of moral evil. Schwager's own aversion to "physical" (ontologized) theories of salvation is obvious, and while he has been seen as reworking an Abelardian theory of atonement and treating Christ principally as a moral exemplar,[74] he, like Girard, has nonetheless recalled an important element in New Testament teaching on redemption and reconciliation.[75] Certainly the idea of atonement as a reversal of moral evil was not lost on Maximus himself:

[Christ] purified nature from the law of sin (Rom. 7:23, 25; 8:2) in not having permitted pleasure to precede his incarnation on our behalf. Indeed his conception wondrously came about without seed, and his birth took place supernaturally without corruption: with God being begotten of a mother and tightening much more than nature can the bonds of virginity by his birth. He frees the whole of nature from the tyranny of law which dominated it in those who desire it and who by

---

[72] Von Balthasar, *Cosmic Liturgy*, 271; cf. Marion, "Les deux volontés du Christ," 59–60.

[73] "Das Mysterium der übernatürlichen Natur-Lehre: Zur Erlöngslehre des Maximus Confessor," in *Der Wunderbare Tausch: Zur Geschichte und Deutung der Erlösungslehre* (Munich: Kösel-Verlag, 1986), esp. 135–60.

[74] See Michael Winter, *The Atonement* (Collegeville, MN: Liturgical Press, 1995), 82.

[75] On the *Christus Victor* motif in the NT as already demanding attention to the existential reversal of moral evil, see Colin Gunton, *The Actuality of Atonement* (Grand Rapids, MI: Eerdmans, 1989), 74–82.

mortification of the sensuality of their earthly members (Col. 3:5) imitate his freely chosen death. For the mystery of salvation belongs to those who desire it, not to those who are forced to submit to it.[76]

Schwager, though frustrated by Maximus' "naturalizing" of atonement, alleging that he is still tied to older Greek patristic notions of "physical" redemption through divine incarnation itself, nonetheless credits the Confessor with making progress toward understanding the role of the mimetic reversal of evil, particularly by enhancing Christ's work in alleviating the internal burden of the law of sin and effecting the transformation of irrational passions.[77] Schwager avers that Maximus undermined himself, however, by pinning everything on the deified *natural* will of Christ and denying him *gnômê*, the gnomic will being the primary agent of human egoism and rivalry. How could Maximus have recognized the redemptive role of gnomic will and free choice (προαίρεσις) in Christ in his early writings only to reverse himself later on?[78] Specifically, how in his debate with Pyrrhus could he collapse all virtue into "natural" volition when elsewhere he has clearly factored *gnômê* into the formation of virtues?[79] Even admitting the role of *gnômê* in precipitating and perpetuating the fall of humanity, *quod non est assumptum, non sanatum*.[80] Schwager will not allow, then, that Christ is a "concrete universal" in any abstract sense. His atonement must address the concrete particularity of individuated human beings, through whose gnomic wills the legacy of sin and violence viciously endures.

Earlier I mapped the controversy surrounding gnomic will in Christ and I will not revisit it here.[81] But the soteriological question stands. How could Christ redirect and redeem the differentiated gnomic wills of all individual rational creatures, or how could he effect the "gnomic surrender" (ἐκχώρησις γνωμική) of creatures to

---

[76] *Or. dom.* (CCSG 23:30–1, ll. 77–85), trans. Berthold, 104.

[77] "Das Mysterium der übernatürlichen Natur-Lehre," *Der Wunderbare Tausch*, 151, 158ff. Michael Hardin, in a different study, claims to discern in Maximus' *Chapters on Love* a rich mimetic paradigm and a profound insight into the nature of human violence. See his "Mimesis and Dominion: The Dynamics of Violence and the Imitation of Christ in Maximus Confessor," *St. Vladimir's Theological Quarterly* 36 (1992): 375–85.

[78] "Das Mysterium der übernatürlichen Natur-Lehre," *Der Wunderbare Tausch*, 141–7.

[79] Ibid., 145–6 (citing *Disp. Pyrr*, PG 91:309B–312A).      [80] Ibid., 157–8.

[81] See pp. 156–65 in this volume.

the unifying will of God,[82] without himself penetrating the gnomic mode of volition? If he was tempted like we are save without sin (Heb. 4:15), would it not be the case that even consistently resisting and overcoming temptation still entailed a mental process of weighing prospective pain or pleasure? A disposition of sheer imperviousness could scarcely suffice as redemptive of human passibility, any more than *apatheia*, in Maximus' ascetical teaching, could be reduced to a state of unfeeling detachment. Certainly, as observed in Chapter 4, we must acknowledge that for Maximus *gnômê* increasingly connoted a weakness and vacillation inappropriate to the integrity and resolve of the Savior.[83] Since, moreover, Christ did not have a separate human hypostasis, he did not exercise *gnômê*. But this too easily dismisses the positive implication of gnomic intentionality to which Maximus consistently refers in his early writings.[84] As Philipp Gabriel Renczes remarks, "Γνώμη is the authority that humanity has to contribute voluntarily to the movement that moves, with God's grace, toward its divine goal, deification."[85] One whole dimension of Christ's salvific work in the Confessor's early writings is not only the recovery of "natural" will and desire for God but also bringing clarity and orientation to the ambiguity of human passibility such that, far from being dismissed as a tragic failure, it enriches the path to deification.

Various attempts to resolve this issue in Maximus' soteriology have been proposed. Lars Thunberg downplays the problem by insisting that the "natural will" of Jesus in the Confessor's anti-monothelete works effectively functioned in the same way that Jesus's already unique and perfect *gnômê* had operated according to his early writings.[86] Certainly Maximus did not admit to any grand reversal in his christological thinking as a result of finally denying *gnômê* in Christ. Ian McFarland has concluded that once he settled on the deified natural will of Jesus as capable of representing how the freedom of individual human beings should operate in anticipation of the eschaton, *gnômê* simply ceased to be christologically relevant even if it still retained anthropological import.[87] Larchet

---

[82] *Amb. Jo.* 7 (PG 91:1076B).     [83] See pp. 164–5 in this volume.
[84] In *Epistle* 2 (PG 91:396C–D), for example, Maximus had envisioned love as persuading *gnômê* to conform to the *logos* of human nature, creating a beautiful scenario in which all *gnômai* would be united with God and each other, and the very law of human nature would be renovated.
[85] *Agir de Dieu et liberté de l'homme*, 276.     [86] *Microcosm and Mediator*, 215.
[87] "'Naturally and by Grace,'" 427–9; id., "'Willing is Not Choosing,'" 11–16.

similarly emphasizes that the *tropos* of Christ's *deified* human will precluded a gnomic mode.[88] Basil Studer, on the other hand, suggests that Maximus simply left unclear "how the vacillation and hesitation of the human will were abolished in the [composite] hypostasis without these not already being the natural principle of the inner life of Jesus's soul. But with that it also remains an open question how the human Jesus resisted sin in carrying out his own freedom, (and) on the other hand, how the hypostasis in the God-man is perfected without in turn being affected by Christ's progress."[89]

Still another perspective is that of Joseph Farrell, who claims to discern in Maximus "a mystical theology of free choice, an eschatological state of synergy."[90] In this case the Confessor's eventual denial of *gnômê* in Christ is, as in McFarland, a function of the *eschatological* mode of willing already realized in Jesus. Maximus' Christ, however, has not only precluded the eschatological carryover of *gnômê*, he has also positively inaugurated the way for human beings, as willing and choosing creatures *by their indissoluble nature*, to extend their freedom in the age to come. Maximus indicates this as a "mystical enjoyment" ($\mu\nu\sigma\tau\iota\kappa\grave{\eta}$ $\mathring{\alpha}\pi\acute{o}\lambda\alpha\nu\sigma\iota\varsigma$) wherein humans will no longer use the "media" ($\tau\grave{\alpha}$ $\mu\acute{\epsilon}\sigma\alpha$) of judgment and decision concerning goods and their opposite, but instead experience an "infinite stretching" ($\grave{\epsilon}\pi$' $\mathring{\alpha}\pi\epsilon\iota\rho\sigma\nu$ $\grave{\epsilon}\pi\acute{\iota}\tau\alpha\sigma\iota\varsigma$) of their natural desire toward its permanent enjoyments.[91] In this sublime state, Farrell argues, Maximus imagined that human choice would not endure as a selection between alternatives, nor would it stall because of a satiety ($\kappa\acute{o}\rho\sigma\varsigma$) of the good, but would embrace the *multiple goods* of God in the form of the *logoi*, his "uncreated energies" and vehicles of eternal well-being.[92] While Farrell's view is difficult to prove since Maximus deals very little with free choice in an eschatological mode, it is at least compatible with his vision of the afterlife as a sublime spiraling "around God" ($\pi\epsilon\rho\grave{\iota}$ $\theta\epsilon\acute{o}\nu$) in a state of eternally progressing enjoyment and sabbath.

[88] *La divinisation de l'homme*, 239–47.
[89] "Zur Soteriologie des Maximus Confessor," *MC*, 246.
[90] *Free Choice in Maximus the Confessor* (South Canaan, PA: St. Tikhon's Seminary Press, 1989), 112.
[91] *Opusc.* 1 (PG 91:24B–C).
[92] *Free Choice in St. Maximus the Confessor*, 110–42.

CHRIST'S CONQUEST OF EVIL AND DEATH:
GROUNDS FOR A UNIVERSAL *APOKATASTASIS*?

In concluding this chapter I want to return to the *Christus Victor* motif and its implications in Maximus' vision of eschatological salvation. Playing off of the Pauline paradox of divine strength through weakness,[93] the Confessor envisioned Christ's redemptive victory as an active passivity, an embrace of perfect submission to the will of the Father, not only by outward obedience but also by inwardly conforming his passibility—his susceptibility to passions, suffering, *and death*—to the *logos* of his human nature as united perfectly with the Godhead. When he speaks of Christ having descended into the lower parts of the earth,[94] and of "having put death to death" (θανατώσας τὸν θάνατον),[95] echoing the Paschal Troparion of Orthodox liturgical tradition, Maximus is referencing Christ's conquest of the fatality of death; but when he also speaks of Christ *using* death, he specifies his aggressive conversion of death into an instrument of life.[96] That conversion begins with Christ entering passible flesh in its trajectory toward death, transforming that passibility from within,[97] using a new repertoire of sanctified passions, and at last making the starkest passion/passivity of death itself a basis for the sublime "passion" of deification.[98] When Maximus notes that Christ's death was the single guiltless or "uncaused" (ἀναίτιος) death, a death not punitive but wholly transformative since it broke once for all the law of pain and pleasure commanding human mortality, he stresses its character as pure gift, an expression of utter *philanthrôpia*.[99]

In stressing the element of *finality* in Christ's triumph over death and the moral evil for which it was punishment, the question inevitably presents itself whether this finality had eschatological effect, extending into the age to come. Simply put, did Maximus project the possibility of a restoration of all things (ἀποκατάστασις παντῶν), a recuperation of every creature of reason and conscience, as part of God's cruciform

---

[93] Maximus explicitly references this paradox in *LA* (CCSG 40:31) and *Amb. Jo.* 71 (PG 91:1409A–C).

[94] e.g. *Q. Thal.* 22 (CCSG 7:139); ibid. 64 (CCSG 22:197).

[95] *Opusc.* 3 (PG 91:48B); cf. *LA* (CCSG 40:31); *Amb. Jo.* 21 (PG 91:1252A–B).

[96] *Q. Thal.* 42 (CCSG 7:285); ibid. 61 (CCSG 22:89–91, 93–5).

[97] Ibid. 21 (CCSG 7:87).

[98] On the "suffering" or "passion" (πάθος) of deification, see *Q. Thal.* 22 (CCSG 7:141, ll. 82–98).

[99] Ibid. 21 (CCSG 7:87–9); cf. ibid. 61 (CCSG 22:89–95).

plan for the world? Indeed, the question has been posed more than once in Maximus scholarship and I reopen it here because of its persistence and its significance for an overall assessment of the Confessor in his theological context. Eugène Michaud prompted modern discussion by concluding that Maximus had indeed affirmed an *apokatastasis*,[100] while von Balthasar understood him to treat the issue dialectically but sympathetically, and with reticence to divulge his true sentiments.[101] Polycarp Sherwood likewise acknowledged Maximus' dialectical approach, and, while admitting the lack of a frontal assault on the doctrine in Maximus, inferred from his rejection of the Origenists' primordial unity (ἑνάς) of pre-incarnate spiritual beings that the recovery of such a unity or bodiless *stasis* was out of the question.[102] Sherwood for his part determined that universal restoration or reconciliation of creatures to God for Maximus was at most an open-ended *hope* (i.e. not ecclesiastical dogma).[103]

There is not the space here to analyze all the relevant texts concerning *apokatastasis* that have been identified from Maximus' corpus in these and other studies. A fair sampling would first have to reference the numerous texts where he appears to uphold the prospect of eternal punishment of the wicked. The most ominous is a passage in *Ambiguum* 65 describing how, on the eschatologically perpetual "eighth day," the sabbatical of creation, God will grant "eternal well-being" (τὸ ἀεὶ εὖ εἶναι) to those who by free choice (προαιρετικῶς) have conformed themselves to the *logos* of their nature, but "eternal ill-being" (τὸ ἀεὶ φεῦ εἶναι) to those who have deliberately (γνωμικῶς) abused their principle of being.[104] Michaud explained away such passages as being a function of the Confessor's moral pedagogy rather than dogmatic pronouncements on unending punishment.

Texts that seem unqualifiedly to affirm a universal restoration are rare but striking. In the opening of his *Commentary on Psalm 59*, Maximus sets out the eschatological significance of the Psalm on the basis of its title:

The present psalm is inscribed with the opening words *Unto the end, for those who shall be changed* (εἰς τὸ τέλος, τοῖς ἀλλοιωθησομένοις) in view

[100] "Saint Maxime le Confesseur et l'apocatastase," *Revue Internationale de Théologie* 10 (1902): 257–72.
[101] See *Cosmic Liturgy*, 354–8.   [102] *The Earlier Ambigua*, 205–22.
[103] Ibid., 222, citing *Car.* 1.71 (PG 90:976B–C).
[104] *Amb. Jo.* 65 (PG 91:1392D). Similarly, cf. *Ep.* 4 (PG 91:416D–417A). On the threat of hell, cf. *Ep.* 24 (PG 91:612B–C).

of the transformation and change in deliberative will and in free choice (διὰ τὴν . . . γνώμικην τε καὶ προαιρετικὴν μεταβολὴν καὶ ἀλλοίωσιν) from infidelity to faith, from vice to virtue, and from ignorance to knowledge of God, which have come about for humanity at the end of time (cf. 1 Cor. 10:11) through the advent of Christ. [It is also thus inscribed] in view of the natural change and renewal which will later, in grace, transpire universally at the end of the ages through the very same Savior and God, when all the human race shall be translated from death and corruption to immortal life and incorruption through the antici-pated resurrection. *For an inscription of a title to David*: that is to say, to Christ himself, in view of the destruction of evil which, in the divine incarnation, itself a kind of "inscription," Christ accomplished in him-self as our *Leader and Savior* (Acts 5:31), and which he effects in those who with him live piously in the manner of Christ (cf. 2 Tim. 3:12; Titus 2:12). Yet this phrase also has in view the complete and final disappearance of death and corruption which is yet to happen through Christ.[105]

Interestingly here, Maximus at once declares that Christ's destruction of evil is effected in those who live in devout imitation of him, and that his complete destruction of evil and corruption remains for a future time in which the entire human race will benefit. But the element of moral admonition is virtually overshadowed by the pro-jection of a complete victory in the end, benefiting all.

Brian Daley claims that such "optimism" is not typical for Maximus, and yet von Balthasar has pointed to passages in which, much like Gregory of Nyssa with his concept of the "fullness" (πλήρωμα) of humanity in Adam and in Christ,[106] the Confessor appears to assert Christ's solidarity with the whole human race in the economy of salva-tion. Jonah's descent into the deep prefigures, among other things, how Christ "descended willingly into the heart of the *earth* (Jonah 2:7, LXX), where the Evil One had swallowed us through death, and drew us up by his resurrection, *leading our whole captive nature up to heaven*."[107] And yet some of von Balthasar's conclusions are overdrawn. For example, in *Questions and Responses to Thalassius* 47 Maximus imagines the Logos (Christ) speaking through Paul, as *becoming all things to all human*

---

[105] *Exp. Ps.* 59 (CCSG 23:3–4, ll. 7–23), trans. Paul Blowers, "A Psalm 'unto the End,'" 270.

[106] See esp. *Hom. opif.* 22 (PG 44:204D).

[107] *Q. Thal.* 64 (CCSG 22:195, ll. 147–51), trans. Blowers and Wilken, 150 (emphasis added). For similar texts, see von Balthasar, *Cosmic Liturgy*, 355–6 and esp. n. 293.

*beings, so that I might save all* (1 Cor. 9:22). Maximus' New Testament text has the variant "all" (πάντας) rather than "some" (τινάς).[108] Von Balthasar understands this passage at face value as supporting universal salvation,[109] but ignores the larger passage in which it is found, where Maximus stresses how the Logos becomes all things to all human beings "proportionately in each one" (κατὰ τὴν ἀναλογίαν ἑκάστου).[110]

Von Balthasar's most adventurous suggestion is that Maximus secretly admired Origen's discernment of a message of universal restoration in his allegorical interpretation of the crucifixion of the King of Ai on a "double" or forked tree (Josh. 8:29, LXX), taken to symbolize the co-crucifixion of Christ and the Devil whose power he despoiled (Col. 2:14–15), thus subsuming the *tree of the knowledge of good and evil* into the true *tree of life* once and for all.[111] Because Maximus speculated on the distinction between the trees along moral-spiritual lines,[112] and because he held room for a more mystical interpretation of the *tree of the knowledge of good and evil* that he chose to "honor in silence,"[113] and finally because he reflected at length on the despoiling of the demonic powers in Colossians 2:14–15 with the possibility of a more mystical sense of this text, von Balthasar concludes that Maximus held Origen's theory in reverent reserve for those mature enough to handle it.[114] Daley has judged this conclusion far-fetched,[115] though von Balthasar has answered Daley's criticisms in kind.[116]

Meanwhile, however, it has largely been taken for granted that Maximus spurned the prospect of *apokatastasis* along Origenist lines. This is certainly true of the Confessor's attitude toward the more recent monastic Origenism that had interpreted the end of the world strictly as a reduplication of the original unity of *disembodied* spiritual beings.[117] But as recent studies of Origen's own eschatology have

---

[108] *Q. Thal.* 47 (CCSG 7:325, ll. 225–6).　　[109] *Cosmic Liturgy*, 356 and n. 302.
[110] *Q. Thal.* 47 (CCSG 7:325, ll. 214–16).
[111] See Origen, *Hom. in Jesu Nave* (GCS 30:341–2).
[112] *Q. Thal.* 43 (CCSG 7:293–7).
[113] Ibid. Intro. (CCSG 7:37, ll. 350–3); cf. ibid. 43 (p. 293, ll. 6–11).
[114] *Cosmic Liturgy*, 356–7.
[115] "Apokatastasis and 'Honorable Silence,'" *MC*, 320–1; cf. Sherwood, *The Earlier Ambigua*, 210–14.
[116] *Dare We Hope: "That All Men Be Saved?"* (San Francisco: Ignatius Press, 1988), 64, n. 38.
[117] Most recently Ilaria Ramelli has argued that Maximus may have refuted the eschatological doctrines (and "automatic" *apokatastasis*) of Origenist extremists closer to his own time but did not fundamentally dispute Origen's own true teaching.

shown, taking more serious account of the fourth-century defenses of Origen by Pamphilius and Rufinus, he himself ostensibly did not settle on a totally unqualified universal salvation of creatures that included the Devil himself,[118] nor a final state of absolute disembodiment. Origen resisted impositions both on the Creator's freedom and the creature's. As a devotee of the Alexandrian soteriological model of perpetual divine pedagogy through the ever-active Logos, Maximus echoed Clement and Origen in projecting an open-ended future in which creaturely freedom still had to be trained and honed to appropriate the fullness of divine grace. The *hope* of universal restoration was still vivid and valid, but it demanded to be sobered by constant attention to the precariousness of striving after virtue and overcoming sin. Georges Florovsky suggested that for Maximus, probably due to his ascetical experience, human "nature" would be altogether restored in the eschaton while human freedom still had to find its way, with the righteous enjoying "eternal *well*-being" but all others having only "eternal being," God's will for them remaining totally extrinsic and unfulfilled.[119]

The mediating influence of Gregory of Nyssa is crucial. Morwenna Ludlow has proven Nyssen's unmistakable commitment to universal salvation,[120] not without some qualifications of his own. There will be, for example, posthumous purification of *all* creatures (not purgatory in the medieval sense, since *all* creatures will undergo it) en route

See her *The Christian Doctrine of Apokatastasis: A Critical Assessment from the New Testament to Eriugena* (Leiden: Brill, 2013), 738–57.

[118] For this rethinking of Origen's eschatology, see Tom Greggs, *Barth, Origen, and Universal Salvation* (Oxford: Oxford University Press, 2009), 68–73; also Frederick Norris, "Universal Salvation in Origen and Maximus," in Nigel M. de S. Cameron, ed., *Universalism and the Doctrine of Hell: Papers Presented at the Fourth Edinburgh Conference in Christian Dogmatics, 1991* (Carlisle: Paternoster Press, 1992), 35–72. Cf. also Ramelli, *The Christian Doctrine of Apokatastasis*, 119–815.

[119] *Byzantine Fathers of the Sixth to Eighth Century*, trans. Raymond Miller et al. (Vaduz: Büchervertriebsanstalt, 1987), 244–5. The distinction is valid insofar as Maximus seems not purely to equate "eternal being" and "eternal well-being." Cf. also Dumitru Staniloae, *The Experience of God: Orthodox Dogmatic Theology*, vol. 6: *The Fulfillment of Creation*, trans. Ioan Ionita (Brookline, MA: Holy Cross Orthodox Press, 2013), 44–5, 50–1.

[120] *Universal Salvation: Eschatology in the Thought of Gregory of Nyssa and Karl Rahner* (Oxford: Oxford University Press, 2000), 77 111. Ludlow sees Gregory's most direct statements in *De anima et res.*, ed. Franz Oehler (Leipzig: Wilhelm Engelmann, 1858), 341, l. 41–342, l. 2; 366, ll. 27–35; *De vita Moysis* (GNO 7/1:57, l. 8–58, l. 3); and *De inscriptiones psalmorum* (GNO 5:174, l. 15–175, l. 2).

to their final restoration.[121] And even though Gregory envisioned the plenitude (πλήρωμα) of humanity, created altogether in the image of God, being destined to perfect fulfillment of that image,[122] Gregory does not, says Ludlow, typically apply this idea soteriologically. Instead, he insists on individual human beings purifying themselves through appropriate use of their free will, the preeminent goal being *participation* (μετουσία) *in* God rather than union with God.[123] Maximus unquestionably knew Gregory's statements on universal salvation. In the *Questions and Uncertainties* he considers some of the meanings of ἀποκατάστασις, such as the "restoration" of individual persons in the *logos* of virtue, the "restoration" of all human nature in the resurrection, and the "restoration" of the soul's powers to their original orientation.[124] Maximus mentions the last as most frequently used by Nyssen, but this is comparative, for he knows Gregory employed ἀποκατάστασις in the other two senses as well, and he clearly implies that all of these were valid interpretations on the bishop's part.[125]

Rather than expanding Gregory's own universalism, however, Maximus chose to build on his message of all humanity's summons to forward moral and spiritual progress, a perennial striving or straining (ἐπέκτασις) toward perfection in virtue and knowledge, whereby any stalling would only give evil (nothingness) a new beginning.[126] For both writers, posthumous existence is an upward spiraling around (περί) the divine essence; and yet this sublime orbit is unimaginable save as a constant synergy of grace and free will,[127] with grace drawing human nature to ever new heights of assimilation to, and participation in,

---

[121] Cf. *De anima et res.* (Oehler, 373, ll. 18–20); *Or. catech.* 26 (GNO 3/4:66–7), cited and analyzed by Ludlow, *Universal Salvation*, 84–5.

[122] e.g. *De mortuis* (GNO 9:63, ll. 8–11).

[123] Ludlow, *Universal Salvation*, 92.

[124] *QD* 19 (CCSG 10:17–18). For good analysis of this text and of Maximus' dialectical approach to *apokatastasis*, see Andreas Andreopoulos, "Eschatology in Maximus the Confessor," *OHMC*, 325–33.

[125] On the resurrection as an *apokatastasis* of all human nature to its primordial perfection in Gregory, see esp. *De mortuis* (GNO 9:51, ll. 16–18); *Hom. in Ecclesiasten* (GNO 5:296, ll. 16–18).

[126] See esp. *Q. Thal.* 17 (CCSG 7:111–15), which clearly depends on Gregory's *De vita Moysis*. See also Blowers, "Maximus the Confessor, Gregory of Nyssa, and the Concept of 'Perpetual Progress,'" 154–65.

[127] Larchet, in particular, has rightly emphasized how divine "respect" for creaturely freedom remains intrinsic to Maximus' vision of deification (*La divinisation de l'homme*, esp. 659–62).

God.[128] In his own "realized" eschatology, Maximus imagines Christ creating an overlap of time and eternity—and of the "ages" of incarnation and deification[129]—that already situates creatures in a transtemporal trajectory toward deification but with the prospect of righteous judgment.[130] For now, Maximus, like Gregory, admonishes individuals to use the powers and freedom of their nature wisely, in anticipation either of full enjoyment of God or estrangement from God "for infinite ages,"[131] "hell" being a nickname for those who through sin relapse into non-existence.[132] Sherwood is quite right, I think, that Maximus abbreviates his view in an aphorism on indiscriminate divine love:

> our Lord Jesus Christ, manifesting his love for us, suffered for all humankind and granted to all equally the hope of resurrection, though each one renders himself or herself worthy either of glory or of punishment.[133]

Overall, then, we may fairly conclude that Maximus' teaching on eschatological salvation in Christ unsystematically combines the following: (1) confidence in the Creator's love for all human beings equally and his unrelenting desire to save all;[134] (2) rejection of any monistic or purely spiritualizing theory of *apokatastasis*; (3) zealous *hope* for the final transformation of all creatures, even non-human ones;[135] (4) existential sobriety about the future of creaturely freedom; and (5) the conspicuous absence of hardened schemes of eschatological closure, especially if that closure entails solely a return to lost paradise and not the revelation of a new, unprecedented glory for creatures inaugurated by the New Adam.

---

[128] *Q. Thal.* 59 (CCSG 22: 53–5, ll. 122–59).     [129] Ibid. 22 (CCSG 7:137–43).
[130] On this prospective judgment, see esp. *QD* 173 (CCSG 10:120).
[131] *Amb. Jo.* 21 (PG 91:1252A–B).     [132] Ibid. 20 (1237C).
[133] *Car.* 1.71 (PG 90:976B–C), trans. Berthold, 43 (altered); cited by Sherwood, *The Earlier Ambigua*, 222.
[134] In addition to *Car.* 1.71, Maximus profusely extols the relentless divine *philanthrôpia*: e.g. *Amb. Jo.* 44 (PG 91:1349D–1352A); ibid. 53 (1373A–B); *Amb. Th.* 5 (PG 91:1048C). See the trenchant commentary in Daley, "Apokatastasis and 'Honorable Silence,'" 328–39; and Larchet, *La divinisation de l'homme*, 652–62.
[135] The eschatological transformation even of non-human creatures, particularly as the outcome of the Logos's immanence or incarnation in the diverse *logoi* of beings, is suggested in numerous texts, including *QD* 173 (CCSG 10:120); *Q. Thal.* 2 (CCSG 7:51); *Amb. Jo.* 7 (PG 91:1089A–B). I fully concur with Larchet on this point (*La divinisation de l'homme*, 663–5). See his fuller list of relevant texts, ibid., 663, n. 996.

# 8

Love, Desire, and Virtue: Transfigured
Life in Christ and the Spirit

Theology knows what love is all about; but it knows it too well
ever to avoid imposing on me an interpretation that comes so
directly through the Passion that it annuls my passions—
without taking the time to render justice to their phenomenality,
or to give a meaning to their immanence.

—Jean-Luc Marion[1]

## THE QUESTION OF LOVE

Jean-Luc Marion's arresting statement comes in the context of eliciting
the failure of theology, right alongside philosophy, poetry, literature,
and psychology to engage the enigma or "question" of love. Indeed,
Christian theology can all too easily force the issue of the irreducible
essence of love communicated in the suffering and death of Jesus Christ
without giving voice to primally experienced human love (and *pathos*)
in its variant forms, which problematizes but also invariably factors into
articulating any sense believers have of love, including the love of Christ.
Primal *erôs*, Marion argues, is the key to "being" (effectively "I love
therefore I am"), not vice versa, and so when we attempt to rationalize
or reduce love to a concept or a metaphysics of love, love absconds.[2]

---

[1] *The Erotic Phenomenon*, trans. Stephen Lewis (Chicago: University of Chicago
Press, 2007), 1.
[2] Ibid., 1–10.

Marion is a postmodern phenomenological philosopher-theologian. Maximus is not. And yet the Confessor shares something of the same dilemma. Love is the *telos*, but it is also already the *archê*. "I love therefore I am" must nevertheless be revised to "God loves" followed by either "... therefore I love" or "... therefore I am," since the creature's loving and well-being (τὸ εὖ εἶναι) are of a piece. The mystery of divine love, and derivatively of human love, pervades Maximus' whole understanding of the created cosmos and of the Christian's participation in the transfiguration of the cosmos by love in the work of Jesus Christ and the Holy Spirit. I wish to show in this chapter how, in developing his spiritual anthropology and asceticism, Maximus was pursuing less a religious or theological conceptualization of love, or an ontology per se of love, than a highly nuanced demonstration of love's "economy" (οἰκονομία) in believers' appropriation of redemptive grace and their aspiration to deification. Love, the secret to the conversion of the passible moral self, is for Maximus the catalyst of the whole life of Christian virtue in response to the ineffable love of God.

In the opening of *Epistle 2*, one of the most incisive (and concise) discourses on love in all of patristic literature, Maximus extols his addressee, John the Chamberlain, for "suffering" (πάσχειν) love, that is, rendering himself passive to "this divine thing, which in its power defies circumscription and definition" (τοῦτο θεῖον ... τὸ κατ᾽ ἀρετὴν ἀπερίγραφον καὶ ἀόριστον). This love, says Maximus, is the very "form of divine grace" (θείας χάριτος μορφή) conspicuous in John's demeanor and words, and basic, under the "law of grace," to their "bond of friendship" (δεσμὸς φίλιος).[3] Love must be approached, then, from the standpoint of what John (or by extension Maximus) has experienced, the gracious activity, and indeed *affect*, of divine love that has formed or taken possession of him over time, rather than from the standpoint of an antecedent love-logic.

Dwelling further on the mystery of love, Maximus describes how love (ἀγάπη) subsumes and interconnects with all other goods and virtues, of which it is both the goal (τέλος) and the cause (αἴτιον).[4] "Everything is circumscribed by love according to God's good pleasure in a single form (μονοειδῶς), and love is dispensed in many forms (πολυτρόπως) in accordance with God's economy (κατ᾽ οἰκονομίαν)."[5] Acknowledging that love stands as the last of the so-called theological

[3] *Ep.* 2 (PG 91:393A; also 408A–B).     [4] Ibid. (393C–396B; cf. 400A).
[5] Ibid. (393C), trans. Louth, *Maximus the Confessor*, 86.

virtues along with faith and hope (1 Cor. 13:13), he explains its primacy still:

> For faith is the foundation of everything that comes after it, I mean hope and love, and firmly establishes what is true. Hope is the strength of the extremes, I mean faith and love, for it appears as faithful by itself and loved by both, and teaches through itself to make it to the end of the course. Love is the fulfilment of these, wholly embraced as *the ultimate desire* (τὸ ἔσχατον ὀρεκτόν), and furnishes them rest from their movement. For love gives faith the reality of what it believes and hope the presence of what it hopes for, and the enjoyment of what is present.[6]

Love, moreover, operates simultaneously in macrocosm and microcosm. At the level of the *macrocosm*, it binds divided creatures together in a common "inclination" (γνώμη).[7] It supremely "levels off and makes equal any inequality or difference in inclination in anything, or rather, binds it to that praiseworthy inequality, by which each is so drawn to his neighbor in preference to herself or himself, and so honors the neighbor before himself or herself, that each one is eager to spurn any obstacle in the desire to excel."[8] Rowan Williams in this regard sees Maximus as projecting a "universal eschatological 'culture'" (not incompatible with what I am calling his cosmo-politeian vision) in which the mutual self-giving of human creatures and the shared realization of their common "nature" go hand in hand. Negatively, this means thwarting those passions wherewith we look on an "other" merely as an object to be used self-servingly; but positively, it means loving that other as one who, like ourselves, is being propelled, at the level of deep-seated desire or *erôs*, to the intentional (gnomic) communion of creatures and the full participation in the Logos that constitute the eschatological actualization of human nature.[9]

At the level of the *microcosm*, meanwhile, love realigns the misdirected powers of the individual soul: converting reason itself from ignorance to the pursuit of God; converting desire (ἐπιθυμία) from

---

[6] Ibid. (396B–C), trans. Louth, *Maximus the Confessor*, 86 (slightly altered; emphasis added); cf. *Q. Thal.* 49 (CCSG 7:353–5).

[7] *Ep.* 2 (PG 91:396C); cf. *Q. Thal.* 2 (CCSG 7:51).

[8] *Ep.* 2 (PG 91:400A), trans. Louth, *Maximus the Confessor*, 88 (slightly altered).

[9] Rowan Williams, "Nature, Passion and Desire: Maximus' Ontology of Excess," in Markus Vinzent, ed., *Studia Patristica* 68 (Leuven: Peeters, 2013), 267–72. Williams, like Loudovikos, rightly underscores Maximus' dynamic definition of human "nature." Nature is a "project," "a mutual process of shaping towards eschatological mutuality" (p. 271).

self-love to longing for God; converting temper (θυμός) from the urge
to dominate to the struggle to attain to God alone.[10] Divine love, says
Maximus, *both forms and is formed by* these reorientations and
thereby reveals one to be a *friend of God* (φιλόθεον, cf. James 2:23)
and indeed "God" by deification.[11] It deifies precisely by extending to
us the love embodied and dramatized in the incarnation, when the
Son, *though he was in the form of God, did not count equality with
God a thing to be grasped, but emptied himself, taking the form of a
servant* (Phil. 2:6–7) so as to give ultimate *form* to our own love and
servanthood; and thus the *formation* of love in the believer is but the
embodiment or "incarnation" of God—who *is* love (1 John 4:8)—
within her or his virtues.[12]

One cannot mistake the consistent language of "form" (both μορφή
and εἶδος) in Maximus' many elucidations of love in *Epistle* 2. It is
invariably tied up with the kaleidoscopic Beauty of God. Love is both
singular in form and polymorphous. It contains the form of all goods
and virtues but its own beauty, its own form, is transcending and
inexhaustible. It is sheer abundance, generosity, freedom—and we
might even be able to include here Marion's "givenness." But unlike
Marion and other postmodern thinkers (mainly Jacques Derrida)
vexed by the philosophical aporia that a true "gift" is impossible
because inevitably it sets up an economy of response or "exchange"
that undermines its gratuity, Maximus assumes, as we have seen, that
the ultimate gift of love, Christ's passion, elicits precisely a "wondrous
exchange" in which the receiver's reciprocal love fulfills the Giver's
gratuity. Unlike Marion, furthermore, Maximus is not quite willing to
suspend a *metaphysics* of love. While divine love as pure gift cannot
be conceptually contained or "possessed," since it is itself containing
and possessing, it nonetheless crucially defines created "nature" itself
as a permeable register of divine grace and activity, and imbues the
*logos* of a creature's nature, its ontological predisposition toward
deification. Is not the Logos's embodiment in the *logoi* of beings
already an act of *kenotic love* as well as the basis of the moral
intelligibility of the cosmos?

Love's immanence in nature is evidenced in the figure of Abraham,
who exemplifies the hard existential work of conforming one's deep
desire (ἔρως) and individual inclination (γνώμη) to the *logos* of

[10] *Ep.* 2 (PG 91:397A–B).     [11] Ibid. (397B).
[12] Ibid. (397B–C, 401B, 404C).

human nature, thereby giving over his "private" freedom to the very
principle that binds creatures of the same nature to one another in
love. In his familiar active/passive dialectical language, Maximus
describes this as Abraham simultaneously "receiving God" (τὸν θεὸν
ἀπολαβών) and "being given back to God" (ἀποδοθείς τῷ θεῷ).[13]

> As man he was made worthy to see God (cf. Gen. 17:1; 18:1), and to
> receive him, since he lived naturally in accordance with the perfect
> natural *logos* through love for humankind (φιλανθρωπίας). He was led
> up (ἀνήχθη) to this, having relinquished the individuality of what
> divides and is divided, no longer ruling (ἡγούμενος) another human
> being different from himself, but knowing all as one and one as all. This
> is clearly not a matter of inclination, about which there is contention
> and division, while it remains irreconcilable with nature, but of nature
> itself.[14]

Maximus most likely knows Gregory of Nyssa's famous condemnation
of slavery,[15] and it is plausible in this passage that he is acknowledging
Abraham's having "ruled" slaves. But in his *philanthrôpia* Abraham
forfeited this dominion over others and took on a newfound servanthood acknowledging equality and solidarity with all people sharing the
same nature. Familiar here is the Stoic idiom of moral living "according
to nature" (κατὰ τὴν φύσιν), but the content has changed. Christian
sages who live in accordance with nature are, like Abraham, caught up
in or raptured by a love greater than themselves.

## THE TRANSFORMATION AND DEIFICATION
## OF HUMAN DESIRE

### Erôs and the Reorientation of the Soul

For Maximus, the "question of love" (to borrow Marion's phrase), is
not so much "What is love?" He spends precious little time discussing
love in the abstract. Other questions—primal Adamic questions, in
effect—already weigh on the Christian believer or ascetic in the fray of
moral struggle, such as, "What do I *do* with this *erôs* deep within me?"

---

[13] Ibid. (400A–C).
[14] Ibid. (400C), trans. Louth, *Maximus the Confessor*, 89 (slightly altered).
[15] *Hom. in Ecclesiasten* 4 (GNO 5:334–8).

"Is this *erôs* a curse or a gift?" "If this *erôs* is instrumental to my very identity and destiny, what (or who) will ultimately satisfy its yearning?" "Who will ravish it?"—for *erôs* will be ravished one way or another. At the center of Maximus' teaching on the spiritual and ascetical life of the Christian, in turn, is a close identification of *erôs* and *agapê*, signaling his effort thoroughly to align deep-seated human desire—and indeed all the resources of the passible self—with the *logos* of nature already infused with *agapê*.

The Christian transformation of *erôs* began long before Maximus, being especially well attested in the exegetical works of Origen and Gregory of Nyssa on the Song of Songs. These writers knew even from Plato that *erôs* was not reducible to purely sexual passion but bespoke the soul's visceral craving for transcendent Beauty.[16] Catherine Osborne has persuasively shown that the *erôs* inherited by Christian writers was not a purely acquisitive or possessive love such as derives from too narrow a reading of Plato and his major interpreters. Already Platonic and Neoplatonic commentators had begun to pair the self-interested and selfless motives of *erôs* in ways that prompted Christian authors to combine *erôs* and *agapê*.[17] Maximus speaks straightforwardly of *erôs* as a gift to creatures:

> God gave to us lowly human beings, as a generous master, a natural longing (πόθον) and desire (ἔρωτα) for him, combining this naturally with the power of reason, so that we might easily be able to know the ways by which this longing might be satisfied, and not fail to attain what we are striving for due to some mistake on our part. Being moved, therefore, by this longing for the truth itself and for the wisdom that is manifested in the orderly governance of all things, we are urged on to our goal, striving all the more because of these things, to attain that for the sake of which we have received this longing. Having secretly come to learn this, those who are studious and zealous lovers of truth set before themselves one sole task and activity, namely, arduous labor (ἄσκησιν) in the service of this desire.[18]

Maximus concedes here that *erôs*, while natural and capable of operating in harmony with reason, is intrinsically *non-rational*. Indeed, it is ecstatic in the sense that it can transfix rational creatures

[16] e.g. *Phaedrus* 249E.
[17] Catherine Osborne, *Eros Unveiled: Plato and the God of Love* (Oxford: Oxford University Press, 1994), 52–70.
[18] *Amb. Jo.* 48 (PG 91:1361A–B), trans. Constas II, 213.

on sensible realities, but also draw minds toward "the ineffable *erôs* of divine Beauty" (ὁ ἄρρητος τῆς θείας καλλονῆς ἔρως).[19] Paradoxically *erôs* encompasses both the lowest and the most sublime aspects of creaturely passibility and desire. It is that element of creaturely nature most elusive of immediate control but most potent in commanding the orientation of movement in relation to God. Through habitual temperance or modulation, there can be "a spiritual, life-giving fecundity (γονιμότητος) . . . an eternal effervescence of erotic enchantment in one's desire for the Divine."[20] Though desire cannot reach the divine essence itself, it continues to be inflamed and "encouraged" (παραμυθεῖται) by God's attributes, his uncreated energies.[21] But as a gift to the created soul-body alliance, *erôs* can neither be sublimated nor thoroughly "rationalized"—let alone disembodied—in view of its unique power to launch the whole creature (spirit, soul, and body) toward a horizon of divine Beauty in which it will be infinitely enriched. This horizon is not simply "upward," toward the intelligible world, otherwise *erôs* would become by default purely a pining after transcendence. Keeping in mind Maximus' teaching on the transformation of human passibility,[22] the horizon of Beauty already unfolds in the ascetical labor of engaging all psychosomatic faculties, including the passions, in the mystery of deification, the very mystery that discloses all the latent beauties of creaturely nature.

And yet the deeper interior mystery of *erôs* for Maximus, as for Dionysius, is the Creator's own erotic outreach, or ecstasy, toward creation. In *Ambiguum* 71 on the Logos's robust "play" in creation, he quotes Dionysius's provocative description of the *mutual* ecstasy between Creator and creature, in which the Creator,

> in the overflow of his passionate goodness (ἐρωτικῆς ἀγαθότητος) is drawn outside himself in his provident care for everything. Beguiled, as it were, by his own goodness, love, and sheer yearning (ἔρωτι), he is enticed away from his dwelling place above and beyond all things, condescending to penetrate all things according to an ecstatic and supernatural power wherewith he can still remain within himself.[23]

---

[19] Ibid. 13 (1209A–B).  [20] Ibid. 21 (1245B–C).
[21] *Car.* 1.100 (PG 90:981D–984A). On this important text, see Thunberg, *Microcosm and Mediator*, 321–2, 358–9.
[22] See pp. 206–11 in this volume.
[23] Dionysius, *Div. nom.* 4.13 (PTS 33:159, ll. 9–14), quoted by Maximus in *Amb. Jo.* 71 (PG 91:1413A–B).

Such language of divine ecstasy graphically affirmed "motion" from within the immovable Trinity, an issue that Maximus also addressed in elucidating Gregory Nazianzen's striking claim that with God, "One is moved (κινηθεῖσα) toward the Two, until coming to rest in the Three."[24] Rather than dwelling on this as an issue of immanent motion within the Trinity, Maximus relates it to the *oikonomia*, proposing that the "movement" is purely a function of indicating how the attributes or "effects" are often accredited to their "cause" as well. Here again he quotes the Areopagite for help but adds his own clarifications:

"What do the theologians mean when at one time they call the Divine 'Desire' (ἔρωτα) and 'Love' (ἀγάπην), and at another, 'Desired' (ἐραστόν) and 'Beloved' (ἀγαπητόν)?" and [Dionysius] answers by saying, "For by the one he is moved, but by the other he moves."[25] To put it more clearly, insofar as the Divine is "desire" and "love," it is moved, but as "desired" and "beloved," it moves to itself all things capable of desire and love. And to be even clearer: the Divine is moved to the extent that it creates an innate relation of desire and love (σχέσιν ἐνδιάθετον ἔρωτος καὶ ἀγάπης) among beings capable of receiving them, and it moves insofar as it naturally attracts the yearning of those who are being moved to it (κινεῖ δὲ ὡς ἑλκτικὸν φύσει τῆς τῶν ἐπ᾽ αὐτῷ κινουμένων ἐφέσεως). And again, it moves and is moved, since it "thirsts to be thirsted for,"[26] desires to be desired, and loves to be loved.[27]

Nikolaos Loudovikos argues from this text that this is not an asymmetrical but a *symmetrical* reciprocity being established between divine and human loves. God has created "a stable relationship of love outside Himself... a conscious otherness outside Himself that responds to His call to this relationship."[28] I would qualify this only by noting that what for human beings is passive here—"being moved"

---

[24] *Or.* 29.2 (SC 250:180), as in *Amb. Jo.* 7 (PG 91:1257C); Maximus also expounds this phrase in *Amb. Th.* 1 (CCSG 48:3–5).

[25] Quoting Dionysius *Div. nom.* 4.14 (PTS 33:160, ll. 4–5).

[26] Quoting Gregory Nazianzen, *Or.* 40.27 (SC 358:260).

[27] *Amb. Jo.* 23 (PG 91:1260B–C), trans. Constas II, 7 (slightly altered). Cf. *Amb. Th.* 1 (CCSG 48:7, ll. 32–8; PG 91:1036C), trans. Constas I, 11: "If, finally, having heard the word 'movement,' you wondered how the Godhead, which is beyond infinity, is said to 'move,' understand that movement is something that happens to us, and not to the Godhead. For first we are illumined by the principle of its being, after which we are enlightened regarding the mode of its subsistence, for the fact of being is always grasped before the manner of being. Thus the 'movement' of the Godhead is the knowledge—through illumination—of its existence and how it subsists, manifested to those who are able to receive it."

[28] *A Eucharistic Ontology*, 173; also 188, n. 70.

by love—is thoroughly *active* in God (especially as viewed through the "active passivity" of Christ). The erotic and agapic motion of God is the pure and prevenient action in which the creature's *erôs* and *agapê*, mutually insinuated,[29] are caught up. But the converse side of this rapture is a *voluntary* self-giving, a rallying of desire and all the interconnected passible faculties. Again, as noted above, Abraham through love *received God* (actively) precisely in also *being given back to God* (passively). Loudovikos is correct, then, insofar as the Creator for Maximus dignifies the creature's love and freedom in an existentially symmetrical reciprocity grounded in the *nature* of the Creator and the *nature* of the Creator's "other." A bold statement to this effect appears in *Ambiguum* 10:

> For they say that God and humanity are paradigms (παραδείγματα) of each, so that as much as humanity, enabled by love, has divinized itself for God, to that same extent God is humanized for humanity by his love for humankind; and as much as humanity has manifested God who is invisible by nature through the virtues, to that same extent humanity is rapt by God in spirit to the unknowable.[30]

All the while Maximus, like Dionysius, guards the mysteriousness of God's own *erôs*. There is no demythologizing it, since such would be vainly attempting to conceptualize the Creator's freedom to be moved (= to move) ecstatically beyond himself in fully revealing his passion for the creature.

## The Dialectics and Therapeutics of Desire

As powerful and strategic as *erôs* (allied with *agapê*) is in converting creatures to the divine will and enabling communion between rational beings and God, "desire" as such is not restricted to *erôs* in the drama of salvation and deification. For Maximus, desire—both as a faculty (= ὄρεξις; τὸ ἐπιθυμητικόν) and as the activity itself of longing (πόθος; ἔφεσις) after a targeted goal—cuts across the whole psychosomatic constitution of the human moral self, a microcosm of the macrocosm's "longing" for the Creator. In Chapter 3, I painted in broad strokes the drama of freedom and desire that animates

---

[29] See *Car.* 3.67 (PG 90:1037A–B), where Maximus calls even *agapê* itself a "blessed passion" (πάθος).

[30] *Amb. Jo.* 10 (PG 91:1113B–C), trans. Constas I, 165 (slightly altered).

Maximus' cosmology, while in Chapter 6 I explored desire and passibility in the context of his anthropology and doctrine of the fall. Now I turn to the retraining and healing of desire so crucial to progress in the moral and spiritual life. For clarity, however, let us briefly recall and review the different contexts and dialectical aspects of Maximus treatment of human desire (see Figure 4), many of which I have already detailed earlier.

As conveyed prominently in *Ambiguum 7*, the dialectics of desire begins, cosmologically, with the tension between divine immobility (stability) and creaturely mobility (vulnerability).[31] At this level, because God's activity precedes and grounds both the potency (δύναμις) and subsequent actuality (ἐνέργεια) of creatures[32] and underlies their *logoi*, their natural impulse (ὁρμή) and desire (ὄρεξις) are already predisposed and projected toward God. They are already, in principle, suffused and prepossessed by the generous object of their eschatological longing. This natural and motile goal-directedness, while reminiscent of the Aristotelian ἐντελέχεια,[33] represents more importantly for Maximus the *graced* state of being which, distending the creature's "natural" development, opens the creature toward the future glory of supernatural deification while simultaneously anticipating the dynamic interplay of divine grace with the creature's own *energeia*, its own desire and volition.

Thus emerges the next major tension in Maximus' dialectics of desire, that between the *natural* creaturely passibility (πάθος) or passivity[34] that characterizes human nature at its genesis, and the postlapsarian *pathos* manifest as a liability to potentially deviant passions (πάθη) connected with the body.[35] This latter *pathos*, both a curse and a blessing (as symbolized in the "tunics of skins," Gen. 3:21[36]), in turn sets up certain anthropological, psychological, and ascetical tensions which factor significantly in Maximus' spiritual doctrine: the classic tension between the body as instrumental to the soul's healthy desire and

---

[31] Ibid. 7 (1069B, 1072B–C); ibid. 8 (1101D–1105B); ibid. 10 (1177A, 1184B–D, 1185B); ibid. 15 (1217A–B); *Cap. theol.* 1–10 (PG 90:1084A–1088A). On the vulnerability and penchant for "deviance" (τροπή) in creaturely movement, see esp. *Ep.* 6 (PG 91:432A–B).

[32] On this motif in Maximus, see Renczes, *Agir de Dieu et liberté de l'homme*, pp. 54–9.

[33] See Renczes, ibid., pp. 50–60, 143–4, 146–7, 365–8.

[34] *Amb. Jo.* 7 (PG 91:1072B, 1073B–C).

[35] On the providential superaddition of the passions, see Q. *Thal.* 1 (CCSG 7:47–9), where Maximus expresses his reliance on Gregory of Nyssa.

[36] See pp. 207, 210–11 in this volume.

### The Dialectics of Desire in Maximus the Confessor

*Cosmological / Historical Dialectic*

| | |
|---|---|
| Divine immobility and stability | Creaturely mobility, passibility, and "vulnerability" |
| Natural creaturely passibility (πάθος) and the capacity for spiritual pleasure | Unnatural postlapsarian liability to vicious passions introduced when Adam lapsed the instant he was created |

*Anthropological / Psychological / Ascetical Dialectic*

| | |
|---|---|
| The body as agent of the soul's true desire and pursuit of virtue | The body as register of the soul's subjection to the contingent "law" of pleasure and pain |
| Natural passions connected with bodily survival (desire for food, fear of pain or death, etc.) | Purely carnal passions (gluttony, lust, etc.) |
| Affections or passions conducive to virtue, reflective of good "use," χρῆσις of the possible faculties    ←ἐπιθυμία→    ←θυμός→ | Vicious affections or passions, reflective of "ill use," παράχρησις of the possible faculties |
| Natural desire (ὄρεξις; πόθος ἔφεσις) and "natural will" (θέλημα φυσική) of humanity for God | The "gnomic" mode of individual desire and volition |
| Gnomic will (γνώμη) as servant of the natural desire for God (the "gnomic surrender," *Amb. Jo.* 7, PG 91:1076B) | Gnomic will as slave to individual self-interest and self-love (φιλαυτία) |

*Christological Dialectic*

| | |
|---|---|
| Christ's embodiment of a new and eschatological mode (τρόπος) of human desire, emotion, and will | Christ's appropriation (οἰκείωσις) of humanity's fallen, passible nature |

*Eschatological Dialectic*

| | |
|---|---|
| Deification as the resting or final sating of all human desire and passion | Deification as unending desire and striving (ἐπέκτασις) for God |

ἔκστασις

**Fig. 4.**

cultivation of virtues[37] and the body as registering the soul's subservience to the circumstantial but remedial "law" of pleasure and pain;[38] the tension between natural bodily passions, or survival instincts, and the carnal passions that are a function of the pursuit of pleasure or avoidance of pain;[39] the tension between passions useful for virtue and the vicious passions—with the lower passible faculties of desire (ἐπιθυμία) and temper (θυμός) poised for conversion or "use" (χρῆσις) either way; the tension between the soul's natural desire (ὄρεξις) or will (θέλησις) and the "gnomic" mode (γνώμη) of desiring and willing; and derivatively the tension between gnomic desire or will as allied with natural desire or will, in "surrender" to God's universal purposes, and the same as commandeered by individual self-interest and self-love (φιλαυτία).[40]

To carry through this dialectics of desire, we would need to set in relief its *christological* dimension, which for Maximus frames all the preceding tensions in the light of the mysterious and salutary tension within Christ's composite hypostasis between his embodiment of a new and eschatological mode (τρόπος) of human desire, emotion, and will, and his appropriation (οἰκείωσις) of human nature in its fallen passible condition.[41] Finally, we would need to add the properly eschatological tension in Maximus' teaching (under the influence of Gregory of Nyssa) between deification as the resting or final sating of desire and deification as an endless, insatiable desire for God—likewise the tension in the fulfillment of deification between pure passivity to the divine *energeia* and the sublime activity of graced human nature.

The healing and retraining of desire runs the gamut of all these dialectical tension-points, but along the way certain reconditioning "therapies" especially stand out. For one, the soul's basic appetency (ὄρεξις) must constantly be dilated and rendered malleable. Desire is disastrously narrowed when it deviates from its natural course and fixates on base infatuations, while the Origenist postulate that a rational creature could actually experience a satiety (κόρος) of the divine Good, as if that Good was itself too narrow for the soul's ambitious desire, is a farce.[42] In *Ambiguum 7*, Maximus envisions

---

[37] *Amb. Jo.* 7 (PG 91:1088C,1092B–C, 1096D, 1100A–B).
[38] *Q. Thal.* 61 (CCSG 22:85–7, 95–7), and pp. 210–11, 247, 265 in this volume.
[39] Ibid. 55 (pp. 487–9).
[40] See pp. 119–24, 207–11, 236–7, 256–7 in this volume.
[41] See Maximus' nuanced interpretation of Christ's assumption of human passibility in *Q. Thal.* 21 (CCSG 7:127–33).
[42] *Amb. Jo.* 7 (PG 91: 1084D–1085A, 1089C); ibid. 10 (1112A–B).

the infinite God able to stretch to infinity (ἐπιτείνειν πρὸς τὸ ἀόριστον) the desire of those who enjoy him through participation (διὰ μετοχῆς),[43] and similarly in greeting his friend Marinus credits him with a feverish desire for God that is "stretching out (συμπαρεκτείν-ων) alongside God's infinity."[44] In fact "whoever conquers the soul's propensity for the body becomes boundless (ἀπερίγραφος), for the God who attracts the desirer's longing is surpassingly higher, and does not allow the desirer to affix her or his longing to any of the things that rank after God."[45] In a creature's experiential history, the "middle" (μεσότης) between its beginning and end, desire must therefore always expand rather than attenuate.[46] "For customarily the mind is expanded (πλατύνεσθαι) toward those things to which it devotes its time, and when it expands toward them, it also turns its desire and love (ἐπιθυμίαν καὶ τὴν ἀγάπην) toward them, whether these be divine and spiritually proper and noetic things, or carnal things and passions."[47]

The mind (νοῦς), in fact, must lead the way in refining and refocus-ing as well as stretching human desire. In the hierarchy of the mind–soul–body trichotomy, the mind's higher spiritual appetency naturally must prevail, especially insofar as seeking after God consists precisely in a *desirous* motion (μετ᾽ ἐφέσεως κίνησις) of the mind.[48] If deviant desire can cause the soul to "slip down from above" (in Nazianzen's words),[49] the mind's desire can raise it up, rallying the support of the lower powers. "Our whole intellect should be directed toward God, tensed by our incensive faculty (τῷ θυμικῷ) as if by a nerve, and fired with longing (ἐπιθυμίας) by our desire at its most ardent (τῇ κατ᾽ ἄκρον ἐφέσει)."[50] As well, the "relative knowledge" (σκετικὴ γνῶσις) of God, based on reason and concepts, feeds desire (ἔφεσις), which in turn intensifies the urge toward a higher, experiential and participative knowledge of God in deification.[51] In indwelling and stretching all

---

[43]   Ibid. 7 (PG 91:1089B).

[44]   *Opusc.* 1 (PG 91:9A). The verb συμπαρεκτείνειν is almost certainly inspired by a passage in Gregory of Nyssa's *Life of Moses* depicting those who participate in the divine Good having their desire endlessly distended with the divine infinity (*V. Moysis*, lib. 1 (GNO 7/1:4)).

[45]   *Capita XV* 15 (from the *Diversa Capita*) (PG 90:1185B).

[46]   See *Q. Thal.* 55 (CCSG 7:525).        [47]   *Car.* 3.71 (PG 90:1037C–D).

[48]   *Q. Thal.* 59 (CCSG 22:65). Maximus adds here that the mind's "seeking out" (ἐκζήτησις) of God is characterized by "burning desire" (μετὰ τινος ζεούσης ἐφέσεως).

[49]   *Amb. Jo.* 7 (PG 91:1084D).        [50]   *Or. dom.* (CCSG 23:58, ll. 542–5).

[51]   *Q. Thal.* 59 (CCSG 22:55–9); ibid. 60 (p. 77).

the natural faculties, which fully retain their capacity (ἕξις) and integrity while cooperating with divine grace, the Spirit specifically instills an "impassible desire" (ἀπαθὴς ἔφεσις) in the questing mind.[52] Deification ultimately includes

the ascent of believers to their proper beginning as defined by their end (ἀρχὴν κατὰ τὸ τέλος).

The ascent of believers to their proper beginning as defined by their end is, in turn, the fulfillment of their desire.

The fulfillment of their desire is, in turn, the ever-moving repose of desirers in relation to the object of their desire.

The ever-moving repose of desirers in relation to their object of desire is, in turn, the uninterrupted and continuous enjoyment of the object of desire.

The uninterrupted and continuous enjoyment of the object of desire consists, in turn, in the participation in supernatural divine realities.[53]

At this level, in concert with faith and hope, *agapê* as the ultimate theological virtue prepares the mind to become sublimely immovable in God's loving affection (στοργή), affixing the mind's entire faculty of desire (ἡ τῆς ἐφέσεως δύναμις) to the longing (πόθος) for God.[54]

Of course this is the high end, as it were, of the healing and reorienting of desire, but all this is unimaginable apart from the prior endeavor of contemplation and asceticism that occupies much of the moral and spiritual life of the Christian. The soul finds itself bombarded by competing urges and desires, and is swarmed by manifold objects of those desires.[55] Simultaneously the lower psychic drives of *epithymia* and *thymos* generate passions or emotions that obfuscate the soul's moral vision. Despite the hegemony of the mind (νοῦς), which holds the supreme power of seeing through to worthy ends of human desire, much of the real psychological work of healing and realigning desire is carried out by sanctified reason.

Therapeutically, reason plays the strategic role in the soul of mediating between the mind and the lower passible faculties, and negotiating the soul through the barrage of passions or emotions. Standing within a long tradition of patristic appropriation of Hellenistic moral psychology, Maximus and his ascetical forebears inherited different views of the origins and nature of the passions, stemming mainly from debates

[52] Ibid. (p. 47, l. 50).   [53] Ibid. (p. 53, ll. 127–34).
[54] Ibid. 49 (CCSG 7:351–3).   [55] *Car.* 3.64 (PG 90:1036C).

within Platonic and Stoic ethics. By one account, the passions were perturbations or diseases of the soul outside of reason's immediate command; by another account, they were misfiring "judgments" of the mind itself (lest one not be held morally responsible for them).[56] Maximus, who technically defines a culpable passion as "a movement of the soul contrary to nature,"[57] draws heavily from Evagrius's connection of the passions to idle or vicious "thoughts" (λογισμοί) and even more vivid "mental representations" (νοήματα) arising and abounding in the soul, often spurred by demonic seduction.[58] The challenge for reason is not simply to thwart vile thoughts/passions before they fully develop and spill over into action, but to trump vile ones with godly ones or at least salvageable ones. Discretion (διάκρισις) is key because thoughts/passions can mutate as they proliferate, and because their moral coloring can change in an instant (added to the instantaneousness of the thoughts/passions themselves).[59] Evagrius, for example, notes how the seemingly godly thought of hospitality can quickly transmute into the thought of hospitality for mere display of piety, effectively subverting it with the passion of vainglory.[60] Maximus observes how even as apparently virtuous a thought as *agapê* can potentially become a culpable (ψεκτόν) passion if not targeted to a morally upright end.[61] Reason thus acts as the "interpreter and exegete (ἑρμενεὺς καὶ ἐξηγητής) of the virtues."[62]

Though it works in league with the mind, reason is already, by the constitution of the soul, implicated with the other two powers of *epithymia* and *thymos*. It is not a matter, then, simply of "rationalizing" the passions and emotions but of reconditioning *epithymia* and *thymos* and directing each "irrational impulse and sudden surge" (ἄλογος ὁρμὴ καὶ συντυχία)[63] to salutary ends. The soul, for example, can have an

[56] For some of the key sources in these debates, see Blowers, "Gentiles of the Soul," 58–9 and nn. 3–5.

[57] *Car.* 2.16 (PG 90:988D–989A).

[58] For Evagrius's teaching on the λογισμοί see esp. his *De malignis cogitationibus* (SC 438), trans. Sinkewicz, *Evagrius of Pontus*, 153–82. In Maximus, who speaks as much of νοήματα as λογισμοί, see e.g. *Car.* 2.31 (PG 90:993C); ibid. 2.71–3 (1008A–B); ibid. 2.78 (1009A); ibid. 2.84 (1009D–1012A); ibid. 3.20 (1021B–D).

[59] On discretion, *Car.* 2.26 (PG 90:992B–C); ibid. 4.91–2 (1069C–1072A); *Th. Oec.* 2.33 (PG 90:1140C).

[60] *De diversis malignis cogitationibus* 7 (SC 438:174–6).

[61] *Car.* 3.71 (PG 90:1037C–D).

[62] *Th. Oec.* 1.14 (PG 90:1088C). On reason's agency in virtue, see also *Q. Thal.* 16 (CCSG 7:105); ibid. 18 (p. 117); ibid. 54 (pp. 445, 461, 493); ibid. 55 (p. 497).

[63] *Car.* 1.51 (PG 90:969D).

impulse of pain (λύπη) associated purely with deprivation of delectable passions or material objects; but the wise and undeterred soul makes that pain profitable (ὠφέλιμος), reading it as a signal of sensual pleasure trying to prevail over rational discretion.[64] Maximus thoroughly exploits and develops the Stoic ethical principle of reason's good or bad "use" (χρῆσις) of impulses and thoughts which are in themselves morally neutral (μέσα; ἀδιάφορα).[65] This use is directed, teleologically, at the realization of true *agapê*;[66] indeed, the right use of things is already a "work of love" (ἔργον ἀγάπης).[67] The concept of use, already reworked by some of the Confessor's cherished predecessors,[68] presumes that individual passions or emotions have moral histories, as it were, or, as Martha Nussbaum suggests, that they even take on a moral "intelligence" of their own (a point to which I shall return momentarily).

> The passions... become good in those who are spiritually earnest once they have wisely separated them from corporeal objects and *used* them to gain possession of heavenly things. For instance, they can turn desire (ἐπιθυμία) into the appetitive movement of the mind's longing for divine things, or pleasure (ἡδονή) into the unadulterated joy of the mind when enticed toward divine gifts, or fear (φόβος) into cautious concern for imminent punishment for sins committed, or grief (λύπη) into corrective repentance of a present evil. In short, we can compare this with the wise physicians who remove the existing or festering infection of the body *using* the poisonous beast, the viper. The spiritually earnest *use* the passions to destroy a present or anticipated evil, and

---

[64] Q. Thal. 58 (CCSG 22:37); see also Hausherr, *Philautie*, 148–51.

[65] See esp. Car. 2.75–6 (PG 90:1008C–1009A); also 1.92 (981B); 3.40 (1028D–1029A); 4.91 (1069C–D). In his ΧΡΗΣΙΣ: *Die Methode der Kirchenväter im Umgang mit der antiken Kultur* (Basel: Schwabe, 1984), 96, Christian Gnilka notes Maximus' modification of the Stoic principle of χρῆσις: "What for [the Stoic] Epictetus is the use of 'appearances' (φαντασιῶν) is for Maximus the use of thoughts (χρῆσις νοημάτων): the one like the other lies within human power, and determines the moral quality of a usage and the value of the things used." Nevertheless, "*chrêsis* in the church father's view is set out in an entirely different framework from that of Epictetus." For further analysis of χρῆσις in Maximus, see Blowers, "Gentiles of the Soul," 71–9.

[66] Car. 4.91 (PG 90.1069C–D).     [67] Ibid. 1.40 (968C).

[68] Cf. Basil, *Hom. adversus eos qui irascuntur* 5 (PG 31:365C–D); similarly on good use of "hatred," see his *Hom. in Psalmos* 44.8 (PG 29:405B); Gregory of Nyssa, *De virginitate* 18 (GNO 8.1:317–19); *De anima et res.* (PG 46:61B, 65B–68A, 88D–89A); *De mortuis* (GNO 9.1:61); *Hom. opif.* 18 (PG 44:193B–C). Evagrius Ponticus promotes the utility of *anger* in battling demons in *Practicus* 24 and 42 (SC 171:556, 596), in fighting for virtue (ibid. 86, p. 676), and in engendering courage and patience (ibid. 89, p. 682); he also affirms the utility of *desire* in longing for virtue (ibid. 86, p. 676) and in producing temperance, charity, and continence (ibid. 89, pp. 680–2).

to embrace and hold to virtue and knowledge. Thus, as I have already suggested, the passions become good when they are *used* by those who take *every thought captive in order to obey Christ* (2 Cor. 10:5).[69]

Maximus frequently refers to these good uses of the passions and their underlying faculties such as enrich the spiritual life. Through good use *epithymia* can be transmuted into *agapê*, and *thymos* into joy (χαρά).[70] But epithymetic desire can also be changed into sheer *erôs*, while temper can be converted into "spiritual fervency" (ζέσις πνευματική), "red-hot eternal movement" (διάπυρος ἀεικινησία), and "temperate madness" (σώφρων μανία).[71] Maximus speaks alike of the healthy or unhealthy use of the impassioned thoughts (λογισμοί) or mental representations (νοήματα) and of the objects themselves of passion,[72] and most basically the underlying drives themselves.[73]

> The incensive power (θυμός) and desire (ἐπιθυμία) . . . are to be treated like the servant and the handmaid of another tribe (cf. Lev. 25:41–2). The contemplative intellect, through fortitude and self-restraint, subjugates them forever to the lordship of the intelligence, so that they serve the virtues. It does not give them their complete freedom until the law of nature is totally swallowed up by the law of the spirit, in the same way as the death of an unhappy flesh is swallowed up by infinite life (cf. 2 Cor. 5:4), and until the image of the unoriginate kingdom is clearly revealed, mimetically manifesting itself in the entire form of the archetype. When the contemplative intellect enters this state it gives the incensive power and desire their freedom, transmuting desire into the unsullied pleasure and pure enravishment of an intense love for God and the incensive power into spiritual fervor, an ever-active fiery *élan*, a self-possessed frenzy.[74]

The depiction of *epithymia* and *thymos* as foreign servants fits with Maximus' allegorization of the passions themselves as "gentiles" of

---

[69] *Q. Thal.* 1 (CCSG 7:47–9, ll. 18–33), trans. Blowers and Wilken, 98.

[70] *Amb. Jo.* 6 (PG 91:1068A).

[71] *Q. Thal.* 55 (CCSG 7.499, ll. 311–15); cf. also *Ep.* 2 (PG 91:397B); *Car.* 2.48 (PG 90:1000C–D).

[72] *Car.* 2.73 (PG 90:1008A–B); ibid. 2.77–8 (1009A); 2.82 (1009C); ibid. 3.1 (1017B); ibid. 3.86 (1044B); ibid. 4.91 (1069C–D); *LA* (CCSG 40:17, ll. 110–20).

[73] *Car.* 2.75 (PG 90:1008C); ibid. 3.3–4 (1017C–D). Cf. *Amb. Jo.* 7 (PG 91:1097C), where Maximus contrasts "healthy use" (εὐχρηστία) and "misuse" (παραχρηστία) of natural human faculties.

[74] *Centuries of Various Texts* 3.54, attributed to Maximus in the *Philokalia*. See G. E. H. Palmer, Philip Sherrard, and Kallistos Ware, eds. and trans., *The Philokalia: The Complete Text* (London: Faber & Faber, 1981), 2:223 (emphasis added). It is possible that this passage was composed by a scholiast working on Maximus.

the soul, ostensibly alien and having a "contingent existence" (παρ-υπόστασις) and yet, through the economy of incarnational grace, redeemed teleologically to the great advantage of the Christian's moral and spiritual development.[75]

## VIRTUE AND VIRTUOSITY

Maximus was the beneficiary, as we have observed earlier,[76] of a rich and diverse tradition of Greek monastic *philosophia* that drew both from Greco-Roman moral philosophy and from biblical, martyrological, and hagiographical *exempla* of the "philosophical life" (βίος φιλοσοφικός). Within this tradition, the healing and transforming of desire so crucial to human deification were unthinkable apart from the sustained cultivation of virtues that stabilize desire and habituate its orientation to worthy ends. Virtues are morally upright dispositions of the soul, but much more than that, since they integrate mind, will, desire, and the body, and align them in relation to a common *telos* in cooperation with divine grace. Virtue is a matter of *character* (χαρακτήρ) inscribed on the moral self through the power of God (Heb. 1:3).[77]

Echoes of Aristotelian virtue ethics resound in Maximus, such as the idea that virtue is an acquired *habitus* (ἕξις) of the moral subject,[78] that it intrinsically leads to *eudaimonia*,[79] and that virtue is by definition a "mean" between dispositional extremes of excess and defect.[80] And yet Maximus departs from Aristotle, as Torstein Tollefsen and others point out, in seeing virtue as altogether *natural* to human beings.[81] Aristotle

[75] *Q. Thal.* 51 (CCSG 7.405, l. 186); cf. ibid. 58 (CCSG 22.33, ll. 95–6), where deviant sensible pleasure is described as ontologically "non-existent" (ἀνυπόστατος). See also Blowers, "Gentiles of the Soul," 71, 84–5.

[76] See pp. 66–77 in this volume.　　　　[77] *Amb. Jo.* 10 (PG 91:1108B).

[78] The term ἕξις is pervasive in Maximus' teaching on the virtues. See the abundant references and analysis in Renczes, *Agir de Dieu et la liberté de l'homme*, 267–313.

[79] e.g. *Amb. Jo.* 10 (PG 91:1172D–1173A). Maximus refers here to *eudaimonia*, but like other patristic authors prefers the more biblical language of "blessedness" (μακαριότης).

[80] e.g. *Q. Thal.* 40 (CCSG 7:271); ibid. 64 (CCSG 22:211).

[81] See Tollefsen, *Christocentric Cosmology*, 121–2; id., *Activity and Participation in Late Antique and Early Christian Thought* (Oxford: Oxford University Press, 2012), 176–8; Andrew Louth, "Virtue Ethics: St. Maximos the Confessor and Aquinas Compared," *Studies in Christian Ethics* 26 (2013): 354–8; Lollar, *To See into the Life of Things*, 185–6. On virtue as "natural" in Evagrius, see Julia Konstantinovsky,

denies this because nature as such is fixed and cannot be altered by habituation.[82] For Maximus virtue is natural because it draws out the potential for assimilation to God already embedded in human nature.[83] Virtue is the vehicle of human participation in divine Good,[84] indeed in God's own infinite Virtue which has no temporal beginning.[85] To say that virtue is natural is not, then, to nullify the operation of grace. Far from it. As we have seen before in Maximus, nature (φύσις) is already graced with an openness to transformation and deification, but this potential is only realized within a history and an economy, the drama of the Creator's interaction with the creature. Virtue is "natural" for Maximus analogous to the way that the "natural law," which informs virtue, does not stand purely on its own but is ever implicated in the "written law," that is, the scripturally-narrated economy of creation and redemption, and in the spiritual "law of grace" perfectly embodied and fulfilled in Jesus Christ.[86] In this way virtue is definitive of the christoform *politeia* of the believer, the parameters and protocols of her or his moral and spiritual "performance" within the theo-drama of Christ.

Virtue, then, is natural but does not spontaneously appear. It has to be elicited, cultivated, conditioned, perfected. The Christian, moreover, is called not simply to virtues but to *virtuosity*, the imitation of the saints' aptitude in sustaining godly character and ultimately the imitation of God's own creativity and resourcefulness in realizing his Good in the world. Rowan Williams similarly describes in Maximus the "artistry" of human beings working to align their desire and virtue with the divinely endowed desire (*erôs*) of all creation for "mutual relatedness," thus adding their own moral creativity to the overarching cosmic work of the Logos.[87] In Maximus' teaching I find three

"Evagrius Ponticus on Being Good in God and Christ," *Studies in Christian Ethics* 26 (2013): 318–20.

[82] *Ethica Nicomachea* 1103A.

[83] *Disp. Pyrr.* (PG 91:309B–312A). Cf. *Amb. Jo.* 10 (PG 91:1108B–1109A), indicating that bodily asceticism does not create virtue but "manifests" it (i.e. as naturally arising from the well-ordered soul).

[84] See Salés, "Divine Incarnation through the Virtues," 166–76.

[85] *Th. Oec.* 1.48 (PG 90:1100C–1101A).

[86] On the interplay of the three laws, see *Q. Thal.* 19 (CCSG 7:119); ibid. 39 (p. 259); ibid. 64 (CCSG 22:233–7). See also von Balthasar, *Cosmic* Liturgy, 291–314; Blowers, *Exegesis and Spiritual Pedagogy in Maximus the Confessor*, 117–22.

[87] "Nature, Passion and Desire: Maximus' Ontology of Excess," 270, 271.

significant (though not exclusive) dimensions of this virtuosity: first, the development of intellectual and contemplative virtues conducive to the ethical virtues; second, the nurturing of virtuous passions or emotions; and third, the shaping and sharpening of virtues within disciplinary and liturgical-communal contexts.[88]

## Intellectual and Contemplative Virtue

Virtue is a matter of *seeing* well, not just of desiring, willing, or doing well. While Maximus hardly believes that only the most spiritually astute Christian (the *gnostikos*) can exercise sufficient insight and foresight to cultivate virtue, he does assume that a maturing intellectual judgment is requisite for determining the appropriate ends that govern the virtuous life and one's individual moral acts. Much of the real mental labor in turn consists in conforming the mediate ends of the particular intellectual, volitional, affective, and bodily operations that cumulatively make up that virtuous life to its indisputably perfect end, the triune God. Even if this supreme *telos* is encoded in the very nature of a human being, and is discernible through reason and contemplation, the mind even of the advanced ascetic is invariably beclouded, as I noted above, by distracting thoughts, errant mental representations of reality, and unhealthy passions in the making. The mind ($\nu o \hat{v} s$) must cut through this psychological morass, overcome its alienation from itself, and see everything, within the soul and without, in the perspective of divine Wisdom.[89] It must deploy its spiritual eyes.[90] Such requires, at bottom, engendering virtues at the level of perception itself, such as self-mastery ($\dot{\epsilon}\gamma\kappa\rho\acute{a}\tau\epsilon\iota a$), and especially prudence ($\varphi\rho\acute{o}\nu\eta\sigma\iota s$), which Maximus dubs the foundation of reason

---

[88] In what follows here, I am drawing from my earlier essay, "Aligning and Reorienting the Passible Self: Maximus the Confessor's Virtue Ethics," *Studies in Christian Ethics* 26 (2013): 333–50.

[89] *Car.* 1.96 (PG 90:981C) 1.100 (981D–984A); *Myst.* 5 (CCSG 69:21–31). See also A. N. Williams, *The Divine Sense: The Intellect in Patristic Theology* (Cambridge: Cambridge University Press, 2007), 190–231, for background on Greek monastic notions of the intellect's functions.

[90] Maximus occasionally uses the language of spiritual senses, including "spiritual eyes" ($\nu o\epsilon\rho o\grave{\iota}$ $\check{o}\mu\mu a\tau a$, Q. Thal. 17, CCSG 7:111, ll. 19–20) and "eyes of the mind" ($\nu o\grave{o}s$ $\grave{o}\varphi\theta a\lambda\mu o\acute{\iota}$, *Myst.* 23, CCSG 69:49, l. 785), appropriating Dionysian terminology: cf. *Div. nom.* 4.5 (PTS 33:149, l. 14); *Cael. hier.* 1.2 (PTS 36:8, l. 4); 3.3 (p. 19, l. 12); *Eccl. Hier.* 3.3.12 (PTS 36:92, l. 9); ibid. 4.3.6 (p. 100, l. 9). For analysis, see esp. Aquino, "Maximus the Confessor," in Gavrilyuk and Coakley, *The Spiritual Senses*, 104–20.

and the very "act and manifestation of wisdom,"[91] just as virtue itself is
the "concrete realization" (ὑπόστασις) of this wisdom and wisdom itself
is "the essence of virtue."[92] "The beauty of wisdom," says Maximus, "is
knowledge embodied in practice, or practice informed by wisdom,
whose common characteristic (inasmuch as it is completed through
both) is the principle of divine providence and judgment."[93]

Such wisdom requires taking command of sense experience (αἴσθ-
ησις) and the individual senses *from the inside out.* "Every passion,"
Maximus posits, "is invariably an interconnected composite of a sensible
object, sense itself, and a natural faculty . . . temper (θυμός), desire
(ἐπιθυμία), or even reason (λόγος) deviated from its natural function."
By a kind of intro-circumspection, the mind can nonetheless contemplate the true "synthetic end" (κατὰ σύνθεσιν τέλος) of the sensible object,
sense itself, and the implicated faculty, and thus remove the soul's
"impassioned disposition" so as to see all of these clearly according to
their *natural* purpose, which also has the effect of clarifying the image of
God within the mind itself.[94] Self-knowledge and the contemplation of
external sensible and intelligible reality are intrinsically connected.

The mind in this process is thus no passive receptor. Its "seeing"
(θεωρία) is active, probing, discerning, which is more plausible on the
analogy of ancient notions of physical optics, whereby vision went out
from the eyes like a beam and returned again with perceptions.[95] But

---

[91] *Myst.* 5 (CCSG 69:25–6, 28); cf. *Car.* 2.26 (PG 90:992B–C), referring prudence to
the practical (πρακτική), and knowledge to the contemplative (θεωρητική) life of the
Christian. On the intellectual virtues in Maximus, see Frederick Aquino, "The *Philokalia* and Regulative Virtue Epistemology: A Look at Maximus the Confessor," in
Bingaman and Nassif, *The Philokalia: Exploring the Classic Text of Orthodox Spirituality*, 240–51; id., "The Synthetic Unity of Virtue and Epistemic Goods in Maximus
the Confessor," *Studies in Christian Ethics* 26 (2013): 378–90. On Maximus' dependence on Nemesius of Emesa in connecting contemplative and practical reasoning in
Maximus, see Steel, "Maximus Confessor on *Theory* and *Praxis*," 235–8.

[92] *Secunda epistula ad Thomam*, Prol. (CCSG 48:37).

[93] *Amb. Th.* Prol. (CCSG 48:3, ll. 9–11), trans. Constas II, 3. On the crucial
importance of wisdom for Maximus vis-à-vis both contemplation and praxis, see
Marcus Plested, "Wisdom in St Maximus the Confessor," in Frances Young and Mark
Edwards, eds., *Studia Patristica* 42 (Leuven: Peeters, 2006), 205–9; Vladimir Cvetko-
vić, "Wisdom in St. Maximus the Confessor Reconsidered," in Dragiša Bojović, ed.,
*Saint Emperor Constantine and Christianity: International Conference Commemorat-
ing the 1700th Anniversary of the Edict of Milan* (Niš, Serbia: Centre of Church
Studies, 2013), 2:197–214.

[94] *Q. Thal.* 16 (CCSG 7:109).

[95] See Nemesius of Emesa, *De natura hominis* 7, ed. Moreno Morani (Leipzig:
Teubner, 1987), 57–62. Maximus used this treatise extensively.

like other ascetics of his time, Maximus knew that physical sight, with its moral precariousness, could muddle clear intellectual vision.[96] In order to see through to appropriate moral ends, the mind's eye requires its own conditioning, not only by intellectual virtues like prudence but even more basically by faith itself, which Maximus calls "true knowledge from undemonstrated principles, since it is the substance of realities that are beyond intelligence and reason (cf. Heb. 11:1)."[97] Faith provides the mind its bearings as it contemplates the tremendously diverse *logoi* of created things and begins to fathom the Creator's economy and one's place within that economy. Rather than simply scoping out "evidences" of a Creator, natural contemplation is a sanctified intuition of the strategy of divine activity, providence, and judgment, and of the intended relations among created beings. The goal of natural contemplation, which stops short of direct knowledge of the Creator,[98] is the *cosmic* perspective or spiritual vision necessary to forming virtues.[99] The contemplation of Scripture ($\theta\epsilon\omega\rho\acute{\iota}\alpha$ $\gamma\rho\alpha\varphi\iota\kappa\acute{\eta}$), moreover, is bound up with natural contemplation both because Scripture contains the so-called "*logoi* of the commandments,"[100] the deeper divine instruction of the Logos immanent in the various virtues,[101] and because Scripture narrates how virtue and the knowledge of God have been concretely embodied by exemplary saints.[102]

---

[96] *Car.* 2.53 (PG 90:1001C).

[97] *Th. Oec.* 1.9 (PG 90:1085C–D); cf. also *Q. Thal.* 33 (CCSG 7:229–31); *Myst.* 5 (CCSG 69:25–6).

[98] See *Amb. Jo.* 10 (PG 91:1108B–1109A); also *Car.* 3.45 (PG 90:1029B–C): "Virtues are based on knowledge of created beings; knowledge is based on a knower; the knower depends on him who is unknowably known, him who himself knows beyond all knowledge."

[99] Maximus frequently pairs the *logoi* grasped by contemplation with the *tropoi*, or modes, of the virtues: e.g. *Q. Thal.* 51 (CCSG 7:397, 399–401, 407); ibid. 52 (pp. 425–7); ibid. 54 (pp. 457, 461); ibid. 56 (CCSG 22:9, 11). Joshua Lollar explores Maximus' instruction on the role of natural contemplation in forming virtues in his *Seeing into the Life of Things*, 203–52; cf. Thunberg, *Microcosm and Mediator*, 343–52; Larchet, *La divinisation de l'homme*, 488–94.

[100] e.g. *Q. Thal.* 54 (CCSG 7:461). He also speaks often of the *logoi* of the virtues grounded in the natural order or law: e.g. ibid. 25 (CCSG 7:163); ibid. 34 (p. 235); ibid. 54 (p. 463); ibid. 55 (p. 497).

[101] Ibid. 7 (CCSG 7:319). The self-differentiation of the Logos in the virtues is also his active "procession" ($\pi\rho\acute{o}o\delta o\varsigma$) into the commandments (ibid. 62, p. 121).

[102] On the interrelation between contemplation of Scripture and contemplation of nature, see Blowers, *Exegesis and Spiritual Pedagogy in Maximus the Confessor*, 117–22; id., "The World in the Mirror of Holy Scripture," 408–26; also pp. 82–5 in this volume.

This profound interconnection between *practicing* the virtues and *contemplating* their underlying reality is accented in a comment of Maximus on the "seven spirits" of Isaiah 11:2–3:

> We go from abstention from evils through *fear* to the practice of the virtues by *strength*; from the practices of the virtues to the discretion of *counsel*; from discretion to the habitus (ἕξιν) of the virtues, or *knowledge-by-experience* (ἐπιστήμην); from the habitus of the virtues to the *knowledge* (γνῶσιν) of the principles (λόγων) in the virtues; from this knowledge to the habitus transformed to the principles so known, which is the same as *understanding*; and from this understanding to the simple, precise contemplation of universal truth . . . Ascending through the eyes of faith, or illuminations, we are drawn together toward the divine unity of *wisdom*. And we ourselves gather this differentiation of gifts, which was instituted for us, together with the particular ascents in the virtues, toward the [divine] Cause of those gifts, and, in cooperation with God, neglect none of them, lest by becoming gradually negligent, we make our faith blind and sightless, devoid of illuminations by the Spirit through our works.[103]

## Cultivating Virtuous Emotions

In English colloquial usage, many virtues sound simply like healthy emotional states. The Christian virtues that Maximus sees comprehended under the supreme virtue of love—hope, humility, meekness, self-mastery, patience, longsuffering, kindness, peace, joy[104]—all conjure up not simply dispositions of character but identifiable emotions. Rosiland Hursthouse notes that a virtue, as a deeply entrenched disposition to act in a certain way, actually presupposes a host of interrelated activities: "emotions and emotional reactions, choices, values, desires, perceptions, attitudes, interests, expectations and sensibilities. To possess a virtue is to be a certain sort of person with a certain complex mindset."[105] For Aristotle too, she suggests,

> The virtues (and vices) are all dispositions not only to act, but to feel emotions, as reactions as well as impulses to action . . . In the person

---

[103] *Q. Thal.* 54 (CCSG 7:463, ll. 336–55). On the deep mutual insinuation of virtuous practice (πρᾶξις) and contemplation (θεωρία), see also ibid. 58 (p. 31).
[104] See *Ep.* 2 (PG 91:393C–396B).
[105] "Virtue Ethics," § 2, *Stanford Encyclopedia of Philosophy* (online: <http://plato.stanford.edu/entries/ethics-virtue>).

with the virtues, these emotions will be felt on the *right* occasion, toward the *right* people or objects, for the *right* reasons.[106]

Aristotle, and later on the Stoics who critically built on his virtue ethics, aspired to mental "techniques" to recognize, modulate, and control emotions, and patristic moralists, including Maximus and his ascetical forebears, were well aware of these.[107] But while Stoics were realists about the emotions, and conceded that they could not be thoroughly eradicated, and that some—the so-called *eupatheiai*[108]—could even be relatively useful, we find little concentration on cultivating virtuous emotions as vital to moral wisdom and comportment.

Maximus and other Christian ascetical writers nonetheless explored whether emotions could enrich the believer's moral and spiritual experience by conditioning virtues and moral character with appropriate *affect*. While the actual physiological duration of any emotion is remarkably brief, emotions have histories, or "scripts" as classicist Robert Kaster has observed from Greco-Roman moral philosophy.[109] They register acquired and engrained values within a moral culture, and though emotions can quickly mutate, cross-fertilize, and cancel each other out, their resilience and sustained effect/affect feed moral memory (recall of virtuous or vicious thoughts and motives) and can foster moral imagination.[110] Maximus certainly realized, as did Evagrius, the deep interconnection between passions and memory (μνήμη)—whether for ill or for good—in the continuum of moral experience.[111] But he also realized the

---

[106] Rosiland Hursthouse, *On Virtue Ethics* (Oxford: Oxford University Press, 1999), 108.

[107] See Richard Sorabji, *Emotions and Peace of Mind: From Stoic Agitations to Christian Temptations* (Oxford: Oxford University Press, 2003).

[108] See e.g. Diogenes Laertius 7.115; Cicero, *Tusculanae disputationes* 4.12.

[109] *Emotion, Restraint, and Community in Ancient Rome* (New York: Oxford University Press, 8–9, 85, 132–3; id., "*Invidia*, νέμεσις, φθόνος, and the Roman Emotional Economy," in David Konstan and N. Keith Rutter, eds., *Envy, Spite and Jealousy: The Rivalrous Emotions in Ancient Greece* (Edinburgh: Edinburgh University Press, 2003), 253–76.

[110] Indeed, as Martha Nussbaum has asserted from her study of therapeutic moral psychology in Greco-Roman sources, the emotions can have a "moral intelligence," an interpretive value of their own, and are not simply "blind surges of affect." See her *Upheavals of Thought: The Intelligence of Emotions* (Cambridge: Cambridge University Press, 2001), 19–237; ead., *The Therapy of Desire: Theory and Practice in Hellenistic Ethics* (Princeton: Princeton University Press, 1994), 38, 369.

[111] Cf. *Cur.* 1.84 (PG 90:980B–C); ibid. 2.19 (989B–C); ibid. 2.74 (1008B); ibid. 2.85 (1012B–C); ibid. 2.92 (1016A–B); ibid. 3.90 (1044C–D); *Th. Oec.* 2.82 (PG 90:1164A); *Amb. Jo.* 10 (PG 91:1197C); ibid. 58 (1381C).

power of a "virtuous" emotion, a secured alignment of contemplation, reason, and pathos in a concrete practical setting. Here I can offer just two examples from the Confessor's repertoire of virtuous emotions: empathetic mercy, and the preeminent of ascetical "emotions," *apatheia* (which I will rename "engaged dispassion"). Both of these reveal virtue aspiring to virtuosity.

Pity or mercy (ἔλεος) had a long history of interpretation in Greco-Roman antiquity, but its status as a virtue was suspect. Aristotle described its function as a catharsis of the fear of suffering, at a distance sufficient for emotional comfort; but Stoics, foreshadowing Nietzsche, viewed pity as potentially depressing and weakening the will of the moral sage, valid only under controlled circumstances ("taking" pity as opposed to "feeling" it).[112] By Maximus' time, of course, mercy was a venerable Christian virtue both in its properly eleemosynary expression (concern for the poor, almsgiving, etc.) and in its role in the forgiveness of sin. And yet the problem of mercy lapsing into pity "at a distance" persisted. Maximus presses toward a deeper dimension of mercy more along the lines of what we now call empathy. Gregory of Nyssa had described mercy as "voluntary misery" (ἑκούσιος λύπη) and "loving self-identification" (ἀγαπητικὴ συνδιάθησις) with the other.[113] Maximus combines these by specifying empathetic mercy as "voluntary self-identification" (ἑκούσιος συνδιάθησις) with the suffering other,[114] adding that through mercy we proactively acknowledge kinship (τὸ συγγενές) and a filial bond (τὸ ὁμόφυλον) with those in crisis.[115]

The particular quality of mercy for Maximus is twofold. First, it is grounded in the divine *gift* of human equality. Mercy embodies an ethics that assumes this equality as ontological fact while acknowledging still the existential inequalities that attend human life. Expanding on Paul, Maximus admonishes believers to fill up others' deficiencies with their own abundances (2 Cor. 8:14), which is an ascetical labor that goes beyond acts of kindness to include

---

[112] On this pre-Christian history of pity (with references), see Paul Blowers, "Pity, Empathy, and the Tragic Spectacle of Human Suffering: Exploring the Emotional Culture of Compassion in Late Ancient Christianity," *Journal of Early Christian Studies* 18 (2010): 5–10.

[113] *Hom. in Beat.* 5 (GNO 7.2:126); similarly Basil, *Hom. in Ps.* 22.3 (on Ps. 114) (PG 29:489B), defines pity in terms of being "sympathetically disposed" (συμπαθῶς διατιθεμενῶν).

[114] *Myst.* 24 (CCSG 69:67, l. 1111).     [115] *Ep.* 2 (PG 91:396A).

self-mortification as a counterbalance to bodily inequalities wherever they exist.[116] The ascetic's self-deprivation is the suffering other's abundantly more. Second, this mercy for Maximus enacts an incarnational grace, a kenosis on behalf of the suffering other which has as its complement the "incarnation" of Christ in the virtue of the one who reveals this mercy:

> If the poor person is "God," it is because of God's condescension in *becoming poor for our sake* (cf. 2 Cor. 8:9) and in taking upon himself by his own suffering the sufferings of each one *until the end of time* (cf. Matt. 28:20), always suffering mystically out of goodness in proportion to each one's suffering. So all the more will that person be "God" who, in imitation of God's philanthropy, personally heals by his or her own initiative, but in a deiform way, the afflictions of those who suffer, and who exhibits in his or her merciful disposition the very same power of God's sustaining providence that operates in proportion to need.[117]

Paradoxically the other sterling example of a virtuous emotion in Maximus, constituting the pinnacle of the ascetical life, is *apatheia*, which has so often been translated "impassibility" or "detachment," both of which fail, however, to convey that *apatheia*, while rising above the fray of unstable passions, and achieving an inner stability akin to *hesychia*, is much more than a state of imperturbability, and even requires constant and sober remembrance of one's weakness and need of divine power.[118] For *apatheia* is never a state of being closed off from the neighbor, the "other." It is conditioned precisely by the inward *and outward* alignment of the passible self, and by the deeper reality of *agapê*. Despite love's priority to all the virtues, Maximus on occasion credits *apatheia* as the matrix of *agapê* insofar as it nurtures the love of all human beings equally.[119] And with *apatheia*, as with empathetic mercy, the indwelling of Christ is the inner mystery of the realization of emotional virtuosity.

> Whoever is perfect in love, and has reached the height of dispassion, knows no distinction at all between his own (ἰδίου) and another's, or

[116] See esp. *Amb. Jo.* 8 (PG 91:1104A–B); *Ep.* 2 (PG 91:400A); also Blowers, "Bodily Inequality, Material Chaos," 54–6.
[117] *Myst.* 24 (CCSG 69:68–9, ll. 1125–34). On the "incarnation" of Christ in the virtues of the believer, see p. 141, at n. 20 in this volume.
[118] *Car.* 2:67 (PG 90:1005B–C).
[119] Ibid. 1.2 (961B); ibid. 1.25 (965B); ibid. 1.81 (977C–D); ibid. 2.30 (993B); 4.91 (1069D).

between her own (ἰδίας) and another's, or between the faithful and the
faithless, or between slave and free, or between male and female. Rather,
having risen far above the tyranny of the passions and focused on the
one nature of human beings, he or she looks upon all as equals and is
equally disposed toward all. For in this person there is no Greek and
Jew, no male and female, no slave and free, but Christ is all and in all
(Gal. 3:21; Col. 3:11).[120]

This positive depiction of the *(com)passionate* face of *apatheia* in its
intrinsic relation to *agapê* had profound influence in subsequent
ascetical traditions in Byzantine Christianity, as attested in various
writers in the *Philokalia* who knew and absorbed Maximus' work,
and who associated *apatheia* with a host of virtuous emotions or
fruits of the Spirit.

## The Formation of Virtue within Disciplinary and Liturgical Community

For Maximus, the reorientation of human desire and the cultivation of
salutary emotions, both constitutive for forming and habituating
Christian virtues, presupposed certain protocols of imitation (μίμησις),
accountability, compassion, and traditioned moral wisdom available
only within communities, monastic and ecclesiastical. Whether monk,
non-monastic layperson, or cleric, every Christian had to look to exemplars, icons of the virtuous life, and time-tested templates of moral and
spiritual growth reinforced through catechesis, preaching, worship, and
the sacraments.

Before we speak of monastic or ecclesiastical communities incul-
cating Christian virtues, it is good to recall Maximus' larger cosmo-
politeian vision, his sense that the whole cosmos is already a grand
theatre of imitation in contemplating and performing the Good. Even
if he does not expand on the Dionysian language of hierarchies,
Maximus embraces the idea that divine Virtue and all the attributes
or energies of God give rise to a cosmic mimesis in which higher
creatures, in their own imitation of God (Christ), exemplify virtue for
lower ones. Human beings are called to the imitation of angels and

---

[120]  Ibid. 2.30 (993B).

not just other human beings,[121] as Paul himself modeled in his worthiness to encounter the three-fold ranks of angels, the "third heaven" (2 Cor. 12:2).[122]

Obviously, however, more approachable exemplars than the angels were requisite. For Maximus, one source was spiritual friendship, the advantage of which was an intimacy in which virtues (and vices) were more vividly in view and more readily brought to fruition.[123] Maximus so often praises the imitable virtues of the addressees of his writings, though he was certainly conscious of reciprocally setting his own example for them. But the context of monastic community naturally intensified the regimen of emulation. As I noted in Chapter 2, Maximus' asceticism presupposes the Eastern desert tradition, where the wisdom and virtue of the elders were passed on, through aphorisms and object lessons, to monastic disciples held in rigorous account for their every thought and action.[124] His *Dialogue on the Ascetical Life* powerfully echoes this tradition, and yet this work, a *tour de force* on imitating Christ through the saints, is almost certainly aimed not only at monastics but all within the Church. It is a veritable catechism in the life of repentance and renewal in the Spirit, saturated with Old and New Testament texts containing exempla and instruction in an asceticism applicable to all Christians. Early in the work, the elder quotes Jesus's commission to his disciples and declares that *everyone* who is baptized is called to obey *all* the commandments (cf. Matt. 28:19–20), as summed up in the love of God and love of neighbor (Luke 10:27).[125] Paul is an especially important exemplar since he expressly instructed Christians to imitate him as he imitated Christ (1 Cor. 4:16; 11:1).[126]

> Let us emulate the holy athletes of the Savior. Let us imitate their combats, *forgetting the things that are behind, and stretching forth to those that are before* (Phil. 3:13). Let us imitate their tireless course, their flaming eagerness, their perseverance in continence, their holiness in chastity, their nobility in patience, their endurance in long-suffering,

---

[121] Ibid. 3.33 (PG 90:1028B); ibid. 3.80 (1041B); ibid. 3.94 (1045B); *Amb. Jo.* 10 (PG 91:1168A); ibid. 20 (1241A); ibid. 41 (1305D, 1308A); ibid. 50 (1368B); *LA* (CCSG 40:121–3).

[122] *Amb. Jo.* 20 (PG 91:1240C).

[123] *Car.* 3.79 (PG 90:1041B); 4.93 (1072A); 4.99 (1072D). See also Manuel Mira Iborra, "Friendship in Maximus the Confessor," in Markus Vinzent, ed., *Studia Patristica* 68 (Leuven: Peeters, 2013), 273–80.

[124] See pp. 69–71 in this volume.          [125] *LA* (CCSG 40:7–9, 15).

[126] Ibid. (pp. 11, 121).

their pity in compassion, their imperturbed meekness, their warmth in zeal, their unfeignedness in love, their sublimity in lowliness, their plainness in poverty, their virility, their kindness, their clemency.[127]

The vast majority of Christians in Byzantium, of course, learned about—and from—the hovering *cloud of witnesses* (Heb. 12:1), the biblical and ecclesiastical saints, not through intimate spiritual directors but through the Church's liturgy, hymnody, and iconography; and even within the monasteries, where such direction was built into the life of the community, liturgy still played a vital role in identifying moral and spiritual exempla. Derek Krueger, in a fine recent monograph, has detailed the multiple ways that Byzantine liturgy and hymnody, beginning in the fifth and sixth centuries, decisively shaped the Byzantine religious "self" (monastic and non-monastic) by holding up the biblical paragons of penitential virtue who could revamp the Christian conscience, articulating its guilt and contrition but also its imagination of salvation and its gratitude for prospective mercy.[128] As we have already seen,[129] Maximus follows Dionysius in understanding the Church, with its liturgy, to mirror the cosmos as a school of virtue. Most of his own teaching on imitating the saints' virtues comes not from his commentary on the liturgy, but from his ascetical writings; nevertheless, the *Mystagogia* certainly assumes that the rhythms and rituals, the readings of Scripture, the chants and hymns, the creed, and the dramatic elements of the Eucharistic service all draw the Christian into the cloud of witnesses, the procession of the faithful extending through salvation history and anticipating its eschatological outcome.

Worship itself is for Maximus a protracted conversion of the free will to deifying virtue. It begins in baptism, which comprises two

[127] Ibid. (p. 121, ll. 1024–33), trans. Sherwood, Ancient Christian Writers 21, 135 (slightly altered).
[128] *Liturgical Subjects: Christian Ritual, Biblical Narrative, and the Formation of the Self in Byzantium* (Philadelphia: University of Pennsylvania Press, 2014). Krueger analyzes, for example, the *kontakia* (sermonic hymns) of Romanos the Melodist, the greatest of Byzantine hymn writers a few generations before Maximus, which often included highly stylized dialogues or monologues placed in the mouths of biblical characters and aimed at plumbing their inner consciences and likewise drawing audiences into close identification with their penitential plight (esp. pp. 1–65). The liturgical calendar itself, preaching, hymns, and the Eucharistic anaphoras all served the purpose of establishing profiles and protocols of repentance and personal reformation in engagement of the biblical narratives.
[129] See pp. 178–80 in this volume.

modes: "the one bestows the grace of adoption, which is entirely present in potency (δυνάμει) in those who are born of God; the other introduces, wholly by active exertion (κατ' ἐνέργειαν), that grace which deliberately (γνωμικῶς) reorients the entire free choice of the one being born of God toward the God who gives birth."[130] Participation in the Church's liturgy—the worship engaging all the saints, in heaven and on earth, in the imitation of Christ—nurtures this flowering of baptismal grace and conversion of the ungodly, all believers of greater or lesser sin.

> For entrance into the church [for the liturgy] signifies not only the conversion of infidels to the *true and only God* (John 17:3) but also the emendation of each one of us who believe but who yet violate the Lord's commandments under the influence of loose and indecent life. Indeed, when any person is a murderer, or adulterer, robber, *haughty, boastful, insolent* (Rom. 1:30), ambitious, greedy, slanderous, resentful, inclined to outbursts and anger, a drunkard, and in a word . . . when someone is entangled in any kind of vice but should cease voluntarily to be held by its attention and deliberately to act according to it and changes his or her life for the better by preferring virtue to vice, such a person can be properly and truly considered and spoken of as entering with Christ our God and High Priest into virtue, which is the church understood figuratively.[131]

---

[130] *Q. Thal.* 6 (CCSG 7:69, ll. 9–13), trans. Blowers and Wilken, 103; cf. *Myst.* 24 (CCSG 69:66).

[131] *Myst.* 9 (CCSG 69:38–9, ll. 624–40), trans. Berthold, 198–9 (slightly altered).

# Part IV

# Maximus' Afterlife East and West

# 9

## Recontextualizations of Maximus
## East and West

After his ignoble death in 662 while exiled in Lazica, Maximus' name became an embarrassment to the Byzantine imperial authorities and the Patriarchate of Constantinople, so much so that it was not even mentioned in the formal decrees of the Council of Constantinople in 680–1, even though the council vindicated dyothelete orthodoxy. As I noted at the end of Chapter 1, however, Maximus' cult as a Byzantine saint began to take shape early on in Georgia, where he was buried. And in due course his theological and ascetical legacies would be registered far and wide in the Christian world, East and West.[1] The present chapter is by no means an exhaustive survey of Maximus' *Nachleben*, but a sampling of the more salient attempts to recontextualize his oeuvre in an array of new theological settings and controversies. Whether we can speak of "Neo-Maximian" theologies in the same way that we identify Neo-Augustinian or Neo-Thomist ones remains to be seen, but there is no doubt that Maximus has proven (and still proves) to be the subject of consistent ecumenical retrieval and *ressourcement*.

---

[1] For good introductory explorations of Maximus' *Rezeptionsgeschichte* East and West, see Maximos Constas, "St. Maximus the Confessor: The Reception of His Thought in East and West," in Vasiljević, 25–53; and Deno Geanakoplos, "Maximus the Confessor and His Influence on Eastern and Western Theology and Mysticism," in his *Interaction of the "Sibling" Byzantine and Western Cultures in the Middle Ages and Italian Renaissance (330–1600)* (New Haven: Yale University Press, 1976), 133–45. Also of interest is Edmond Voordeckers, "L'iconographie de saint Maxime le Confesseur dans l'art des églises de rite byzantin," in Schoors and van Deun, *Philohistôr*, 339–59.

## MAXIMUS' LEGACY IN THE EARLY
## MEDIEVAL WEST

It is little surprise that, in the wake of the monothelete controversy and the new confidence of the papacy in its resistance to Byzantine imperial authority, the Roman Church seized upon Maximus' prestige as leader of the Greek monastic opposition to Constantinople, hoping to keep alive this unprecedented Eastern alliance with the Roman see. The pivotal mediator here was Anastasius Bibliothecarius (*c*.800–79), who, after a stormy early career and even a stint as an anti-pope in 855, eventually became both head of the papal archives and papal legate to Constantinople amid the increased alienation between Rome and Byzantium. Working for a time under the ambitious Pope Nicholas I (r. 858–67), who envisioned the Roman Church as the model for the Church universal,[2] Anastasius's goal was to recontextualize Maximus as an Eastern adjudicator of the papal primacy. To this end, being thoroughly proficient in Greek, he translated into Latin the biographical and hagiographical documents connected with the demise of Maximus and Pope Martin I, both revered as champions of Roman orthodoxy against the Byzantine emperor and the Patriarchate of Constantinople. What more effective way could there be to bolster the Roman primacy than to register Maximus' purported Eastern witness in the papal dossier? In fact, one of the other works translated by Anastasius was the classic *Life of John the Almsgiver* by the Cypriot bishop Leontius of Neapolis (seventh century), a work that supplemented the earlier *Life* of John produced by John Moschus and Maximus' one-time spiritual father, Sophronius. Bronwen Neil is surely correct that this is no coincidental choice on Anastasius's part, as he sought to muster other Eastern "pro-Chalcedonian, anti-imperial" sources associated with Maximus in support of papal claims.[3]

Turning north in the same period to the Carolingian Dynasty, Maximus found an even more robust intellectual legacy in the work of John Scottus Eriugena (*c*.815–77), the most accomplished philosophical

---

[2] On Anastasius's assistance in adducing Nicholas I's claims to universal episcopal primacy, see Walter Ullmann, *The Growth of Papal Government in the Middle Ages*, 3rd edn., reprinted (London: Routledge, 2013), 191–3; Neil, *Seventh-Century Popes and Martyrs*, 5–9; and on his turbulent but illustrious career and his fluency in Greek, see also Allen and Neil, 32–5; Neil, *Seventh-Century Popes and Martyrs*, 11–34.

[3] Neil, *Seventh-Century Popes and Martyrs*, 44–5.

theologian of the Carolingian Renaissance, who translated into Latin both the *Corpus Areopagiticum* and Maximus' two longest works, the *Ambigua to John*[4] and the *Questions and Responses for Thalassius*.[5] Both Eriugena and Anastasius esteemed Maximus as an interpreter of Dionysius, thus assuring close connection of the pair in their medieval Western reception. Anastasius actually produced a revision of Eriugena's translation of Dionysius along with scholia on the Areopagite attributed to Maximus and to the Palestinian bishop John of Scythopolis. He also translated sections of Maximus' *Mystagogia*, which was already closely associated with Dionysius's *Ecclesiastical Hierarchy* as a commentary on the liturgy.[6]

Eriugena's translation of Maximus, commissioned by and dedicated to the Emperor Charles the Bald (Charlemagne's grandson), was wooden and literalist, and roundly assailed by Anastasius, who deemed John a rustic upstart over his head in daring to render Maximus' sophisticated Greek into Latin.[7] But one cannot depend on John's often verbatim translations to grasp his larger interpretation of Maximus,[8] which was part of his campaign to reconcile Western (namely Augustinian) doctrine with the Eastern Fathers (namely Gregory of Nyssa, Dionysius, and Maximus) for the sake of a revised Christian-Neoplatonic system of thought. Though too complex to detail here,[9] John's interpretation of

---

[4] For Eriugena's Latin translation of the *Amb. Jo.*, see CCSG 18 (ed. Édouard Jeauneau).

[5] Eriugena's Latin translation of the *Q. Thal.* is included with the Greek critical edition by Carl Laga and Carlos Steel, CCSG 7 and 22. Interestingly, John's translations predate the earliest Greek MSS of Maximus. On Eriugena's translation work, see John O'Meara, *Eriugena* (Oxford: Oxford University Press, 1988), 51–79; Eligius Dekkers, "Maxime le Confesseur dans la tradition Latine," in Carl Laga et al., eds., *After Chalcedon: Studies in Theology and Church History offered to Albert van Roey* (Leuven: Peeters, 1985), 83–7.

[6] Anastasius's Latin translation of the *Mystagogia* is included with the Greek critical edition, CCSG 69. For background, see also Neil, *Seventh-Century Popes and Martyrs*, 80–5; Constas, "St. Maximus the Confessor: The Reception of His Thought in East and West," 26–30; Dekkers, "Maxime le Confesseur dans la tradition latine," 87–90.

[7] *Ep.* 13 (Anastasius to the Emperor Charles the Bald), Monumenta germaniae historica, Epistolarum tom. 7 (Berlin: Weidmann, 1928), 431, ll. 18–20 (referring to John as a *vir barbarus*).

[8] See Édouard Jeauneau, "Jean l'Érigène et les *Ambigua ad Iohannem* de Maxime le Confesseur," *MC*, 343–64.

[9] For overviews of Eriugena's reworking of Maximus and his other patristic sources, see Catherine Kavanagh, "The Impact of Maximus the Confessor on John Scottus Eriugena," *OHMC*, 480–99; Dermot Moran, *The Philosophy of John Scottus Eriugena: A Study of Idealism in the Middle Ages* (Cambridge: Cambridge University Press, 1989), 116–20.

Maximus surfaces principally in his great work of philosophical and theological cosmology, the *Periphyseon*. Here Eriugena, like Dionysius and Maximus, describes the hierarchy of being not for its own sake but as a function of theophany (or especially in Maximus' case, Christophany). The Creator–creation relation bases itself in the strict division between uncreated and created nature, and from the notion, attributable to Dionysius and Maximus but developed much more extensively by John, that the "nothing" (*nihil*) from which God created the world was but the negation of the ineffable divine being (the divine "no-thing"). The nothing signals the Creator's transcendence of all being, while affirming still that he causes and funds created being. God the Creator

> is deservedly called 'nothing' by virtue of his excellence (*per excellentiam nihilum non immerito vocitatur*). But in truth, when he begins to appear in his theophanies, he is said to proceed, as it were, from nothing into something (*ex nihilo in aliquid*), and what is properly considered beyond all essence is perceived in every essence. And for that reason, every visible and invisible creature is a theophany, that is, every single creature can be called a divine appearance. For the more each order of created natures from top to bottom—that is, from the celestial essences down to the lowliest visible body of this world—is understood to be hidden, the more it is seen to approximate the splendor (*claritati*) of God.[10]

John's robust sense that creation *ex nihilo* is creation *ex Deo*, and that God not only causes but *is* his creation, inspired later accusations of pantheism, especially as he claimed that "we must not understand God and creation as two distinct things but as one and the same, since creation subsists in God and God creates himself in the creation (*in creatura . . . creatur*) in a wondrous and ineffable manner."[11] And yet Eriugena doubtless assumed he was faithfully interpreting Dionysius and Maximus, for whom the Creator (Christ), though beyond being, is free to *be* all as well as be *in* all (cf. 1 Cor. 15:28; Col. 3:11) without violating his transcendence, in virtue of his gracious immanence and his securing of the unity of creation amid its diversity.[12] More problematic from a Maximian perspective, however, is John's additional caveat that in explicating the divine "self-creation in creation" he is *not* referencing

---

[10] *Periphyseon* 3.19 (CCCM 163:88–9, ll. 2549–58). For Maximus' own view of God as "no-thing" in virtue of his transcendence, see *Myst.* prooemium (CCSG 69:9); also pp. 125–6 in this volume; and Blowers, *Drama of the Divine Economy*, 181–4.

[11] *Periphyseon* 3.17 (CCCM 163:85, ll. 2443–6).

[12] Cf. Maximus, *Amb. Jo.* 7 (PG 91:1092C); ibid. 22 (1257A); Dionysius, *Div. nom.* 7.3 (PTS 33:198).

the incarnation of the Logos but only the "ineffable condescension of the ultimate Good, which is Unity and Trinity."[13]

Eriugena also considered Maximus' doctrine of the five cosmic polarities[14] in the light of his own fourfold division of *naturae*.[15] The difference is that for Maximus these are ontological structures in their own right, the coherence of which is immediately tied to the historical incarnation of Jesus Christ, who ultimately and perfectly embodies divine Wisdom in creation.[16] In John's system, they are revelations of God to the contemplative human mind. Dermot Moran avers that John's "seemingly *objective hierarchical* scheme of nature is counterbalanced by an *antihierarchical subjectivist* tendency, which may indeed be termed 'idealist,'" since the putative hierarchies of nature are "mind-dependent," and since the mind (as image of God) is to be given direct access to God and to the essences of things without intermediaries.[17]

In comparing John with Maximus, von Balthasar thus considered Eriugena a "cosmic gnostic" and throwback to radical Origenism whose metaphysics was fully detached from Christology.[18] Of late, John Gavin, in one of the only studies of Eriugena's own Christology, nevertheless suggests more fidelity to Maximus. He points out, for example, Eriugena's reiteration of the Maximian doctrine of the multiple "incarnations" of the Logos. John the Evangelist calls the Word's assumption of human substance in Jesus the incarnation proper, while the Word is *quasi incarnatus* in scriptural language and in the forms and orders of visible things.[19] This seems a departure, however, from Maximus' view that while the historic incarnation is unique and supreme, all his incarnations are eschatologically simultaneous, and it is precisely the Logos *qua Christ* who is fully present in all of them. Gavin goes far to vindicate Eriugena's Christology, but the incarnation proper remains decisive for the Irish sage primarily for human restoration within the redemptive *oikonomia*. Cosmologically, it *complements* the revelatory work of the transcendent Logos but still does not seem to figure as the deepest "rationale" or plan (βουλή) of creation itself, as is the case in Maximus.

---

[13] *Periphyseon* 3.17 (CCCM 163:85, ll. 2455–7).
[14] *Amb. Jo.* 41; see p. 127 and Figure 2 in this volume.
[15] Ibid. 2.3–13 (CCCM 162:9–24).     [16] See esp. *Amb. Jo.* 41 (PG 91:1313B).
[17] *The Philosophy of John Scottus Eriugena*, 95.     [18] *Cosmic Liturgy*, 85
[19] *Comm. in Johannem* 1.29 (SC 180:154–6); cited by John Gavin, *A Celtic Christology: The Incarnation according to John Scottus Eriugena* (Eugene, OR: Cascade Books, 2014), 43.

MAXIMUS' LEGACY IN MIDDLE
BYZANTINE SCHOLASTICISM

Earlier I discussed Averil Cameron's thesis that already in Maximus'
time were the makings of a scholasticism representing the essentially
defensive cultural posture assumed by Byzantium in the face of the
internal threat of schism and heresy, and the external specter of
Islam.[20] This scholasticism nonetheless found its real traction in the
Middle Byzantine period (ninth through early thirteenth centuries),
though it extended even to the collapse of the empire in 1453. Its hallmark
was a broad-based reappropriation of the Hellenic and Christian intellectual sources of Byzantine cultural identity, part of a continuing process
of cultural self-definition in relation to political and cultural "others."[21]
Henceforth the retrieval of Maximus' legacy was tied to the compiling of
authorities for purposes of preserving theological orthodoxy. Just as
Maximus had himself compiled florilegia to support dyothelete Christology, he would be included as a source in later florilegia, as well as in
catena commentaries on Scripture.[22] But in the works of Byzantine
humanists, his legacy was also tied to enduring debates over the relation

---

[20]  See pp. 64–5, 96–8 in this volume.
[21]  On the complexity of that Hellenic identity amid the ethnic and cultural diversity
of Byzantium, see Averil Cameron, *Byzantine Matters* (Princeton: Princeton University Press, 2014), 46–67. For an excellent survey of the themes and literary genres of
Byzantine philosophy from 730 to 1453, see Katerina Ierodiakonou and Börje Bydén,
"Byzantine Philosophy," *Stanford Encyclopedia of Philosophy* (online: <http://plato.
stanford.edu/entries/byzantine-philosophy>); for a fuller treatment, see Basil Tatakis,
*Byzantine Philosophy*, trans. Nicholas Moutafakis (Indianapolis: Hackett Publishing,
2003 [1949]). On the scholastic culture of "collecting, summarizing, excerpting and
synthesizing earlier texts" in this era, see Paul Magdalino, "Byzantine Encyclopaedism
of the Ninth and Tenth Centuries," in Jason König and Greg Woolf, eds., *Encyclopaedism from Antiquity to the Renaissance* (Cambridge: Cambridge University Press,
2013), 219–31. See also Peter van Deun and Caroline Macé, eds., *Encyclopedic Trends
in Byzantium? Proceedings of the International Conference Held in Leuven, 6–8 May
2009* (Leuven: Peeters, 2011).
[22]  See Peter van Deun, "Les citations de saint Maxime le Confesseur dans le florilège
palamite de l'Atheniensis, Bibliotheque nationale 2583," *Byzantion* 57 (1987): 127–57;
Bram Roosen and Peter van Deun, "Les collections des définitions philosophico-
theologiques appartenant à la tradition de Maxime le Confesseur: Le recueil centré
sur *ΟΜΩΝΥΜΟΝ, ΣΥΝΩΝΥΜΟΝ, ΠΑΡΩΝΥΜΟΝ, ΕΤΕΡΩΝΥΜΟΝ...*," in
Michel Cacouros and Marie-Hélène Congourdeau, eds., *Philosophie et sciences à Byzance
de 1204 à 1453* (Leuven: Peeters, 2006), 53–76 (and the substantial further studies listed
at p. 54, n. 2). See also Aloys Grillmeier, *Christ in Christian Tradition*, vol. 2, pt. 1, trans.
Pauline Allen and Paul Cawte (Atlanta: John Knox Press, 1987), 73–6.

of theology to philosophy amid new passion for philosophy, and disputes as to whether Platonism or Aristotelianism held supremacy as Byzantium's canonical philosophical idiom—though Aristotelianism, with Neoplatonic reworkings, was destined to win the day.[23]

Transitionally crucial here is John Damascene (*c*.646–749), the prolific monastic theologian of Mar Sabas monastery in the Judean desert, whose reputation soared because of his highly articulated defense of icons in another culturally defining event in Byzantium, the iconoclastic controversy (726–843). Beyond this, however, John's trilogy summarily titled *The Fountain of Knowledge* is a monument of zeal for religious and cultural definition. It begins with the *Dialectica*, a treatise of philosophical terminology for theological usage that bears the influence of Porphyry's *Isagoge* and Aristotle's logical works. More than likely it was not the Damascene's original work but a prior compilation that he endorsed, and similar handbooks are ascribed to Maximus too.[24] Next is *On Heresy*, which catalogs and targets not only internal heretics, old and new, but also the latest external one: "Ishmaelites" (Muslims). John caps the trilogy with his magnum opus *On the Orthodox Faith*, a rhetorically dry but substantive synthesis of Greek patristic theology heavily, though certainly not exclusively, dependent on Maximus' prior work.

Most notably in the christological sections of his summa, John resonated Maximian distinctions and definitions, like those concerning the dual energies and wills of Christ,[25] and the attributes of Christ's psychological constitution and appropriation of human nature.[26] But the Damascene is an interpreter, not a slavish duplicator.[27] On the Dionysian "new theandric energy," for example, Maximus had emphasized the exchange ($\dot{a}\nu\tau\acute{\iota}\delta o\sigma\iota s$) of properties in the composite person of Christ, while John applies to it Maximus' closely related notion of the "circumincession" ($\pi\epsilon\rho\iota\chi\acute{\omega}\rho\eta\sigma\iota s$) of natures.[28] On the vexed question of

---

[23] See Klaus Oehler's still useful overview, "Aristotle in Byzantium," *Greek, Roman, and Byzantine Studies* 5 (1964): 133–46.

[24] See Andrew Louth, *St. John Damascene: Tradition and Originality in Byzantine Theology* (Oxford: Oxford University Press, 2002), 42–6.

[25] *De fide orthodoxa* 3.14 (PTS 12:137–44). According to Boniface Kotter, critical editor of the PTS edition, there are 70 citations of Maximus on the wills and energies of Christ in this work. See also Grillmeier, *Christ in Christian Tradition* 2/1, 76, § 2.

[26] *De fide orth.* 3.20–5 (PTS 12:162–8).

[27] See Louth, *St. John Damascene*, esp. 84–189.

[28] *De fide orth.* 3.19 (PTS 12:160); cf. Maximus, *Amb. Th.* 5 (CCSG 48:32–3).

gnomic will, however, John fully knows that Maximus denied *gnômê* in Christ because Christ did not waver in choosing the good,[29] and yet he finds an alternative meaning of the semantically pliable *gnômê* that still could apply: namely, *inclination* toward the commonly *willed objective* (τὸ θελητόν) of the divine and human natures.[30] Reintroducing *gnômê* to Christ in this restricted sense, John undoubtedly believed he was still faithful to Maximus, who, in expounding the Gethsemane prayer, quoted Cyril of Alexandria precisely to the effect that Christ invariably willed the same thing (τὸ θελητόν) as the Father.[31]

After John, who further enhanced the Confessor's prestige in Orthodoxy's theological archive, fresh interpretation of Maximus was limited principally to ascetical and spiritual theology in the Middle and Late Byzantine periods. He never addressed the legitimacy of religious iconography as it was not in question, so his name did not significantly emerge in the iconoclastic controversy, though his theological articulations of the relation of image and prototype may have positively informed the defense of icons.[32] In the ninth century, Maximus was admired by the Patriarch, theologian, and encyclopedist Photius of Constantinople, who included him in his famous "reading list," the *Myriobiblion* (*Bibliotheca*),[33] even though some of his most memorable remarks are his virulent criticisms of Maximus' prolixity of language and style.[34] As Andrew Louth has characterized him, however, Photius was essentially a lay theologian, a man of tremendous learning but quickly ordained and advanced in ecclesiastical office.[35] His primary audience was educated laity for whom he

---

[29] *De fide orth.* 2.22 (PTS 12:91–2); ibid. 3.14 (p. 143).

[30] Ibid. 2.22 (PTS 12:92).

[31] *Opusc.* 15 (PG 91:165A). Cf. *Opusc.* 3 (48B–C), indicating Christ's sharing of the Father's will (βουλή, Eph. 1:11; cf. Acts 2:23). See also Paul Blowers, "Maximus the Confessor and John of Damascus on Gnomic Will (γνώμη) in Christ: Clarity and Ambiguity," *Union Seminary Quarterly Review* 63 (2012): 44–50.

[32] See V. M. Zhinov, "The *Mystagogia* of Maximus the Confessor and the Development of the Byzantine Theory of the Image," *St. Vladimir's Theological Quarterly* 31 (1987): 349–76.

[33] See *Myriobiblion*, cdd. 192–5, which include comments on the *Q. Thal.*, various *Epistulae*, the *LA* and various of the *Th. Oec.*, and "two letters to Thomas" (i.e. *Amb. Th.* and *Epistula secunda ad Thomam*).

[34] As assessed by Carl Laga, "Maximus as a Stylist in *Quaestiones ad Thalassium*," *MC*, 139–46. See p. 94 in this volume.

[35] "Photius as Theologian," in Elizabeth Jeffreys, ed., *Byzantine Style, Religion and Civilization: In Honour of Sir Steven Runciman* (Cambridge: Cambridge University

was committed to clarifying the *aporiae* of Scripture and inherited theological tradition. An innovative interpreter of Maximus he was not. Perhaps an exception, pointed out by Louth, is Photius's resumption of the issue of gnomic will in Christ in his *Amphilochia*, a treatise on scriptural and theological ambiguities. Photius used both Maximus' work on this and the Damascene's. Most interestingly, Photius recognized the very dilemma that I discussed earlier: if the gnomic will is fallen human will in need of redemption, how can it be healed unless Christ assumes it? Ultimately, however, after exploring various scriptural texts, he concurred with Maximus that Christ had no gnomic will since it is not, strictly speaking, proper to human nature.[36]

Turning to the eleventh century, in the heyday of Byzantine humanism, Maximus and other Greek patristic authors came under increasing scrutiny by quasi-secularizing scholars keen on measuring them up to the standards of good philosophy. Michael Psellos (1018–*c*.1080), who rose to prominence as the imperially-appointed Consul of the Philosophers, superintendent of philosophical education in Constantinople, wrote, among other things, a set of theological and exegetical *Opuscula* heavy on the interpretation of Scripture and the Fathers. In this collection, for example, Psellos subjects Christian interpretation of the transfiguration, via John Damascene's canon on it, to the criterion of what Michael believed was the pure Neoplatonic mysticism of Proclus.[37] Psellos holds especially great interest in the *Orations* of Gregory Nazianzen, whom he clearly esteems as a rhetorical genius. He is interested in "Maximus the Philosopher," as he calls him, partly because he is a fellow interpreter of Gregory, such as on the allegorical meaning of certain New Testament passages in Nazianzen's preaching.[38] In a few instances, however, Psellos appeals to Maximus'

---

Press, 2006), 206–23; id., *Greek East and Latin West: The Church AD 681–1071* (Crestwood, NY: St. Vladimir's Seminary Press, 2007), 159–62.

[36] *Amphilochium* 80, ed. L. G. Westerink, *Photii patriarchae Constantinopolitani Epistulae et Amphilochia* 5, BSGRT (Leipzig: Teubner, 1986), 112–28. See also Louth, "Photius as Theologian," 219–20.

[37] *Opusc.* 11, ed. Paul Gautier, *Michaelis Pselli theologica*, BSGRT (Leipzig: Teubner, 1989), 1:43–7. For analysis see Frederick Lauritzen, "Psellos the Hesychast: A Neoplatonic Reading of the Transfiguration on Mt. Tabor (*Theologica* I, 11 Gautier)," *Byzantinoslavica* 70 (2012): 167–79.

[38] Cf. *Opusc.* 43 (*Michaelis Pselli theologica* 1:162–5), referring to various of the *Amb. Jo.*

opinion on its own terms, as when he discusses Jesus's enigmatic statement, "My Father is working still, and I am working (John 5:17)."[39] *Opusculum* 108 is a reflection "on the mystery of the cross and burial of Christ," in which, for the sake of pursuing "more exalted thoughts" on its meaning, Michael references Maximus' celebrated dictum that the cross and the resurrection hold the key to the knowledge of sensible and intelligible creatures and of scriptural figures and enigmas.[40] Psellos's engagement of these revered patristic authorities like Gregory, Maximus, and John Damascene is fascinating to follow, insofar as he rarely if ever concealed his desire to harmonize them with the finest Neoplatonic thinkers, all the while having to exonerate himself of suspicions of his own theological orthodoxy.

Also in the eleventh century, the Emperor Alexius I Comnenus's older brother Isaac ("the Sebastocrator"), another Neoplatonic enthusiast, extensively integrated Maximus (less so Dionysius) into his treatises on providence, determinism, and the subsistence of evil, in a bid to balance out his dependence on Proclus. Carlos Steel has identified two especially salient examples of Isaac's synthesizing of Maximus and Proclus. In one case Isaac takes Proclus's doctrine of five ascending modes of knowledge and insinuates into it Maximus' five modes of natural contemplation set forth in *Ambiguum* 10 (PG 91:1133A–1137C). In another case Isaac replaces Maximus' phrase "the one nature of the cosmos" (ἡ μία τοῦ κόσμου φύσις) with "the logos of every nature" (ὁ τῆς φύσεως λόγος), the latter representing the fact that the Logos/logos is the real causal principle within each and every natural creature—a view thoroughly congenial with Maximus' doctrine of the *logoi* of beings.[41] Isaac is thus a splendid study, like Michael Psellos, in the urge of Byzantine humanists to reconcile the Church Fathers, in our case Maximus, with the philosophical tradition in the effort to galvanize a body of wisdom enhancing Byzantium's cultural glory.

---

[39] Ibid. 79 (*Michaelis Pselli theologica* 1:319, ll. 73–89), referring to *Q. Thal.* 2 (CCSG 7:51).

[40] *Opusc.* 108 (*Michaelis Pselli theologica* 1:428–9, ll. 1–38), referring to *Th. Oec.* 1.66 (PG 90:1108A–B) and ibid. 1.36–43 (1097A–1000A).

[41] Carlos Steel, "Un admirateur de S. Maxime à la cour des Comnènes: Isaac le Sébastocrator," *MC*, 365–73; id., "Maximus Confessor on *Theory* and *Praxis*," Appendix, 255–7.

## MAXIMUS IN THE FRAY OF EAST–WEST SCHISM: THE *FILIOQUE* CONTROVERSY

Maximus did not live long enough to see the *Filioque* become a consuming point of contention between the Eastern and Western Churches. Having roots in Latin patristic theology, this principle affirming the Holy Spirit's procession from the Father *and from the Son* did not begin to appear in Western versions of the Nicene-Constantinopolitan Creed until the late sixth century, and thus was thoroughly overshadowed in Maximus' time by the monothelete controversy, with its own East–West fallout. Not until the so-called Photian Schism of the ninth century did the wound opened by the *Filioque* truly begin to fester ecumenically.[42] As Patriarch of Constantinople, Photius judged it a Western aberration in the context of fending off not only a papal bid to judge his legitimacy as patriarch but also an incursion of Roman missionaries in Bulgaria, who introduced the Creed with the *Filioque* to an infant church still struggling to find its ecclesiastical and theological bearings.

It would be wrong, however, to infer that there was no real debate on the issue before or during Maximus' time.[43] And his status in the gradually intensifying controversy was assured because of a relatively brief but striking reflection on the procession of the Holy Spirit that he left in a letter to Marinus the Cypriot priest (= *Opusculum* 10, *c.*645). He had learned that certain critics from Constantinople rebuked two sections of the Synodical letters of "the current most holy Pope" (ostensibly Theodore), one of which included his claim that "the Holy Spirit proceeds also from the Son" (ἐκπορεύεσθαι κἀκ τοῦ Υἱοῦ τὸ Πνεῦμα τὸ ἅγιον).[44] Maximus postured himself in defense of the Pope, declaring that his teaching was consonant not only with the "Roman Fathers" but also with the Eastern luminary Cyril of Alexandria,[45] all of whom

---

[42] On the larger *Filioque* controversy, see A. Edward Siecienski, *The Filioque: History of a Doctrinal Controversy* (New York: Oxford University Press, 2010); Peter Gemeinhardt, *Filioque-Kontroverse zwischen Ost- und Westkirche im Frühmittelalter* (Berlin: Walter de Gruyter, 2002).

[43] See Jean-Claude Larchet, *Maxime le Confesseur, médiateur entre l'Orient et l'Occident* (Paris: Cerf, 1988), 11–75, esp. 14–18.

[44] *Opusc.* 10 (PG 91:133D–136A).

[45] Maximus only mentions (ibid., 136A) that Cyril's view came from a work on the Gospel of John. Larchet (*Maxime le Confesseur, mediateur*, 44–52) identifies some relevant passages from Cyril's *Comm. in Johannem*.

showed that they were not making the Son the cause of the Spirit, for they knew that the Father alone is the cause of the Son and the Spirit: of the Son by generation (κατὰ τὴν γέννησιν), of the Spirit by procession (κατὰ τὴν ἐκπόρευσιν). Rather, they demonstrated the advance (τὸ προϊέναι) of the Spirit through the Son, and thereby proved that they were conjoined and indistinguishable in essence.[46]

Predictably, much interpretation has focused on the meaning of this *advance* (τὸ προϊέναι) of the Holy Spirit *through* (δία) the Son, though Maximus does not nuance its meaning. His thorough confidence in the ecumenically established fact that the Father is the unique cause of the Son's eternal begetting and the Spirit's eternal procession suggests that in this instance he was speaking not in the register of *theologia* but of *oikonomia*, and was assuming the same for Pope Theodore and the other authorities. The Spirit's advance through the Son refers not to intra-trinitarian relations but to their cooperative endeavor in the economy of salvation.[47] This perspective is supported by an earlier but relevant text in *Questions and Responses for Thalassius* 63, where Maximus posits that in the mystery of the Church, Christ the Word is the Head, being the one who has the Spirit and who grants to the Church the Spirit's "energies" or "gifts" (χαρίσματα), though in the very same passage he says that the Spirit himself, who "ineffably proceeds (ἐκπορευόμενον) in essence from the Father through the begotten Son," grants those energies to the Church.[48]

Maximus went out of his way to insist that the pope and the Latins were being unjustly accused of theological error on the Spirit's procession, whereas their critics in Constantinople were without excuse for what they themselves had covertly introduced (i.e. the monothelete error).[49] Maximus continues to Marinus:

But as you requested, I have urged the Romans to translate their own terms for the sake of avoiding obscurities in what they suggest. But since they legitimately followed the procedure of composing and sending

---

[46] *Opusc.* 10 (PG 91:136A–B).

[47] So Siecienski, *The Filioque*, 74–86, esp. 84–5; Larchet, *Maxime le Confesseur, médiateur*, 19–21, 52–75.

[48] *Q. Thal.* 63 (CCSG 22:153–5). As Larchet points out, Maximus here has taken ἐκπορευόμενον as synonymous with the τὸ προϊέναι of *Opusc.* 10, at a time when the patristic vocabulary of the procession was quite fluid. He also exhibits other relevant texts from Maximus that articulate his position on the *Filioque* (*Maxime le Confesseur, médiateur*, 52–64).

[49] *Opusc.* 10 (PG 91:136B).

[Synodical letters], I know not whether they will ever comply. Besides, it is also the case that they cannot precisely convey their meaning in words and language other than their own mother-tongue, any more than we could do the same in a foreign language.[50]

Whatever his good will, Maximus recognized that there was a linguistic fault-line on the *Filioque*, and sought a remedy that actually placed the burden more on the Latins than the Greeks to achieve clarity and consensus.

For subsequent Greek interpreters, including Photius, Maximus' adjustment of the *Filioque* along the lines of the *oikonomia* of the Spirit's procession *through the Son* held great promise, though there was little openness to it in the West, with the exception of Eriugena, who thoroughly sympathized with it. "We very much indeed believe and understand that the Holy Spirit proceeds from the Father through the Son (*a Patre per Filium . . . procedere*), and yet we are obliged to accept not that the Holy Spirit has two causes, but one cause alone, the Father, with the Son being generated from him and the Holy Spirit proceeding from him through the Son."[51] Centuries later, in the fateful Council of Ferrara/Florence (1438–45), which began with high hopes for ecclesiastical reconciliation but resulted in an even deeper alienation of Eastern and Western Churches, Maximus' letter to Marinus (*Opusc.* 10) came up in debate over the *Filioque*, an inevitably crucial issue in discussions of reunion.[52] Maximus proved in this context to be, as Edward Siecienski puts it, "a sword that could cut both ways."[53]

Well before the Council, Nilus Cabasilas (1298–1363), one time Bishop of Thessaloniki and for a while a champion of East–West reconciliation, had turned strongly against the Latin defenses of the *Filioque*, and appealed to, among other Greek patristic sources, Maximus' letter to Marinus as an anti-*Filioque* text.[54] His treatise on the Holy Spirit in turn served as the principal florilegium for Byzantine representatives at Ferrara/Florence, though they did not all agree on Nilus's own view of

---

[50] Ibid. (136B–C).     [51] *Periphyseon* 2.32 (CCCM 162:479, ll. 6085–92).
[52] For what follows here I am especially indebted to Edward Siecienski, "The Use of Maximus the Confessor's Writing on the *Filioque* at the Council of Ferrara-Florence (1438–1439)" (Ph.D. dissertation, Fordham University, New York, 2005), 161–211; also Joseph Gill, *The Council of Florence* (Cambridge: Cambridge University Press, 1958).
[53] Siecienski, "The Use of Maximus the Confessor's Writing on the *Filioque*," 162.
[54] See Nilus Cabasilas, *De processione Spiritus Sancti* 5.4–7, Greek text ed. Théophile Kislas, *Nil Cabasilas: Sur le Saint-Esprit* (Paris: Cerf, 2001), 376–80.

Maximus. The leading anti-unionist at the Council, Mark Eugenicus, Bishop of Ephesus, who brought his own florilegium, confidently cited not only the letter to Marinus but also the passage cited earlier from the *Questions and Responses to Thalassius* 63 as irrevocable evidence of Maximus' denial of a double-origin of the Spirit's procession. Moderate, pro-union Byzantine representatives nevertheless cited these texts as well, believing that Maximus' instruction on the procession of the Spirit through the Son could provide a *modus vivendi* between staunch Latin defenders of the *Filioque* and the Greeks. Interestingly, then, the arguments rotated not just around Maximus' precise position on the *Filioque*, but his strategic political importance as a mediator who had once sided with Rome on Christology and distanced himself from the monothelete radicals in Constantinople.

Meanwhile, Latin conservatives had left Maximus out of their own argumentation, having already concluded that his letter to Marinus, if authentic, did not support their own interpretation of the *Filioque* (allowing for the Son's causation of the Spirit). Only Andrew of Rhodes, an ethnic Greek who had become a Dominican friar and eventual Latin Bishop of Rhodes, brought forward the letter to Marinus as congenial to the Latin position; but he was quickly overrun by his Latin colleagues who wanted Maximus kept out of the discussion.[55] An ostensive breakthrough occurred when the Latin delegate John of Montenero reintroduced the letter to Marinus and affirmed that Maximus' real point was that the Romans themselves believed in the Spirit's procession from the Father alone. The Greeks took note and, at the bidding of the Emperor John VIII Palaeologus, who was with the Byzantine delegation, decided, according to the Greek *Acta*, to put forward Maximus' letter as a formal grounds for reunion:

> And everyone together [in the Byzantine caucus] said, "If the Latins are persuaded by this epistle, then nothing else is required for us to unite with them" . . . Therefore the synod designated the emperor to go to the pope and ask if he received the epistle and confession of Saint Maximus.[56]

Siecienski indicates from the *Memoirs* of Sylvester Syropoulos, however, that there was substantial division in the caucus over this strategy, and that Mark Eugenicus balked:

[55]  Siecienski, *The Filioque*, 154.

[56]  *Acta graeca* (of the Council of Florence), cited and trans. Siecienski, "The Use of Maximus the Confessor's Writing on the *Filioque*," 173.

How can we unite with them when they accept, in word alone, the statement of Holy Maximus while among themselves they opine the opposite, even proclaiming it openly in their churches? No, they must first confess our teaching—clearly and without ambiguity. Only in this way will we consummate the union with them.[57]

Mark's chief opponent in the Byzantine delegation, the strong pro-unionist Basil Bassarion (an Orthodox bishop who eventually was appointed a Cardinal in the Roman Church), insisted that Maximus' letter to Marinus did make room for the Son's secondary causality of the Spirit, and proposed it on that basis to the Romans as a vehicle of reunion. Eugenicus continued to maintain the anti-*Filioque* reading of Maximus. George Scholarius stepped in to arbitrate, but to no avail, as the Latins ultimately refused to admit Maximus' letter, read either way, as a formula for unity.

By the end of the council, pressure from the emperor and from Joseph, the Patriarch of Constantinople, led all the Byzantine delegates except Eugenicus to sign off on an agreement stating that the Son was indeed *a* cause (though not *the* cause) of the Spirit's procession. Florence was a complete victory for the Romans, and the Byzantine delegation returned to Constantinople soured by their own capitulation. Siecienski is certainly right that Maximus' letter to Marinus may not have provided a satisfactory basis for reconciliation, but discussion of it went far to clarify substantive differences of perspective East and West on the procession of the Spirit.[58] Siecienski's rightly judges, furthermore, that a great opportunity was lost by the failure of the two sides to come to terms with the spirit of Maximus' letter, which in its simplicity and economy of words still exemplified a real common ground.[59]

## MAXIMUS' LEGACY IN THE HESYCHAST CONTROVERSY

The fourteenth-century hesychast controversy was a critical cross-roads in the spiritual theology of Eastern Christianity, but it was more

---

[57] Mark Eugenicus, in Syropoulos's *Memoirs*, quoted and trans. Siecienski, *The Filioque*, 160.
[58] *The Filioque*, 198–206.     [59] Ibid., 206–11.

than that, for it overlapped with the larger debate in the Byzantine scholastic age over the relation between theology and philosophy.[60] Indeed, it interfaced with philosophical interest in the character of mystical experience and religious epistemology, and thus played its own contributing role in cultural self-definition in the late Byzantine period.[61] As Antoine Lévy notes, moreover, this debate foregrounded the basic issue of *who* truly had the ability to speak authoritatively of things divine (i.e. the monastic sage, the academic theologian or philosopher, the cleric?).[62] The controversy even bled over into the political arena, since powerful monks like Gregory Palamas carried great weight in the attempt to negotiate peace amid a political coup and resultant civil war (1341–47).[63]

The hesychast controversy pitted two immense figures against each other: Gregory Palamas (1296–1359), the preeminent exponent of hesychasm, a monk of Mt. Athos and eventual Metropolitan of Thessaloniki; and Barlaam the Calabrian (*c*.1290–1349), a Greek monk-scholar from southern Italy who came to Constantinople and won imperial favor for his expertise in Aristotelian philosophy.[64] While it is inaccurate to caricature this as a simple clash between mysticism and rationalism (as it has sometimes been cast), there is no question that two seemingly irreconcilable approaches to sublime knowledge of God collided. Standing in the tradition of Symeon the New Theologian and other great hesychasts before him, Palamas envisioned a spiritual serenity (ἡσυχία) engaging the whole body, and the whole panoply of psychosomatic faculties, in the quest for

---

[60] See Gerard Podskalsky, *Theologie und Philosophie in Byzanz: Die Streit um die theologische Methodik in der spätbyzantinischen Geistesgeschichte (14./15. Jh.): Seine systematischen Grundlagen und seine historische Entwicklung* (Munich: C. H. Beck, 1977), 124–80.

[61] On this interface, see Niketas Siniossoglou, *Radical Platonism in Byzantium: Utopia and Illumination in Gemistos Plethon* (Cambridge: Cambridge University Press, 2011), 93–124; Tatakis, *Byzantine Philosophy*, 217–30.

[62] *Le créé et l'incréé: Maxime le Confesseur et Thomas d'Aquin* (Paris: Vrin, 2006), 10.

[63] On Gregory Palamas's role in the political turbulence in Constantinople (1341–7), see John Meyendorff, *A Study of Gregory Palamas* (Crestwood, NY: St. Vladimir's Seminary Press, 1998), 63–85.

[64] On the broader hesychast controversy, see John Meyendorff, *St. Gregory Palamas and Orthodox Spirituality* (Crestwood, NY: St. Vladimir's Seminary Press, 1974), 71–172; id., *A Study of Gregory Palamas*, 42–62, 134–56, 202–27; Dirk Krausmüller, "The Rise of Hesychasm," in Michael Angold, ed., *The Cambridge History of Christianity*, vol. 5: *Eastern Christianity* (Cambridge: Cambridge University Press, 2006), 101–26.

sublime encounter with God—indeed, a robust physical and spiritual vision of the glorious light of the transfiguration. Besides lampooning certain hesychastic practices like the navel-focused "prayer of the heart," Barlaam rebuked Palamas and his disciples for claiming the possibility of direct knowledge of God and unmitigated vision of uncreated divine light. An interpreter of Dionysian apophaticism through a strict philosophical key, Barlaam took the Areopagite's negative theology to the extreme of denying both conceptual *and experiential* access to the inner reality of God. Looking much the philosophical nominalist, he insisted that access to God could normatively come only through careful logical inference from creation and scriptural revelation. Palamas, though respectful of Aristotelian logic, did not believe it could dictate the terms of divine transcendence and immanence. Gregory's own celebrated distinction between the inaccessible divine essence and the uncreated but participable "energies" of God, which allow a relative but gracious access to God's nature,[65] framed his robust perspective on the experience of deification. The advantage of this distinction was that it safeguarded the divine transcendence but also affirmed the freedom of God to be "really" present in his energies (i.e. virtues, attributes, intentions, activities *ad extra*), the latter being verified in the incarnation itself.[66]

Not without justification, Palamas read Maximus as a faithful hesychast, and numerous Maximian emphases reappear in Gregory's theological anthropology and ascetical doctrine.[67] In his *Triads* and other works, Palamas appealed to Maximus in opposing Barlaam and his disciples. One such appeal was to support his differentiation of divine essence and uncreated divine energies, a doctrine that is rather basic in the Confessor though not developed with the intensity we find in Palamas himself.[68] It seems odd that he did not exploit, in this

---

[65] *Triads* 3.1.23; 3.2.5–18; 3.3.6–10, Greek text ed. John Meyendorff, *Grégoire Palamas: Défense des saints hesychastes* (Leuven: Spicilegium Sacrum Louvaniense, 1959), 601, 651–77, 707–15.

[66] See *Triads* 3.3.5 (Meyendorff, 703–5).

[67] In *Triads* 2.2.19 (Meyendorff, 361–3), for example, Gregory appropriates Maximus' notion of *apatheia* as a positive reorientation of the soul's faculties, and reiterates the beneficial "use" (χρῆσις) of the epithymetic and thymetic drives in providing momentum for the pursuit of virtue and deification.

[68] Ibid. 3.2.7, 9 (Meyendorff, 655–6, 661), citing Maximus, *Th. Oec.* 1.48–50 (PG 90:1100C–1101B). The most extensive attempt to trace the development of the distinction of divine essence and energies in Maximus is Karayiannis, *Maxime le Confesseur: Essence et énergies de Dieu*.

connection, Maximus' doctrine of the *logoi*. This can be explained, however, first by the fact that nowhere does Maximus explicitly equate the *logoi* with God's *uncreated* energies, although some interpreters have considered them virtually the same.[69] Second, as Maximos Constas observes, exploiting Maximus' doctrine of the *logoi* could easily play into Barlaam's hands since the Calabrian had already laid claim to the doctrine, proposing that the *logoi*, being grounded in the Creator's mind, have corresponding "images" in the soul which, if epistemically apprehended, lead the reasoning mind to the knowledge of God.[70] Among the specific texts in play, one was Maximus' statement that "he who has been rendered worthy to be in God will, by a certain simple and undivided knowledge, come to perceive as preexisting in God all the principles of created things."[71] Another was his assertion that only in gazing on—and aspiring to nuptial union with—the Logos immanent in created reality would one so advanced acquire knowledge of the *logoi*.[72] These are among Palamas's few references to Maximus' theory of *logoi*, and it appears that he is countering Barlaam's appeal to the same texts. As Gregory clarifies, he and Maximus concur that this is a special, graced vision of God granted to the spiritual senses of those being deified,[73] not an intelligence acquired by human reason.

Palamas was also keenly aware of Maximus' evocative interpretation of the transfiguration, believing it to support his projection of a sublime participation in the glorious, uncreated light of God for those deemed worthy. Barlaam too had claimed Maximus' authority here, focusing on the Confessor's description of the transfigured face of Jesus as a "symbol of his divinity"[74] as proof that he too believed that the disciples, and by extension the hesychasts, could only encounter the light indirectly and symbolically. Having cited other patristic authorities to oppose the idea that the light was merely a created symbol, Gregory responded that Maximus was using "symbol" in a very specific sense, akin to how he used it elsewhere in his interpretation of the transfiguration, when he

[69] e.g. Karayiannis, *Maxime le Confesseur: Essence et énergies de Dieu*, 207. See also pp. 112–13 in this volume.
[70] "St. Maximus the Confessor: The Reception of His Thought East and West," 44–6.
[71] *Th. Oec.* 2.4 (PG 90:1128A), quoted by Palamas, *Triads* 3.3.10 (Meyendorff, 713).
[72] *Myst.* 5 (CCSG 69:30), quoted by Palamas, *Triads* 3.3.10 (Meyendorff, 713).
[73] *Triads* 3.3.10 (Meyendorff, 713–15).
[74] *Amb. Jo.* 10 (PG 91:1128A); ibid. (1165D). See also Meyendorff, *A Study of Gregory Palamas*, 196–8.

spoke of the light as symbolic of the two modes of theology, apophatic and kataphatic, in order to make an epistemological point, not to deny the experienced reality of uncreated light.[75] The light belongs to those participable realities "around God" (περὶ θεόν) which have no beginning or end.[76]

The overriding issue here was the nature of deification itself. John Meyendorff has emphasized in his extensive work on Palamas and the hesychast controversy that Gregory found in Maximus a precedent for his bold realism in depicting deification, especially as grounded in the mystery of the incarnation.[77] He drew, for example, upon Maximus' description of deification as "unoriginated" (ἀγένητος), which a scholiast (possibly Maximus himself) defined as "enhypostatic (ἐνυπόστατον) illumination from the Godhead, such as has no origin but registers incomprehensible for those deemed worthy of it."[78] By *enhypostaton* here, the scholiast was indicating not that a divine hypostasis subsumes the human hypostasis of the deified believer, but that the beginningless divine energy *in reality* (i.e. as grounded in the divine essence) penetrates that person in a way that defies his or her own comprehension.[79] This parallels the fact that deification is a sheer gift of divine grace. Otherwise put, deification transforms human nature but is not naturally acquired. Christians derivatively share, moreover, in the ultimate circumincession (περιχώρησις) of the divine and the human accomplished once for all in Jesus Christ, a participation sustained through the indwelling of the Holy Spirit.

In hindsight, we must acknowledge that Palamas's battle, of course, was not Maximus'. Maximus had no proxy of Barlaam against whom he had to elaborate and defend his views of human transformation through the grace of the incarnate and transfigured Lord. His extensive teaching on deification arose, as Jean-Claude Larchet has ably shown, from every

---

[75]  *Triads* 3.1.13 (Meyendorff, 583–5).

[76]  Ibid. 3.1.19 (Meyendorff, 595). Gregory appears to be citing *Th. Oec.* 1.48 (PG 90:1000D), but there the participable realities are not explicitly said to be "around God." The phrase is nonetheless consistent with Maximus' usage elsewhere, e.g. *Car.* 2.27 (PG 90:992C-D), where the things περὶ θεόν include his eternity, infinity and illimitability, goodness, wisdom, and power as Creator; also *Amb. Jo.* 15 (PG 91:1220C), referring to the "infinity around God" that is not God himself.

[77]  See *A Study of Gregory Palamas*, 175–8, 181.

[78]  *Q. Thal.* 61 (CCSG 22:101, ll. 296–7) and Schol. 16 (p. 111, ll. 71–3); cited by Palamas, *Triads* 3.1.28 (Meyendorff, 611).

[79]  On this language of *enhypostaton* in Maximus and Palamas, see Meyendorff, *A Study of Gregory Palamas*, 216–18.

major domain of his thought.[80] Apart from its role in his reprimand of radical Origenists,[81] however, it was rarely polemically charged. It is because, drawing on his own diverse array of sources (Origen and Clement, Pseudo-Macarius, the Cappadocians, Evagrius, Dionysius, et al.), Maximus positively framed a vision of the ascetical and contemplative life within a refreshed Christology and a highly nuanced and multifaceted doctrine of deification that he became a vital link in the pre-Palamite history of hesychasm and a foundational source for Gregory himself. Since, moreover, councils at Constantinople in 1341 formally vindicated Palamas and censured Barlaam, Maximus' privileged place in the hesychast tradition was secured all the more.

## MAXIMUS IN THE TRADITION
## OF THE *PHILOKALIA*

An effective measure of Maximus' long-term legacy in the Eastern monastic tradition, a crucially important channel of his posthumous influence, is his status in the *Philokalia*, Orthodoxy's spiritual treasury and handbook compiled at Mount Athos in the eighteenth century by Nicodemus of the Holy Mountain and Macarius of Corinth. The *Philokalia* was more an attempt to pan-contextualize than to recontextualize Maximus and other monastic sages, since its ethos was the recovery and perpetuation of an ascetical and contemplative wisdom that its editors believed speaks timelessly to monastics and non-monastics alike.[82] Maximus was, with Peter of Damascus (twelfth century), the writer allotted the most space among the *Philokalia*'s more than thirty contributing authors, which can hardly be coincidental. Indeed, Kallistos Ware, one of the editor-translators of the *Philokalia* in English, maintains that its very nucleus is "the Evagrian-Maximian orientation" in which the

---

[80] *La divinisation de l'homme*, passim. See also Norman Russell, *The Doctrine of Deification in the Greek Patristic Tradition* (Oxford: Oxford University Press, 2004), 262–95.

[81] See esp. *Amb. Jo.* 7 (PG 91:1072D–1077B).

[82] On the background and editorial ethos of the *Philokalia*, see Kallistos Ware, "St. Nikodemos and the *Philokalia*," in Bingaman and Nassif, *The Philokalia*, 9–35; John McGuckin, "The Making of the *Philokalia*: A Tale of Monks and Manuscripts," ibid., 36–49.

spiritual life is ordered to the threefold regimen of ascetical practice (πρᾶξις), contemplation of nature (θεωρία φυσική), and mystical theology (θεολογία).[83]

The *Philokalia* reproduced Maximus' *Chapters on Love*, *Chapters on Theologia and Oikonomia*, an anthology of *varia* from other works (*Q. Thal., Ep., Amb.*, and some anonymous scholia attributed to Maximus), and lastly the *Commentary on the Lord's Prayer*.[84] Here in effect were works definitive of a "philokalic" theology and worldview. While I cannot analyze at length Maximus' strategic importance in the *Philokalia*, a few general observations are in order about why the Confessor's work enjoyed special esteem. The first is obvious enough from the priority given his *Chapters on Love*. At one level, the *Philokalia* ("Love of Divine Beauty") is itself a vast exploration of the polymorphous gift of divine love, goodness, and wisdom, and of the ways that these form and condition human disciplines of prayer and hesychasm, self-mortification, the practice of charity and the virtues in the imitation of Christ, the contemplation of natural and scriptural revelation, and the relentless mystical quest for (and experience of) deification. Maximus, as we observed in the preceding chapter, couched his own teaching on love, and so too his entire asceticism, within a highly articulated theological anthropology that envisioned the transformation of the whole of human nature, including the passible and emotional self, the *desiring* self in all its complexity. The notion of the virtuous "use" of desire, anger, and other passions is fairly pervasive in the *Philokalia*, as is the revision of *apatheia* as "engaged dispassion," a revision to which he was a pivotal contributor.[85]

Doubtless another reason for Maximus' prominence in the *Philokalia* is that he was considered a key reviser of the Clementine–Origenian–Evagrian heritage of "gnostic" contemplation and spiritual *paideia*, all the more so since the Cappadocian Fathers, who had also reworked that tradition, were not included in the anthology. Even if Origenist cosmology and eschatology were scarcely at issue by the time the *Philokalia* was produced, Evagrius's austere terminology and recondite teaching on contemplation (θεωρία) and spiritual

---

[83] "St. Nikodemos and the *Philokalia*," 29–31.

[84] See Palmer, Sherrard, and Ware, *The Philokalia: The Complete Text*, 2:49–50 and Appendix, 391–5.

[85] See my analysis with citations in Paul Blowers, "Hope for the Passible Self: The Use and Transformation of the Human Passions in the Fathers of the *Philokalia*," in Bingaman and Nassif, *The Philokalia*, 216–29.

knowledge (γνῶσις) were easily offputting for non-monastic audiences. That certain of his works were included at all, however, indicates that the editors recognized his incisiveness as an ascetical theologian.[86] Several *Philokalia* authors, like John Cassian, Diadochus of Photiki, Thalassius the Libyan (Maximus' famous correspondent), Peter of Damascus, and others incorporated significant elements of Evagrian asceticism. Maximus too drew heavily from Evagrian teaching on the struggle with "thoughts" (λογισμοί) and passions, on natural contemplation and *gnosis*, on the doctrine of *logoi*, and on the principle of "pure prayer."[87] It is an oversimplification to pit Maximus' "incarnational" spirituality against Evagrius's "intellectualism,"[88] but Maximus definitely engages Evagrius critically and modifies aspects of his moral psychology and spiritual instruction.[89] And yet Maximus, unlike other authors dependent on Evagrius, had left behind a substantial criticism and correction of monastic Origenism, elaborated in the *Ambigua to John*, and, in a condensed form, in the *Chapters on Theologia and Oikonomia* that were incorporated into the *Philokalia*.[90]

Finally, while the *Chapters on Theologia and Oikonomia* (called Maximus' "most starkly challenging work" by von Balthasar[91]) still mirror Evagrius's severity respecting the struggles of acquiring spiritual knowledge (γνῶσις), and while Maximus prefaced his *Chapters on Love* with a warning that some of them would require great diligence to understand,[92] the theological anthropology of Maximus

[86] See Julia Konstantinovsky, "Evagrius in the *Philokalia* of Sts. Macarius and Nicodemus," in Bingaman and Nassif, *The Philokalia*, 175–92.
[87] The groundbreaking studies were Marcel Viller, "Aux sources de la spiritualité de saint Maxime: les oeuvres d'Évagre le Pontique," *Revue d'ascétique et de mystique* 11 (1920): 156–84, 239–68, 331–6; and Irénée-Henri Hausherr, "Ignorance infinie," *Orientalia Christiana Periodica* 2 (1936): 351–62; also Völker, *Maximus Confessor als Meister des geistlichen Lebens*, passim.
[88] This tendency appears with von Balthasar's fairly dismissive early attitude toward Evagrian spiritualism and anti-materialism. See his "Die Metaphysik und Mystik des Evagrius Ponticus," *Zeitschrift für Aszese und Mystik* 14 (1939): 31–47. Later he was willing to concede some edifying influence of Evagrius on Maximus (*Cosmic Liturgy*, 47, 62–3). For a more balanced assessment of Maximus' relation to Evagrius, see Marcus Plested, "The Ascetic Tradition," *OHMC*, 165–8; and Thunberg, *Microcosm and Mediator*, 233–4, 248–59, 284–98, 302–22, 355–68.
[89] For a demonstration of this, see Maximos Constas, "Evagrios Pontikos, St. Maximos the Confessor, and the *Chapters on Love*" (unpublished essay available online: <https://independent.academia.edu/FrMaximosConstas>).
[90] Sherwood (*Date-List*, 35) and von Balthasar (*Cosmic Liturgy*, 344–5) have both viewed *Th. Oec.* 1.1–10 as a kind of précis of Maximus' anti-Origenist position.
[91] *Cosmic Liturgy*, 344.     [92] *Car.* Prol. (PG 90:960B).

engrained in his ascetical writings reached beyond monastics to a broader audience. Maximus' "cosmo-politeian" vision enjoined on all creatures an appropriate and proportionate asceticism,[93] with human beings uniquely positioned as the key link in creation and as participants in Christ's cosmic ministry of mediation and reconciliation.[94] In the *Commentary on the Lord's Prayer*, the last of his works appearing in the *Philokalia*, Maximus specifically depicted the Prayer as instruction from Christ, the mediator between God and the world who both revealed the Father and gave access to him through the Holy Spirit. In the *Commentary* Maximus sought to unfold the Prayer's deep integration of *theologia* and *oikonomia*, and of divine incarnation and human deification, in a way that framed the ascetical and contemplative disciplines of *all* Christians who collectively voice the Prayer in worship and in life.

## MAXIMUS IN MODERN EASTERN ORTHODOX THEOLOGY

Even if Maximus was of little interest to post-Tridentine Catholic theologians and to the Protestant Reformers and their heirs in the early modern period, new seasons of reengagement awaited his legacy in modern Orthodox thought.[95] An especially intriguing admiration for Maximus developed, for example, among some of the Slavophile philosophers and theologians in nineteenth-century Russia who were already avid readers of the *Philokalia* in its Slavonic translation from 1793 (though Maximus' works, amazingly, were not in this version). The pioneering Slavophile littérateur and philosopher Ivan Kireevsky (1806–56) gravitated to Maximus while reading him under the spiritual direction of two elders (*startsi*), Philaret of the Novospassky Monastery in Moscow, and particularly Makary of the revered Optina Pustyn Monastery southwest of Moscow. He even strengthened his competence in Greek specifically to refine Russian translation of the

---

[93] See pp. 130–4 in this volume.     [94] See pp. 127–8 in this volume.
[95] For an extended survey of Maximus' reception in modern Orthodox thought, see Andrew Louth, "Maximus the Confessor's Influence and Reception in Byzantine and Modern Orthodoxy," *OHMC*, 500–15.

Confessor.[96] At one time beguiled by German Romanticism and Idealism (he had met Hegel in person and diligently read Schelling), the mystically-inclined Kireevsky re-envisioned the Gospel through the lens of the Greek Fathers. Maximus and other patristic thinkers, with their deep sense of the "wholeness" of the human self as the subject and contemplator of revelation, provided Kireevsky a salutary alternative to the grievous Western enthronement of critical reason above all other elements of the self in its encounter with divine truth. They provided the model of a philosophical hesychasm, as it were, that integrated the mind's highest philosophical quest with the aspiration of faith arising from out of the psychosomatic unity of human nature.[97]

In the next generation of Slavophile sages, Vladimir Soloviev (1853–1900) also absorbed Maximus and, though discouraging a mere reduplication of the Confessor's project in the changed context of nineteenth-century Russia,[98] factored Maximus' "theandric" principle in Christology and soteriology into his own developed notion of "Godmanhood" (*bogochelovechestvo*). Soloviev's engagement of Maximus on this theme is more associative than demonstrable since he does not routinely cite the Confessor (or other patristic sources), but he extolled Maximus' philosophical and mystical achievement and wrote an encyclopedia essay on him,[99] and numerous scholars have affirmed Maximus' deep influence.[100] In his *Lectures on Godmanhood*

---

[96]   Nikolay Lossky, *History of Russian Philosophy* (London: Allen & Unwin, 1952), 15.

[97]   See esp. Kireevsky's essay "On the Necessity and Possibility of New Principles in Philosophy" (1856), trans. Boris Jakim and Robert Bird, in *On Spiritual Unity: A Slavophile Reader* (Hudson, NY: Lindisfarne Books), 234–73.

[98]   "On Spiritual Authority in Russia," trans. Vladimir Wozniuk, in *Freedom, Faith, and Dogma: Essays by V. S. Soloviev on Christianity and Judaism* (Albany: SUNY Press, 2008), 26.

[99]   On this essay ("Maksim Ispovednik") for the Russian *Brockhaus and Efron Encyclopedic Dictionary*, see Manon de Courten, *History, Sophia and the Russian Nation: A Reassessment of Vladimir Solov'ëv's Views on History and His Social Commitment* (Bern: Peter Lang, 2004), 113–16. Courten notes that Soloviev focused mainly on two themes: (1) Maximus' battle with monotheletism, evincing his commitment to the preservation of human freedom in Christ; and (2) his favorable attitude toward the papacy (which Soloviev aimed against the anti-Catholicism of his arch-conservative Orthodox peers in Russia).

[100]   Cf. M.-J. Le Guillou, "De Maxime le Confesseur à Vladimir Soloviev," Preface to Garrigues, *Maxime le Confesseur*, 7–22; von Balthasar, *The Glory of the Lord: A Theological Aesthetics*, vol. 3: *Studies in Theological Style: Lay Styles*, trans. Andrew Louth et al. (San Francisco: Ignatius Press, 2004), 288, 310–11, 315, 338; Richard Gustafson, "Soloviev's Doctrine of Salvation," in Judith Kornblatt and Richard

(delivered 1877–84), Soloviev reflected on the inner "necessity" of divine self-revelation, and argued that its trinitarian form included the Divine's self-possession (Father), the Divine's counterposing to itself, realizing itself as self-determining and as an object of itself (the Son/ Word), and the Divine's asserting and preserving itself, and finding itself in its "other" returning to it (the Spirit).[101] This may appear quite foreign to Maximus' own trinitarian teaching, but its christological correlate is congenial, for Soloviev claimed that in Jesus Christ alone the Divine was "realized" or revealed as "all," embracing plurality, differentiation, and particularity while also being the principle of unity and wholeness.[102] The miracle, for Soloviev, is that this revelation is not an abstraction but a "living (and 'universal') organism,"[103] the "spiritual man," the Second Adam, the theandric person intervening in the very middle of history as the fullest and final theophany.[104] Like Maximus (and Irenaeus), then, Soloviev candidly declared that the incarnation of Jesus Christ was originally essential to the very plan of creation.[105] He also reclaimed the identification of Christ, the "universal organism," as the divine *Wisdom* (*Sophia*) as well as Word (*Logos*), and as the "ideal of perfect humanity," who restores creation to its true beginning and inaugurates the mystery of deification.[106]

The prolific émigré theologian Sergius Bulgakov (1871–1944), an ex-Marxist and a keen disciple of Soloviev's work, found in Maximus' conception of the cosmic *logoi* an inspiration for his controversial Sophiology, which envisioned the divine Wisdom, transcendent but also immanent in the world, intervening "between" (μεταξύ) eternity and temporality, between being and nothing, embodying God's gracious solidarity with his creation, and providing the condition for the cosmos, through humanity, to reciprocate with its own creaturely wisdom and

Gustafson, eds., *Russian Religious Thought* (Madison: University of Wisconsin Press, 1996), 45–7.

[101] *Lectures on Godmanhood*, trans. Peter Zouboff (London: D. Dobson, 1948; reprinted San Rafael, CA: Semantron, 2007), Lecture 6, 130–44; Lecture 7, 145–50.

[102] Ibid., Lecture 7, 152–7.     [103] Ibid., 153, 154, 155.

[104] *The Spiritual Foundations of Life* (1882–1884), trans. Donald Attwater under the title *God, Man and the Church* (Cambridge: James Clarke, 1937), 113–31; *Lectures on Godmanhood*, Lectures 11–12, 192–6.

[105] *The Spiritual Foundations of Life* (= *God, Man and the Church*), 118.

[106] *Lectures on Godmanhood*, Lecture 7, 154–5; Lecture 8, 159–64; Lecture 9, 165–75; Lectures 11–12, 192–207.

freedom, the fulfillment of its vocation.[107] Bulgakov explicitly says of Maximus that "his 'logology' is essentially a sophiology."[108]

Bulgakov was also drawn to the apophaticism of Dionysius and Maximus, in particular their shared principle of the divine "no-thing" that defies all essence or being, subverts the pretentions of reason and metaphysics, and abolishes the delusion of pantheism.[109] Bulgakov revered the fact that a "dogmatic" and "kataphatic" theologian like Maximus conveyed an "alogical" and "adogmatic" mysticism (i.e. a mysticism akin to Neoplatonism and not necessarily conditioned by Christian faith) while also demonstrating that such mysticism did not exhaust religious experience. "Accompanying that NOT towards which [Maximus'] negative theology and mysticism lead is the YES of religion, the Word uttered by Divinity and filling the universe with its thunder."[110] Like Soloviev, Bulgakov understood that Christian apophaticism carried inseparably with it a gospel of divine condescension and incarnation, and of Wisdom empowering the creature toward authentic freedom and fullness. Bulgakov was not all positive, however, about Maximus' Christology, arguing that his dispute with monotheletes was largely "academic," that his grounding of will in nature rather than in "the life of the spirit" was faulty, and that his denial of gnomic will in Christ bordered on destroying Christ's real human freedom.[111]

Thematic echoes from Maximus resound throughout Bulgakov's work, even when he is not declaring an immediate dependence on the Confessor. For example, Bulgakov argues that the very basis of divine creation of the world is the Creator's sacrificial love for an "other" displayed most perfectly in the cross—a perspective strongly reminiscent of Maximus and Irenaeus alike.

> The creation of the world by God, the self-bifurcation of the Absolute, is the sacrifice of the Absolute for the sake of the relative, which becomes for it "other" (*thateron*), a creative sacrifice of love. Golgotha was not only eternally pre-established at the creation of the world as an event in time, but it also constitutes the metaphysical essence of creation. The

[107] Cf. *Sophia, the Wisdom of God: An Outline of Sophiology* (1937), trans. Patrick Thompson et al. (reprinted Hudson, NY: Lindisfarne Press, 1993), 63–6; id., *Unfading Light: Contemplations and Speculations* (1917), trans. Thomas Allan Smith (Grand Rapids, MI: Eerdmans, 2012), 214–83; id., *The Lamb of God* (1933), trans. Boris Jakim (Grand Rapids, MI: Eerdmans, 2008), 89–156.
[108] *The Lamb of God*, 126, n. 6.   [109] *Unfading Light*, 103–10, 125–30.
[110] Ibid., 130.   [111] *Lamb of God*, 76–9.

divine "it is accomplished" proclaimed from the cross, embraces all being, refers to all creation ... The world is founded by the cross, taken upon himself by God in the name of love.[112]

Bulgakov resumed another striking Maximian theme as well—the divine "play" in creation—and with something of the same force. God's creativity is a form of play, not as a mere show of omnipotence but as a function of "ecstatic" love and a bid for fellowship with the creation.

It is not this *jeu divin* [of displayed omnipotence] that God's love wants in creating the world, and in Scripture "play" is ascribed not to God but to his Wisdom which by perceiving the revelation of divine creativity, feels joy and rapture through it. In creating, the trihypostatic God summons polyhypostaseity to life; he wants to multiply in the "children of God," to find friends for himself among them. But a son and friend is not a toy or object: once having called him to life, God himself respects his freedom and takes it into account. Having recognized this freedom and introduced it as one of the defining forces in the life of the world, God seemingly limits his omnipotence in its ways for the sake of humankind.[113]

Whereas Bulgakov interprets the divine "play" and "rapture" sophiologically, Maximus had ascribed them to the Creator himself in terms of the folly/wisdom (1 Cor. 1:19ff.) of divine incarnation, the mutual ecstasy of Creator and creation, and the ongoing providential work of the Logos to "tease" the freedom of creatures to their own benefit.[114]

The next significant Eastern interpreter of Maximus was Bulgakov's younger fellow-émigré and one-time colleague at the St. Sergius Institute in Paris, Georges Florovsky (1893–1979), an inspirer of the "neo-patristic synthesis" in twentieth-century Orthodox theology.[115] Like Bulgakov, Florovsky benefited greatly from the groundbreaking work on Maximus' doctrine by the Ukrainian historical theologian Sergius Epifanovich (1886–1918).[116] Florovsky, under Epifanovich's

---

[112] *Unfading Light*, 185.     [113] Ibid., 343.

[114] *Amb. Jo.* 71 (PG 91:1408C–1416D); also Blowers, "On the 'Play' of Divine Providence in Gregory Nazianzen and Maximus the Confessor;" and pp. 86–7 in this volume.

[115] On Florovsky and the development and diversification of the neo-patristic movement in modern Orthodox theology, see Paul Ladouceur, "Treasures New and Old: Landmarks of Orthodox Neopatristic Theology," *St. Vladimir's Theological Quarterly* 56 (2012): 191–227.

[116] *Prepodobnyi Maksim Ispovednik i vizantiiskoe bogoslovie* (*The Blessed Maximus the Confessor and Byzantine Theology*) (Kiev, 1915). On Epifanovich and modern

influence, deemed Maximus the capstone of the Greek patristic synthesis of scriptural revelation and Hellenic philosophical tradition, and judged Maximus' work a parallel to his own "new Christian synthesis" responding to new challenges.[117] Florovsky's most concentrated analysis of Maximus, in a volume on the Byzantine Fathers, argued that the doctrine of revelation was a crucial theme in the Confessor's thought—perhaps not surprising in a period when, in the West, Karl Barth's theology was coming to the forefront. Like Bulgakov, Florovsky acknowledged Maximus' uncompromising apophaticism coupled with deep conviction about God's condescension to engrace and enrapture the creature; so too he determined that Maximus had recovered the Logos of pre-Nicene theology, the Logos who through the *logoi* brings creatures into existence from nothing (τὸ μὴ ὄν) and reveals his will for the world, even though the full revelation awaits the incarnation of the Word.[118] Absent from Florovsky, however, was Bulgakov's sophiological reinterpretation of creation and revelation in Maximus.[119] Sophiology undoubtedly detracted, in Florovsky's perspective on Maximus, from the absolute primacy of Jesus Christ as the mediator of creation and redemption and as the supreme content of divine self-revelation.[120] Florovsky also insisted that the interpretation of Maximus required due attention to his asceticism as a crucial register of his dogmatic theology, calling his overall achievement a "symphony of spiritual experience" rather than a doctrinal system as such.[121]

Another instrumental figure in the neo-patristic synthesis, Vladimir Lossky (1903–58), referenced Maximus abundantly in his highly influential reconstruction of the principal features of Eastern Christian mystical theology.[122] In the latter twentieth century, however, the Romanian theologian Dumitru Staniloae (1903–93), another

---

scholarship on Maximus in Russia, see Grigory Benevich, "Maximus' Heritage in Russia and Ukraine," *OHMC*, 460–79.

[117] So suggests Paul Gavrilyuk, "Georges Florovsky's Reading of Maximus: Anti-Bulgakov or Pro-Bulgakov," in Vasiljević, 410–11.

[118] *The Byzantine Fathers of the Sixth to Eighth Century*, 215–18, 222–4.

[119] On the difference between Bulgakov and Florovsky here, see Gavrilyuk, "Georges Florovsky's Reading of Maximus," 414–15.

[120] See *The Byzantine Fathers of the Sixth to Eighth Century*, 226–46.

[121] Ibid., 213.

[122] *The Mystical Theology of the Eastern Church*, passim; id., *The Vision of God*, trans. Ashleigh Moorhouse, 2nd edn. (Leighton Buzzard, UK: Faith Press, 1973), 99–110.

contributor to the neo-patristic synthesis, emerged as arguably the most incisive interpreter of Maximus for contemporary Eastern Orthodoxy. Early on Staniloae composed a monograph on Maximus' Christology (1943), translated and annotated works of Maximus in Romanian, and incorporated his translation into the Romanian version of the *Philokalia*.[123] His scholia on the *Ambigua* remain among the finest commentaries on the text.[124] Staniloae also had Maximus as a formative source for his multi-volume *Orthodox Dogmatic Theology*, with hopes of recontextualizing the Confessor's christocentric cosmic theology for Orthodox churches faced with all new cultural, social, and ethical challenges. Familiar themes from Maximus resurface, such as the cruciformity of creation,[125] the *logoi* as divine "intentions" (which Staniloae saw as embodying the "malleable rationality of the world" and the Creator's freedom to effect new possibilities in the world through humanity),[126] and the exalted role of humanity as the micro-cosm of creation.[127]

The technical features of the Christology of Maximus (on natures, wills, hypostasis, etc.) were largely definitive for Staniloae,[128] but he sought to retrieve as well Maximus' emphasis on Christ's remaking of the human being as a participating agent in the renewal and trans-formation of creation. Under Maximus' inspiration, furthermore, Staniloae unapologetically affirmed the anthropocentricity of created nature itself, and nature's intrinsic "elasticity" vis-à-vis the unfolding rationality of the world as a whole, in keeping with the Creator's dynamic relationship with his creation.[129] Indeed Staniloae, more than any other modern interpreter except Loudovikos, enhanced the Max-imian view of nature as fecund gift and as reflecting the infinite resourcefulness and creative prowess of the triune God.[130] Ascetically,

---

[123] See Calinic Berger, "A Contemporary Synthesis of St. Maximus' Theology: The Work of Fr. Dumitru Stăniloae," in Vasiljević, 389–95.

[124] A French translation by Aurel Grigoras of the Romanian original of these annotations appears as an appendix to Emmanuel Ponsoye, trans., *Saint Maxime le Confesseur: Ambigua* (Paris and Suresnes: Éditions de l'Ancre, 1994), 373–540.

[125] See *The Experience of God: Orthodox Dogmatic Theology*, vol. 2: *The World: Creation and Deification*, trans. Ioan Ionita and Robert Barringer (Brookline, MA: Holy Cross Orthodox Press, 2000), 21–7.

[126] Ibid., 2:15, 16, 27–43, 45.      [127] Ibid., 2:18–19.

[128] See *The Experience of God: Orthodox Dogmatic Theology*, vol. 3: *The Person of Jesus Christ as God and Savior*, trans. Ioan Ionita (Brookline, MA: Holy Cross Orthodox Press, 2011), 25–84.

[129] *The Experience of God*, 2:7–19, 21–63, 80–112.

[130] See esp. ibid. 2:1–7, 21–4.

human beings, as the image of God, are to "use" their own shared nature
(in its present passible and mortal condition) in building each other up
and mirroring the perfection of their nature realized by Christ.[131] But
Staniloae extended that asceticism to the responsible Christian use of
created nature as a whole, undertaken in science, technology, and the
arts, and in this connection he began to articulate a Christian theology
of work.[132]

In Orthodoxy more recently, the Greek theologians John Zizioulas
(1931–) and Christos Yannaras (1935–) have drawn considerable
attention to their rereading of Maximus in terms of a Personalist
philosophy critical of Greek metaphysics.[133] Earlier I noted Zizioulas's
claim that Maximus helped achieve a breakthrough, elevating the
uniquely Christian notion of "person" above the Greek notion of
"nature," seeking to exalt the principles of freedom and communion
above all "ontological necessity."[134] In his book *Being and Communion*
(1985), Zizioulas writes:

> The idea of *ekstasis* signifies that God is love, and as such He creates an
> immanent relationship of love *outside Himself*. The emphasis placed on
> the words "outside Himself" is particularly important, since it signifies
> that love as *ekstasis* gives rise not to an emanation in the neoplatonic
> sense, but to an otherness of being which is seen as responding and
> returning to its original cause. In Maximus this idea receives a more
> complete and definite treatment, because his approach is not ultimately
> related to cosmology, as in Dionysius, but to the trinitarian being of
> God. Likewise, the distinction between essence and energy in God
> serves to indicate the relationship between God and the world as
> ontological otherness bridged by love, but *not* by "nature" or by
> "essence" . . . The principal object of [apophatic] theology is to remove
> the question of truth and knowledge from the domain of Greek theories
> of ontology in order to situate it within that of love and communion.[135]

Later, in his *Communion and Otherness* (2007) Zizioulas enhanced
his attribution to Maximus of the idea of an otherness and personhood piercing the constraints of nature. Here he deduces that for the
Confessor, it was the Logos *as Person*, not as divine Mind or some

---

[131]  Ibid., 2:86–112.      [132]  Ibid., 2:2–7, 43–63.
[133]  On the Personalism of Zizioulas and Yannaras in context, see Ladouceur,
"Treasures New and Old," 206–9.
[134]  See my discussion on pp. 155, 185–6, 205–6 in this volume.
[135]  Zizioulas, *Being as Communion*, 91, 92.

other "natural" property of God, who contained the *logoi* of creatures and enabled "the intervention of personhood between God and creation."[136] The composite hypostasis of Jesus Christ was itself the ultimate liberation from the force of nature.

Zizioulas's critics, among the most incisive being Nikolaos Loudovikos and Jean-Claude Larchet, have disputed his approach to Maximus and the Greek Fathers on several points, suggesting that he anachronistically superimposes modern existentialist-personalist categories on these ancient writers, and identifies "nature" more as an ontological yoke than as a gift supporting personhood. In place of the ontological necessity of nature that he targets, Loudovikos charges, Zizioulas appears to assert a new ontology of "dictated otherness" that actually undermines real communion between uncreated and created *natures*.[137] I have already offered my own criticism that Zizioulas's interpretation obscures Maximus' dialectical approach to "nature," inviting a confusion between nature as essence and nature as the condition or force of biological necessity. In my view Zizioulas also obfuscates Maximus' doctrine of divine and human *ekstasis*, which is an ecstasy *of* nature rather than purely *from* nature in the reciprocal communion that leads to deification. Zizioulas has answered his critics by arguing that unless the unique *person* of Christ (and the graced human person) is the locus of salvation and deification, and unless "the person leads [and] the natures follow," and unless will has priority to nature in Maximus' definition of "natural will," then a (Greek) *essentialist* rather than a (biblical) *relational* ontology wins the day.[138] Nature, meanwhile, remains merely a functional "abstract universal," registering the fact that persons exercise their freedom in relation to all other persons who share that nature.[139]

---

[136] *Communion and Otherness*, 19–32, 64–8, 72–3.

[137] Loudovikos, "Person Instead of Grace and Dictated Otherness: John Zizioulas' Final Theological Position," *Heythrop Journal* 48 (2009): 1–16; id., *A Eucharistic Ontology*, 9–10. See Larchet's extensive criticisms of the "existentialisme" and "hyper-personnalisme" of Zizioulas and Yannaras in his *Personne et nature: La Trinité—le Christ—l'homme* (Paris: Cerf, 2011), 207–396.

[138] Zizioulas, "Person and Nature in the Theology of St. Maximus the Confessor," esp. 96–100. Cf. Yannaras, *Person and Eros*, 232: "The ecstatic otherness of the person is not defined by its nature, since it transcends (as otherness) the fixed boundaries of the common attributes that constitute the nature. But the person fixes the boundaries of its nature or essence, since it constitutes nature's mode of existence." Freedom is "determination of the nature by personal otherness" (p. 233).

[139] Ibid., 89, 101. Cf. Yannaras, *Person and Eros*, 232–3: "We know the Being of humanity (the mode by which a human being *is*) as personal otherness, but the

Christos Yannaras's interpretation of Maximus likewise concentrates on the release of human beings to true personhood in Christ. To this he brings a highly developed criticism of "Western" onto-theology and its negative effects on Orthodoxy, as well as a nuanced philosophical articulation of personhood in his magnum opus, *Person and Eros*, the book in which he draws most heavily from the Confessor. Yannaras's depiction of the "ecstasy" of the person as the overcoming of the individual (egocentric) self, transcending the nothingness that is being or nature without person, is exceedingly eloquent, though he too, like Zizioulas, is fighting a philosophical battle that is not Maximus' own. Albeit sharing with Zizioulas the idea that "nature" for humanity entails a "biological necessity" to be overcome, Yannaras conveys—more in keeping with Maximus—that human ecstasy is still *nature's own potential* to "stand outside" itself in relation to God, with personal will revealing *nature's own* aspiration, and Christ fulfilling nature's own ecstatic potentiality by inaugurating a new *tropos* of human nature.[140] Also more compelling in the Maximian perspective is Yannaras's dramatization of the "erotic" dimension of personal communion. Citing Maximus, he calls *erôs* a truly natural as well as personal faculty that overcomes the "oblivion of non-relation" and empowers authentic, ecstatic love.[141]

Loudovikos has challenged Zizioulas (less so Yannaras) by arguing from Maximus that the communion of persons is not purely and simply hypostatic, an interplay of wills or freedoms, but grounded in the "dialogue" between the Logos and created *natures* through the *logoi*, which are not static but "dynamic proposals from God's personal will . . . toward entities, waiting for human will/logos/response in order for creation to advance to the eschatological fullness of the 'eighth day.'"[142] Loudovikos, who has garnered some criticism of his own,[143] does not undermine the theological importance of "person"

---

personal otherness is instantiated in respect of the identity of the common characteristics of our nature in the fact of a single human existence."

[140] *Person and Eros*, 258, 262–3, 268–9.       [141] Ibid., 144–5.

[142] *A Eucharistic Ontology*, 92.

[143] e.g. Alexis Torrance, "Personhood and Patristics in Orthodox Theology," *Heythrop Journal* 52 (2011): 700–7. Torrance argues that Loudovikos has misread certain of Zizioulas's statements on "nature" and "necessity;" but I would hasten to add that Zizioulas's confusion about nature—at least in his interpretation of Maximus—easily generates criticisms like Loudovikos's since nature so routinely carries negative implications.

for Maximus, but more faithfully represents the ontological simultaneity of nature and person, and nature's enrichment of person (not just vice versa) at the levels of his Christology, cosmology, and anthropology. Ultimately Loudovikos is no less passionate about discerning a "relational" ontology in Maximus, grounded in *nature* as already imbued with the grace of potential formation and transformation in the theatre of creatures' interaction with one another and with the Creator. For now, he argues, "the Eucharist remains the *locus par excellence* of this dialogical/synergistic encounter of human logos/will with divine logical providence/judgment, which asks for this dialogue."[144]

## THEOLOGICAL RETRIEVALS OF MAXIMUS
## BEYOND THE ORTHODOX FOLD

Theological retrieval of Maximus outside the Orthodox tradition has both intensified and diversified in the last few decades. Again, I can only provide a cursory sampling. The modern critical scholarship on the Confessor, meanwhile, is far too vast to review here.[145]

### Hans Urs von Balthasar as Interpreter of Maximus

Hans Urs von Balthasar's investment in patristic theology was enormous,[146] and his devotion to Maximus was rivaled only by his keen attention to Irenaeus, Origen, Gregory of Nyssa, Augustine, and Dionysius the Areopagite. As one of the most prolific Roman Catholic thinkers of the twentieth century, with a growing non-Catholic readership as well, his work on Maximus has gone far to

---

[144] *A Eucharistic Ontology*, 93. See also pp. 186–8, 194 in this volume.

[145] For surveys of the modern critical scholarship, however, see Andrew Louth, "Recent Research on St. Maximus the Confessor: A Survey," *St. Vladimir's Theological Quarterly*, 42 (1998): 67–84; Aidan Nichols, *Byzantine Gospel: Maximus the Confessor in Recent Scholarship* (Edinburgh: T. & T. Clark, 1996); and Joshua Lollar, "The Reception of Maximian Thought in the Modern Era," *OHMC*, 564–80.

[146] On this work, see Werner Löser, *Im Geiste des Origenes: Hans Urs von Balthasar als Interpret der Theologie der Kirchenväter* (Frankfurt: Knecht, 1976), esp. on Maximus, 181–212.

correct the neglect of the Confessor in modern Western Christian thought. His *Cosmic Liturgy* (first German edition, 1941; second edition, 1961) culminated his early concentrated work on patristic theology and, as Brian Daley observes, revealed already his signature habit, more obvious in his later writing, of employing perspectives from classical and modern European literature, art, drama, and music in elucidating traditional theological themes.[147]

That said, von Balthasar's reading of Maximus in *Cosmic Liturgy* has its idiosyncrasies. In the book's very opening line, he references the Catholic theologian Franz Staudenmaier's aspiration, in nineteenth-century Germany, to counteract Hegel's pantheism by retrieving the Christian Neoplatonism of Eriugena.[148] This segues into his claim that Maximus achieved a superior synthesis and articulation of the Christian *Weltbild*, and a better answer to Hegel,[149] who reappears intermittently in *Cosmic Liturgy*, whether implicitly in von Balthasar's consistent use of a Hegelian dialectics to describe the development of Maximus' synthetic metaphysics, or explicitly in musings of often grandiose scope:

> Maximus can clearly be seen as a thinker standing between East and West. By elevating both the contemplative quest for freedom from desire, characteristic of Buddhism and Gnosticism, and the drive to construct a titanic synthesis, characteristic of Hegel, into Christian love, Maximus finds the "higher midpoint" for both approaches. Like the Buddha, he calls for an attitude toward creatures that has freed itself from self-seeking, from passion, from worldliness, but he interprets it in a Christian way as the love demanded by the Sermon on the Mount, a love like God the Father's for all creatures, both good and evil. Like Buddha and Hegel, he calls for a power of the critical and synthetic intelligence that comes within a hair's breadth of pure idealism, but he

[147] Daley, Translator's Foreword to *Cosmic Liturgy*, 15–16.
[148] *Cosmic Liturgy*, 29.
[149] See ibid., 207: "Maximus looks straight in the eye of Hegel, who clearly derived his synthetic way of thinking from the Bible—more precisely from the anthropological antitheses of the Old Testament and from that between the Bible and Hellenism, as well as from the reconciling synthesis of Christ, understood principally from a Johannine (and thus, in effect, from an Alexandrian) perspective. The difference is that the theological starting point in Hegel is kept in the shadows, while in Maximus it remains luminously open: everyone recognizes that his ontology and cosmology are extensions of his Christology, in that the synthesis of Christ's concrete person is not only God's final thought for the world but also his original plan."

situates it, too, within the sustaining power of love: more precisely, in the redeeming love of Christ, whose self-emptying indifference and conceptual openness are revealed to be—far more deeply than with Hegel or in the abstract quest for Nirvana—the almighty power that preserves the individual and personal by elevating it into the divine. This mighty fusion of Asia and Europe, which subjects all speculative power to the law of self-emptying revealed in the Incarnation, was achieved by Maximus in full consciousness of what he was doing; it allowed him, in a feat of ultimate daring, to surpass and so to overcome two opposed brands of pantheism—that of India and China, which dissolves all things in God, and that of Hegel, which constructs God out of all things.[150]

Amid postmodern suspicion of totalizing discourses and comprehensive metanarratives, von Balthasar's assertions about the breadth of Maximus' synthesis can appear overdrawn, but in his own time he was responding to a theological culture already increasingly allured to "theologies of" this and that, a culture gradually shying away from capacious syntheses and summas. Accordingly, one may fault von Balthasar for anachronistic claims about Maximus' achievement, like the claim that he paved a via media between Buddhism and Hegel. Brian Daley remarks that in the light of von Balthasar's abiding intrigue with Hegel alongside Maximus, "the ever-present danger is a gnosis, an idealism that refuses to take seriously and to value reverently the finite, ontologically dependent concrete reality of individual things."[151] Von Balthasar shows awareness of this danger, as when he states that "universal being" is "always newly brought into being from particularity."[152] And describing how the synthesis of all things in Jesus Christ is the *skopos* of the universe, he writes:

All this may seem very abstract and unpromising, but the constant repetition of this, the most universal law of being, remains nonetheless the great achievement of Maximus the Confessor. Not only did he construct here an apologia for finite, created being in the face of the overwhelming power of the transcendent world of ideas; the application of this principle to the relation between God and the world, in the hypostatic union, finally assures the world itself—even in, and precisely because of, its difference from God—a permanently valid claim to being and to a "good conscience."[153]

Certainly von Balthasar cannot be faulted for missing a point of historical fact, that Maximus was a "cosmic theologian" genuinely motivated to describe how all things ultimately fit together and find their meaning in Jesus Christ. His intellectual *habitus* may not have anticipated German idealism, but it was a contemplative-theological counterpart of Hawking's aspiration to a "theory of everything" in physics.

Von Balthasar certainly affirmed, with Lars Thunberg and others, that there was a guiding "Chalcedonian logic" operative in Maximus.[154] But he was also insistent that Maximus' christocentric cosmology grew first and foremost out of deep identification with the Gospels' narratives of the "destiny" of Jesus. Already in *Cosmic Liturgy* we see adumbrations of a "theo-dramatic" reading of Maximus that was more overt in von Balthasar's later work. As I noted in Chapter 3, Maximus does not figure nearly as prominently in the Aesthetics series (*The Glory of the Lord*) of his trilogy as in the *Theo-Drama* series.[155] In the latter series, setting in relief Jesus Christ as the preeminent hero and *persona dramatis* in the unfolding drama of creation and redemption, von Balthasar stressed Maximus' importance in moving post-Chalcedon beyond "political formulas for unity" and an orthodoxy-amid-schism to what was really needed, namely, a refocus on the biblically-elicited mystery of Christ the God-man.[156] Maximus sees through to the Jesus dramatized in the Gospels, destined for the cross, as the key to creation itself.[157] Even his more technical Christology, von Balthasar suggested, was aimed to unveil the intensity of the drama of the incarnational economy:

> If Maximus' portrayal of the reciprocal immanence of finite and infinite freedom seems somehow undramatic, we must remember two things: first,

---

[154] See pp. 135–6 in this volume.

[155] In *The Glory of the Lord*, vols. 2 and 3: *Studies in Theological Style*, trans. Andrew Louth et al. (San Francisco: Ignatius Press, 1984, 1986), Maximus does not receive his own chapter treatment, as do Irenaeus and Dionysius. Cf., however, von Balthasar's *Theo-Drama: Theological Dramatic Theory*, vol. 1: *Prolegomena*, trans. Graham Harrison (San Francisco: Ignatius Press, 1988), 249; ibid., vol. 2: *The Dramatis Personae: Man in God* (San Francisco: Ignatius Press, 1990), esp. 12, 201–2, 215–16, 222; 328, 359, 378–80, 382; ibid., vol. 3: *The Dramatis Personae: The Person in Christ* (San Francisco: Ignatius Press, 1992), esp. 215, 217, 257–8; ibid., vol. 4: *The Action* (San Francisco: Ignatius Press, 1994), esp. 252–4, 259, 364, 380–3; ibid., vol. 5: *The Last Act* (San Francisco: Ignatius Press, 1998), 220, 318, 385, 405, 466.

[156] *Theo-Drama*, 2:215.

[157] Von Balthasar, *Mysterium Paschale*, 21–2, referencing *Th. Oec.* 1.66 (PG 90:1108A–B).

that the *analogia entis* (the irreducible "otherness" of created nature) excludes any kind of fusion or confusion in this ever-intensifying reciprocal interpenetration: each increase in "divinization" on the part of the creature also implies an increase of its own freedom. This guarantees the abiding and ever-increasing vitality of the dramatic relationship between God and the creature. Second, . . . finite freedom, once it has been redeemed and liberated, is now in danger of being able to utter a heightened No, even to the extent of making a total and irrevocable refusal of grace . . .[158]

With what he calls the "play of freedoms,"[159] von Balthasar sought to augment Maximus' portrayal of how, in Jesus Christ, the infinite divine freedom liberates finite human freedom. Christians not only imitate the incalculable love of Christ, they also participate in the whole new eschatological *tropos* of human existence that Christ has inaugurated. Maximus helped inspire von Balthasar's vision of discipleship in its theo-dramatic framework, wherein the audiences of God's revelatory drama are called *on stage*, as it were, as the latest *dramatis personae* who must grow into their roles (their freedom and virtuosity) in the forward movement of historical existence leading to the full consummation of the work of Christ and the Spirit.[160] Herein all the virtues of Christ, nurtured in the Spirit, bring definition to the "characters" in the drama.

Von Balthasar's reading of Maximus has registered itself in certain of his own devotees, such as the phenomenologist and philosopher-theologian Jean-Luc Marion. Marion, who wrote an early essay on the two wills of Christ in Maximus, has maintained in his mature career a keen interest in patristic thought, especially Dionysius and Augustine. Joshua Lollar suggests, I think rightly, that Marion's thinking on "distance" and "difference," such as enable the possibility of authentic love, echoes motifs from von Balthasar's interpretation of the Confessor.[161] Apart from von Balthasar, however, Marion shows his own independent interest in Maximus' apophaticism, though largely as a function of his more intensive work on Dionysius.[162]

---

[158] *Theo-Drama*, 4:383. I quoted part of this passage in earlier discussion at p. 242 in this volume.

[159] Ibid., 2:63.

[160] On this integration of believers/communities into the drama of Christ, see ibid., 2:62 89, also 173 334 (on infinite and finite freedom in theo-dramatic context); ibid. 3:122–48, 263–461, 513–14, 532–5.

[161] "The Reception of Maximian Thought in the Modern Era," 571.

[162] See pp. 125–7, 128, 173 in this volume.

## Retrievals of Maximus in Ecological Theology

Despite the frequent disparagement of the Fathers by many ecological philosophers and theologians, who see them as affirming an omnipotent Deity who tames the world and gives humanity privileged place therein,[163] a new generation of Christian scholars writing on environmental concerns have been drawn to Maximus as a cosmic theologian. This is not a totally Western development. With the strong advocacy of Mar Paulos Gregorios, the "Green" Ecumenical Patriarch Bartholomew I, John Chryssavgis, Bruce Foltz, Elizabeth Theokritoff, and others, environmental theology has grown exponentially in modern Eastern Orthodoxy, much of it focusing on Maximus and his vision of humanity as a responsible "mediator" of creation.[164] Here I would mention as well the work of Alexei Nesteruk, who has analyzed Maximus' cosmic theology (and doctrine of the *logoi*) in conversation with contemporary physics and cosmology.[165]

Outside the Orthodox fold, a leading voice in retrieving Maximus for ecological theology is Celia Deane-Drummond, who seeks to recover the primacy of divine Wisdom in creation approached from a stance of contemplation, wonder, and wisdom.[166] She reads Maximus through von Balthasar, finding in the Confessor a perspective in which the Creator thoroughly identifies with creation in its tragic, compromised state, all the while maintaining the "sacramentality" of creation as a medium of grace, and the interrelatedness and interdependence of all

[163] On this issue, see Blowers, *Drama of the Divine Economy*, 353–5.

[164] Cf. Paulos Gregorios, *The Human Presence: An Orthodox View of Nature* (Geneva: World Council of Churches, 1978), 73–8; John Chryssavgis, ed., *Cosmic Grace, Humble Prayer: The Ecological Vision of the Green Patriarch Bartholomew*, revised edn. (Grand Rapids, MI: Eerdmans, 2009), esp. 24–5, 83–4, 123ff., 188, 285–6, 329, 359; John Chryssavgis and Bruce Foltz, eds., *Toward an Ecology of Transfiguration: Orthodox Christian Perspectives on Environment, Nature, and Creation* (New York: Fordham University Press, 2013), passim; Andrew Louth, "Man and Cosmos in St. Maximus," in Chryssavgis and Foltz, *Toward an Ecology of Transfiguration*, 59–71; Elizabeth Theokritoff, *Living in God's Creation: Orthodox Perspectives on Ecology* (Crestwood, NY: St. Vladimir's Seminary Press, 2009); Radu Bordeianu, "Maximus and Ecology: The Relevance of Maximus the Confessor's Theology of Creation for the Present Ecological Crisis," *Downside Review* 127 (2009): 103–26.

[165] See his *Light from the East: Theology, Science, and the Eastern Orthodox Tradition* (Minneapolis: Augsburg Fortress, 2003); id., *The Universe as Communion: Toward a Neo-Patristic Synthesis of Theology and Science* (London: T. & T. Clark, 2008).

[166] See her *Creation through Wisdom: Theology and the New Biology* (Edinburgh: T. & T. Clark, 2000), esp. 77–8, 81, 85.

creatures.[167] Deane-Drummond is drawn as well to Maximus' theory of Logos and *logoi*, and sympathizes with the view that the *logoi* have both an uncreated and created dimension, mediating the Creator's transcendence of, and immanence in, the world.[168]

Christopher Southgate, who, like Deane-Drummond, brings expertise in the biological sciences to environmental theology, similarly discerns great ecological promise in Maximus' doctrine of the *logoi*, insofar as they signal the Creator's dynamic relation with the unfinished creation. Maximus conceives the *logoi*, says Southgate, "not as static aesthetic ideals but dynamically in terms of peaks in fitness landscapes, peaks that shift over time as God draws the biosphere onward."[169] They embody the Logos's own freedom to work in and through the natures of created species in ways that answer the need for an evolutionary theodicy and that encourage human participation in the stewardship of creation. In a separate study, I myself have engaged with Southgate's work and explored how Maximus' doctrine of creation can prospectively support an evolutionary theodicy.[170]

Still another environmental theologian, Willis Jenkins, aspires to "explore the ecological promise of Maximian deification by turning to modern Russian theology . . . [and by] tracing the ecological promise of Maximus through Sergei Bulgakov, testing and developing the strategy of ecological spirituality within the tradition of deification."[171] Jenkins finds in Maximus the paradigmatic form of Eastern Orthodoxy's intrinsic fusion of grace and nature, wherein human deification (inaugurated through the incarnation) carries with it humanity's participation in the transformation of all creation. He identifies in Maximus three crucial "mysteries" that articulate the way of the world into union with God. First is the mystery of *createdness* itself, the ontological otherness that establishes the possibility of communion between creation and

---

[167] *Christ and Evolution: Wonder and Wisdom* (Minneapolis: Fortress Press, 2009), 149–51.

[168] *Eco-Theology* (Winona, MN: Anselm Academic, 2008), 61–3.

[169] *The Groaning of Creation: God, Evolution, and the Problem of Evil* (Louisville: Westminster John Knox, 2008), 61. On the notion of "fitness landscapes," see ibid., 159–60, n. 40.

[170] "Unfinished Creative Business: Maximus the Confessor, Evolutionary Theodicy, and Human Stewardship in Creation," in David Meconi, ed., *On Earth as It Is in Heaven: Cultivating a Contemporary Theology of Creation* (Grand Rapids: Eerdmans, 2016), 174–90.

[171] *Ecologies of Grace: Environmental Ethics and Christian Theology* (New York: Oxford University Press, 2008), 109.

Creator—a communion perfected in the incarnation of the Logos. Not surprisingly, Jenkins broaches Maximus' teaching on the *logoi* in this same connection.[172] Second is the mystery of *personhood*, as the tension between *hypostasis* and *physis* charges personal activity with a creative responsibility to realize the real nature of things, manifested perfectly in Christ. Christ's own *hypostasis* confirms the embrace and synthesis of multiplicity in creation, thus sanctioning human engagement with non-human creatures. Personhood reveals the "plasticity" of nature conducive to communion.[173] Third, Jenkins proposes, is the mystery of the *theurgical Church*, the communing body of those who gather with all creatures as *liturgical* subjects in the cosmic liturgy. In this communion, authored by Christ, there is no competition amid the "divinizing union of freedoms." "Christ's freedom does not act against passively inert natures, but brings to expression nature's inner glory, thus liberating its own 'voice,' realizing its own mode of existence."[174]

Jenkins concludes: "So Maximus anticipates the peaceable kingdom of the ecclesial economy, where Christians reconcile the world as they dwell within it, transfiguring creation through worship, offering the world to God as they enter into the communion of the cosmos."[175] That said, Jenkins suggests that among Maximus' later readers, Staniloae, but even more so Bulgakov, astutely conveyed his ecological promise. Jenkins ignores the dissonances between the Christologies of Maximus and Bulgakov and chooses instead to harmonize Maximus with Bulgakov's Sophiology insofar as both writers gave primacy to the incarnate Christ's role in liberating the human microcosm (and *person*) into communion with the whole creation.[176]

The retrieval of Maximus for contemporary ecological theology is likely to continue for the foreseeable future, as indicated in the recent study of Brock Bingaman, comparing Maximus and Jürgen Moltmann on the "trinitarian-christocentric" basis of the human vocation in creation, and demonstrating how both writers provide richly "contemplative" perspectives on humanity's role in the world that enhance human servanthood and asceticism in and for the world.[177]

---

[172] Ibid., 191–2.      [173] Ibid., 193–4.      [174] Ibid., 194–6.
[175] Ibid., 195–6.      [176] Ibid., 196–216.
[177] Brock Bingaman, *All Things New: The Trinitarian Nature of the Human Calling in Maximus the Confessor and Jürgen Moltmann* (Eugene, OR: Wipf and Stock, 2014).

## Maximus in the Revival of Virtue Ethics

In recent decades, moral philosophy and theology have seen a noticeable revival of virtue-based ethics, due largely to fatigue with neo-Kantian approaches and renewed interest in Aristotle's *Ethics* and in the theological ethics of Thomas Aquinas. Integration of the Greek Fathers into conversations on virtue ethics has been slow in coming, owing in part to the perception of virtue ethicists that patristic moralists treated the virtues primarily ascetically and pastorally, not theoretically.[178] Orthodox scholars like Perry Hamalis and Aristotle Papanikolaou have tried to remedy the situation and to bring Eastern Christian perspectives into conversation with the work of Alasdair McIntyre and other leading virtue ethicists in the West.[179]

Instruction in the virtues was of course a stock element in the moral psychology and spiritual anthropology of many Greek monastic writers (including Evagrius and most other authors in the *Philokalia*). But Maximus has emerged as exemplary for various reasons. First, as I myself have argued elsewhere, his teaching on the Christian's formation readily meets the virtue ethicist's demand for a coherent "moral narrative" in which virtues are framed and cultivated. In his case it is a "theo-dramatic" construct wherein the Logos, having through the *logoi* already scripted creatures' communion with one another and with God, incarnates himself in Jesus Christ to bring the drama to a head, and in the denouement embodies himself in the virtues of believers who participate in the drama.[180] Second, Maximus' aretology articulates both the properly intellectual and properly performative or embodied dimensions of virtue, and mediates between them. Frederick Aquino has highlighted the relevance of Maximus' teaching on prudence and the other intellectual virtues to contemporary discussion of "virtue epistemology" as a subsidiary of

---

[178] Perry Hamalis and Aristotle Papanikolaou, "Toward a Godly Mode of Being: Virtue as Embodied Deification," *Studies in Christian Ethics* 26 (2013): 273–4, referencing the view of the Catholic virtue ethicist Jean Porter.

[179] Such was the purpose of their edited special issue of *Studies in Christian Ethics* 26/2 (2013): "Modes of Godly Being: Reflections on the Virtues from the Christian East," collecting essays of Orthodox and non-Orthodox scholars alike. See also Joseph Woodill, *The Fellowship of Life: Virtue Ethics and Orthodox Christianity* (Washington, DC: Georgetown University Press, 1998), 90–1 (on Maximus); Demetrios Harper, "The Analogy of Love: The Virtue Ethic of St. Maximus the Confessor" (Ph.D. dissertation, University of Winchester, 2015).

[180] Blowers, "Aligning and Reorienting the Passible Self," 335–7.

virtue ethics.[181] Luis Salés has illuminated how for Maximus the
whole of the embodied moral self is integrated into the performance
of virtue, paralleling insights from behavioral neurobiology with
Maximus' teaching on *gnômê*, the passions, and virtuous habitudes
in the interest of "a virtue ethics which is concerned with the totality
of a human person."[182] Third, Maximus' teaching on virtue makes for
a compelling Eastern comparison with that of the towering figure of
Aquinas, particularly in the consideration of whether virtues
are "natural" or "habitual," and whether, if habitual, the *habitus*
(ἕξις) is itself natural or supernatural.[183] Finally, and more generally,
Maximus' aretology both informs, and is informed by, an extensive
consideration of the nature of human desire and freedom,[184] abiding
themes in contemporary theological ethics.

[181] "The *Philokalia* and Regulative Virtue Epistemology: A Look at Maximus the
Confessor," 240–51; id., "The Synthetic Unity of Virtue and Epistemic Goods in
Maximus the Confessor," 378–90.
[182] "Maximos and Neurobiology: A Neurotheological Investigation of Asceticism
as Erosion of the Passions and the Gnomic Will," in John McGuckin, ed., *Orthodox
Monasticism: Past and Present* (New York: Theotokos Press, 2014), 324–31; also id.,
"Divine Incarnation through the Virtues," 159–76. On the Orthodox side, considering
virtue to be "embodied deification," see Papanikolaou, "Learning How to Love: Saint
Maximus on Virtue," in Vasiljević, 241–50.
[183] See Andrew Louth's comparison, "Virtue Ethics: St. Maximos the Confessor
and Aquinas Compared," 351–63; Papanikolaou, "Learning How to Love," 239–41.
[184] See Blowers, "The Dialectics and Therapeutics of Desire in Maximus the
Confessor," 425–51.

# Epilogue: A Confessor for East, West, and Global South

It is a point of historical fact, not of retrospective eulogy or nostalgia, that Maximus the Confessor was one of the few genuinely ecumenical theologians of the late-ancient and early-medieval age.[1] His profile staggeringly contrasts, of course, with that of reputed ecumenical theologians of our own time, who carry on their work in the shadow of sizable networks of organized endeavor toward global Christian unity, such as both benefit and problematize their prophetic witness. Though empirically the Church of Maximus' time was far less fragmented than it appears today, he knew the harsh sting of alienation within the Christian *ekklêsia*, whose unity in the seventh century was complicated not only by polarizing doctrinal conflict and ecclesiastical rivalries but also by imperial interventions therein. He earned his epithet "Confessor" honestly. Monastic community, far from being a haven from the world, launched him for a career that resulted in high-profile public confrontations with ecclesiastical and imperial powers alike, confrontations that cost him his life, a martyr[2] for convictions only posthumously vindicated.

Von Balthasar, for all the virtues of his interpretation of Maximus, exaggerates the image of the Confessor as a man of "destiny" aware of his place in Christian intellectual history and his mediating role between East and West. He finds in Maximus the kind of person who "has seen his own star rising beyond all the cultural and political

---

[1] For a good review, see Andrew Louth, "St. Maximus the Confessor between East and West," in Elizabeth Livingstone, ed., *Studia Patristica* 32 (Leuven: Peeters, 1997), 332–45.

[2] The term applied to Maximus ostensibly for the first time by Theodore Spudaeos, *Hyponesticon* §5 of Allen and Neil, 154.

configurations and weaknesses of his time and follows it with a freedom that overcomes the world."[3] There is, however, little evidence from Maximus' own writings of a heightened self-consciousness of heroically rising above the fray. Von Balthasar himself qualifies his bold image by suggesting that Maximus shrank from any pretense of authority and "did nothing to give power to his own achievement," instead acting out of "passionate vulnerability" and "evangelical love," a "humble monk."[4] But this too may exaggerate, since at times Maximus revealed strong charismatic authority and an extraordinary capacity to wield influence.[5]

Without desiring to underplay Maximus' robust persona in his own context, I would hasten to revise von Balthasar's portrait in more sobering terms. Maximus scarcely lacked a sense of his own acquired "clout" in the definitive situations of his career, be it communicating intimately with friends as a spiritual advisor, corresponding with civil authorities and confidants, interpreting the authoritative doctors of the faith for a new day, debating a former Patriarch of Constantinople, aligning himself christologically with the papacy, or rallying Greek monks against the doctrinal pretensions of the Byzantine imperial establishment. In the story of his trials and exiles by imperial prosecutors, moreover, Maximus appears fully cognizant of the weight of the moment, the high stakes of his convictions and the price to be paid for them. He knows himself to be a player in what God has preordained before the ages[6]—and if that is what von Balthasar means by a sense of "destiny," so be it. All the while, there is no signal from Maximus whatsoever that, once embroiled in the monothelete controversy, he has moved beyond his original monastic vocation or that there is some existential fault-line to be crossed from the life of a non-ordained monk to that of a thoroughly public exponent of christological orthodoxy interacting with imperial officials and with bishops and patriarchs. Indeed, in Lazica the circle of his life is perfectly closed, as the exile of the defamed political

[3] *Cosmic Liturgy*, 29–30.       [4] Ibid., 30.

[5] On Maximus and authority, see Christian Boudignon, "Le pouvoir de l'anathème ou Maxime le Confesseur et les moines palestiniens du VIIe siècle," in Alberto Complani and Giovanni Filoramo, eds., *Foundations of Power and Conflicts of Authority in Late-Antique Monasticism: Proceedings of the International Seminar, Turin, December 2–4, 2004* (Leuven: Peeters, 2007), 245–74.

[6] *Ep. Maximi ad Anastasium monachum discipulum*, in Allen and Neil, 122.

prisoner and the *xeniteia*[7] of the monk finally appear as one and the same.

In earlier chapters, I have described Maximus' *Weltbild* as a "theo-drama," or better still a "christo-drama," focused on the resourcefulness of the Creator and the initiative of the Logos-Christ in the freedom and fullness of his incarnational manifestation—his aspiration to "embody himself" in all things. I have also described Maximus' worldview as the articulation of a "cosmo-politeian" vision, one in which *all* rational creatures are called to particular "ascetical" roles in the universe, as participant actors in the cosmic drama whose central plot is the full fruition of the *politeia* of Jesus Christ.[8] This is how he reads the created world and Scripture alike. All creatures—and even non-rational crea-tures whose "modes of existence" still fall thoroughly within the com-pass of divine providence—contribute, from out of the particularity of their position and vocation, to the cosmic liturgy of praise, and to Christ's cosmic ministry of reconciliation and transformation. Such is the teleological actualization of the vocation encoded for every creature in the *logos* of its nature.

How radical, or even political, is this vision in Maximus' context? The social or cultural historian might argue that it simply gives theological and cosmological sanction to the hierarchies already built into the socio-political fabric of Byzantium, projecting an orderly cosmos for an orderly empire—analogous to how Dionysius's *Celestial Hierarchy* and *Ecclesiastical Hierarchy* were appropriated by medieval European thinkers as theoretical grounding for the ranked social and ecclesiastical order of Western Christendom. More than once I have noted Averil Cameron's compelling portrait of Maximus as a cultural conservative, a proto-scholastic serving the defense of Byzantium's cultural identity in the face of the threats of Islam from without and heresy from within.

But for various reasons such a reading of Maximus' cosmo-politeian vision is unsatisfying. Let us recall the sharp contrast with his contem-porary, George of Pisidia, whose poetry richly deploys cosmological imagery as a framework for glorifying Heraclius's imperial regime.[9] George's Heraclius is Christ's worldwide vice-regent seeking to usher in a "new creation." Maximus discourses little on the Byzantine social and political order as such, and he is a reluctant patriot, to be sure. In

[7] See pp. 32–42 in this volume.  [8] See pp. 130–4 in this volume.
[9] See pp. 15–16, 131 in this volume.

one of his letters to John the Chamberlain, referencing the inevitable postlapsarian necessity of worldly rulers disciplining human beings who are equal by nature but fallen, Maximus nonetheless relativizes the imperial authority. An emperor is only as good as his being "a most faithful servant of the divine will"; otherwise he invests in wicked earthly advisors, makes them his viceroys, and wreaks destruction.[10] This reductive assessment of imperial power is matched by Maximus' exegesis of certain kings in the Bible who were capable of going either way, like the Pharaoh, who symbolized the "law of nature" when he served Israel under the dispensation of Joseph but was a Devil-figure when he set out to destroy God's people in Moses's time.[11] A king or emperor, like every other creature, must fulfill his "natural" vocation or *politeia* in relation to the universal *politeia* of Jesus Christ. But how could an emperor now, in the seventh century, hope to fulfill that vocation if he did not proceed with a clear and true understanding of the person, natures, and wills of Christ? For Maximus, imperial intervention in the monothelete controversy was less the problem than the emperors' inability to see that precision in Christology was bound up with the very way of salvation and deification, and was not just a function of imperial unity. Maximus was accused of being implacable and unaccommodating in his dispute at Bizya at the end of his career,[12] but for him the christocentric asceticism (*politeia*) imposed on all citizens—indeed all creatures—was a heavy yoke to be borne by all alike.

There is an instructive comparison here, I believe, with Maximus' teacher three centuries removed, Gregory Nazianzen. Gregory, of course, was a bishop—albeit it in a very provincial locale before rising to fame in Constantinople in the final climax of the trinitarian controversy. But as Susanna Elm has recently profiled him, Nazianzen was caught up in a fierce battle over very precise language of God that is best described as a "philosophical *agôn*" in which bishops contended with each other but also with the emperor (himself a "philosopher"). For Gregory and for the neo-pagan Emperor Julian alike, writes Elm, "the question was how to guarantee the salvation implicit in the return to the divine, becoming God, to all and not merely to those of higher purity." Bishop and emperor had become the new ascetics and contemplatives, assuming the traditional function of philosophers in

[10] *Ep.* 10 (PG 91:449A–453A).    [11] *Q. Thal.* 26 (CCSG 7:179–81).
[12] See pp. 60–1 in this volume.

society, modeling their *paideia* for all within the *oikoumene*, guiding all within the civil *politeia* toward salvation and deification.[13]

Maximus, a non-ordained monk, did not have Nazianzen's relatively elite status. Despite the Greek *Life*'s dubious claims of Maximus having once been an insider at the imperial court, the predominant pattern of his career was that of the peregrinating monk whose first allegiance was to his original spiritual fathers, principally Sophronius. Indeed, this overall pattern lends credibility to the Syriac *Life*'s claims of his Palestinian monastic provenance. Maximus' early circulation with the intimate Moschus–Sophronius circle (the "Eukratades") prepared him more readily to lead the escalating Greek monastic dissent against the monothelete establishment in Constantinople. In my judgment, it is precisely in this monastic network, and under the mentoring of Sophronius,[14] that we must look for the internal link between the broad cosmo-politeian vision, articulated across Maximus' earlier writings and correspondence, and the narrower, more technical christological discourses of his career from the 640s on. This is the context where rigor about the ascetical *politeia* of every creature—*a fortiori* every Christian human being—was fused with rigor in fathoming the *politeia* of Christ himself. The very mysteriousness of Christ's composite person, and of the eschatological *tropos* of creaturely nature that he opened up with his "new theandric energy," induced more, not less, assiduous aspiration to participate in the mystery in every aspect of one's being and intelligence.[15]

Critically-minded Western moderns, heirs of the hermeneutics of suspicion in the study of history, frequently have great difficulty fathoming the possibility that anyone could act out of sheer theological principle, without ulterior motives supervening. It is not idealizing him to offer Maximus' career as testimony that such suspicion is not always warranted. For him, rigor in christological formulations went hand in hand with plumbing the depths of the *mysterium Christi*, the mystery which, simply put, is the beginning, middle, and end of all things. We

---

[13] Susanna Elm, *Sons of Hellenism, Fathers of the Church: Emperor Julian, Gregory of Nazianzus, and the Vision of Rome* (Berkeley: University of California Press, 2012), esp. 479–86 (quoted at 480).

[14] See Garrigues, *Maxime le Confesseur*, 47–55.

[15] In *Opusc.* 15 (PG 91:184B – ll. 824–7 in Roosen's forthcoming critical edition), a letter to Stephen of Dor, Maximus praises the Palestinian bishop for guiding him and other believers back to "the most divine confession and *politeia* of the Logos," as the two go absolutely hand in hand.

already live and move and have our being within it,[16] whether we choose to recognize it or not. The imperative is actively to embrace that "being" as sheer gift, as christoform and cruciform vocation, as summons to receive "eternal well-being" in Christ's new, transfigured creation.

Such is the christocentric cosmic gospel which the wandering monk Maximus the Confessor carried with him across East, West, and "South" (Africa), in Byzantium's profoundly tempestuous seventh century. Especially in its christological content, it is his legacy today for churches East and West still struggling to recover the unity of the Church grounded in the mystery that is Jesus Christ. Especially in its setting of the lordship of Jesus Christ above all earthly powers-that-be, it is Maximus' legacy for today's postcolonial churches of the "Global South" (or of post-Soviet Georgia, the land of his burial[17]) striving to fathom and interpret the mystery of Christ in their own new contexts. And whatever the differences of circumstance, Maximus' sheer endurance as a Christian witness is encouragement to battered and berated Christians in the land quite possibly of his own nativity, Christians now striving to keep their faith amid their own kinds of exile in "occupied territories" or in the larger war zones of the Middle East.

---

[16]  Acts 17:28, referenced in *Amb. Jo.* 7 (PG 91:1084B).
[17]  See Nino Sakvarelidze, "Contextualization and Actualization of Maximus' Textual and Spiritual Heritage," in Vasiljević, 271–83.

# Select Bibliography

## Primary Works

*Primary Works (Series)*
Corpus Christianorum, continuatio mediaevalis. Turnhout: Brepols, 1966–.
Corpus Christianorum, series graeca. Turnhout: Brepols, 1976–.
Gregorii Nysseni Opera. Leiden: Brill, 1952–.
Griechischen christlichen Schriftsteller der ersten drei Jahrhunderte. Leipzig:
    J. C. Hinrich; Berlin: Akademie-Verlag, Walter de Gruyter, 1897–.
Patrologia Graeca. Paris: J.-P. Migne, 1857–66.
Patrologia Latina. Paris: J.-P. Migne, 1844–55.
Patrologia Orientalis. Turnhout: Brepols, 1903–.
Sources Chrétiennes. Paris: Éditions du Cerf, 1944–.

*Critical Editions and Translations of Other Primary Works*
Allen, Pauline, trans., *Sophronius of Jerusalem and Seventh-Century Heresy:
    The* Synodical Letter *and Other Documents.* Oxford: Oxford University
    Press, 2009.
Anon., *Chronicon Paschale*, Greek text ed. Ludwig Dindorf, 2 vols. Bonn:
    E. Weber, 1832.
Anon., Prologue to John Moschus, *Pratum spirituale.* Greek text ed. Hermann
    Usener, *Der heilige Tychon*, 91–2. Leipzig and Berlin: Teubner, 1907.
*Book of the Pontiffs (Liber Pontificalis)*, trans. Raymond Davis, 2nd edn.
    TTH 6. Liverpool: Liverpool University Press, 2001.
Dionysius the Areopagite, *Corpus Dionysiacum.* Greek text ed. Beate Suchla,
    Günter Heil, and Adolf Martin Ritter. PTS 33 and 36. Berlin: Walter de
    Gruyter, 1990, 1991.
George of Pisidia, *Panegyric Poems.* Greek text ed. Agostino Pertusi, *Giorgio
    di Pisidia Poemi, I. Panegirici Epici.* Murnau, Germany: Buch-Kunstverlag
    Ettal, 1959.
Gregory Palamas, *Triads.* Greek text ed. John Meyendorff, *Grégoire Palamas:
    Défense des saints hesychastes.* Leuven: Spicilegium Sacrum Louvaniense,
    1959.
Neil, Bronwen, ed., *Narrationes sancti papae Martini* (Latin text), in Bronwen
    Neil, *Seventh-Century Popes and Martyrs: The Political Hagiography of
    Anastasius Bibliothecarius*, 166–233. Turnhout: Brepols, 2006.
Nemesius of Emesa, *De natura hominis.* Greek text ed. Moreno Morani.
    BSGRT. Leipzig: Teubner, 1987.

Nicephorus of Constantinople, *Breviarium historicum*. Greek text ed. and
trans. Cyril Mango, *Nikephoros, Patriarch of Constantinople: Short History*.
Washington, DC: Dumbarton Oaks, 1990.

Peeters, Paul, ed., *Vita sancti Martini*, in "Une vie grecque du pape S.
Martin I," *Analecta Bollandiana* 51 (1933): 225–62 (Greek text, 253–62).

Riedinger, Rudolph, ed., *Acta Conciliorum Oecumenicorum*, series secunda,
vol. 1: *Concilium Lateranense a. 649 celebratum*. Berlin: Walter de Gruyter,
1984.

Riedinger, Rudolph, ed., *Acta Conciliorum Oecumenicorum*, series secunda,
vol. 2: *Concilium universal Constantinopolitanum tertium*, 2 parts. Berlin:
Walter de Gruyter, 1990, 1992.

Theophanes, *Chronicle*, ed. and trans. Cyril Mango, Roger Scott, with Geoffrey
Greatrex, *The Chronicle of Theophanes Confessor: Byzantine and Near
Eastern History, 284–813*. Oxford: Oxford University Press, 1997.

*Primary Works of Maximus (and of Maximian Biography)
in Critical Editions*

Allen, Pauline, and Bronwen Neil, eds., *Maximus the Confessor and His
Companions: Documents from Exile*. Oxford: Oxford University Press,
2002.

Allen, Pauline, and Bronwen Neil, eds., *Scripta saeculi VII vitam Maximi
Confessoris illustrantia una cum latina interpretatione Anastasii Bibliothecarii
iuxta posita*. Corpus Christianorum, series graeca 39. Turnhout: Brepols,
1999.

Boudignon, Christian, ed., *Maximi Confessoris Mystagogia una cum latine
interpretatione Anastasii Bibliothecarii*. Corpus Christianorum, series
graeca 69. Turnhout: Brepols, 2011.

Brock, Sebastian, ed. and trans., "An Early Syriac Life of Maximus the
Confessor," *Analecta Bollandiana* 91 (1975): 299–346.

Declerck, José, ed., *Maximie Confessoris Quaestiones et dubia*. Corpus Christianorum, series graeca 10. Turnhout: Brepols, 1982.

Jannsens, Bart, ed., *Maximi Confessoris Ambigua ad Thomam una cum Epistula
secunda ad eundem*. Corpus Christianorum, series graeca 48. Turnhout:
Brepols, 2002.

Jeauneau, Édouard, ed., *Maximi Confessoris Ambigua ad Iohannem iuxta
Iohannis Scoti Eriugenae latinam interpretationem*. Corpus Christianorum,
series graeca 18. Turnhout: Brepols, 1988.

Laga, Carl, and Carlos Steel, eds., *Maximi Confessoris Quaestiones ad Thalas-
sium*, vol. 1: *Quaestiones I–LV una cum latine interpretatione Ioannis Scotti
Eriugenae*; vol. 2: *Quaestiones LVI–LXV una cum latine interpretatione
Ioannis Scotti Eriugenae*. Corpus christianorum, series graeca 7 and 22.
Turnhout: Brepols, 1980, 1990.

Neil, Bronwen, and Pauline Allen, eds. and trans., *The [Greek] Life of Maximus the Confessor: Recension 3*. Strathfield, NSW: St. Paul's, 2003.

Van Deun, Peter, ed., *Maximi Confessoris Liber asceticus*. Corpus Christianorum, series graeca 40. Turnhout: Brepols, 2000.

Van Deun, Peter, ed., *Maximi Confessoris Opuscula exegetica duo*. Corpus Christianorum, series graeca 23. Turnhout: Brepols, 1991.

Vinel, Françoise, ed. and trans., *Questions à Thalassios*. Sources Chrétiennes 529, 554, and 569, with introductions and notes by Jean-Claude Larchet. Paris: Cerf, 2010, 2012, 2015 (uses the Laga-Steel critical text).

*English Translations of Maximus's Writings (and of Maximus's* Vitae*)*

Berthold, George, trans., *Maximus Confessor: Selected Writings*. Classics of Western Spirituality. Mahwah, NJ: Paulist Press, 1985.

Blowers, Paul, trans., *Commentary on Psalm 59*, in "A Psalm 'Unto the End': Eschatology and Anthropology in Maximus the Confessor's *Commentary on Psalm 59*," in Brian Daley and Paul Kolbet, eds., *The Harp of Prophecy: Early Christian Interpretation of the Psalms*, 270–8. Notre Dame, IN: University of Notre Dame Press, 2014.

Blowers, Paul, and Robert Louis Wilken, trans., *On the Cosmic Mystery of Jesus Christ: Selected Writings from St. Maximus the Confessor*. Crestwood, NY: St. Vladimir's Seminary Press, 2003.

Brock, Sebastian, ed. and trans., "An Early Syriac Life of Maximus the Confessor," *Analecta Bollandiana* 91 (1973): 299–364.

Constas, Maximos (Nicholas), ed. and trans., *On Difficulties in the Church Fathers: The* Ambigua *of Maximos the Confessor*. Dumbarton Oaks Medieval Library. Cambridge, MA: Harvard University Press, 2014.

Lollar, Joshua, trans., *Maximus the Confessor: Ambigua to Thomas; Second Letter to Thomas*. Corpus Christianorum in Translation 2. Turnhout: Brepols, 2009.

Neil, Bronwen, and Pauline Allen, eds. and trans., *The [Greek] Life of Maximus the Confessor: Recension 3*. Strathfield, NSW: St. Paul's, 2003.

Palmer, G. E. H., Philip Sherrard, and Kallistos Ware, eds. and trans., *The Philokalia: The Complete Text*, vol. 2. London: Faber & Faber, 1981.

Prassas, Despina, trans., *St. Maximus the Confessor's* Questions and Doubts. DeKalb, IL: Northern Illinois University Press, 2010.

Shoemaker, Stephen, trans., *The Life of the Virgin: Maximus the Confessor*. New Haven: Yale University Press, 2012.

**Secondary Studies**

Alexander, Paul, *The Byzantine Apocalyptic Tradition*. Berkeley: University of California Press, 1985.

Allen, Pauline, "Life and Times of Maximus the Confessor," *OHMC*, 3–18.

Allen, Pauline, and Bronwen Neil, eds., *The Oxford Handbook of Maximus the Confessor*. Oxford: Oxford University Press, 2015.

Andia, Ysabel de, "Transfiguration et théologie negative chez Maxime le Confesseur et Denys l'Aréopagite," in Ysabel de Andia, ed., *Denys l'Aréopagite et sa posterité en Orient et en Occident: Actes du Colloque International, Paris, 21–24 septembre 1994*, 293–328. Paris: Institut d'Études Augustiniennes, 1997.

Andreopoulos, Andreas, "Eschatology in Maximus the Confessor," *OHMC*, 322–40.

Aquino, Frederick, "Maximus the Confessor," in Paul Gavrilyuk and Sarah Coakley, eds., *The Spiritual Senses: Perceiving God in Western Christianity*, 104–20. Cambridge: Cambridge University Press, 2011.

Aquino, Frederick, "The *Philokalia* and Regulative Virtue Epistemology: A Look at Maximus the Confessor," in Brock Bingaman and Bradley Nassif, eds., *The Philokalia: Exploring the Classic Text of Orthodox Spirituality*, 240–51. New York: Oxford University Press, 2012.

Aquino, Frederick, "The Synthetic Unity of Virtue and Epistemic Goods in Maximus the Confessor," *Studies in Christian Ethics* 26 (2013): 378–90.

Athanassiadi, Polymnia, *Vers la pensée unique: La montée de l'intolérance dans l'antiquité tardive*. Paris: Les Belles Lettres, 2010.

Balthasar, Hans Urs von, *Cosmic Liturgy: The Universe according to Maximus the Confessor*, trans. Brian Daley. San Francisco: Ignatius Press, 2003.

Balthasar, Hans Urs von, *The Glory of the Lord: A Theological Aesthetics*, 7 vols., trans. Erasmo Leiva-Merikakis et al. San Francisco: Ignatius Press, 1983–91.

Balthasar, Hans Urs von, *Mysterium Paschale: The Mystery of Easter*, 2nd edn., trans. Aidan Nichols. Grand Rapids, MI: Eerdmans, 1990.

Balthasar, Hans Urs von, *Theo-Drama: Theological Dramatic Theory*, 5 vols., trans. Graham Harrison. San Francisco: Ignatius Press, 1988–98.

Balthasar, Hans Urs von, *Theo-Logic*, vol. 2: *Truth in God*, trans. Adrian Walker. San Francisco: Ignatius Press, 2004.

Bathrellos, Demetrios, *The Byzantine Christ: Person, Nature, and Will in the Christology of St. Maximus the Confessor*. Oxford: Oxford University Press, 2004.

Bathrellos, Demetrios, "Passions, Ascesis, and the Virtues," *OHMC*, 287–306.

Bausenhart, Guido, *In Allem uns gleich ausser der Sunde: Studien zum Beitrag Maximos' des Bekenners zur altchristlichen Christologie*. Mainz: Matthias Grünewald, 1995.

Behr, John, *Irenaeus of Lyons: Identifying Christianity*. Oxford: Oxford University Press, 2013.

Behr, John, *The Mystery of Christ: Life in Death*. Crestwood, NY: St. Vladimir's Seminary Press, 2006.

Benevich, Grigory, "Christological Polemics of Maximus the Confessor and the Emergence of Islam onto the World Stage," *Theological Studies* 72 (2011): 335–44.

Benevich, Grigory, "Maximus' Heritage in Russia and Ukraine," *OHMC*, 460–79.

Berger, Calinic, "A Contemporary Synthesis of St. Maximus' Theology: The Work of Fr. Dumitru Stăniloae," in Vasiljević, 389–405.

Berthold, George, "The Church as *Mysterion*: Unity and Diversity according to Maximus the Confessor," *Patristic and Byzantine Review* 6 (1987): 20–9.

Berthold, George, "The Cappadocian Roots of Maximus the Confessor," *MC*, 51–9.

Bingaman, Brock, *All Things New: The Trinitarian Nature of the Human Calling in Maximus the Confessor and Jürgen Moltmann*. Eugene, OR: Wipf and Stock, 2014.

Bingaman, Brock, and Bradley Nassif, eds., *The Philokalia: Exploring the Classic Text of Orthodox Spirituality*. New York: Oxford University Press, 2012.

Blowers, Paul, "Aligning and Reorienting the Passible Self: Maximus the Confessor's Virtue Ethics," *Studies in Christian Ethics* 26 (2013): 333–50.

Blowers, Paul, "Bodily Inequality, Material Chaos, and the Ethics of Equalization in Maximus the Confessor," in Frances Young, Mark Edwards, and Paul Parvis, eds., *Studia Patristica* 42, 51–6. Leuven: Peeters, 2006.

Blowers, Paul, "The Dialectics and Therapeutics of Desire in Maximus the Confessor," *Vigiliae Christianae* 65 (2011): 425–51.

Blowers, Paul, *Drama of the Divine Economy: Creator and Creation in Early Christian Theology and Piety*. Oxford: Oxford University Press, 2012.

Blowers, Paul, "Entering 'this Sublime and Blessed Amphitheatre': Contemplation of Nature and Interpretation of the Bible in the Patristic Period," in Jitse van der Meer and Scott Mandelbrote, eds., *Interpreting Nature and Scripture: History of a Dialogue in the Abrahamic Religions*, 1:148–76. Leiden: Brill, 2009.

Blowers, Paul, "Exegesis of Scripture," *OHMC*, 253–73.

Blowers, Paul, *Exegesis and Spiritual Pedagogy in Maximus the Confessor: An Investigation of the* Quaestiones ad Thalassium. Notre Dame, IN: University of Notre Dame Press, 1991.

Blowers, Paul, "Gregory of Nyssa, Maximus the Confessor, and the Concept of 'Perpetual Progress,'" *Vigiliae Christianae* 46 (1992): 151–71.

Blowers, Paul, "Hope for the Passible Self: The Use and Transformation of the Human Passions in the Fathers of the *Philokalia*," in Brock Bingaman and Bradley Nassif, eds., *The Philokalia: Exploring the Classic Text of Orthodox Spirituality*, 216–29. New York: Oxford University Press, 2012.

Blowers, Paul, "The Interpretive Dance: Concealment, Disclosure, and Deferral of Meaning in Maximus the Confessor's Hermeneutical Theology," in Vasiljević, 253–9.

Blowers, Paul, "Maximus the Confessor and John of Damascus on Gnomic Will (γνώμη) in Christ: Clarity and Ambiguity," *Union Seminary Quarterly Review* 63 (2012): 44–50.

Blowers, Paul, "On the 'Play' of Divine Providence in Gregory Nazianzen and Maximus the Confessor," in Christopher Beeley, ed., *Re-Reading Gregory of Nazianzus: Essays on History, Theology, and Culture*, 183–201. Washington, DC: Catholic University of America Press, 2012.

Blowers, Paul, "The Passion of Jesus Christ in Maximus the Confessor: A Reconsideration," in M. F. Wiles and E. J. Yarnold, eds., *Studia Patristica* 37, 361–77. Leuven: Peeters, 2001.

Blowers, Paul, "Pity, Empathy, and the Tragic Spectacle of Human Suffering: Exploring the Emotional Culture of Compassion in Late Ancient Christianity," *Journal of Early Christian Studies* 18 (2010): 1–27.

Blowers, Paul, "A Psalm 'Unto the End': Eschatology and Anthropology in Maximus the Confessor's *Commentary on Psalm 59*," in Brian Daley and Paul Kolbet, eds., *The Harp of Prophecy: Early Christian Interpretation of the Psalms*, 257–83. Notre Dame, IN: University of Notre Dame Press, 2014.

Blowers, Paul, "Realized Eschatology in Maximus the Confessor, *Ad Thalassium* 22," in Elizabeth Livingstone, ed., *Studia Patristica* 32, 258–63. Leuven: Peeters, 1997.

Blowers, Paul, "The Transfiguration of Jesus Christ as 'Saturated Phenomenon' and as Key to the Dynamics of Biblical Revelation in St. Maximus the Confessor," in Seraphim Danckaert, Matthew Baker, and Mark Mourachian, eds., *What is the Bible? The Patristic Doctrine of Scripture*. Minneapolis: Augsburg Fortress, forthcoming 2016.

Blowers, Paul, "Unfinished Creative Business: Maximus the Confessor, Evolutionary Theodicy, and Human Stewardship in Creation," in David Meconi, ed., *On Earth as It Is in Heaven: Cultivating a Contemporary Theology of Creation*, 174–90. Grand Rapids: Eerdmans, 2016.

Blowers, Paul, "The World in the Mirror of Holy Scripture: Maximus the Confessor's Short Hermeneutical Treatise in *Ambiguum ad Joannem* 37," in Paul Blowers, Angela Russell Christman, David Hunter, and Robin Darling Young, eds., *In Dominico Eloquio/In Lordly Eloquence: Essays on Patristic Exegesis in Honor of Robert Louis Wilken*, 408–26. Grand Rapids, MI: Eerdmans, 2002.

Booth, Phil, *Crisis of Empire: Doctrine and Dissent at the End of Late Antiquity*. Berkeley: University of California Press, 2014.

Booth, Phil, "On the Life of the Virgin Attributed to Maximus the Confessor," *Journal of Theological Studies* N.S. 66 (2015): 149–203.

Booth, Phil, "Sophronius of Jerusalem and the End of Roman History," in Philip Wood, ed., *History and Identity in the Late Antique Near East*, 1–28. Oxford: Oxford University Press, 2013.

Bordeianu, Radu, "Maximus and Ecology: The Relevance of Maximus the Confessor's Theology of Creation for the Present Ecological Crisis," *Downside Review* 127 (2009): 103–26.

Bornert, René, *Les commentaires byzantins de la divine liturgie du VIIe au XVe siècle*. Paris: Institut Français d'Études Byzantines, 1966.

Boudignon, Christian, "Maxime le Confesseur et ses maîtres: À propos du 'bienheureux ancien' de la *Mystagogie*," in Giovanni Filoramo, ed., *Maestro e Discepolo: Temi e problemi della direzione spirituale tra VI secolo a.C. e VII secolo d.C*, 317–30. Brescia: Morcelliana, 2002.

Boudignon, Christian, "Maxime était-il constantinopolitain?" in Bart Janssens, Bram Roosen, and Peter van Deun, eds., *Philomathestatos: Studies in Greek and Byzantine Texts Presented to Jacques Noret for his Sixty-Fifth Birthday*, 11–43. Leuven: Peeters, 2004.

Boudignon, Christian, "Le pouvoir de l'anathème ou Maxime le Confesseur et les moines palestiniens du VIIe siècle," in Alberto Complani and Giovanni Filoramo, eds., *Foundations of Power and Conflicts of Authority in Late-Antique Monasticism: Proceedings of the International Seminar, Turin, December 2–4, 2004*, 245–74. Leuven: Peeters, 2007.

Bradshaw, David, *Aristotle between East and West*. Cambridge: Cambridge University Press, 2007.

Bradshaw, David, "St. Maximus the Confessor on the Will," in Vasiljević, 143–80.

Brandes, Wolfram, "'Juristische' Krisenbewältigung im 7. Jahrhundert? Die Prozesse gegen Martin I. und Maximos Homologetes," in Ludwig Burgmann, ed., *Fontes Minores* 10, 141–212. Frankfurt: Löwenklau-Gesellschaft, 1998.

Brock, Sebastian, "An Early Syriac Life of Maximus the Confessor," *Analecta Bollandiana* 91 (1975): 299–346.

Bulgakov, Sergius, *The Lamb of God* (1933), trans. Boris Jakim. Grand Rapids, MI: Eerdmans, 2008.

Bulgakov, Sergius, *Sophia, the Wisdom of God: An Outline of Sophiology* (1937), trans. Patrick Thompson. Reprint edition. Hudson, NY: Lindisfarne Press, 1993.

Bulgakov, Sergius, *Unfading Light: Contemplations and Speculations*, trans. Thomas Allan Smith. Grand Rapids, MI: Eerdmans, 2012.

Cameron, Averil, *Byzantine Matters*. Princeton: Princeton University Press, 2014.

Cameron, Averil, *Changing Cultures in Early Byzantium*. Variorum Collected Studies 536. Aldershot: Variorum, 1996.

Cameron, Averil, *Christianity and the Rhetoric of Empire: The Development of Christian Discourse*. Berkeley: University of California Press, 1991.

Cameron, Averil, "The Cost of Orthodoxy," *Church History and Religious Culture* 93 (2013): 339–61.

Cameron, Averil, "Images of Authority: Elites and Icons in Late Sixth-Century Byzantium," *Past and Present* 84 (1989): 3–35.

Cameron, Averil, *Procopius and the Sixth Century*. Berkeley: University of California Press, 1985.

Cattoi, Thomas, *Divine Contingency: Theologies of Divine Embodiment in Maximos the Confessor and Tsong Kha Pa*. Piscataway, NJ: Gorgias Press, 2008.

Cattoi, Thomas, "Liturgy as Cosmic Transformation," *OHMC*, 414–35.

Ceresa-Gastaldo, Aldo, "Tradition et innovation linguistique chez Maxime le Confesseur," *MC*, 123–37.

Chadwick, Henry, "John Moschus and His Friend Sophronius the Sophist," *Journal of Theological Studies* N.S. 25 (1974): 41–74.

Conant, Jonathan, *Staying Roman: Conquest and Identity in Africa and the Mediterranean, 439–700*. Cambridge: Cambridge University Press, 2012.

Constas, Maximos (Nicholas), "Evagrios Pontikos, St. Maximos the Confessor, and the *Chapters on Love*." Unpublished essay online: <https://independent.academia.edu/FrMaximosConstas>.

Constas, Maximos, "The Last Temptation of Satan: Divine Deception in Greek Patristic Interpretations of the Passion Narrative," *Harvard Theological Review* 97 (2004): 139–63.

Constas, Maximos, "St. Maximus the Confessor: The Reception of His Thought in East and West," in Vasiljević, 25–53.

Cooper, Adam, *The Body in St. Maximus the Confessor: Holy Flesh, Wholly Deified*. Oxford: Oxford University Press, 2005.

Cooper, Adam, "Spiritual Anthropology in *Ambiguum 7*," *OHMC*, 360–77.

Cooper, Adam, "St. Maximus on the Mystery of Marriage and the Body: A Reconsideration," in Vasiljević, 195–221.

Costache, Doru, "Going Upward with Everything You Are: The Unifying Ladder of St. Maximus the Confessor" (in Romanian), in Basarab Nicolescu and Magda Stavinschi, eds., *Science and Orthodoxy: A Necessary Dialogue*, 135–44 (Bucharest: Curtea Veche, 2006). Eng. trans. by author online: <https://www.academia.edu/1077440/The_Unifying_Ladder_of_St_Maximus_the_Confessor_Going_Upwards_with_Everything_You_Are>.

Costache, Doru, "Living above Gender: Insights from Saint Maximus the Confessor," *Journal of Early Christian Studies* 21 (2013): 261–90.

Costache, Doru, "Seeking Out the Antecedents of the Maximian Theory of Everything: St. Gregory the Theologian's *Oration* 38," *Phronema* 26 (2011): 27–45.

Croce, Vittorio, *Tradizione e ricerca: Il metodo teologico di san Massimo il Confessore*. Milan: Vita e Pensiero, 1974.

Cvetković, Vladimir, "Wisdom in St. Maximus the Confessor Reconsidered," in Dragiša Bojović, ed., *Saint Emperor Constantine and Christianity:*

*International Conference Commemorating the 1700th Anniversary of the Edict of Milan*, 2:197–214. Niš, Serbia: Centre of Church Studies, 2013.

Daley, Brian, "Apokatastasis and 'Honorable Silence' in the Eschatology of Maximus the Confessor," *MC*, 309–39.

Daley, Brian, "Maximus Confessor, Leontius of Byzantium, and the Late Aristotelian Metaphysics of the Person," in Vasiljević, 55–70.

Daley, Brian, "A Richer Union: Leontius of Byzantium and the Relationship of Human and Divine in Christ," in Elizabeth Livingstone, ed., *Studia Patristica* 24, 239–65. Leuven: Peeters, 1993.

Dalmais, Irénée-Henri, "La manifestation du Logos dans l'homme et dans l'Église: Typologie anthropologique et typologie écclesiale d'après *Qu. Thal.* 60 et la *Mystagogie*," *MC*, 13–25.

Dalmais, Irénée-Henri, "Mystère liturgique et divinisation dans la *Mystagogie* de saint Maxime le Confesseur," in Jacques Fontaine and Charles Kannengiesser, eds., *Epektasis: Mélanges patristiques offerts au Cardinal Jean Daniélou*, 55–62. Paris: Beauchesne, 1972.

Dalmais, Irénée-Henri, "Saint Maxime le Confesseur et la crise de l'origénisme monastique," in *Théologie de la vie monastique*, 411–21. Paris: Aubier, 1961.

Dalmais, Irénée-Henri, "Théologie de l'église et mystère liturgique dans la *Mystagogie* de S. Maxime le Confesseur," in Elizabeth Livingstone, ed., *Studia Patristica* 13, 145–53. Berlin: Akademie-Verlag, 1975.

Dalmais, Irénée-Henri, "La théorie des 'logoi' des creatures chez Saint Maxime le Confesseur," *Revue des sciences philosophiques et théologiques* 36 (1952): 244–9.

Dalmais, Irénée-Henri, "Le vocabulaire des activités intellectuelles, voluntaires et spirituelles dans l'anthropologie de Saint Maxime le Confesseur," in *Mélanges offerts à M.-D. Chenu*, 189–202. Paris: Vrin, 1967.

Dawson, David, *Christian Figural Reading and the Fashioning of Identity*. Berkeley: University of California Press, 2002.

Deane-Drummond, Celia, *Christ and Evolution: Wonder and Wisdom*. Minneapolis: Fortress Press, 2009.

Deane-Drummond, Celia, *Creation through Wisdom: Theology and the New Biology*. Edinburgh: T. & T. Clark, 2000.

Deane-Drummond, Celia, *Eco-Theology*. Winona, MN: Anselm Academic, 2008.

Dekkers, Eligius, "Maxime le Confesseur dans la tradition Latine," in Carl Laga, Joseph Munitiz, and Lucas van Rompay, eds., *After Chalcedon: Studies in Theology and Church History offered to Albert van Roey*, 83–97. Leuven: Peeters, 1985.

Deun, Peter van, "Les citations de saint Maxime le Confesseur dans le florilège palamite de l'Atheniensis, Bibliotheque nationale 2583," *Byzantion* 57 (1987): 127–57.

344     *Select Bibliography*

Deun, Peter van, "Maximus the Confessor's Use of Literary Genres," *OHMC*, 274–86.

Deun, Peter van, and Caroline Macé, eds., *Encyclopedic Trends in Byzantium? Proceedings of the International Conference Held in Leuven, 6–8 May 2009.* Leuven: Peeters, 2011.

Devreesse, Robert, "La fin inédite d'une lettre de saint Maxime: Un baptême forcé de juifs et de samaritains à Carthage en 632," *Revue des sciences religieuses* 17 (1937): 25–35.

Doucet, Marcel, "Est-ce que le monothélisme a fait autant d'illustrés victimes? Réflexions sur un ouvrage de F.-M. Léthel," *Science et esprit* 35 (1983): 53–83.

Doucet, Marcel, "La volonté humaine du Christ, spécialement en son agonie: Maxime le Confesseur, interprète de l'écriture," *Science et esprit* 37 (1985): 123–59.

Drijvers, Jan, "Heraclius and the *Restitutio Crucis*: Notes on Symbolism and Ideology," in Gerrit Reinink and Bernhard Stolte, eds., *The Reign of Heraclius (610–641): Crisis and Confrontation*, 175–90. Leuven: Peeters, 2002.

Ekonomou, Andrew, *Byzantine Rome and the Greek Popes.* Lanham, MD: Lexington Books, 2007.

Elm, Susanna, *Sons of Hellenism, Fathers of the Church: Emperor Julian, Gregory of Nazianzus, and the Vision of Rome.* Berkeley: University of California Press, 2012.

Epifanovich, Sergius, *Prepodobnyi Maksim Ispovednik i vizantiiskoe bogoslovie* (*The Blessed Maximus the Confessor and Byzantine Theology*) (Kiev, 1915). Reprint edition. Moscow: Martis, 1996.

Fantino, Jacques, *La théologie d'Irénée: Lecture des Écritures en réponse à l'exégèse gnostique: Une approche trinitaire.* Paris: Cerf, 1994.

Farrell, Joseph, *Free Choice in St. Maximus the Confessor.* South Canaan, PA: St. Tikhon's Seminary Press, 1989.

Florovsky, Georges, *The Byzantine Fathers of the Sixth to Eighth Century*, trans. Raymond Miller, Anne-Marie Döllinger-Labriolle, and Helmut Schmiedel. Vaduz: Büchervertriebsanstalt, 1987.

Garrigues, Juan Miguel, *Maxime le Confesseur: charité, avenir divin de l'homme.* Paris: Beauchesne, 1976.

Gauthier, R.-A., "Saint Maxime le Confesseur et la psychologie de l'acte humaine," *Recherches de théologie ancienne et médiévale* 21 (1954): 51–100.

Gavrilyuk, Paul, "Georges Florovsky's Reading of Maximus: Anti-Bulgakov or Pro-Bulgakov," in Vasiljević, 407–15.

Geanakoplos, Deno, "Maximus the Confessor and His Influence on Eastern and Western Theology and Mysticism," in *Interaction of the "Sibling"*

*Byzantine and Western Cultures in the Middle Ages and Italian Renaissance (330–1600)*, 133–45. New Haven: Yale University Press, 1976.

Gemeinhardt, Peter, *Filioque-Kontroverse zwischen Ost- und Westkirche im Frühmittelalter*. Berlin: Walter de Gruyter, 2002.

Gnilka, Christian, *ΧΡΗΣΙΣ: Die Methode der Kirchenväter im Umgang mit der antiken Kultur*. Basel: Schwabe, 1984.

Golitzin, Alexander, *Mystagogy: A Monastic Reading of Dionysius Areopagita*. Collegeville, MN: Liturgical Press/Cistercian Publications, 2013.

Gray, Patrick, *The Defense of Chalcedon in the East (451–553)*. Leiden: Brill, 1979.

Grdzelidze, Tamara, "Liturgical Space in the Writings of Maximus the Confessor," in Maurice Wiles and E. J. Yarnold, eds., *Studia Patristia 37*, 499–504. Leuven: Peeters, 2001.

Gregorios, Paulos, *Cosmic Man: The Divine Presence: The Theology of St. Gregory of Nyssa*. New York: Paragon House, 1988.

Gregorios, Paulos, *The Human Presence: An Orthodox View of Nature*. Geneva: World Council of Churches, 1978.

Grillmeier, Aloys, *Christ in Christian Tradition*, vol. 1: *From the Apostolic Age to Chalcedon*, 2nd edn., trans. John Bowden. Atlanta: John Knox Press, 1975.

Grillmeier, Aloys, *Christ in Christian Tradition*, vol. 2: *From the Council of Chalcedon (451) to Gregory the Great*, pt. 1: *Reception and Contradiction: The Development of the Discussion about Chalcedon from 451 to the Beginning of the Reign of Justinian*, trans. Pauline Allen and Paul Cawte. Atlanta: John Knox Press, 1987.

Grillmeier, Aloys, *Christ in Christian Tradition*, vol. 2: *From the Council of Chalcedon (451) to Gregory the Great (590–604)*, pt. 2: *The Church of Constantinople in the Sixth Century*, trans. Pauline Allen and Paul Cawte. Atlanta: Westminster John Knox Press, 1995.

Guillaumont, Antoine, "Le dépaysement (*xeniteia*) comme forme d'ascèse dans la monachisme ancient," in *Aux origines du monachisme chrétien: pour une phénoménologie du monachisme*, 89–116. Bégrolles en Mauges: Abbaye de Bellefontaine, 1979.

Hardin, Michael, "Mimesis and Dominion: The Dynamics of Violence and the Imitation of Christ in Maximus Confessor," *St. Vladimir's Theological Quarterly* 36 (1992): 373–85.

Hatlie, Peter, *The Monks and Monasteries of Constantinople, ca. 350–850*. Cambridge: Cambridge University Press, 2007.

Hausherr, Irénée, *Philautie: De la tendresse pour soi à charité selon Maxime le Confesseur*. Rome: Pontificium Institutum Orientalium Studiorum, 1952.

Hefele, Charles, *A History of the Councils of the Church*, vol. 5, trans. William Clark. Edinburgh: T. & T. Clark, 1896.

Heinzer, Felix, "L'explication trinitaire de l'économie chez Maxime le Confesseur," *MC*, 159–72.

Heinzer, Felix, *Gottes Sohn als Mensch: Die Struktur des Menschseins Christi bei Maximus Confessor.* Fribourg: Éditions Universitaires, 1980.

Heinzer, Felix, and Christoph Schönborn, eds., *Maximus Confessor: Actes du Symposium sur Maxime le Confesseur, Fribourg, 2–5 septembre 1980.* Fribourg: Éditions Universitaires, 1982.

Hofer, Andrew, *Christ in the Life and Teaching of Gregory of Nazianzus.* Oxford: Oxford University Press, 2013.

Hovorun, Cyril, *Will, Action and Freedom: Christological Controversies in the Seventh Century.* Leiden: Brill, 2008.

Howard-Johnston, James, *Witnesses to a World Crisis: Historians and Histories of the Middle East in the Seventh Century.* Oxford: Oxford University Press, 2010.

Iborra, Manuel Mira, "Friendship in Maximus the Confessor," in Markus Vinzent, ed., *Studia Patristica* 68, 273–80. Leuven: Peeters, 2013.

Jankowiak, Marek, "Essai d'histoire politique du monothélisme." PhD dissertation, University of Warsaw, 2009.

Jankowiak, Marek, and Phil Booth, "A New Date-List of the Works of Maximus the Confessor," *OHMC*, 19–83.

Jeauneau, Édouard, "Jean l'Érigène et les *Ambigua ad Iohannem* de Maxime le Confesseur," *MC*, 343–64.

Jenkins, Willis, *Ecologies of Grace: Environmental Ethics and Christian Theology.* New York: Oxford University Press, 2008.

Kaegi, Walter, "Initial Byzantine Reactions to the Arab Conquests," *Church History* 38 (1969): 139–49.

Kaegi, Walter, *Byzantium and the Early Islamic Conquests.* Cambridge: Cambridge University Press, 1995.

Kaegi, Walter, *Heraclius: Emperor of Byzantium.* Cambridge: Cambridge University Press, 2003.

Kaegi, Walter, *Muslim Expansion and Byzantine Collapse in North Africa.* Cambridge: Cambridge University Press, 2010.

Karavites, Peter, "*Gnome's* Nuances: From Its Beginning to the End of the Fifth Century," *Classical Bulletin* 66 (1990): 9–34.

Karayiannis, Vasilios, "The Distinction between Essence and Energy according to Maximus the Confessor," in Constantinos Athanasopoulos and Christoph Schneider, eds., *Divine Essence and Divine Energies: Ecumenical Reflections on the Presence of God in Eastern Orthodoxy*, 232–55. Cambridge: James Clarke, 2013.

Karayiannis, Vasilios, *Maxime le Confesseur: Essence et énergies de Dieu.* Paris: Beauchesne, 1993.

Kavanagh, Catherine, "The Impact of Maximus the Confessor on John Scottus Eriugena," *OHMC*, 480–99.

Krausmüller, Dirk, "The Rise of Hesychasm," in Michael Angold, ed., *The Cambridge History of Christianity*, vol. 5: *Eastern Christianity*, 101–26. Cambridge: Cambridge University Press, 2006.

Krueger, Derek, "Between Monks: Tales of Monastic Companionship in Early Byzantium," *Journal of the History of Sexuality* 20 (2011): 28–61.

Krueger, Derek, *Liturgical Subjects: Christian Ritual, Biblical Narrative, and the Formation of the Self in Byzantium*. Philadelphia: University of Pennsylvania Press, 2014.

Krueger, Derek, *Writing and Holiness: The Practice of Authorship in the Early Christian East*. Philadelphia: University of Pennsylvania Press, 2004.

Lackner, Wolfgang, "Zu Quellen und Datierung der Maximosvita," *Analecta Bollandiana* 85 (1967): 285–316.

Ladouceur, Paul, "Treasures New and Old: Landmarks of Orthodox Neopatristic Theology," *St. Vladimir's Theological Quarterly* 56 (2012): 191–227.

Laga, Carl, "Maximus as a Stylist in *Quaestiones ad Thalassium*," *MC*, 139–46.

Larchet, Jean-Claude, "Ancestral Guilt according to St. Maximus the Confessor: A Bridge between Eastern and Western Conceptions," *Sobornost* 20 (1998): 26–48.

Larchet, Jean-Claude, *La divinisation de l'homme selon saint Maxime le Confesseur*. Paris: Cerf, 1996.

Larchet, Jean-Claude, *Maxime le Confesseur*. Paris: Cerf, 2003.

Larchet, Jean-Claude, *Maxime le Confesseur, médiateur entre l'Orient et l'Occident*. Paris: Cerf, 1988.

Larchet, Jean-Claude, "The Mode of Deification," *OHMC*, 341–59.

Larchet, Jean-Claude, *Personne et nature: La Trinité—Le Christ—L'homme*. Paris: Cerf, 2011.

Lauritzen, Frederick, "Pagan Energies in Maximus the Confessor: The Influence of Proclus in *Ad Thomam* 5," *Greek, Roman, and Byzantine Studies* 52 (2012): 226–39.

Le Guillou, M.-J., "De Maxime le Confesseur à Vladimir Soloviev," Preface to Juan Miguel Garrigues, *Maxime le Confesseur: charité, avenir divin de l'homme*, 7–22. Paris: Beauchesne, 1976.

Léthel, François-Marie, *Théologie de l'agonie du Christ: La liberté humaine du Fils de Dieu et son importance sotériologique mises en lumière par saint Maxime le Confesseur*. Paris: Beauchesne, 1979.

Lévy, Antoine, *Le créé et l'incréé: Maxime le Confesseur et Thomas d'Aquin*. Paris: Vrin, 2006.

Lilie, Ralph-Johannes, *Byzanz: Das zweite Rom*. Berlin: Siedler, 2003.

Lollar, Joshua, "Reception of Maximian Thought in the Modern Era," *OHMC*, 564–80.

Lollar, Joshua, *To See into the Life of Things: The Contemplation of Nature in Maximus the Confessor and His Predecessors*. Turnhout: Brepols, 2013.

Löser, Werner, *Im Geiste des Origenes: Hans Urs von Balthasar als Interpret der Theologie der Kirchenväter.* Frankfurt: Knecht, 1976.

Lossky, Vladimir, *The Mystical Theology of the Eastern Church.* Cambridge: James Clarke, 1957.

Lossky, Vladimir, *The Vision of God,* trans. Ashleigh Moorhouse, 2nd edn. Leighton Buzzard, UK: Faith Press, 1973.

Loudovikos, Nikolaos, *A Eucharistic Ontology: Maximus the Confessor's Eschatological Ontology of Being as Dialogical Reciprocity,* trans. Elizabeth Theokritoff. Brookline, MA: Holy Cross Orthodox Press, 2010.

Loudovikos, Nikolaos, "Person Instead of Grace and Dictated Otherness: John Zizioulas' Final Theological Position," *Heythrop Journal* 48 (2009): 1–16.

Louth, Andrew, "The Ecclesiology of Saint Maximus the Confessor," *International Journal for the Study of the Christian Church* 4 (2004): 109–20.

Louth, Andrew, *Greek East and Latin West: The Church AD 681–1071.* Crestwood, NY: St. Vladimir's Seminary Press, 2007.

Louth, Andrew, "Man and Cosmos in St. Maximus," in John Chryssavgis and Bruce Foltz, eds., *Toward an Ecology of Transfiguration: Orthodox Christian Perspectives on Environment, Nature, and Creation,* 59–71. New York: Fordham University Press, 2013.

Louth, Andrew, *Maximus the Confessor.* London: Routledge, 1996.

Louth, Andrew, "Maximus the Confessor's Influence and Reception in Byzantine and Modern Orthodoxy," *OHMC,* 500–15.

Louth, Andrew, "Recent Research on St. Maximus the Confessor: A Survey," *St. Vladimir's Theological Quarterly* 42 (1998): 67–84.

Louth, Andrew, "St. Gregory the Theologian and St. Maximus the Confessor: The Shaping of Tradition," in Sarah Coakley and David Pailin, eds., *The Making and Remaking of Christian Doctrine: Essays in Honour of Maurice Wiles,* 117–30. Oxford: Oxford University Press, 1993.

Louth, Andrew, *St. John Damascene: Tradition and Originality in Byzantine Theology.* Oxford: Oxford University Press, 2002.

Louth, Andrew, "St. Maximos' Doctrine of the *logoi* of Creation," in Jane Baun, Averil Cameron, Michael Edwards, and Markus Vinzent, eds., *Studia Patristica* 48, 77–84. Leuven: Peeters, 2010.

Louth, Andrew, "St. Maximus between East and West," in Elizabeth Livingstone, ed., *Studia Patristica* 32, 332–45. Leuven: Peeters, 1997.

Louth, Andrew, "The Views of St. Maximus the Confessor on the Institutional Church," in Vasiljević, 347–55.

Louth, Andrew, "Virtue Ethics: St. Maximos the Confessor and Aquinas Compared," *Studies in Christian Ethics* 26 (2013): 351–63.

Ludlow, Morwenna, *Gregory of Nyssa: Ancient and (Post)modern.* Oxford: Oxford University Press, 2007.

Ludlow, Morwenna, *Universal Salvation in the Thought of Gregory of Nyssa and Karl Rahner.* Oxford: Oxford University Press, 2000.

Maas, Michael, *Exegesis and Empire in the Early Byzantine Mediterranean: Junillus Africanus and the* Instituta Regularia Divinae Legis. Tübingen: Mohr Siebeck, 2003.

McFarland, Ian, "'Naturally and by Grace': Maximus the Confessor on the Operation of the Will," *Scottish Journal of Theology* 58 (2005): 410–33.

McFarland, Ian, "'Willing is Not Choosing': Some Anthropological Implications of Dyothelite Christology," *International Journal of Systematic Theology* 9 (2007): 3–23.

McGuckin, John, *Saint Cyril of Alexandria and the Christological Controversy: Its History, Theology, and Texts*. Crestwood, NY: St. Vladimir's Seminary Press, 2004.

McGuckin, John, *Saint Gregory of Nazianzus: An Intellectual Biography*. Crestwood, NY: St. Vladimir's Seminary Press, 2001.

Madden, John, "The Authenticity of Early Definitions of Will," *MC*, 61–79.

Madigan, Kevin, "Ancient and High-Medieval Interpretations of Jesus in Gethsemane: Some Reflections on Tradition and Continuity in Christian Thought," *Harvard Theological Review* 88 (1995): 157–73.

Magdalino, Paul, "Byzantine Encyclopaedism of the Ninth and Tenth Centuries," in Jason König and Greg Woolf, eds., *Encyclopaedism from Antiquity to the Renaissance*, 219–31. Cambridge: Cambridge University Press, 2013.

Magdalino, Paul, "The History of the Future and Its Uses: Prophecy, Policy and Propaganda," in Roderick Beaton and Charlotte Roueché, eds., *The Making of Byzantine History: Studies Dedicated to Donald M. Nichol*, 3–34. Aldershot: Variorum, 1993.

Magdalino, Paul, "Orthodoxy and Byzantine Cultural Identity," in Antonio Rigo and Pavel Ermilov, eds., *Orthodoxy and Heresy in Byzantium: The Definition and the Notion of Orthodoxy and Some Other Studies on the Heresies and the Non-Christian Religions*, 21–46. Rome: Università degli studi di Roma "Tor Vergata," 2010.

Marion, Jean-Luc, *Being Given: Toward a Phenomenology of Givenness*, trans. Jeffrey Kosky. Palo Alto: Stanford University Press, 2002.

Marion, Jean-Luc, "Le deux volontés du Christ selon Maxime le Confesseur," *Résurrection* 41 (1972): 48–66.

Marion, Jean-Luc, *In Excess: Studies of Saturated Phenomena*, trans. Robyn Horner and Vincent Berrand. New York: Fordham University Press, 2002.

Marion, Jean-Luc, *The Idol and Distance: Five Studies*, trans. Thomas Carlson. New York: Fordham University Press, 2001.

Meyendorff, John, *Christ in Eastern Christian Thought*. Crestwood, NY: St. Vladimir's Seminary Press, 1975.

Mcyendorff, John, *Imperial Unity and Christian Divisions: The Church 450–680 A D.* Crestwood, NY: St. Vladimir's Seminary Press, 1989.

Meyendorff, John, *St. Gregory Palamas and Orthodox Spirituality*. Crestwood, NY: St. Vladimir's Seminary Press, 1974.

Meyendorff, John, *A Study of Gregory Palamas*. Crestwood, NY: St. Vladimir's Seminary Press, 1998.

Michaud, Eugène, "Saint Maxime le Confesseur et l'apocatastase," *Revue Internationale de Théologie* 10 (1902): 257–72.

Milkov, Kostake, "Maximus and the Healing of the Sexual Division of Creation," in Vasiljević, 427–36.

Moeller, Charles, "Le Chalcédonisme et le néo-Chalcédonisme en Orient de 451 à le fin du VIe siècle," in Aloys Grillmeier and Heinrich Bacht, eds., *Das Konzil von Chalkedon: Geschichte und Gewart*, 637–720. Würzburg: Echter-Verlag, 1951.

Moran, Dermot, *The Philosophy of John Scottus Eriugena: A Study of Idealism in the Middle Ages*. Cambridge: Cambridge University Press, 1989.

Moreschini, Claudio, "Sulla presenza e la funzione dell'aristotelismo in Massimo il Confessore," *ΚΟΙΝΩΝΙΑ* 28–9 (2004–5): 105–24.

Mueller-Jourdan, Pascal, "The Foundation of Origenist Metaphysics," *OHMC*, 149–63.

Mueller-Jourdan, Pascal, *Typologie spatio-temporelle de l'Ecclesia byzantine: La* Mystagogie *de Maxime le Confesseur dans la culture philosophique de l'antiquité tardive*. Leiden: Brill, 2005.

Neil, Bronwen, "Divine Providence and the Gnomic Will before Maximus," *OHMC*, 235–49.

Neil, Bronwen, *Seventh-Century Popes and Martyrs: The Political Hagiography of Anastasius Bibliothecarius*. Turnhout: Brepols, 2006.

Nellas, Panayiotis, *Deification in Christ: The Nature of the Human Person*, trans. Norman Russell. Crestwood, NY: St. Vladimir's Seminary Press, 1987.

Nesteruk, Alexei, *Light from the East: Theology, Science, and the Eastern Orthodox Tradition*. Minneapolis: Augsburg Fortress, 2003.

Nesteruk, Alexei, *The Universe as Communion: Toward a Neo-Patristic Synthesis of Theology and Science*. London: T. & T. Clark, 2008.

Nichols, Aidan, *Byzantine Gospel: Maximus the Confessor in Recent Scholarship*. Edinburgh: T. & T. Clark, 1996.

Nikolaou, Theodor, "Zur Identität des μακάριος γέρων in der *Mystagogia* von Maximos dem Bekenner," *Orientalia Christiana Periodica* 49 (1983): 407–18.

Norris, Frederick, "Universal Salvation in Origen and Maximus," in Nigel M. de S. Cameron, ed., *Universalism and the Doctrine of Hell: Papers Presented at the Fourth Edinburgh Conference in Christian Dogmatics, 1991*, 35–72. Carlisle: Paternoster Press, 1992.

Oehler, Klaus, "Aristotle in Byzantium," *Greek, Roman, and Byzantine Studies* 5 (1964): 133–46.

Ohme, Heinz, "*Oikonomia* im monenergetisch-monotheletischen Streit," *Zeitschrift für Antikes Christentum* 12 (2008): 308–43.

O'Regan, Cyril, "Von Balthasar and Thick Retrieval: Post-Chalcedonian Symphonic Theology," *Gregorianum* 77 (1996): 227–60.

Osborne, Catherine, *Eros Unveiled: Plato and the God of Love*. Oxford: Oxford University Press, 1994.

Papanikolaou, Aristotle, "Learning How to Love: Saint Maximus on Virtue," in Vasiljević, 241–50.

Patrich, Joseph, *Sabas, Leader of Palestinian Monasticism: A Comparative Study in Eastern Monasticism, Fourth to Seventh Centuries*. Washington, DC: Dumbarton Oaks, 1995.

Pelikan, Jaroslav, " 'Council or Father or Scripture': The Concept of Authority in the Theology of Maximus the Confessor," in David Neiman and Margaret Schatkin, eds., *The Heritage of the Early Church: Essays in Honor of Georges Florovsky*, 277–88. Rome: Pontificium Institutum Orientalium, 1973.

Piret, Pierre, *Le Christ et la Trinité selon Maxime le Confesseur*. Paris: Beauchesne, 1983.

Plested, Marcus, *The Macarian Legacy: The Place of Macarius-Symeon in the Eastern Christian Tradition*. Oxford: Oxford University Press, 2004.

Plested, Marcus, "Wisdom in St Maximus the Confessor," in Frances Young and Mark Edwards, eds., *Studia Patristica* 42, 205–9. Leuven: Peeters, 2006.

Podskalsky, Gerhard, *Byzantinische Reichseschatologie: Die Periodisierung der Weltgeschichte in der vier Grossreichen (Daniel 2 und 7) und dem tausendjährigen Friedensreiche (Apok. 20): Eine motivgeschichtliche Untersuchung*. Munich: W. Fink, 1972.

Podskalsky, Gerhard, *Theologie und Philosophie in Byzanz: Die Streit um die theologische Methodik in der spätbyzantinischen Geistesgeschichte (14./15. Jh.): Seine systematischen Grundlagen und seine historische Entwicklung*. Munich: C. H. Beck, 1977.

Portaru, Marius, "Classical Philosophical Influences: Platonism and Aristotelianism," *OHMC*, 127–48.

Ramelli, Ilaria, *The Christian Doctrine of Apokatastasis: A Critical Assessment from the New Testament to Eriugena*. Leiden: Brill, 2013.

Regan, Geoffrey, *First Crusader: Byzantium's Holy Wars*. New York: Palgrave Macmillan, 2001.

Reinink, Gerrit, "Heraclius, the New Alexander: Apocalyptic Prophecies during the Reign of Heraclius," in Gerrit Reinink and Bernhard Stolte, eds., *The Reign of Heraclius (610–641): Crisis and Confrontation*, 81–94. Leuven: Peeters, 2002.

Renczes, Philipp Gabriel, *Agir de Dieu et la liberté de l'homme: Recherches sur l'anthropologie théologique de Saint Maxime le Confesseur*. Paris: Cerf, 2003.

Riedinger, Rudolf, "Die Lateransynode von 649 und Maximos der Bekenner," *MC*, 111–21.

Riou, Alain, *Le monde et l'église selon Maxime le Confesseur*. Paris: Beauchesne, 1973.

Roosen, Bram, "Maximus Confessor and the *Scholia in Johannem* in Codex *Vaticanus, Bibliothecae Apostolicae Vaticanae, Graecus* 349 [CPG C 147.2]," *Journal of Eastern Christian Studies* 54 (2002): 185–226.

Roosen, Bram, "Maximi Confessoris Vitae et Passiones Graecae: The Development of a Hagiographic Dossier," *Byzantion* 80 (2010): 408–61.

Roosen, Bram, and Peter van Deun, "Les collections des définitions philosophicothéologiques appartenant à la tradition de Maxime le Confesseur: Le recueil centré sur *ΟΜΩΝΥΜΟΝ, ΣΥΝΩΝΥΜΟΝ, ΠΑΡΩΝΥΜΟΝ, ΕΤΕΡΩΝΥΜΟΝ...*," in Michel Cacouros and Marie-Hélène Congourdeau, eds., *Philosophie et sciences à Byzance de 1204 à 1453*, 53–76. Leuven: Peeters, 2006.

Roques, René, *L'univers dionysien: Structure hiérarchique du monde selon Pseudo-Denys*. Paris: Aubier, 1954.

Russell, Norman, *The Doctrine of Deification in the Greek Patristic Tradition*. Oxford: Oxford University Press, 2004.

Sahas, Daniel, "The Demonizing Force of the Arab Conquests: The Case of Maximus (ca. 580–662) as a Political 'Confessor,'" *Jahrbuch der österreichischen Byzantinistik* 53 (2003): 97–116.

Sakvarelidze, Nino, "Contextualization and Actualization of Maximus's Textual and Spiritual Heritage," in Vasiljević, 271–83.

Salés, Luis Joshua, "Divine Incarnation through the Virtues: The Central Soteriological Role of Maximos the Confessor's Aretology," *St. Vladimir's Theological Quarterly* 58 (2014): 159–76.

Sansterre, Jean-Marie, *Les moines grecs et orientaux à Rome aux époques byzantine et carolingienne*. Brussels: Palais des Académies, 1983.

Sarris, Peter, *Empires of Faith: The Fall of Rome to the Rise of Islam, 500–700*. Oxford: Oxford University Press, 2011.

Schneider, Christoph, "The Transformation of Eros: Reflections on Desire in Jacques Lacan," in Adrian Pabst and Christoph Schneider, eds., *Encounter between Eastern Orthodoxy and Radical Orthodoxy: Transfiguring the World through the Word*, 271–89. Farnham: Ashgate, 2009.

Schönborn, Christoph, "Plaisir et douleur dans l'analyse de S. Maxime, d'après les *Quaestiones ad Thalassium*," *MC*, 273–84.

Schönborn, Christoph, *Sophrone de Jérusalem: Vie monastique et confession dogmatique*. Paris: Beauchesne, 1972.

Schulz, Hans-Joachim, *The Byzantine Liturgy: Symbolic Structure and Faith Expression*, trans. Matthew O'Connell. New York: Pueblo, 1986.

Schwager, Raymund, "Das Mysterium der übernatürlichen Natur-Lehre: Zur Erlöngslehre des Maximus Confessor," in *Der Wunderbare Tausch: Zur Geschichte und Deutung der Erlösungslehre*, 135–60. Munich: Kösel-Verlag, 1986.

Sherwood, Polycarp, *An Annotated Date-List of the Works of Maximus the Confessor*. Rome: Herder, 1952.

Sherwood, Polycarp, *The Earlier Ambigua of St. Maximus the Confessor and His Refutation of Origenism*. Rome: Herder, 1955.

Sherwood, Polycarp, "Maximus and Origenism: *APXH KAI TEΛOΣ*," *Berichte zum XI. Internationalen Byzantinisten-Kongress* III, 1, 1–27. Münich, 1958.

Shoemaker, Stephen, "'The Reign of God Has Come': Eschatology and Empire in Late Antiquity and Early Islam," *Arabica* 61 (2014): 514–58.

Siecienski, Edward, *The Filioque: History of a Doctrinal Controversy*. New York: Oxford University Press, 2010.

Siecienski, Edward, "The Use of Maximus the Confessor's Writing on the *Filioque* at the Council of Ferrara-Florence (1438–1439)." Ph.D. dissertation, Fordham University, New York, 2005.

Siniossoglou, Niketas, *Radical Platonism in Byzantium: Utopia and Illumination in Gemistos Plethon*. Cambridge: Cambridge University Press, 2011.

Soloviev, Vladimir, *Lectures on Godmanhood*, trans. Peter Zouboff. London: D. Dobson, 1948; reprinted San Rafael, CA: Semantron, 2007.

Sorabji, Richard, "The Concept of the Will from Plato to Maximus the Confessor," in Thomas Pink and M. W. F. Stone, eds., *The Will and Human Action: From Antiquity to the Present Day*, 6–28. London: Routledge, 2003.

Sorabji, Richard, *Emotions and Peace of Mind: From Stoic Agitations to Christian Temptations*. Oxford: Oxford University Press, 2003.

Southgate, Christopher, *The Groaning of Creation: God, Evolution, and the Problem of Evil*. Louisville: Westminster John Knox, 2008.

Spinks, Bryan. *Do This in Remembrance of Me: The Eucharist from the Early Church to the Present Day*. London: SCM Press, 2013.

Staniloae, Dumitru, "Commentaires" on the *Ambigua* of Maximus, French translation from the Romanian by Père Aurel Grigoras. Appended to Emmanuel Ponsoye, trans., *Saint Maxime le Confesseur: Ambigua*, 373–540. Paris and Suresnes: Les Éditions de l'Ancre, 1994.

Staniloae, Dumitru, *The Experience of God: Orthodox Dogmatic Theology*, vol. 2: *The World: Creation and Deification*, trans. Ioan Ionita and Robert Barringer. Brookline, MA: Holy Cross Orthodox Press, 2000.

Staniloae, Dumitru, *The Experience of God: Orthodox Dogmatic Theology*, vol. 3: *The Person of Jesus Christ as God and Savior*, trans. Ioan Ionita. Brookline, MA: Holy Cross Orthodox Press, 2011.

Staniloae, Dumitru, *The Experience of God: Orthodox Dogmatic Theology*, vol. 6: *The Fulfillment of Creation*, trans. Ioan Ionita. Brookline, MA: Holy Cross Orthodox Press, 2013.

Starr, Joshua, "Note on the Crisis of the Early Seventh Century C.E.," *Jewish Quarterly Review* N.S. 38 (1947): 97–9.

Starr, Joshua, "St. Maximos and the Forced Baptism at Carthage in 632," *Byzantinisch-neugriechische Jahrbücher* 16 (1940): 192–6.

Steel, Carlos, "Un admirateur de S. Maxime à la cour des Comnènes: Isaac le Sébastocrator," *MC*, 365–73.

Steel, Carlos, "Le jeu du Verbe: À propos de Maxime, *Amb. ad Ioh. LXVII [=Amb. 71],*" in Anton Schoors and Peter van Deun, eds., *Philohistôr: Miscellanea in honorem Caroli Laga septuagenarii,* 281–93. Leuven: Peeters, 1994.

Steel, Carlos, "Maximus Confessor on *Theory* and *Praxis*: A Commentary on *Ambigua ad Johannem* VI (10) 1–19," in Thomas Bénatouïl and Mauro Bonazzi, eds., *Theoria, Praxis, and the Contemplative Life after Plato and Aristotle,* 229–57. Leiden: Brill, 2012.

Studer, Basil, "Zur Soteriologie des Maximus Confessor," *MC*, 239–46.

Taft, Robert, "Is the Liturgy Described in the *Mystagogia* of Maximus Confessor Byzantine, Palestinian or Neither?" *Bollettino della Badia Greca di Grottaferrata*, 3rd series 8 (2011): 223–70.

Tatakis, Basil, *Byzantine Philosophy*, trans. from the 1949 French edition by Nicholas Moutafakis. Indianapolis: Hackett Publishing, 2003.

Thunberg, Lars, *Man and the Cosmos: The Vision of St. Maximus the Confessor*. Crestwood, NY: St. Vladimir's Seminary Press, 1985.

Thunberg, Lars, *Microcosm and Mediator: The Theological Anthropology of Maximus the Confessor*, 2nd edn. Chicago: Open Court Publishing, 1995.

Tollefsen, Torstein, *Activity and Participation in Late Antique and Early Christian Thought*. Oxford: Oxford University Press, 2012.

Tollefsen, Torstein, *The Christocentric Cosmology of St. Maximus the Confessor*. Oxford: Oxford University Press, 2008.

Törönen, Melchisedec, *Union and Distinction in the Thought of St. Maximus the Confessor*. Oxford: Oxford University Press, 2007.

Torrance, Alexis, "Personhood and Patristics in Orthodox Theology: Reassessing the Debate," *Heythrop Journal* 52 (2011): 700–7.

Tsakiridou, Cornelia, *Icons in Time, Persons in Eternity: Orthodox Theology and the Aesthetics of the Christian Image*. Farnham: Ashgate, 2013.

Uthemann, Karl-Heinz, "Der Neuchalkedonismus als Vorbereiten des Monotheletismus: Ein Beitrag zum eigentlichen Anliegen des Neuchalkedonismus," in Elizabeth Livingstone, ed., *Studia Patristica* 29, 373–413. Leuven: Peeters, 1997.

Vasiljević, Maxim, ed., *Knowing the Purpose of Creation through the Resurrection: Proceedings of the Symposium on St. Maximus the Confessor, Belgrade, October 18–21, 2012*. Alhambra, CA: Sebastian Press, 2013.

Viller, Marcel, "Aux sources de la spiritualité de saint Maxime: les oeuvres d'Évagre le Pontique," *Revue d'ascétique et de mystique* 11 (1920): 156–84, 239–68, 331–6.

Völker, Walther, *Maximus Confessor als Meister des geistlichen Lebens.* Wiesbaden: Franz Steiner, 1965.

Voordeckers, Edmond, "L'iconographie de saint Maxime le Confesseur dans l'art des églises de rite byzantin," in Anton Schoors and Peter van Deun, eds., *Philohistôr: Miscellanea in honorem Caroli Laga septuagenarii*, 339–59. Leuven: Peeters, 1994.

Wainwright, Geoffrey, *Eucharist and Eschatology*, 2nd edn. New York: Oxford University Press, 1981.

Westphal, Merold, "Transfiguration as Saturated Phenomenon," *Journal of Philosophy and Scripture* 1 (2003): 26–35.

Whitby, Mary, "George of Pisidia's Presentation of the Emperor Heraclius and His Campaigns," in Gerrit Reinink and Bernhard Stolte, eds., *The Reign of Heraclius (610–641): Crisis and Confrontation*, 157–73. Leuven: Peeters, 2002.

Williams, A. N., *The Divine Sense: The Intellect in Patristic Theology.* Cambridge: Cambridge University Press, 2007.

Williams, Rowan, "Macrina's Deathbed Revisited: Gregory of Nyssa on Mind and Passion," in Lionel Wickham and Caroline Bammel, eds., *Christian Faith and Greek Philosophy: Essays in Tribute to George Christopher Stead*, 227–46. Leiden: Brill, 1993.

Williams, Rowan, "Nature, Passion and Desire: Maximus' Ontology of Excess," in Markus Vinzent, ed., *Studia Patristica* 68, 267–72. Leuven: Peeters, 2013.

Williams, Rowan, *The Wound of Knowledge: Christian Spirituality from the New Testament to Saint John of the Cross*, 2nd edn. Cambridge, MA: Cowley Publications, 1990.

Winkelmann, Friedhelm, *Der monenergetisch-monotheletisch Streit.* Frankfurt: Peter Lang, 2001.

Winslow, Donald, *The Dynamics of Salvation: A Study in Gregory of Nazianzus.* Philadelphia: Philadelphia Patristic Foundation, 1979.

Yannaras, Christos, *Person and Eros*, trans. Norman Russell. Brookline, MA: Holy Cross Orthodox Press, 2008.

Yeago, David, "Jesus of Nazareth and Cosmic Redemption: The Relevance of St. Maximus the Confessor," *Modern Theology* 12 (1996): 163–93.

Young, Frances, *Biblical Exegesis and the Formation of Christian Culture.* Cambridge: Cambridge University Press, 1997.

Zhinov, V. M., "The *Mystagogia* of Maximus the Confessor and the Development of the Byzantine Theory of the Image," *St. Vladimir's Theological Quarterly* 31 (1987): 349–76.

Zirnheld, Claire-Agnès, "Le double visage de la passion: malédiction due au péché et/ou dynamisme de la vie: *Quaestiones ad Thalassium XXI, XXII et XLII*," in Anton Schoors and Peter van Deun, eds., *Philohistôr: Miscellanea in honorem Caroli Laga septuagenarii*, 361–80. Leuven: Peeters, 1994.

Zizioulas, John, *Being as Communion: Studies in Personhood and the Church.* Crestwood, NY: St. Vladimir's Seminary Press, 1985.

Zizioulas, John, *Communion and Otherness: Further Studies in Personhood and the Church.* New York: T. & T. Clark, 2006.

Zizioulas, John, *The Eucharistic Communion and the World.* London: T. & T. Clark, 2011.

Zizioulas, John, "Person and Nature in the Theology of St. Maximus the Confessor," in Vasiljević, 85–113.

\*   \*   \*   \*   \*

For a more extensive international bibliography of Maximus the Confessor, see Mikonja Knežević, *Maximus the Confessor (580–662): Bibliography.* Bibliographia serbica theologica 6. Belgrade: Institute for Theological Research, 2012.

# Index

# Index

as *erôs* *see* desire, as *erôs*
"form" of 255, 257
identification of *erôs* and *agapê* 259, 262
mystery of 126, 228, 254–62
of neighbor 202, 203, 256, 279, 281
of self 214, 215, 216, 219, 238, 257, 264, 265
*see also* desire; *Epistle 2*

Macarius of Antioch 62–3
Marinus of Cyprus 49, 77, 93
Maximus' letter to (*Opusculum* 10) 297–9, 300, 301
Marion, Jean-Luc 79–82, 125, 126, 127, 128, 173, 254–5, 257, 323
Mark the Monk 168
marriage 218, 220
Martin I (Pope) 22–3, 54, 56–7, 58, 288
Martina (empress) 37, 40, 49–50
Maurice (emperor) 12
Maximus the Confessor
as abbot of Chrysopolis monastery 27
alignment with papacy on Christology 4, 25, 28, 48, 50, 53, 54, 55–7, 60
alleged as a proto-scholastic 24, 64–5, 96–8
appeal to patristic and conciliar tradition 46, 49, 61, 78, 92, 93, 136
on the Arab invasions 20
authorial kenosis of 71–3
Chalcedonian "logic" of 135–7
on Christ's "new thandric energy" *see* Dionysius the Areopagite; Jesus Christ
in the circle of Eukratas monks 29–30, 34–9, 69
Constantinopolitan provenance of 26–8, 37
"cosmo-politeian" perspective of 6, 101, 131–4, 202, 224, 280–1, 309, 331–3
in Crete 29
debate with Pyrrhus 50–1
deference to a "wise elder" 70–1, 281
dispute at Bizya 60–1, 332
dyenergist and dyothelete Christology of 46–7, 49, 50, 51, 55–6, 63, 93, 97, 137, 157–65, 292
exiles and death of 4–5, 60, 61–2, 63, 287, 330–1
on the *Filioque* 297–9

on the forced baptism of Jews 21
friendship with John the Chamberlain *see* John the Chamberlain
friendship with Peter the Illustrious *see* Peter the Illustrious
as Georgian and Byzantine saint 62, 287
Greek *Life* of 5, 25–6, 26–8, 35, 67
as interpreter of Scripture 78–90
and the Lateran Council (649) 55–6, 57
literary genres of 90–3
literary style of 93–6
as liturgical commentator 166–95
at monastery in Cyzicus 28, 29
neo-Irenaean perspective of 102–9, 138
in North Africa 25, 28, 29, 30–1, 32
on "one incarnate nature of God the Logos" 150
and Origenism 1–2, 5, 26, 34, 36, 66–8, 102, 110, 115, 119–20, 222, 248, 250–1, 265–6, 308
Palestinian provenance of 4, 26, 29, 34–6, 39, 66
recontextualizations of *see* recontextualizations of Maximus the Confessor
relationship with Sophronius 29–30, 32, 34–6, 38, 46, 63
as spiritual advisor to Eparch George *see* George (eparch of Africa)
at synod of Cyprus 29
Syriac *Life* of 5, 25, 26, 29, 34–5, 47, 55, 59, 66, 67, 333
trials of 22, 25, 58–60, 62, 67
vindicated by Council of Constantinople (680–1) 62
mercy 278–9
Messalians 168
miaphysitism 18, 40–1, 48, 136, 150, 155
mind (νοῦς) 68, 75, 90, 96, 117, 123, 133, 144, 160, 161, 169–70, 177, 182, 183, 187, 190, 203, 208, 209, 227, 260, 266–7, 268, 269, 270, 271, 273, 274–5, 291, 304, 310
"mode of existence" (τρόπος ὑπάρξεως) 19, 73, 111, 114, 116, 122, 128–9, 131, 179, 202, 206, 228, 242
*see also* creation, diversity of; particularity of creatures in

Printed and bound by CPI Group (UK) Ltd, Croydon, CR0 4YY